ARCHITECTURAL SYMBOLISM OF IMPERIAL ROME

AND THE MIDDLE AGES

ARCHITECTURAL SYMBOLISM
OF IMPERIAL ROME
AND THE MIDDLE AGES

BY E. BALDWIN SMITH

Hacker Art Books, New York, 1978

Copyright © 1956 by Princeton University Press, Princeton, New Jersey
Reissued 1978 by Hacker Art Books, New York

Library of Congress Catalogue Card Number 76-27052
International Standard Book Number 0-87817-195-9

This book is reissued with the kind permission of Princeton University Press

Printed in the United States of America.

TO MY COLLEAGUES

IN THE

DEPARTMENT OF ART AND ARCHAEOLOGY

AND THE

SCHOOL OF ARCHITECTURE

WHOSE FRIENDSHIP AND COOPERATION

HAVE MADE MY FORTY YEARS

AT PRINCETON SO ENJOYABLE

PREFACE

Now that this study has been terminated, but not finished, I am not entirely clear in my own mind how it came to expand into a sequel to *The Dome*, with many of the same characters but a new plot, when it started as a modest article or so. I would like to believe that it grew naturally; others, including my family and friends, may suspect that it was partly the result of an obsession. The grounds for this suspicion become only too apparent when one tries to explain why an architectural historian should go so far out of his way to invite trouble from numismatists, classical scholars, mediaeval historians, theologians, and Islamic specialists. My only justification for asking new questions and proposing answers is that someone must take a calculated risk and attempt to integrate the scattered evidence if architecture is to recover some of its ancient prestige as the major art.

It is not myself, but my friends and colleagues who have helped me, that I want to protect. It would be most unfortunate if the experts in other fields should assume that they were not aware of my limitations and were in agreement with all my conclusions. It is true that Kurt Weitzmann, after reading the first draft of my manuscript and making many suggestions and corrections, did give me some much needed encouragement. I am equally indebted to Erik Sjöqvist, whose careful reading and many criticisms of the classical material were invaluable in the rewriting. It would, however, be unfair to him if I did not point out that he was frankly skeptical of many of my interpretations and most anxious, as a friend, to protect me from myself. I can only hope that the finished study will justify Weitzmann's encouragement and dispel some of Sjöqvist's doubts.

I am not so troubled about protecting my colleague of much longer standing, A. M. Friend, to whom I have gone, as usual, for information, books and all kinds of assistance in the Byzantine field. After all the years that we have worked together he should have become accustomed to worrying as to whether I was going to get into difficulties with the complexities of Byzantine rituals and theology. My only regret is that no one part of this study was properly finished, and independent of the whole, so that it could be made a part of the Festschrift which was presented to him on his sixtieth birthday.

And now let me pay credit to the graduate student, who is so often the forgotten man in the books of university professors. In his graduate courses, which are the professor's laboratory for testing out theories, he is the unthanked slavey who does much of the preliminary digging and who not infrequently comes up with some of the best finds. Since my teaching days will be over by the time this book is published, it will not prove dangerous for me to acknowledge that a teacher can learn from his students. Much as I would like to, I cannot mention all of the exceptional group on whom I have had the good fortune to try out my ideas. Although I have made no apparent use of Wen Fong's exposition of the cosmic and celestial symbolism expressed in the Imperial Palace at Peking, it showed me that the Chinese ideas, while more developed and complicated, paralleled the palace ideologies of the West. I have also benefited by J. M. Snyder's systematic study of the development of the Carolingian Westwerk and I have taken over L. D. Steefel's interpretation of the poem of Dungal as describing Charlemagne's throne in the Westwerk of St. Denis. I am reluctant to admit how much I have benefited from helping O. Grabar prepare his dissertation on the Umayyads. While I do not wish to saddle the graduate students with any responsibility for the results of their contributions, partly because they were never in a position to be as frankly critical as my colleagues, still I am grateful for having had their full cooperation.

Outside the Princeton group of advanced students, I am indebted to J. Ghaede of New York University, who allowed me to read his thesis on the coins of Charlemagne, and to C. A. Mango at Dumbarton Oaks, who put at my disposal a copy of his French doctoral dissertation on the Chalce at Constantinople.

E. BALDWIN SMITH

Princeton, N.J.

CONTENTS

ARCHITECTURAL SYMBOLISM OF IMPERIAL ROME

AND THE MIDDLE AGES

AN INTRODUCTION TO
ARCHITECTURAL SYMBOLISM

THIS study is not, as its title may imply, an exposition of all the political concepts, spiritual ideas, and popular beliefs that by means of symbolism gave expressive content to the architecture of Imperial Rome and the Middle Ages. Instead, it is an investigation of a group of architectural features, all directly or indirectly related to the city-gate and palace entrance, and the ceremonies which gave the forms so much of their royal and divine significance in the popular imagination. The burden of proof is naturally upon anyone who endeavors to go back of the very limited documentary evidence and tries to trace the development of an architectural ideology from the sequence of monuments in Antiquity and the Middle Ages. The problem of presenting a convincing exposition of symbolic intent that is seldom specifically stated is made difficult by the modern conviction that architecture, apart from its figurative sculptures, has always been created for utilitarian and aesthetic reasons. Even when dealing with the buildings of the Middle Ages, there has been a prevailing tendency to disregard the political issues involved in the symbolism and to minimize the spiritual connotations as mystic, vague, and nonessential to appreciation. This means that architectural symbolism will continue to seem artificial as long as the buildings that embodied it are divorced from the history of ideas, and as long as it is assumed that the motivating factors of architectural creation were always, as they are today, only structural necessity, utility, decorative desire, and a particular kind of taste.

There is, unfortunately, no easy way of modifying this preconception regarding the expressive function of architecture and of setting buildings back into their original climate of ideas. Anyone who feels that art is necessarily blighted by "kunsthistorische" methods should be warned that only by the machinery of scholarship can one begin to demonstrate the extent to which the controlling patrons of architecture, the State and the Church, succeeded in conveying ideas of heavenly powers, universal authority, and awe-inspiring grandeur by means of architectural forms that we today have come to believe, because of changing interests and repetition, were never anything more than conventions of design. Also, without any intention of begging the issue with the scholarly critics who are historically trained to be suspicious of any interpretations of the past which are not fully substantiated by documentary evidence, it must be pointed out that symbolism in an art as abstract as architecture was always most effective at a popular, instinctive, and illiterate level. This meant during the centuries when the ordinary man was so dependent upon the arts for his conceptual imagery, that symbolism was usually taken for granted and was only expounded, as in the case of the Church Fathers, when it was being readapted to different ideals.

Therefore, during the Roman Empire, when the State was cultivating by every means at its command a kind of monumental propaganda to impress the masses throughout the provinces, many of the accepted implications of architectural forms, which were based upon instinctive habits of thought, are only partially reflected in the literature. Later in the Middle Ages, when there are so many references to the Christian import of architecture, the documents, always written by churchmen, give little intimation of the extent to which the symbolism was based upon pagan and imperial precedents and seldom reveal the motivating ideas, sometimes more political than spiritual, which the emperors and popes in their conflicting claims to being God's supreme representative on earth intended to have associated with a traditional symbolism that they were consciously taking over from the past.

It has come to be recognized that the insignia, rituals, ceremonies, and palace architecture of the Roman Court, which had developed over the centuries from Hellenistic and Eastern customs in order to present the Imperator as a divine Kosmokrator, had a lasting influence upon the symbolic art and rituals of the Christian Church.[1] It is not so clearly realized that Christian architecture, with its mystic intent to express the invisible by means of the visible, appropriated the ideological concepts already associated with imperial Roman architecture. Because it is assumed that the Romans, as we know them in their literature, were too practical a people to be influenced by architectural symbolism, it is not commonly understood how much the Christian desire to make the church an apparent "Gate of Heaven," and impregnable "Stronghold," a "City of God," and a replica of God's cosmic dwelling was inspired by the ideas and ceremonies which had long been associated with the towered gateways, triumphal arches, and sacred palaces of the Roman emperors.

From earliest times the palaces, temples, and fortified enclosures in the eastern provinces of the Roman Empire, which were the impressive abodes and sacred strongholds of those superior beings who controlled the life and destiny of men, were the only comprehensible realities by means of which the common man could visualize the splendors of a heavenly domain. The primitive instinct to conceive of the unknown in terms of the known, to think of the world as an ancestral shelter or cosmic house, and to formulate conceptions of heaven as a stronghold, palatium, and walled enclosure guarded by a "Royal Gate," had not been changed by the upper-class rationalism of Classic culture. Over the centuries the forms of architecture continued to have ideational values and overtones of meaning in the minds of the credulous masses, who looked with awe and reverence upon all monumental structures.

Monumental construction in carved stone was by necessity the creation of the ruling

---

[1] G. Bandmann, *Mittelalterliche Architektur als Bedeutungsträger*, 1951; L. Bréhier and P. Batiffoll, *Les survivances impérial romain*, 1920; L. Hautecoeur, *Mystique et architecture, symbolisme du cercle et de la coupole*, Paris, 1954; A. Grabar, *L'Empereur dans l'art byzantine*, 1936; P. Lemerle, "Apropos des origines de l'édifice culturel chrétien," *Bulletin de la classe des lettres del'Ac. Royale de Belgique*, xxxiv, 1948, pp. 306-328; E. Lohmeyer, *Christus Kult und Kaiser Kult*, 1919; H. Sedlmayr, *Die Enstehung der Kathedrale*, 1950, pp. 141-143; J. Sauvaget, *La mosquée omeyyade de Médine, Étude sur les origines architecturales de la mosquée et de la basilique*, 1947; A. Strange, *Das frühchristliche Kirchengebäude als Bild des Himmels*, Cologne, 1950; a dissertation by L. Kitschelt (Munich, 1938) discusses the Early Christian basilica as a representation of the Heavenly Jerusalem.

order, because it was dependent upon wealth, skill, quarries, transportation, and organized labor. Hence its forms, which transcended anything within the attainment of the ordinary man, were the most memorable means by which the people could visualize the grandeur, power, and superhuman authority of their earthly and spiritual lords. For centuries, therefore, when the illiterate masses were unable to think in the abstractions of verbal imageries, architectural symbolism was a natural way of imaginative thinking because it was only by means of comprehensible forms that ideas, intuitions, and beliefs could have any convincing reality and popular validity. In the evolution of thought symbolism was for a long time just as necessary and intuitive in the arts as was the habit in philosophical reasoning of transferring thought-patterns, which were based upon customary social and technomorphic forms, to the exposition of concepts regarding religion and the cosmic order.[2]

The Romans had their own symbolic traditions long before they learned from the Hellenistic East the value of impressive architectural forms as a means of conveying ideas and strengthening popular beliefs. It was only after the solemn deliberation of the Senate that Caesar was granted the honor of having a gabled roof (*fastigium*) on his dwelling. At the beginning of the Empire the shrewd Augustus saw the value of architecture when he established the policy of building monumental gateways at the entrance to his provincial cities to commemorate his rule and celebrate his Adventus. Before the end of the Empire, when everything associated with the emperors had become sacred, this architectural symbolism, especially as it pertained to the palatium, was systematically cultivated by the State, and was always most effective in the provinces where the people were accustomed to see in the grandeur of the temples, gateways, public buildings, and palaces a manifestation of the *providentia* and heavenly authority of a divine sovereign.

The exact intent of this imperial symbolism is difficult to interpret because the separate architectural features, when removed from the beliefs and public ceremonies which gave them their content, look to our rational and unimaginative age like mere conventions of design. Nevertheless, when such elements as the city-gate, towered façade, castrum, cupola, orbis, royal ciborium, and domical vestibule are seen as forms of palace symbolism and are reviewed as historical ideas from their inception down to their adaptation by the Christian Church, they reveal a consistent use and persistent expressive intent. It is the purpose of this study to demonstrate, if possible, that when these motifs are considered as significant forms in the figurative imagery and rituals of both Antiquity and the Middle Ages, are recognized as something more than representational conventions on Roman coins and mosaics, and are seen persisting as celestial and cosmic symbols in Christian art and architecture, they begin to complement one another, revealing a pattern which links together in one tradition the thinking of the mediaeval period with that of Rome and the Hellenistic East.

A pattern by itself is not convincing if, by chronological sequence, it shows nothing

[2] E. Topitsch, "Society, Technology and Philosophical Reasoning," *Philosophy of Science*, 24, 1954, pp. 275-296.

5

more than a continuity of architectural forms. The mere repetition of motifs does not reveal expressive content and prove that the same ideas continued to be associated with identical forms. It is not enough to piece together from the records a sketchy indication of what the forms were meant to convey in each successive period. Before the fragmentary evidence derived from documents and ceremonies ceases to appear artificial and dubious, there is the necessity of escaping from the limitations of our own rational logic in order to sympathize with the habits of thought and incentives which kept alive a symbolic tradition. The fact that architectural symbolism was always intuitive at the popular level, and for that reason dependent upon traditional forms and customary ideas, helps to explain why the Christian churchmen took over, both consciously and unconsciously, so much from the past and, often with very little change in the meanings, made use of pagan symbolism, imperial forms, and palace conventions to present in convincing terms the spiritual beliefs and heavenly rewards of the new faith.

At the present time, when kings are looked upon as ordinary mortals who acquire their power from the people rather than from God, it is difficult to appreciate the incentives which impelled the great patrons of architecture, regardless of whether they were Roman emperors, mediaeval kings, papal prelates, or Islamic caliphs, to turn back to the past for the symbolic means of expressing, and also of justifying, their claims to universal and divine authority. Much of what they insisted upon in their architecture, ceremonies, titles, and trappings now seems little more than an empty formalism, or at best comparable to our own use of ideological propaganda. While accepting the fact that Eastern monarchs, triumphant Republican generals and Roman emperors were looked upon as deities, that Nero and Domitian wanted to be recognized in their palaces as a Ptolemaic sun-king and living god, and that Caracalla, Severus Alexander, and Gallienus tried to revive in their own persons the cult of Alexander the Great, we consider it to have been irrational and vain stage acting. Therefore, all the symbolic means, which were used to make their parts look real, seem like obvious scenery, now that the actors have left the stage. Much the same is true when we read about the rulers of the Middle Ages who, within the framework of the Christian faith, wore the vestments of a Kosmokrator, still accepted the flattery of the old imperial sun-symbolism, enacted the part of the Son of God, were accepted as a throne-sharer with God, identified themselves with the great world rulers of the past, and by their policy of *imitatio imperialis* endeavored to preserve, or revive, all the formal manifestations of the old imperial claims to universal and heavenly authority.

Any modern effort to follow the long and bitter struggle in the West between the emperors and popes, as to which should be accepted by all men as the Vicar of God and the heir to the supreme powers of the Roman Augustus, is likely to underestimate the importance of symbolism if, by reducing the issues to only feudal power politics, it disregards the underlying and inherited religious convictions regarding kingship. It is easy to overlook the very essence of the imperial contentions when we sympathize logically with the papal opposition to the efforts of the northern rulers to be recognized as the "Royal Christ" and to insist that the Palatium in all matters, both spiritual and secular, was over the Church. At the same time we are likely to attribute only nonspiritual motives to the popes who, in the creation of an ecclesiastic principality at Rome, adopted the imperial ceremonies, regalia, titles, and architectural insignia of a pagan past. The necessity of symbolism in the Middle Ages should not be misinterpreted because the papal policy of *imitatio imperialis* sank to a purely mundane level when it impelled Bonifice VIII to make his arrogant statement, *Ego sum caesar, ego sum imperator.*

These related royal and ecclesiastic policies of *imitatio imperialis* indicate that there was a consistent pattern of ideas underlying the continuity of architectural motifs. They do not, however, explain why both rulers and churchmen continued to seek precedent in the past and to attach so much importance to vestments, rituals, ceremonies, and palace forms of architecture, which they felt were convincing manifestations of divine pre-eminence. Both were influenced by the universal beliefs in the mystical nature of kingship. Ever since the Roman emperors adopted the forms and ideas of the Hellenistic kings, which had been based upon the Egyptian, Persian, and Mesopotamian conceptions of the ruler as a divine Kosmokrator, kingship was a religion in the popular mind, regardless of whether it was over, combined with, or secondary to the other cults. Such was its appeal that it was a long time before Christianity, nationalism, and representative government could divest the monarch of his relationship to God. In a way that was comparable to the antique acceptance of triumph and coronation as implying deification, everyone during the Middle Ages believed that purification and consecration by anointment invested a ruler with divine attributes.

The desire, therefore, of successive monarchs from Alexander the Great down to Frederick II to be immersed for apotheosis in the ceremonial stream of world rulership was not all vanity and empty formality. The mediaeval rulers still believed in their spiritual relationship in the "World Family of Kings," for very much the same instinctive reasons that the people wanted to see and adore something supernatural in the head of the State.[3] Even though we may sense a longing for immortality, and hence a belief in reincarnation, in the efforts of successive Roman and mediaeval emperors to affiliate themselves in every way possible with an Alexander the Great, Caesar, Augustus, Constantine, King David, and Charlemagne, there was nearly always behind them a faith and conviction that heavenly authority was transmitted with the purple and that divine powers resided in the symbolism and rituals of the kingly tradition.

The modern age should have regained some insight into the magic of this mystical

[3] G. A. Ostrogorsky, "Die Byzantinische Staatenhierarchie," *Seminarium Kondakovianum,* VIII, 1936, pp. 41-61; R. Holtzmann, "Der Weltherrschaftsgedanke des Mittelalterlichen Kaisertums und die Souveränität der Europapäischen Staaten," *Historische Zeitschrift,* CLIX, 1938-39, pp. 251-264; F. Dölger, "Die 'Familie der Könige' im Mittelalter," *Historische Jahrbuch,* LX, 1940, pp. 397-420.

faith now that it has witnessed in two dictators how vain and ambitious mortals can become obsessed with a veneration of the past and in the end, regardless of their motives, become deluded by their re-enactment of a part. The interest of Hitler and Mussolini in traditional architecture as a setting for ceremonies, and the Communist efforts to revive a ruler-cult, should help us to understand the necessity of symbolism and the instinct to turn back to the past for precedent in any age when the theophanic ideas regarding the Crown transcended the rational. As long as the concepts of kingship were something more than a secular ideology the Court, like the Church, had to find expression for its beliefs in ceremonies, rituals and monumental symbols. Furthermore, in attempting to trace the persistence of imperial symbolism, it should be kept in mind that rulers have most emphatically reverted to the prestige of the past when their position was being challenged, as by the Church during the Middle Ages, when new aspirants to universal ruler came to power, or when conquerors, like the Islamic Caliphs, Ottoman Sultans and Indian Moghuls, sought to justify their claims to being the Voice and Shadow of God.[4]

It remains to be seen whether by starting with the history of the city and palace gateways it is possible to expand this limited approach to include all that the introduction has implied and to meet the criticisms of those who are reluctant to accept the mediaeval repetition of motifs as evidence of an earlier Roman ideology. At no stage in the investigation is the proof conclusive, since it is only by the cumulative weight of the evidence that it is possible to show that from ancient times down to the end of the Middle Ages, in both the Christian West and Islamic East, there was a persistent and consistent interrelation between similar gateway features, ruler ceremonies, and popular beliefs regarding the heavenlike abode of a divine ruler. Within the pattern of gateway symbolism, as it influenced palaces, temples, numismatics, and the representational arts, it is the striking parallels and recurrent relations between forms and ceremonies which justify the use of both prototypes and survivals as a means of reformulating the content and intent of various architectural motifs.

In spite of the gaps in the evidence it is difficult to disregard the existence of a continuum when, for example, in the sequence of time it is seen: a) that the Mesopotamians attributed anagogical values to the towered façade of their kingly strongholds and transferred this gateway feature to their palaces and temples; b) that the

[4] Recent studies of kingship, many of which are summarized by I. Engnell (*Studies in Divine Kingship in the Ancient Near East*, Uppsala, 1951), make it apparent that from the beginnings of kingship there has been a universal desire on the part of the uneducated to see in the ruler a priest-god-king and godlike father endowed with the physical and supernatural powers to provide for them and to control an incomprehensible world. The significance of ruler worship may have been overemphasized by A. M. Hocart (*Kingship*, Oxford University Press, 1927, p. 7) when he wrote, "The earliest known religion is a belief in the divinity of kings"; but its importance to the history of ideas has been reaffirmed in more restricted statements by Engnell (p. 31) and G. Widengren (*Hochgottglaube im alten Iran*, Uppsala, 1928, p. 395). Difficult as it is for an enlightened age to explain the striking similarities of the forms, customs and ceremonies in the long history of ruler worship, there is gradually emerging evidence from the Roman, Holy Roman, Byzantine and Islamic empires to show that the beliefs back of the conventions of kingship, even when they seem to have been imposed by vain rulers on the ruled, actually reflect a persistent and instinctive willingness on the part of the people to see a supernatural, cosmic, and divine Father in their king.

Egyptians made the towered pylon a palace, temple and cosmic symbol; c) that the Syrians in the Roman period added towers over the entrance to the temples of their sky-gods; d) that the Christians in Syria made use of towers to transform the primitive church into a Royal House of God; e) that the late Roman and Byzantine architects and artists made the towered façade a symbol of the *Sacrum palatium*; and f) that the Carolingian emperors constructed a towered façade over the entrance to their royal abbey churches as a ceremonial *locus regalis* and a monumental assertion that the Palatium was over the Church.

Whether or not the overall uniformity and cumulative consistency of the evidence regarding the ideological and ceremonial association of domical towers, domical vestibules, and domical baldachins with palace entrances warrant a reconsideration of how the now destroyed Roman and Byzantine palaces should be restored must remain a problematical question until the conclusions of this study have been tested, modified, and corrected. While it will be obvious that a detailed investigation of architectural motifs and their expressive connotations does not result in light reading, it is to be hoped, nevertheless, that this study may contribute to the realization that the history of architecture involves much more than structural and descriptive facts made palatable by a personal and contemporary veneer of aesthetic appreciation.

I · THE CITY-GATE CONCEPT

THE first architectural element to be considered is the city gateway with its towered façade, archway, and vestibule. Because of its ceremonial importance in the religious and public life of a city, its forms all acquired divine, royal, and celestial meaning, and hence came to influence the development of architectural expression throughout Antiquity and the Middle Ages. Studies of the towered façade, disregarding its gateway origin and ceremonial importance, have given little intimation of why this apparently utilitarian element of construction was taken over from defensive portals to be transformed into the monumental entrance of palaces, temples, and churches.[1] Usually the decorated towered gateways of Roman cities have been looked upon as examples of Rome's somewhat ostentatious insistence upon display; their representation on the coins of Thrace and Asia Minor have been literally interpreted as only a means of depicting a *civitas* or *oppidum*; and the ultimate transference of its towers from the castrum, as the seat of imperial government in the provinces, to the royal entrance of late Roman palaces, and subsequently to the entrance of royal churches has been generally accepted as little more than a matter of design. There is the possibility, however, that this purely factual and descriptive approach has resulted in imposing upon the past our own modern attitude towards architecture, leaving us with little understanding of how men thought of august structures when they embodied the ideas and authority of the State.

From the remote time when walled towns and royal strongholds were first built it was instinctive for men to attribute anagogical, allegorical and topological meanings to gateways, and especially to the "King's Gate," because they were the dramatic and memorable stage-sets for so much of the ceremonial life of the people. In the Ancient East the gateway was a symbol of heavenly authority just because it was the entrance to the domain and dwelling of both godlike kings and kinglike gods. Its arcuated portal and towered bulwark continued to have ideological values throughout Antiquity and the Middle Ages because it was the place where the populace received with dramatic pageantry their ruler as a divine being, a triumphant victor, and a potential savior. Under the Romans a similar imagery became customary in all parts of the Empire where the theophanic implications of the *Adventus Augusti* and of triumphal entries gave a celestial import to the towered portal of the castrum and the triumphal arch. By the Late Empire, when everything pertaining to the emperors was revered, the gateway surmounted by either towers or ciborium cupolas had become the most memorable feature of an imperial stronghold. Its forms and its ceremonies of welcome were incorporated into the palace tradition with the result that the gateway became a kind of architectural ideogram denoting a *Sacrum palatium*

[1] H. Schaefer, "The Origin of the Two-towered Façade in Romanesque Architecture," *Art Bulletin*, XXVII, 1945, pp. 85-108; R. Schultze, "Die römische Stadttore," *Bonn. Jahrb.*, CXVIII, 1909, pp. 280-352; Schultze, "Das römische Stadttor in der kirchlichen Baukunst des Mittelalters," *Bonn. Jahrb.*, CXXIV, 1917, pp. 17-52; E. Weigand, *Byz. Zeit.*, XXVII, 1927, pp. 155-157.

as the seat of government and the place from which emanated the divine wisdom of the State.

Both the nature and importance of this imperial concept can be most clearly seen in the influences which the Roman ruler rituals and architectural symbolism had upon church architecture in the Carolingian and Byzantine empires. Because the towered façade of the castrum had been a symbol of THE PALATIUM, the Carolingian kings, for political reasons, made it the dominant feature on the façade of the royal abbey churches of those monasteries where they periodically resided with their courts. At the same time that these mediaeval rulers were endeavoring to make the towered "Westwerk" a manifestation of their claims to authority over the Church, Byzantine architecture gradually developed a monumental baldachin over the entrance to the palace churches at Constantinople as a chapel for the Basileus and as an emblem of his dominant position in the Church.

1. In the Ancient and Christian East

Every primitive culture attached a special sanctity and ritual to the doorway and portal, but many of the most lasting ideas associated with the sacral gateway in the Roman Empire and Middle Ages went back in origin to the fortifications of Mesopotamia, Palestine, and Egypt, where the walled and towered enclosure was the stronghold of a divine king and his gods.[2] Throughout the Hellenistic East, where it had long been customary to adore a ruler as an exalted being, the towered façade and archway of the city-gate had a celestial meaning because they were the monumental features of the ceremonial entrance to cities, palaces, and temples, where the populace welcomed their kings and god-images as heavenly beings. Hence in the Roman provinces of the East the Royal Gate was by tradition the place where a resplendent and godlike king was received by his subjects, where he sat in judgment and where, after his appearance and reception, he withdrew like the sun at night into his impregnable and heavenlike stronghold.

Everywhere in the ancient Orient the city-gate was the center of public and ceremonial life, comparable in many ways to the agora and forum of the Greeks and the Romans.[3] At an early date its towered façade, rising to heaven and dominating the city, became a symbol of royal and divine authority and was, therefore, transferred to the entrance of palaces and temples, which were themselves the fortresslike dwellings of men's earthly and heavenly masters. Although nothing was conceivably more awe-inspiring than the king's citadel, the ordinary man's knowledge of it was limited to its towered portal. Hence, because it was the most memorable feature and the place where the king's business was transacted, "gateway" in the East became by metonymy

[2] A. J. Evans, *Journal of Hellenistic Studies*, XXI, 1901, pp. 181ff.; M. Rostowzew, *Röm. Mittl.*, XXVI, 1911, p. 132; E. L. Highbarger, "The Gates of Dreams," *The Johns Hopkins Univ. Studies in Archaeology*, No. 30, 1940.

[3] F. Vigouroux, *Dictionnaire de la Bible*, I, 1895, "aire," p. 324.

a synonym for "palace."[4] This usage as a synecdoche reflected the same habits of thinking which resulted in the Egyptian king being called the Pharaoh, or "Great House," the Roman royal family being designated as the *Domus divina*, and the Turkish government being called the "Sublime Porte."[5] Also it helps to explain why a gateway continued to be, during Antiquity and the Middle Ages, a natural ideogram with which to symbolize a city, stronghold, and palace, and at the same time to indicate the divine power invested in the ruler of the State.

The instinctive habit of transferring the attributes of rulers to the architecture is reflected in the statement of an Akkadian official who wrote, "The King's majesty I equated to that of a god and reverence for the palace I inculcated in the troops."[6] At the same time it must be realized that the resplendent and sacred Gate of Ishtar was decorated with golden rosette-stars on a sky-blue ground because the inhabitants of Babylon for centuries had looked upon an arched and towered portal as a celestial form, a replica of the arch of heaven. In the literature of Mesopotamia it was customary, as in the hymn to the Sun-god, to speak of "The Towers of Heaven,"[7] to refer in both hymns and oracles to "The Door of Heaven Thou do'st open,"[8] to write "Out of the great gate of Heaven I proclaimed aloud,"[9] and to identify the gateway with the Lord of Heaven and Earth, as in the hymn to the deified King, Ur-Engur, which reads:

> Thy gate, "Thy God is a Great God," I name;
> Its shining doors like the Sun-god at midday radiate light.
> Where . . . decrees fate, where the gods determine justice,
> (There) Ur-Engur, God of Heaven and Earth, sits as Counsellor.[10]

The same ideological and ceremonial veneration for the gateway existed among the Egyptians, who believed that the flanking towers of the pylon at the entrance to their palace-temples represented the "Horizon of Heaven," an all-inclusive cosmic house and the bounding limits of North and South between which the Sun-god rose and set.[11] "Such cosmic symbolism made the doorway of the pylon of both palaces

---

[4] From ancient times down to the use of "Porte" to designate the Turkish government, "gateway" and "Door of the King" have been used to signify the Court and the seat of the ruler (*op.cit.*, v, "Porte," pp. 553-554), while in the Old Testament "gate" is frequently used by metonymy for palace (J. H. Hastings, *A Dictionary of the Bible*, II, 1898, p. 12).

[5] See pp. 195, 205.

[6] J. B. Pritchard, *Ancient Near Eastern Texts*, 1950, p. 434.

[7] T. Dombart, "Das Babylonische Sonnentor und die 'Sage' des Sama," *Journal of the Society of Oriental Research*, XII, 1928, p. 2; Dombart, *Der Sakralturm*, 1920; in the Hymn to the Sun it reads, "May the gate of Heaven be thy bond" and "In the Great Gate of the shining heavens" (A. H. Sayce, *Origin and Growth of Religion*, 1888, p.

171; 1891, p. 513); Highbarger, *op.cit.*, pp. 15-22.

[8] Hymn to Shamash (Jastrow, *Religion of Babylonia and Assyria*, 1898, pp. 301-303).

[9] Oracles of Esarhaddon (Jastrow, *op.cit.*, p. 345); also "The Heavens are made firm by two gates."

[10] S. Landon, "Three Hymns in the Cult of the Deified Kings" *Proceedings of the Society of Biblical Archaeology*, XL, 1918, p. 47; also in the Hymn to Innini as Venus (p. 53), "May thy temple star-like constructed shine in splendour for thee; May thy heavenly house lift up its head for thee."

[11] T. Dombart, "Der zweitürmige Tempel-pylon altaegyptischer Baukunst und seine religiöse Symbolik," *Egyptian Religion*, I, 1933, pp. 87-98; "Horizon," or the towered pylons, not only represented heaven, the celestial dwelling of the Sun, the king's palace and a temple, but it symbolized

and temples the Gate of Heaven through which, from the East in most temples, emerged the Shining One and his divine and equally resplendent representative on earth." An Alexandrian coin (Fig. 47), issued in honor of Trajan, is evidence of the persistence of this imagery, for it shows Isis rising like the Sun over the gateway, between the towers of the pylon, as she comes forth to meet the Roman ruler of heaven and earth. It is also comparable to the figure of Constantine, all glorious like the "Invincible Sun" over the *Porta Incluta* of his city of Treves (Fig. 50), and the imperial "Day Star" over the castrum-portal on the other Constantinian coins (Figs. 42-46).

Every culture in Antiquity was influenced by the gateway concept which had originated in a remote past when men began to live in walled cities. The Greeks as early as Homer referred to the "Gate of Hades" and in the "Gate of the Sun" saw a resplendent portal separating heaven and earth; later, Virgil in presenting his prophecy of an ideal empire made use of gateway symbolism in his reference to "The Ivory Gate."[12] But it was not its importance in literature which kept alive the gateway imagery in all parts of the Roman world. Everywhere the people who lived under the protection of walled cities and who still considered it the ordained condition of men to be ruled by superior and godlike beings retained very similar ideas to those of the Mesopotamians and Egyptians in regard to the gateway as the place where all-powerful gods and kings entered and came forth.

By Roman times the Near East had various ancient gateway traditions which had become enriched in content during the Classical period by the continued ceremonial importance of the city entrance in the religious festivals, the Royal Epiphany, the Roman Triumph and the Imperial Adventus. In those regions that had once been part of the late Hittite Empire a ceremonial structure known as an *hilani* had taken over the towers of the Assyrian "gate of Heaven," thereby giving rise, as at Sindjerli, to palaces with a towered façade.[13] Under the Romans the religious architecture of Syria and the Hauran attached a celestial value to a gateway, especially as the mark of a heavenly stronghold and triumphal entrance on temples dedicated to sun and sky worship. At Sî', in the first century B.C., the sanctuary of Ba'al Shamin, the supreme solar deity, had a towered façade.[14] The monumental propylaea at the entrance to

the "Throne of the World." This explains the words of Sinuhe, servant of the palace, who says, "I found his Majesty on his great throne in the golden gateway" (A. Erman, *The Literature of the Egyptians*, trans. by A. M. Bachman, 1927, p. 26; E. B. Smith, *Egyptian Architecture*, 1938, p. 153).

[12] E. K. Rand, *The Building of Eternal Rome*, 1943, pp. 115-125; E. H. Highbarger, *The Gates of Dreams, An Archaeological Examination of Virgil, Aeneid VI*, 1940, pp. 893-899.

[13] The problem of the so-called *hilani* and the question of whether the towered gatehouses and palaces at Sindjerli should be called an *hilani* are in need of further study: A. Bell, *Palace and Mosque at Ukaidir*, 1914, ch. IV; R. Bernheimer, "Oriental Source of Sacred Christian Architecture," *A.J.A.*, XLIII, 1939, p. 654; Koldewey, *Ausgrabungen in Sindschirli*, II, pp. 188ff.; Oelmann, "Hilani und Liwan Haus," *Bonn. Jahrb.*, CXXVII, 1922, pp. 188-236; Wachtsmuth, "Zum Problem der Hethitischen und Mitannischen Baukunst," *Jahrb. d. D. Arch. Inst.*, XLVI, 1931, pp. 32ff. For the Persian palace see F. W. Bissing, "Der Persische Palast und die Turmbasilika," *Studien zur Kunst des Ostens*, 1923, pp. 40ff.

[14] H. C. Butler, *Ancient Architecture in Syria*, II, A, p. 374, ill. 325.

the sacred precincts of such sky deities as Jupiter Heliopolitanus at Ba'albek, Jupiter at Damascus and Bel at Palymra had flanking towers in combination with some of the decorative features of a triumphal arch.[15]

The most significant extant structure in Syria is the little temple at Djmer (Fig. 1), finished and consecrated on October 15, A.D. 245, which was dedicated to Zeus and has in it an inscription of A.D. 216, referring to a judgment of Caracalla.[16] Unlike the temples of Greece, it has on its classical and gabled roof towers at all four corners. In its gable is the traditional Window of Appearance from which the priests spoke for the god. A recent study of temples with staircases leading to the roof lists more than twenty known sanctuaries in Syria which were presumably similar to Djmer in having one or two pairs of towers on the roof.[17] That these Syrian towers, rising heavenward, were ritualistically associated with the worship of a supreme sky-god is most clearly indicated in the Great Temple of Bel at Palmyra by the staircases at either end of the cella: these go up to what were once towers at the four corners of the roof and flank a *thalamos* which is sculpturally decorated with a flat astronomical dome and other celestial symbols.[18] This Eastern custom of having towers at all four corners not only made the towered façade a traditional feature of the entrance to a divine and royal residence, but it also gave to the sanctuary the form of a stronghold, making it comparable to an Assyrian palace-temple, a castrum type of Roman palace and to the derivative Christian conception of a church and "the City of God" as a heavenly fortress.

In addition to the customary relation in the Orient between palaces and temples there is conclusive evidence from both the Hellenistic and the Late Antique periods to show that this towered type of structure in the Near East, whether used as a palace or temple, was always thought of as a Royal House. From the second century B.C. (c. 182-175 B.C.) at Arak el-Emir (ancient Tyrus), which lies east of the Jordan, the ruins of the Ḳaṣr il-ʿAbd ("Castle of the Slave"), which de Vogüé first recognized as having been a palace, are similar to the Syrian temples in having had the foundations of towers at the four corners, in which there are staircases leading to the roof.[19] Re-

---

[15] Baalbek (T. Wiegand, *Baalbek*, I, 1921, pp. 103-109, Taf. 16); Palmyra (Wiegand, *Palmyra*, I, 1932, pp. 146-150, Taf. 100); R. Dussaud ("Le temple de Jupiter Damascénien," *Syria*, III, 1922, pp. 219ff.) restored the propylaea with towers and published a coin of Caracalla (p. 230, fig. 4) which shows the temple at Abila with a towered façade.

[16] Butler, *Architecture and the Other Arts*, 1903, p. 406, fig. 144; P. Roussel and F. de Visscher, "Les Inscriptions du temple," *Syria*, XXIII, 1942-43, pp. 173-200.

[17] R. Amy, "Temples à escaliers," *Syria*, XXVII, 1950, pp. 82-136, figs. 1-3.

[18] H. Seyrig, "Antiquities syriennes," *Syria*, XIV, 1933, pp. 238ff., fig. 1; Wiegand, *Palmyra*, Taf. 71.

[19] De Vogüé, *Voyage au Terre Sainte*, 1860, p. 224; Butler, *Ancient Architecture in Syria*, 1907, II, A, I, pp. 1-19, ill. 2; L. H. Vincent, *Rev. Bibl.*,

XVII, 1920, pp. 182ff.; F. Oelmann, *Bonn. Jahrb.*, CXXVII, 1922, p. 202, Abb. 9; C. Watzinger, *Denkmäler Palästinas*, II, 1933, p. 13; Sauvaget, *La mosquée omeyyade*, p. 181; the Hellenistic use of βᾶρις for a fortresslike structure, whether a palace or a temple, when considered in relation to the ancient ideas of towers as heavenly symbols, the concept of the tower as "the house which is the link of heaven and earth" (G. E. Wright, "The Temple in Palestine-Syria," *The Biblical Archaeologist*, III, 1944, p. 67), and the Biblical and Christian use of *turris* to symbolize a divine person and the church as a fortress, all implies not so much a verbal derivation as a persistent conceptual tradition in which "tower," like "gateway," was visualized as the equivalent of either a divine or royal stronghold. For possible derivations see: E. Littmann, *Princeton Expedition to Syria*, III, A, p. 6;

gardless of whether this building was a temple, as some have thought, or more probably a palace, it is interesting to note that the historian Josephus uses the Greek word for *turris* for it when he wrote, "He (Hyrkanos) also erected a mighty building (βᾶρις)," with great *aulai* and spacious gardens. The persistence of this palace tradition is illustrated by the palaces and temples at Aksum, which were constructed between the fourth and the seventh centuries A.D., for they all presumably had massive towers at the corners of the divine and royal residences, and in two of the towers of the Palace of Enda Mikael there are still great staircases.[20]

Against this background it is not surprising that the Christians towards the close of the fourth century began to think of their ecclesia as a royal structure which they called a "basilica."[21] It was not, however, until the last half of the fifth and the beginning of the sixth century that they undertook to transform their place of worship into a more monumental and royal *Domus Dei* by erecting towers not only over the façade, i.e., at either side of the "Royal Door," but also over the prothesis and diaconicon which flanked the apse that they called "Heaven."[22] As early as Eusebius, who wrote of "The Temple of Heavenly Types" and said, "He adorneth (it) with a single mighty gateway, even in praise of the one and only God, the universal King," the Syrian churchmen were formulating the symbolic conception of the church as a cosmic house. They were fully aware of the various implications of the city-gate tradition, especially as it pertained to the Epiphany of a Royal Savior, the entrance of a Triumphant Lord, and the Advent of a Universal King of Kings, for they had

---

C. B. Welles, *Royal Correspondence in the Hellenistic Period*, 1934, pp. 320-321); for the Hellenistic and Roman use of "turris" see: P. Grimal, "Les maisons à tours hellénistiques et romains," *Mélanges d'arch. et d'hist.*, LVI, 1939, pp. 28-59; for Christian usage: Du Cange, *Glossarium Lat.*, "Turres"; Auber, *Histoire et théorie du symbolisme religieux*, 1884, pp. 116-120; Sauer, *Symbolik des Kirchengebäudes*, 1902, pp. 137, 140-143; Hastings, *A Dictionary of the Bible*, 1902, IV, p. 800. The influence of this tower imagery on Roman architectural symbolism is indicated by the way Tacitus (*Hist.*, III, 38) uses *turris* to designate a palace near Horti Serviliani, and Horace (*Odes*, 1, 4, 13) writes, *Pallida Mors aequo pulsat pede pauperum tabernas regumque turris* ("Pale Death with foot impartial knocks at the poor man's cottage and at princes' palaces"); for the importance of towers on Roman villas: P. W. Lehmann, *Roman Wall Paintings from Boscoreale in the Metropolitan Museum of Art*, Cambridge, 1952, pp. 99-106; for the use of terra-cotta towers as lanterns and tomb offerings: F. Oelmann, "Die tönerne Porta des Ilarus von Intercisa," *Festschrift für Rudolf Egger*, Klagenfurt, 1952, pp. 114ff.

[20] D. Krencker, *Deutsche Aksum Expedition*, II, 1913, pp. 112ff., Taf. 19; Oelmann, *Bonn. Jahrb.*, CXXVII, 1922, p. 192, Abbs. 6, 7; for survivals of this type of castrum palace with corner towers as mediaeval churches in the region see D. R. Buxton, *Archaeologia*, XCII, 1947, pp. 1-42.

[21] A. M. Schneider, "Die altchristliche Bishofs und Gemeinde-kirche und ihre Benennung," *Nachrichten d. Ak. d. Wissenschaften in Göttingen*, I, Phil-hist. Klasse, 1952, pp. 153-161. For the various theories regarding why it came to be believed, as Isidore of Seville (*Etym.*, 15,4,11) says, that "*Basilica* was formerly the name of the King's residence, which is how it got its name, for *Basileus* means king and *Basilica* the king's house," see: E. Langlotz and F. Deichmann, *Reallexikon für Antike und Christentum*, I, 1950, cols. 1225-1259; Langlotz, "Der architektonische Ursprung der christlichen Basilica," *Festschrift für Hans Jantzen*, Berlin, 1951, pp. 30-36; J. Ward Perkins, "Constantine and the Origins of the Christian Basilica," *Papers of the British School at Rome*, XXII, 1954, pp. 69-90.

[22] The mystic conception of the church as a cosmic house is described in some detail by the Patriarch Iso 'jahb III (d. A.D. 660), who based his exposition on earlier Nestorian sources of the fifth century. In the *Expositio* he contrasts the apse, as the "Place of Heaven," with the *katastroma* in the nave, as the "Place of Paradise" (R. H. Connolly, *Expositio officiorum ecclesiae*, I, p. 196).

already begun to see in the church a Royal House, a *Templum regium* and a *Porta coeli*.[23]

The earliest representation of the House of God with a towered façade is the panel of the doors of Santa Sabina. It is our first evidence that back of the Christian's conception of the church as a *Porta coeli* and the adoption of the towered façade was an imperial ceremonial tradition; for Kantorowicz has pointed out that the panel represents an Epiphany scene, the Advent of what he calls the Messianic world ruler in which the Lord, like a Hellenistic king and Roman emperor, is depicted with an angel, or what had been in imperial iconography the winged victory, receiving the adoration of the *acclamantes* at the gate of the Templum.[24] It is still a question, as Delbrueck has pointed out, whether the bearded figure with the angel is the Lord or the Emperor; but the subsequent history of the motif is proof that the towered setting was meant to refer to the *Templum regium* as a gateway where all were received with royal honors into the heavenly palatium and, by extension, into the City of God and the Church itself.

The adoption of the towered façade on Syrian churches was undoubtedly related to the Christian policy, which had taken shape by the fifth century, of appropriating from the palace tradition everything, including ceremonies, insignia, regalia, acclamations, music, and decorations, which would present the Son of God and his Royal House in the impressive terms of a divine Imperator. At the same time the churchmen, when they began to make the towered façade so important, were influenced by the fortresslike character of the pagan palaces and temples with towers at the four corners and by the Late Roman type of castrum-palace representing the seat of divine authority, for Christian architecture, like Christian thinking, was the result of an assimilation of concurrent ideas.[25] That the Syrian churchmen by the second half of the fifth century had begun to think of God's temple as a heavenly castrum is indicated by many of their sanctuaries. The Church of the Prophets, Apostles, and Martyrs erected at Gerasa in A.D. 464-465 had towers at the four corners and a central

[23] For references to tower symbolism in the early church writings see: J. Sauer, *Symbolik des Kirchengebäudes*, 1902, pp. 103-105, 140-143; Auber, *Histoire et théorie du symbolisme religieux*, 1884, II, pp. 54, 112, 350-390 and III, pp. 116, 120; and for bibliography on the Church as the *Porta coeli* see H. Sedlmayr, *Die Entstehung der Kathedrale*, pp. 124, 141-143.

[24] E. H. Kantorowicz, "The 'King's Advent' and the Enigmatic Panels in the Doors of Santa Sabina," *Art Bulletin*, XXVI, 1944, pp. 207-231. R. Delbrueck ("The Acclamation Scene on the Doors of Santa Sabina," *Art Bulletin*, XXXI, 1949, pp. 215-217) suggests that the bearded figure with the angel is not the Lord, but either the emperor, perhaps Theodosius II, or his imperial representative, visiting the church, and that the towers "belong to the monumental turret-system of the gate to the town or palace." Much the same royal interpretation has been advanced by K. Wessel, "Der Kaiser und die

Kirche," *Jahrb. d. D. Arch. Inst.*, 65/66, 1950-51, pp. 317-323. The fact that churchmen, especially in the East, were opposed to representations of God strengthens Delbrueck's interpretation.

[25] Several Syrian churches of the sixth century were located inside a walled enclosure with towers at the four corners, which, because of their location and small dimensions, could not have been for defensive purposes but must have been intended to symbolize the City and Stronghold of God. The best example of this type of heavenly castrum is the South Church at il-Anderin, which was located within the city and yet had towered walls that probably enclosed a cemetery (Butler, *Ancient Architecture in Syria*, II, B, 1908, pp. 58-59, ill. 54). Another church with a castrum wall was at il-Habbat (*op.cit.*, p. 102, ill. 119) which Butler calls a fort, but which seems too small to have had any defensive value.

tower that was perhaps domical; the basilica church at Dair Solaib had fortresslike towers at the four corners; and on the Syrian mosaic from Khirbit Mukhayyat (Fig. 2) the same type of sanctuary is pictured.[26] This Syrian representation is very important in showing that the towers derived their celestial significance from the imperial castrum, because later it will be seen that the cupolas which it depicts on the towers flanking the entrance to the basilica were royal and divine emblems taken over from the palace symbolism of the Late Empire.[27]

It must be realized that Christianity was only following precedent in adapting the symbolic forms and glory of palace concepts to the service of God, for there had always been in the East a close correlation in men's minds between palaces and temples, kings and gods. This does not mean, however, that we can accept without any qualifications the recent theories that the Christian church in all its parts was copied directly from the pagan palace.[28] The towered façade is a case in point. The Syrian theologians, who were endeavoring to present the "Royal House" of God in imperial terms which would be readily comprehensible to the people, were not by necessity copying either Roman palaces or temples. The Hebrew veneration of city-gates went back to the writers of the Old Testament who, following Babylonian precedent, customarily visualized Heaven as a fortified city and Paradise as a walled garden protected by a series of gateways.[29] Both Esther and Daniel, who vividly remembered the years of their captivity, refer to the "King's Gate" as synonymous with palace,[30] for to the Jews, as to all the peoples of Egypt, Mesopotamia, and Persia, the gateway was the place where the king's business was transacted. In the Bible, Jerusalem is figuratively referred to as "The Gates of Sion," for they were "the Gate of the Lord" into which the righteous were allowed to enter; and it was within the Gates of Sion that were set "the thrones of judgment, the thrones of the house of David."

The custom, old and universal in the East, of setting up the king's throne in the gateway of his city, or palace, explains why the Royal Gate had come to acquire so

---

[26] Gerasa (J. W. Crowfoot, *Early Churches in Palestine*, 1941, pp. 85ff., fig. 8; E. B. Smith, *The Dome*, p. 112, figs. 175, 177); Dair Solaib (Mattern, *Mélanges de l'Université Sainte-Joseph*, XXII, 1939, p. 6); Khirbat Mukhayyat mosaic (P. Lemaire, *Rev. Bibl.*, XLIII, 1934, pp. 385-401, pl. XXVI/1; Smith, *The Dome*, p. 42, fig. 44).

[27] See p. 61.

[28] A. Strange, *Das frühchristliche Kirchenbäude als Bild des Himmel*, 1950; G. Bandmann, *Mittelalterliche Architektur als Bedeutungsträger*, 1951, pp. 90-91; Sauvaget, *La mosquée omeyyade*, 1947, pp. 122-157.

[29] In the "Creation of the World" (L. Ginsberg, *The Legends of the Jews*, I, 1942, p. 19) the Hebrew records tell how "Two gates of carbuncle form the entrance to Paradise"; and in the "Book of Adam" (*op.cit.*, p. 69) it was at the first portal of the seven gates of Paradise that the soul was welcomed; Enoch in the book of "The Ten Gener-

ations" (pp. 132-133) was shown "the six gates in the east of the fourth heaven by which the sun goes forth, and the six gates in the west where it sets."

[30] In the Old Testament "gate" is frequently used for "palace" (Hastings, *A Dictionary of the Bible*, II, 1898, p. 112): according to Esther, "all the King's servants, that were in the King's Gate (palace), bowed and reverenced Haman" (3:2), and "Hatach went forth to Mordecai unto the street of the city, which was before the King's Gate (4:6); "Esther put on her royal apparel, and stood in the inner court of the King's house (in Susa), over against the King's house, and the King sat upon his royal throne in the royal house, over against the gate of the house" (5:1); and after his elevation to power Mordecai the Jew sat at the King's Gate (5:13), while as ruler of the whole province of Babylonia under Nebuchadnezzar, "Daniel sat in the gate of the King" (Daniel 2:49).

much distinction as the symbol of supreme and heavenly omnipotence.[31] The public appearance of a ruler under a ceremonial covering at the gateway may later help to account for the eventual use of the dome, as a permanent version of the throne canopy, over the vestibule at the entrance to Roman and Byzantine palaces. The *'adr*, or canopy, in the poem from Ras Shamra under which Daniel sat in judgment at the city-gate is now thought to have been similar to the Assyrian *adru*, which was a ritualistic canopy used for the public reception of a city's god.[32] Evidence of the importance of the Royal Gate was uncovered at Assur where in the vestibule of the principal gate of the city the excavators found an enthroned statue of King Salmanassar III (859-824 B.C.), his embrasure decorated in imitation of heaven with colored tiles and reliefs.[33] Throughout the ancient East elaborate ceremonies of welcome for kings and gods took place at the entrance to cities, palaces, and temples. By the Hellenistic period, when the *parousia* of a king was religiously comparable to the Epiphany of a God, the *apantesis*, or official reception, was celebrated by a prescribed ritual in which the statues of the city's gods were sometimes brought forth to meet the ruler and the whole population bedecked their city, strewed palms, chanted their hymns of welcome, and shouted forth their acclamations as they bowed down or prostrated themselves in adoration.

The lasting imprint which this religious tradition had upon the popular imagination during both Antiquity and the Middle Ages can be explained by the way in which the Royal Epiphanies, and the seasonal festivals of welcome accorded to local gods, were transformed into imperial ceremonies and then re-adapted to Christian rituals and celebrations. Also for the Christians the Epiphany concept was given a new and lasting content by the influence which the Hebrew ceremonies had had upon the verbal imagery in the Bible. In many parts of the Old Testament the presentation of God as a glorious and triumphant Lord, who is greeted by the inhabitants of his city with music and praise, is a direct reflection of the ritual commonly accorded to a divine ruler, a resplendent Sun-god, at the time of his victorious entry. Inasmuch as the Biblical intent was anagogical, the picture of the King's Advent is always fractional until the passages based upon it are visualized in some such order: "Awake, awake . . . put on thy beautiful garments, O Jerusalem" (Is. 52:1); "Clap your hands, all ye people, shout unto God with the voice of triumph" (Ps. 47:1); "Sing unto the Lord" (Ps. 95:1); "Bow down . . . kneel before the Lord" (Ps. 96:2); for

[31] The titles "Gate of the King" and "Audience Gate" came from the Eastern tradition of an entrance court, or vestibule, in which the king's throne was set up so that he might "sit as Counsellor," give audiences and conduct his public business (W. Otto, *Hermes*, LV, 1920, p. 222; LVI, 1921, p. 104). In the Old Testament "The King of Israel and Jehosephat, the King of Judah, sat each on his throne, having put on their robes, at the threshing floor, in front of the entrance to the gate of Samaria" (I Kings 22:10); in Jeremiah (38:7) "the King then sitting in the gate of Benjamin" and "all the princes of the King of Babylon came in,

and sat in the Middle Gate" (39:3); and in Ezekiel it says of the closed, temple gate, "It is for the prince; the prince he shall sit in it to eat bread before the Lord" (44:3) and "the prince shall worship at the threshold of the gate" (46:2). In Palestine the threshing floor, or *goren*, which was located in front of the city-gate, was a sacred place used for public and religious rites and was the place where a ruler sat in judgment under a ceremonial covering (See Ch. IV nn. 27, 28).

[32] See Ch. IV nn. 27-30.

[33] W. Andrae, *Das Wiedererstandene Assur*, 1938, pp. 9, 146, Abbs. 4, 60.

when the gates are opened and "the everlasting doors" have been lifted up, then "the King of Glory shall come in" (Ps. 24:7, 9). Actually this Old Testament ritual of welcome was based upon the New Year Festival of the Israelites, when on the first day of the Feast of Tabernacles the kingship of Jahweh was celebrated (S. W. Hooke, *Myth and Ritual*, pp. 122-135). It was primarily derived from the Babylonian *akitu* festival and was originally held in honor of a sun-god before his worship was adapted to Jahweh. Nevertheless, it presents the same ceremonial features and "king-god ritual pattern" which were taken over with almost no changes for the Royal Epiphanies of the Hellenistic Sun-kings.

2. In relation to the Hellenistic Epiphany, Roman Adventus, and triumphal arch

It is not only the Old Testament references to the Coming of the Lord which reflect the influence of the Royal Epiphany upon men's imagery. Throughout the Empire and the Middle Ages many of the most lasting symbolic ideas associated with the gateway and the ritual of ruler-worship were derived from the elaborate ceremonies with which the cities of the Hellenistic and Roman East welcomed their rulers at the gateway as a resplendent Sun-god, a universal "Master of Heaven and Earth" and a "Savior" destined, it was hoped, to bring peace, prosperity, and happiness to their adoring subjects. Back, however, of the Hellenistic Epiphany and Roman Adventus was a much older and more universal religious tradition. To the Greeks an Epiphany, or "Appearance," was at first a purely religious event pertaining to the manifestation, anniversary and seasonal coming of a god.[34] Its ritual in most instances had been taken over from the older religions of the ancient East, where at the beginning of the new year, or on the occasion of a seasonal festival, the populace met their god-image at the gateway, escorted it with music, dancing, and acclamations through the city to its temple-palace, and finally celebrated the event with feasting. For centuries these Eastern religious rites, which at the festival of the New Year dramatized the return, or rebirth, of the god responsible for the renewed fertility of the land, had royal implications because in Egypt, Mesopotamia, and Palestine the king frequently took the part of the deity in the ceremonies.

All the cults and cities of the Near East continued to preserve some variation of this type of ceremony. At Assur, for example, Andrae has reconstructed from the records an account of what might be called an Assyrian Epiphany.[35] At the time of the god's annual festival his statue, after it had spent the night outside the city in its garden festival-house, was mounted under a baldachin on a wheeled ship and brought into the city with rejoicing. Always in Mesopotamia great importance was attached to "The Opening of the Gate" and in some rituals to its closing until such

---

[34] Pfister, Pauly-Wissowa, *Real-Encyclopädia*, Suppl., IV, 1924, pp. 277ff.
[35] Andrae, *op.cit.*, pp. 37-45.

time as the deity should again come to the city; and an Akkadian record tells how at Uruk "after (the statue of) the god Anu has left the chapel Enamenna and has reached the Exalted Gate," the brewers, especially honored, were harnessed to the crossbeam of the wagon on which the god made his ceremonial procession "from the Royal Gate to the Akitu House, the house of worship."[36]

By the Hellenistic period, when Alexander the Great and his successors had adapted themselves to the Eastern conception of a ruler as a divine world-master, all these Oriental and Greek festivals celebrating the Appearance of a God were long established and popular ceremonies, readily transformed into a Royal Epiphany. There had always been in the Near East, and especially in Egypt, a close parallel between the ritual of receiving gods and kings. The Egyptian Pharaoh, whom the Ptolemaic kings and Roman emperors were to emulate, was the heir of all the gods, publicly recognized as an incarnate Amon-Ra, identified with the shining Sun-god Horus as "The Master of the Sky" and given the official title of "The Son of Ra."[37] At the time of his periodic *heb-sed* festivals the Pharaoh's divinity and immortality were solemnly proclaimed in public before delegates from all the towns of Egypt; panegyrics were addressed to the "Golden Horus" in his festival hall; the event was celebrated "in the whole earth"; and throughout the kingdom his statues, like those of the later Roman emperors, were received, honored, and adored by the people in the cities.[38] As early as the Middle Kingdom we are told how the Pharaoh when he visited the cities of his kingdom made his appearances on the royal boat as the living Horus in a ceremonial fashion which recalls the later Epiphany and Adventus receptions of the Hellenistic kings and Roman emperors.[39] The manner in which the Egyptian ruler at the time of these public appearances was enthroned under a celestial tent-covering as a symbol of his supernatural nature and the way in which he was greeted by his subjects had a very direct bearing upon the subsequent importance of the ciborium in royal receptions at a city and palace gateway.

The long history of ruler-worship in the East meant that by the time the Greek kings took the titles of "Epiphany," "Savior," and "Lord God," and appeared before their subjects as the incarnation of Zeus-Amon, Apollo-Horus, Helios, and Dionysus, the celebration of their receptions, festivals, and appearances followed established conventions. This universal adoption throughout the Near East of the royal *parousia*, or Epiphany, marked the beginning of a new era in the Classical world; for it was then that the Greek cities not only accepted the Oriental forms of ruler-worship but began to compete with one another in the religious way they honored their deified masters.[40] At Athens the *parousia* of Demetrius Poliorketes, whom the Athenians called "the Savior-king," is described as follows: "They even went out to meet him with

[36] J. B. Pritchard, *Ancient Near Eastern Texts*, 1950, pp. 342-343.

[37] A. Moret, "Du Caractère religieux de la royauté pharaonique," *Annales du Musée Guimet*, xv, 1902, pp. 5-10 ("heir of all the gods"), 11 ("Son of the Sun"), 18 ("Master of the Sky"), 19 ("Son of Ra"), 22 ("Horus of gold").

[38] Moret, *op.cit.*, pp. 238-255, panegyrics (p. 256).

[39] K. H. Sethe, *Der dramatische Ramesseumpapyrus, ein Spiel zur Thronbesteigung des Königs*, 1928.

[40] Pfister, *op.cit.*, p. 311.

hymns, and choruses, and ithyphalli, and dancing and singing, and saying that he was the only true god. . . . And they fell at his feet and addressed supplications and prayers to him" (Athenaeus, *The Deipnosophists*, VI, 62).

Unfortunately there is much about the Hellenistic Epiphany that the fragmentary evidence fails to record in regard to its ceremonial provisions and its relation to the Roman Adventus.[41] In discussing the Graeco-Oriental origins of the Adventus, Kantorowicz wrote, "The King's appearance at the gate of the city compared with, or was, the Epiphany of a god."[42] These public welcomes of a divine ruler were not limited to periodic festivals celebrating the birthday, accession, and deification of a "Kyrios," but in both the Hellenistic and Roman world had become a prescribed part of the ruler-cult which the cities followed at the time of a royal visitation. Also, if we can judge by the emperor liturgies at the Byzantine and Germanic Courts there were various kinds of public receptions which were formally a part of all visitations, anniversaries, religious festivals, and even of the daily appearances of a sovereign at the entrance to his cities, palaces, and places of worship.

What made the Epiphany and Adventus so important to the history of art were their survival in the Middle Ages, their influence upon Christian imagery, and the way in which their pageantry and theology of ruler-worship gave symbolic values to the gateways and palace entrances where they took place. At the Byzantine Court the ritual of ingress and egress and the participation of the emperors in the religious festivals preserved many of the traditional forms of the Hellenistic Epiphany; throughout Europe all royal, ecclesiastical, and monastic ceremonies of welcome were based upon the *Adventus Augusti*; and down to the end of the Renaissance the public celebration of royal visitations, coronations, and triumphs followed Roman precedents. Inasmuch as the Roman custom of erecting free-standing arches to victorious generals and emperors was an important factor in the development of architectural symbolism, some consideration must be given to the rites of the Latin Triumph and the relation of the triumphal arch to the city-gate tradition.

A. THE ROMAN TRIUMPH

The Roman Triumph, especially as it influenced popular ruler-concepts and gateway symbolism, had much in common with the Hellenistic Epiphany and Imperial Adventus. All were ceremonies of welcome whose rites of deification gave a celestial

[41] A. Alföldi, *Hermes*, LXV, 1930, pp. 369-384; Alföldi, "Die Ausgestaltung des monarchischen Zeremoniells am römischen Kaiserhof," *Röm. Mittl.*, XLIX, 1934, pp. 88-89; E. Beurlier, *Essai sur le culte rendu aux empereurs romains*, 1890; A. Deissmann, *Light from the Ancient East* (trans. Strachan), pp. 372ff.; F. Kampers, "Die Geburtsurkunde der abendländischen Kaiseridee," *Hist. Jahrb.*, 1915, p. 255; E. H. Kantorowicz, *Art Bulletin*, XXVI, 1944, pp. 207-231; Kantorowicz, "Laudes Regiae," *University of California Publications in History*, XXX, 1946, pp. 63ff.; J. Kroll, "Gott und Hölle, der Mythos vom Descensuskampfe," *Studien der Bibliothek Warburg*, XX, 1932, pp. 37, 39, 42, 195, 278, 287, 358, 467, 480-486; E. Lohmeyer, *Christus Kult und Kaiser Kult*, 1919; Pfister, *Real-Encyclopädie*, "Epiphanie," Suppl., IV, 1924, pp. 277-323; E. Petersen, "Die Einholung des Kyrios," *Zeitschrift f. systematische Theologie*, VII, 1930, pp. 682-702; P. Roussal, *Bull. Corr. Hell.*, LV, 1931, pp. 95ff.; G. Strom, *Demos und Monarch*, 1922, p. 117; J. M. C. Toynbee, *The Hadrianic School*, 1934, note 38; O. Weinreich, "*Antikes Gottmenschentum*," *Neue Jahrb.*, II, 1926, pp. 633-650.

[42] Kantorowicz, *Art Bulletin*, XXVI, 1944, p. 212.

content to the arcuated portal. Scholars, however, have not agreed as to whether the triumphal arch with its rites of entry went back in origin to the city-gate and its Eastern antecedents. Some theories regarding the origin of the *fornix* have entirely disassociated it from the arcuated gateway and insisted that it was little more than a pedestal, invented during the Republic, to carry trophies and sculptures.[43] All agree that the honorific *arcus* was a Roman creation, influenced undoubtedly by the decorative and sculptural conventions of Hellenistic art. In addition to the fact that Rome had a *Porta Triumphalis*, there are many reasons why it is impossible to disregard the relation of the free-standing arch to the city-gate and all that the Roman Triumph came to have in common with the Imperial Adventus. Only the common factors in the long history of the Roman ceremonies explain the way in which, during the Empire, the arch was used to memorialize both the Triumph and Adventus[44] and the manner in which the city-gates in the Eastern cities, where the Epiphany receptions had customarily taken place, were in the course of the Empire rebuilt or redecorated like a triumphal arch.[45]

Since so many manifestations of the Roman emperor-cult seem to have had a Ptolemaic origin, it is interesting to note that the Egyptian Pharaohs enjoyed elaborate triumphal ceremonies at the pylon gateways of their temple palaces in which they appeared in a golden loggia, or "Window of Appearances," as a Sun-god, reviewed the presentation of their spoils, enjoyed games of celebration, and recorded their victories by sculptures on the towered pylons of the "Horizon of Heaven."[46] At Rome, however, the Republican Triumph was a Latin adaptation of a royal Etruscan rite in which the Triumphant One was received as the image of a god, the ruler of Heaven, who was joyously welcomed by the populace after the Oriental custom with musicians and dancers.[47]

These reminiscences of the ancient religious Epiphanies of the East persisted during the Republic in the way the Triumphator was met at the *Porta Triumphalis*, was painted, dressed, and crowned to resemble Jupiter returning to his temple on the Capitoline, was received by the people as a god for the duration of the ceremony,

[43] For bibliography see: H. Kaehler, "Triumphbogen," *P-W, Real-Encyclopädie*, 2nd Ser., VII, 1939, pp. 371-491; A. B. Cook, *Zeus*, II, pp. 359, 1131; M. P. Nilsson, *Bull. Corr. Hell.*, XLIX, 1925, p. 143; Nilsson, *Corolla Archaeologica*, 1932, pp. 132-139.

[44] "By the second century the Adventus had become an integral and independent element within the imperial theology of triumph and victory" (Kantorowicz, *op.cit.*, p. 214). For further evidence on the relation of the two ceremonies see notes 52, 53.

[45] E. Wiegand, "Propylon und Bogentor in der Östlichen Reichskunst," *Wiener Jahrb.*, V, 1928, pp. 85ff.

[46] The Egyptian Pharaohs of the New Kingdom enjoyed elaborate triumphal ceremonies in the forecourt of their palaces and temples, and presumably at the entrance to their cities (H. H. Nel-son, "Medinet Habu Reports," *The Oriental Institute Reports*, No. 10, 1931, pp. 21-27). Since these Egyptian triumphal processions came into the forecourt of the palaces and temples through the pyloned gateway, called the "Horizon of Heaven" and "Golden Gateway," on which the Pharaohs recorded their victories and in front of which they set up their statues, we may suspect that the Hellenistic kings continued the tradition of setting up their statues and figures of their divinities at the city and palace gateways in order to commemorate their Triumphs and Epiphanies.

[47] A. Bruhl, "Les Influences hellénistiques dans le triumph romain," *Mélanges d'arch. et d'histoire.*, XLVI, 1929, p. 80; L. Deubner, "Die Tracht des römischen Triumphators," *Hermes*, LXIX, 1934, pp. 316-323; C. Barini, *Triumphalia*, 1952; E. Pais, *Fasti triumphales populi romani*, I, 1920, pp. xxvi-lvi.

and was then looked upon as a demigod for the rest of his life.[48] Before the end of the Republic the Triumph was directly influenced by the traditional receptions of the deified Hellenistic kings.[49] Following the conquest of the Near East when the Republican generals in their victorious entries were accorded divine honors, crowned like kings, and flattered with all the formal adulation which had characterized the *parousia* of the Greek monarchs, the Roman Triumph became still more similar to the Eastern Royal Epiphany, especially in the way both ceremonies attached theophanic attributes to the events. In Asia Minor, "when Antony made his entry into Ephesus, women arrayed like Bacchus and men and boys like Satyrs and Pans led the way before him, and the city was full of ivy and thyrsus-wands and harps and pipes and flutes, the people hailing him as Dionysus, Giver of Joy and Beneficent."[50]

Antony, we are told, was not only "called the New Dionysus" and Cleopatra "the New Isis," but in 34 B.C., when Antony celebrated his Armenian victory at Alexandria, his triumph was comparable to a Hellenistic Epiphany.[51] After having entered the city through the "Golden Gate" he drove in his chariot to the center of the city, which was probably the entrance to the palace, where he endeavored to make his captives do reverence to Cleopatra enthroned as Isis; and in the festivals which followed, he and Cleopatra, like divinities, sat together on a silver dais in the stadium where their golden thrones, it must be assumed, were covered with baldachins in much the same way that the Apollo-ruler is presented under a ciborium in a *Porta regia* on the Pompeian fresco (Fig. 113). Even at Rome, as early as 61 B.C., the influence of the Hellenistic ritual is reflected in the way Pompey at his triumph was compared, like one of the Diodochi, to Alexander the Great, Hercules, and Dionysus.

In contrast to the Triumph the *Adventus Augusti*, which was the public celebration of the official coming, or visitation, of an emperor and was presumably a Roman version of the Hellenistic Royal Epiphany, does not appear until after Augustus returned from the East and established the Empire. Although there was a definite distinction between the two types of reception during the first two centuries of the Empire, it has become apparent that there was more than one kind of Adventus and that as early as Domitian there was a military Adventus which was closely related to the Triumph. On the Flavian reliefs from the Palazzo della Cancelleria, Domitian, in the company of Victory, Mars, and Minerva, is shown being met at the city-gate by delegates of the Senate, representatives of the Roman people, and by the personification of Roma, while on a second relief the "civil Adventus" of Vespasian is presented with the Emperor being received by representatives of the Senate, the people, and the Vestal Virgins.[52] Another indication that there was a link between the two ceremonies is the Adventus medallion of Marcus Aurelius on which the Emperor is shown

---

[48] F. Noack, "Triumph und Triumphbogen," *Vorträge d. Bibl. Warburg*, 1925-26, pp. 150-160.

[49] A. Bruhl, *op.cit.*, pp. 77-97; Pais, *op.cit.*, pp. xlviii ff.

[50] Plutarch, *Anthony*, XXIV.

[51] Bruhl, *op.cit.*, p. 92; Plutarch, *Anthony*, L, 2;

Dio Cassius, XLIX, 40-42; L. R. Taylor, *The Divinity of the Roman Emperor*, 1931, pp. 126-130.

[52] F. Magi, *I Rilievi flavi del Palazzo della Cancelleria*, pp. 98-124; P. G. Hamberg, *Studies in Roman Imperial Art*, 1945, pp. 50ff.

being crowned by Victory as he advances towards the triumphal arch of Domitian which was built into the opening of the *Porta Triumphalis*.[53] While neither the exact prototypes of the Adventus nor the stages by which it was absorbed into the Triumph are clear, it is very evident that both ceremonies, in combination with the theology of victory and the idea of victorious coronation, placed much the same emphasis upon deification and consecration by apotheosis.[54] The way in which these public manifestations of the Coming of a *Divus* influenced architectural symbolism will be considered later.

What is of primary importance is still the question of the origin of the free-standing triumphal arch at Rome. This cannot be explained by the fact that at an early date Rome outgrew her fortified limits and down to the time of Aurelian was an open city, because there was at Rome and in the other Italian cities an old and established relation between a triumph and a city-gate. From the third century B.C., when towers and arcuated portals were first introduced from the Hellenistic East into the fortifications of the Latin cities, the city-gate had a direct influence upon the development of the honorific *arcus*.[55] This influence is best illustrated by the Porta Marzia (Fig. 3) which was built into the old walls of Perugia towards the close of the Republican period.[56] Both the ceremonial and symbolic significance of the archway are evident from the way there looks down from the loggia over the portal, as from Olympus, the figure of Jupiter the Thunderer, flanked by Castor and Pollux, the warrior demigods, who throughout the Empire were worshiped as intermediaries between heaven and earth and were later translated into saints by the Christians.[57]

Another Hellenistic factor in the development of the triumphal arch is suggested by the fact that it was not until after Octavian returned from his triumphs and receptions in the East that the Italian cities began to erect stone arches to him as the "Savior of the Empire."[58] It is equally significant, especially when we note how the city-gate is presented as a triumphal arch on the Roman coins of Thrace, that so many of the earliest Augustan stone arches were built into existing gateways.[59] Inasmuch, therefore, as the Republican triumphal arches at Rome were presumably only semipermanent structures of wood we may suspect that in origin they were not unlike the wooden ceremonial arches which have decked the processional way in European triumphs and coronations ever since the Middle Ages, and perhaps since Roman and even Hellenistic times. Rome, however, had in her *Porta Triumphalis* an official ceremonial gateway. Hence it is reasonable to assume that the Republican Romans erected a *fornix* to commemorate an individual triumph because they considered it neither feasible nor

[53] Magi, *op.cit.*, p. 99, fig. 58.

[54] J. Gagé, "La Théologie de la victoire impériale," *Revue hist.*, CXXI, 1933, pp. 26ff.; "La Victoire Auguste," *Mélanges d'arch. et d'hist.*, XLIX, 1923, p. 68.

[55] F. E. Brown, *Mem. Amer. Ac. in Rome*, XX, 1951, p. 111; M. E. Blake, *Ancient Construction in Italy*, 1947, pp. 203-209.

[56] I. A. Richmond, *Journal of Roman Studies*,

XXIII, 1933, pp. 161-174.

[57] F. Chapouthier, *Les Dioscures en service d'une déesse*, 1935; J. R. Harris, *The Dioscuri in the Christian Legends*, 1903; E. Lucius, *Les Origines du culte des saints*, 1908, p. 32.

[58] Nilsson, *Corolla archaeologica*, 1932, p. 139.

[59] I. A. Richmond, *op.cit.*, fig. 5 (Mintorno), fig. 6 (Fano) and fig. 7 (Rimini).

even appropriate to set up statues and trophies at the gateway in the same way that the Hellenistic cities were presumably accustomed to honor their divine kings.

The *Porta Triumphalis*, located in the Campus Martius,[60] was the place where all the imperial triumphs started before their processions passed through certain of the circuses and theatres, circled the Palatine, and then by way of the Via Sacra traversed the Forum Romanum before reaching the Temple of Jupiter on the Capitoline.[61] This Porta, as can be seen on the stone map of Rome (Fig. 4), had the customary flanking towers of a city gateway into which Domitian built his triumphal arch, which was later known as the *Arcus Divorum*.[62] It was just outside the *pomerium*, which was the traditional boundary line of the ancient city, and was adjacent to the *Villa Publica*. By the time of the Empire the *Villa Publica* was a kind of state palace with a garden where, in a ceremony which curiously recalls the old Assyrian festival celebrating the seasonal coming of a city's god, the Triumphator spent the night and probably breakfasted before being received at the Triumphal Gate. After making his entry into the *Porticus Divorum*, he made sacrifices at the two small temples, located at either side of the entrance, which were dedicated to the Divi Vespasian and Titus. The *Porticus Divorum*, as built by Domitian and depicted on the plan, was a great rectangular court open in the center, and colonnaded down both sides and perhaps planted with rows of trees, where the throng of participants could receive the Imperial Triumphator as a *Divus* and see him mount the platform at the south end of the enclosure. Beyond the platform was a temple, probably of *Fortuna Redux*, which was a shrine of the divinity responsible for the happy return and protection of the emperor. According to the *Forma urbis* this shrine had an exceptional horseshoe apse which recalls the almost circular apses of certain Syrian *Tychaia*.

[60] Kaehler, *op.cit.*, p. 490.

[61] E. Makin, "The Triumphal Route," *Journal of Roman Studies*, XI, 1921, pp. 25ff.; Noack, *Vorträge d. Bibl. Warburg*, 1925-26, pp. 147-151.

[62] C. Huelsen, *Röm. Mittl.*, XVIII, 1903, pp. 17-57, pl. I; L. Lundstrom, *Svenskt Arkiv. for Humanistika, Abhandlungen*, II, 1929, pp. 110-128; G. Gatti, *Atti Pontificia Acc. Romana di Arch.*, XX, 1943-44; E. Sjöqvist, *Opuscula Archaeologica*, IV, 1946, pp. 99-121. Since by the beginning of the Empire so many features and provisions of the Roman Triumph indicate the influence of Ptolemaic Egypt, attention should be called to an article of E. Sjöqvist in the new *Opuscula Romana*, I, 1954, pp. 86-108: in this study on "The Kaisarion" he points out that the *Porticus Divorum* of the *Porta Triumphalis* with its porticos, altar platform and temple to the personal divinity of the emperors was like the *quadriporticus* of the Forum Iulia with its sanctuary to the divine ancestress of Caesar and the similar colonnaded Forum of Augustus with its temple of Augustus as the Avenging Mars; he concludes that the *quadriporticus* type of structure dedicated to the Cult of the Caesars, was based upon the "Kaisarion of the Landing Caesar" at Alexandria, which was a monument commemorat-ing the triumphal Epiphany of Caesar and a sanctuary (*Augusteum*) where the subsequent emperors were worshiped; he also shows that the famous Alexandrian *Kaisarion* was presumably a Hellenistic version of the older Nilotic provisions for ruler-worship; and even his suggestion that the uneven rows of spots in the plan of the *Porticus Divorum* on the map of Rome (Fig. 4) were probably shade trees strengthens the Egyptian link, because in Egypt it had long been customary to plant and water rows of trees, as a desirable paradise, in front of the palace and mortuary residences of the divine Pharaohs. It should be added, what Sjöqvist has pointed out to me but not included in his article, that there is an interesting survival of the Pharaonic-Roman tradition of the *quadriporticus* type of structure being used for ruler-worship to be seen in the way the soldiers of Diocletian, when they constructed their castrum around the Temple of Amon at Luxor, made use of the colonnaded forecourt and hypostyle hall of Amenophis II as the processional way leading to their sacellum for the imperial cult in the ancient temple (U. Monneret de Villard, "The Temple of the Imperial Cult at Luxor," *Archaeologia*, XCV, 1953, pp. 85-105).

There are two features of the *Porta Triumphalis* which raise important questions as to the ceremonial provisions and their influence upon the development of architectural ideas. The large platform at the south end of the *Divorum* has columns indicated at the four corners. The columns, as Sjöqvist had suggested, presumably supported a baldachin over the fire altar on the platform, in much the same way that a domical covering is depicted on the fresco of the Domus Vesonius at Pompeii, and is indicated by the sculptures of the Haterii tomb from the Via Labinica. There are two domical baldachins on the reliefs of the Roman tomb, which is generally attributed to the period of Domitian: in the scene of the erection of the tomb the Haterii relief shows a baldachin with scale decorations and an orbis finial over a fire altar on a raised pedestal; and in the middle of the topographical frieze there is a triumphal arch with a tentlike and domical ciborium on a pedestal in front of the archway in which stands a female divinity.[63] Whether or not the goddess is Fortuna Redux, which would imply that the succession of monuments on the Haterii relief was intended to refer to the triumphal way, the evidence from the sculptures and the plan of the Porta Triumphalis is more than an indication that a domical ciborium by the time of Domitian was a feature of a triumphal ceremony.

The other provision which demands special consideration because of its possible influence upon Christian ideas is the circular, and probably domical, structure placed so prominently in the middle of the processional way leading to the Triumphal Gate. This was a fountain tholus, as is indicated by the steps at the four sides of its basin, which came to be known as the *Lavacrum Agrippae*.[64] The location of this tholus directly in front of the Triumphal Gate raises the controversial issue of whether it was not a ceremonial place of ablutions connected with the imperial rite of apotheosis. In his study of the site Sjöqvist has already called attention to the Latin references to a *lavacrum immortale* and *lavacrum mysticum*, suggesting that there may have

[63] The reliefs from the Haterii tomb in the Lateran Museum are best illustrated by F. Castagnoli (*Bulletino della Commissione archaeologica del Governatorato di Roma*, LXIX, 1941, pp. 59-69) who summarizes all the bibliography. It has been suggested that the structures depicted in the topographical frieze only refer to the monuments on which Q. Haterius, a *redemptor*, worked. It may be important to note that by changing the interpretation of only one structure the whole sequence of buildings on the frieze can be related to the triumphal way at Rome. Beginning at the left is the Arch of Isis, which the *Forma urbis* (Fig. 4) shows was adjacent to the *Porta Triumphalis*. This is followed by a building which has usually been called the Colosseum, but because it has a group of horses over its portal it may be the Circus Flaminius, which was the first public grandstand through which the triumphal procession passed. Next to this Circus is a triumphal arch with the figure, perhaps of Fortuna, standing beside a domical ciborium in front of its archway (*op.cit.*, Tav. III). Then follows the "Arcus in sacra via summa" (Augus-

tus?) and finally the Temple of Jupiter on the Capitoline, which was the goal of all triumphal entries. It is possible, therefore, that the frieze refers to a mystic Isis rite, or belief, in which the soul of the dead was to enjoy a triumphal apotheosis.

In the Pompeian fresco from the *Domus Vesonius Primus* with its baldachin over the fire-altar (Rostowzew, *Röm. Mittl.*, XXVI, 1911, p. 44, fig. 24; C. M. Dawson, *Romano-Campanian Landscapes*, 1944, p. 101, fig. 43) the way in which the soldiers have laid down their standards beside the altar and are enjoying with the maidens the idyllic setting makes one suspect that the fire-altar under its celestial ciborium with pine-cone finials was intended to have some association with a triumphal purification and a soldier's future reward in a heavenly paradise.

[64] Sjöqvist, *op.cit.*, pp. 99-115. It is to be noted that the reconstruction of the *Lavacrum Agrippae* by Piero Lugli (*op.cit.*, fig. 37) has a gored dome, which was a Roman method of translating the corrugations and striations of the celestial *skene* into a masonry vault (see p. 190).

been some relation between this imperial tholus as a *lavacrum profanum* and the later Christian baptistery.[65] While it is doubtful whether this *Lavacrum* was the direct prototype of the Christian baptistery, it helps to relate this pagan Roman tholus to the triumphal ceremony if it is realized that purification by water was always considered to be a royal rite, and that the Christians were influenced by existing ideas when they made baptism with the waters of life a means by which an ordinary mortal could be triumphally reborn with Christ, the Heavenly King, in order to enter the City of God.

The Roman army was lustrated *in campo* by means of sacrifices before passing under the Porta Triumphalis and entering the City of Rome. There is also the possibility that purification by water may have been a prescribed rite which prepared the Triumphator for his exalted role as the Olympian King of Heaven.[66] Therefore, it is no flight of fancy to follow up Domaszewski's suggestion that the holy water from the sacred spring which fed the stream called Petronia, or Petronila, separating the Campus Martius from the Porta Triumphalis, had a ceremonial use in the Triumph and, on the basis of Sjöqvist's study, to assume that the domical tholus was a *lavacrum immortale* over the spring in which the emperor and triumphator was prepared for deification.[67] Even though one is hesitant about insisting on this interpretation there are a number of reasons for considering the possibility that the *Lavacrum* of the *Porta Triumphalis* was an imperial *fons vitae aeternae*.

Initiation *per lavacrum*, or "through a font," was a mystic rite of many pagan cults, while consecration by ablution was a royal rite throughout the ancient Orient. It was not only the Hebrews who insisted upon a ceremonial washing or anointment before the ruler could speak for God. In Egypt the Pharaoh underwent a symbolic ablution before his coronation and presentation in the temple as a god, and he was also purified by water before his rebirth and public adoration at the time of his Heb-sed Festival.[68] It is not unlikely, therefore, that the Romans took over this mystic cleansing from the royal ceremonies of the Hellenistic East inasmuch as so many features of their Triumph and their ideas of regal apotheosis seem to lead back to Alexandria and the Nilotic traditions of the Ptolemaic kings.[69]

The presumption of an act of purification prior to a triumphal entry, which would have been an imperial link between the ancient formulas for the sanctification of

[65] Sjöqvist, *op.cit.*, pp. 100-101, 148.

[66] F. Noack, *op.cit.*, pp. 152-160; Domaszewski, *Abh. z. Röm. Religion*, 1909, pp. 16, 217-220; Wissowa, *Religion und Kultus*, 1902, p. 130.

[67] A. v. Domaszewski, "Die Triumpstrasse auf dem Marsfelde," *Archiv. f. Religionswissenschaft*, XII, 1909, pp. 66-82; W. Warde Fowler, *Roman Essays and Interpretations*, 1920, p. 73.

[68] Moret, *op.cit.*, pp. 77 (coronation), 78 (Heb-sed festival); A. M. Blackman, "Sacramental Ideas and Usages in Ancient Egypt," *Rec. de trav. relatifs à la philol. et à archéol. Egypt et Assur*, XXXIX, 1921, pp. 44-78. When the Ethiopian Piankhy vis-

ited the Temple of the Sun at Heliopolis (P. Derchain, *Chronique d'Egypte*, XXVIII, 1953, p. 265), he was purified by water before "going up to the great balcony."

[69] The probable Alexandrian origin of the royal tradition of apotheosis is discussed by E. Brecchia ("Apotheosi," *Enciclopedia italiana*, III, 1929, pp. 716-719) and S. Eitrem (*Symbolae Osloensis*, X, 1932, pp. 31ff.; XI, 1932, pp. 11ff.; and XV/XVI, 1936, pp. 111ff.; J. M. Toynbee, "Ruler-apotheosis in Ancient Rome," *The Numismatic Chronicle*, 1946, pp. 126-149.

rulers and the Christian conception of baptism and anointment as royal sacraments,[70] does not mean that the Christian baptistery in its domical form was by necessity derived from the imperial *lavacrum immortale*.[71] The presence, however, of a domical tempietto as the place in the Roman triumphal liturgy where the victor was mystically prepared for celestial glorification does help to account for the Christian ceremonial emphasis upon a fountain of ablution, a "lavacrum" as it was called at Tebessa, in their adaptation of triumphal symbolism to the church and service of God. It would also establish an imperial precedent for the ritualistic importance of fountains under a domical tholus and with a pine-cone waterspout in the Imperial Palace and palace-churches of Constantinople. And it may even explain the origin of the pine-cone cantharus in the atrium of Old St. Peter's. It has been frequently noted that the processional approach to Old St. Peter's was a kind of *Via Triumphalis* with its monumental gateway, its atrium, and its font of ablutions in the shape of a pine cone, which was under a "tholus" in front of the "Royal Door" leading to the symbolic throne of God.[72]

The mediaeval accounts tell us that the great bronze *pinea aurea* formerly in the atrium of St. Peter's was under a "tholus" which had eight columns of royal porphyry; and Hülsen, arguing from the traditional and persistent association of the *pinea* with the region of the Field of Mars in front of the *Porticus Divorum*, suggested that the Roman pine cone used as a fountain in front of Constantine's church was not the crowning finial from the Pantheon of Agrippa, as a twelfth century document describes it, but instead came from the *lavacrum* of the Field of Mars.[73] It is true that

[70] For the ancient significance of purification and the mediaeval conception of anointment as a mystic means of making the king a divine person, a Son of God who henceforth was to be God's "Office bearer in the world" see: C. J. Gadd, "Ideas of Divine Rule in the Ancient East," *British Ac. Lecture*, 1948, p. 48; A. R. Johnson, "The Role of the King in the Jerusalem Cultus," in S. H. Hooke's *The Labyrinth; Further Studies in the Relation between Myth and Ritual in the Ancient World*, London, 1935, pp. 73-111; F. Kern, *Kingship and Law in the Middle Ages* (trans. S. B. Chimes), 1939, pp. 34-50; C. R. North, "The Religious Aspects of Hebrew Kingship," *Zeitschrift für alttestamentliche Wissenschaft*, L, 1932, pp. 8-38; P. E. Schramm, *The History of the English Coronation*, 1937, pp. 6-8, 115-141; G. H. Williams, *Harvard Theological Studies*, XVIII, 1951, pp. 76-79, 144-167. For further references to the early and almost universal importance of lustration and anointment in royal coronation ceremonies with triumphal connotations of a ritualistic origin see: H. C. Hocart, *Kingship*, London, 1927, Ch. VII, and I. Engnell, *Studies in Divine Kingship*, Uppsala, 1945, pp. 5, 10 (baptism).

[71] For recent discussions of the origins of the domical baptistery see: R. Krautheimer, *Journal of the Warburg and Courtauld Institutes*, V, 1942, p. 22; J. Lassus, *Sanctuaires chrétiens de Syrie*, 1947,

pp. 217-228; Smith, *The Dome*, pp. 56-57; P. Underwood, *Dumbarton Oaks Papers*, No. 5, 1950, pp. 43-138.

[72] Bandmann, *op.cit.*, p. 91; Fuchs, *Die Karolingischen Westwerk*, pp. 45, 80, 82; M. Schwarz, "Das Stilprinzip der altchristlichen Architektur," *Festgabe zum Konstantins-Jubiläum*, 1913, *Röm. Quartalschift*, Suppl., 19, 1913, pp. 340ff.

[73] C. Hülsen, "Porticus Divorum und Serapeum im Marsfelde," *Röm. Mittl.*, XVIII, 1903, pp. 39-46; G. Lacour-Gayet, "La 'Pigna' du Vatican," *Mélanges d'arch. et d'hist.*, 1888, pp. 312-319; E. Petersen, "Pigna-Brunnen," *Röm. Mittl.*, 1903, pp. 312-328. It is difficult to believe that the massive bronze *pigna* of St. Peter's, pierced with water holes, could have originally been a kind of finial on the dome of the Pantheon with its oculus and could have been taken down to be made into a Christian font without suffering some apparent damage. Instead, it seems much more likely that the late mediaeval accounts, like the *Mirabilia Urbis Romae* (Hülsen, p. 41), which say that it came from the Pantheon, were repeating misinformation which had resulted from a very old confusion in the attribution of round buildings in the region of the Field of Mars to Agrippa. When the evidence that even from Roman times the *Lavacrum*, a domical tholus, in front of the *Porta Triumphalis* was attributed to Agrippa is combined

there have been many theories regarding the original use and symbolic significance of this *pinea aurea*. It is only necessary, however, to modify Hülsen's suggestion by assuming that the bronze *pinea* of Old St. Peter's was originally the actual imperial font in the triumphal tholus over the sacred spring in order to have an imperial precedent for the font of ablutions in the Christian *Via Triumphalis* and to account for the persistent association of the pine-cone waterspout with its phiale in the Byzantine palace and palace-churches.[74]

It is evident from the Byzantine "Book of Ceremonies" that mystical phiales had a ritualistic importance in the palace liturgy of the Byzantine emperors.[75] We are told, for example, that the "phiale mysticum" in the Court of the Triconchos of the Great Palace at Constantinople was a pine cone and the place where the emperor went alone when he was presumably enacting the part of Christ in the Triumphal Entry on Palm Sunday. There were also two pine-cone phiales in the atrium of the Nea, which was the great palace-church of Basil I. Something of the importance of fountains in the palace tradition can be seen in the mosaic of St. George at Saloniki (Fig. 74) where the fonts are given so much prominence under the towered façade and in combination with the other palatium motifs which the Christian took over to depict heaven in terms of an imperial palace. Another indication that purification by water was considered an imperial rite is the magnificently decorated phiale over "the life-giving waters" at the entrance to the church of the imperial monastery of the Lavra at Mt. Athos, which has over the actual font the imperial eagle. Further evidence that there was a Roman imperial precedent associating the triumphal coming of an Imperator with a ceremonial fountain of life, which will be discussed more fully in a later chapter, is the Adventuslike reception of the Byzantine Basileus at his palace churches, where he took his seat in a domical phiale at the entrance to the House of God and where he was received and acclaimed by representatives of the political factions. It is also interesting to note that in the account of the Triumphal Arch of Frederick II

---

with the tradition which associated the great domical tholus of the Pantheon with the baths of Agrippa, it is easy to understand how in the course of centuries the *pigna* of St. Peter's, which was known to have come from some tholus in the Field of Mars, was eventually attributed to the one extant and famous domical structure in the region. The arguments of those who insist that the *Pigna* was a symbolic Roman finial fail to take into account the long Christian tradition of having a cantharus, "lavacrum," or fountain of life, in the shape of a pine cone and under a domical tholus, or phiale.

[74] Leclercq in Cabrol's *Dict. d'arch. chrét. et de liturgie*, II², cols. 1955-1969; J. Strzygowsky, "Der Pinienzapfen als Wasserspier," *Röm Mittl.*, XVIII, 1903, pp. 185-206.

[75] See p. 176. We are told that Theophilus sat in judgment under a phiale (A. Rambaud, *Études sur l'histoire byzantine*, 1919, p. 194). The importance of a domical tholus over a font in the imperial tradition is shown by the way in which the Basileus in the Byzantine palace ceremonies, at the time of his "Anniversary festival," received the salutations and acclamations first in the phiale of the Greens and then in that of the Blues (A. Vogt, *Échoes d'Orient*, XXXVI, 1935, pp. 438-440; *Le Livre des cérémonies, Commentaire*, pp. 103-106). The fact that this anniversary festival in honor of the emperor was celebrated at Constantinople on the Sunday after Easter, or at about the same time in the year that the Romans had been accustomed to hold their *Natalis urbis*, when they celebrated the Foundation of the City and the Birth of the Emperor, not only implies a Roman precedent for the Byzantine festival, but also suggests that at Rome the Coming of Venus at the time of the *Natalis* and the birthday Epiphany of the Emperor may have involved a reception in the *Tholus* outside the *Porta Triumphalis*.

at Capua the *Gesta Romanorum* says, "it stood above a fountain of running water."[76]

Throughout this study, in which an effort is made to relate architectural symbolism with public ceremonies, objection may be made to the way in which no clear distinction is preserved between royal Epiphany and imperial Adventus, Adventus and Triumph, and between city-gates, triumphal gateways, and palace portals. One is hesitant to be too explicit not only because the evidence is limited, but also because all the ceremonies, which had so much in common, had a tendency to combine during the Late Empire and Middle Ages. All, however, started at a city-gate and terminated after passing along the processional way at a palace, temple, or church. Since they all became a public means of honoring a divine ruler, whose coming as a Victor and Savior brought a heavenly distinction to the city and joy to the populace, the religious nature of the event gave a celestial content to the portal regardless of whether it was the *Porta aurea* of the city, the *Porta regia* of the palatium or the *Porta coeli* of a church. Also as far as the populace was concerned, the gateway motif had much the same symbolic values when it was used to symbolize a *civitas*, a *castrum* as the seat of government, *Imperium Romanorum*, and a *Palatium*. Later during the Middle Ages it will be seen that the motif could represent at the same time the Palatium, the Church, the City of God, and Heaven.

There is an intimation of why the Roman public associated the archway with heaven in the fact that the *Porta Triumphalis* became known as the *Arcus Divorum*. This kind of imagery, however, was merely the continuation of much earlier ideas. From the time when the cut-stone arch was first introduced into Italy from the Hellenistic East and was used for portals in the existing walls of the Etruscan cities, its shape had acquired ideational values not only from the gateway ceremonies but also from the belief that the arch was the *simulacrum* of Ianus, the ancient sky-deity of the Latins who was "the god of the heavens," a sun-deity comparable to Jupiter, and "the keeper of the gate of heaven."[77] This old and persistent identification of the arch form with the apparent curve of heaven was given more specific overtones of celestial significance by the impressive spectacles of the Triumphant One being received as the King of Heaven after he had passed through the Triumphal Gate. As Cook has pointed out, men visualized the arch as a sky image because they were accustomed to think of the figure of a triumphant general on his arcus as the embodiment of the supreme sky-god on the arch of heaven.[78] During the Empire this

---

[76] See p. 106. Many of the persistent associations of water with kingship, pine-cone fonts with purification and rebirth, fountains with palaces, and phiales with royal ceremonies must have come down as survivals of ruler myths and rituals from the ancient Orient, where the divine king was himself the "Tree of Life" and the mystic "possessor and giver of the waters of life" (I. Engnell, *Studies in Divine Kingship*, pp. 25-28; G. Widengren, "The King and the Tree of Life in Ancient Near Eastern

Religion," *Universitets Årsskrift*, 1951, pp. 5ff.).

[77] W. Deeke, *Etruskische Forschungen*, II, 1876, p. 125; IV, pp. 26, 180; S. Linde, *De Iano summo Romanorum*, 1891, p. 18.

[78] A. B. Cook, *Zeus*, II, pp. 160, 354-365; that the Late Antique world may have attached a heavenly significance to the gateway, as did the Christians, is indicated by the clay model of a city-gate, inscribed "Ilarus fecit porta(m) fel(iciter)," which was found in a grave at Intercisa in Hungary (F.

habit was further strengthened when the Triumph and Adventus had become a form of emperor-worship and the passage through the arch was celebrated as the apotheosis of a divine Augustus. Also it was because of this heritage of ideas that the Christian came to think of the church as a *Porta coeli* and to see in the "triumphal arch" of its crossing a processional way leading to heavenly glories.

When the sculptures of the Porta Marzia (Fig. 3) are seen against the background of the Etruscan and Roman triumphs the figure in the center, flanked by the two demigods and their horses, becomes the actual Triumphator as he appeared to the populace in his role of the King of Heaven looking down from his loggia elevated over the arch as the *simulacrum* of Olympus. If this were so, then the balcony must have had divine and royal significance, as Richmond implied when he described the figures of the Porta Marzia as "like the Saints and Patriarchs on the parapet of Heaven in Mediaeval painting." This analogy between a Republican gateway and the later Christian use of the arcade as a heavenly symbol has a direct bearing upon the subsequent history of the gateway concept, because it raises the question of whether the arched gallery, which became so characteristic of Roman city-gates (Fig. 11) and the later palace façades (Fig. 6), had a ceremonial purpose as the place of royal appearances and hence a symbolic content when present over an imperial portal.

The gallery, which first appeared over Roman portals as a colonnade with arched openings and then became a crowning arcade over imperial gateways and an arched corbel-table on the façade of palaces, has been customarily accepted as a decorative feature of neither conceptual nor ceremonial significance, presumably transferred to monumental gateways from such buildings as the Tabularium at Rome. Even Rivoira attached no ideational values to it when he insisted that it was a derivation from an Etruscan tradition seen in the Porta Marzia and in the single arch over the much rebuilt and so-called "Gate of Augustus" at Perugia.[79] This motif, however, cannot be dismissed in this casual fashion because the whole history of the arcade, even including the curious gaps in the evidence for its architectural development, and especially the widespread importance which was attached to it in Christian architecture and art as a heavenly form, indicate very clearly that it was originally a palace feature and a symbol of *Imperium Romanorum*. Even if it were not taken over directly from the Palatium at Rome, certainly by the Late Empire and throughout the Middle Ages the arcade was recognized as a characteristic feature of the *Sacrum palatium* with all its celestial implications.

The very fact that its sudden appearance over Roman gateways cannot be explained by the assumption that it was an ordinary utilitarian and military feature is evidence of its expressive purpose. Throughout the Empire and the Middle Ages the crenellated battlement, as in the Orient, was always the traditional parapet on purely defensive walls and gateways. The fact that the arcade does not appear over any gateways in

---

Oelmann, *Festschrift für Rudolf Egger*, Klagenfurt, I, 1952, pp. 114-125, Abb. 1; Grenier, *Manuel*

d'archéologie gallo-romaine, V, 1931, p. 575, fig. 226).

[79] Rivoira, *Architettura romana*, 1921, pp. 73-74.

the *Corpus Agrimensorum Romanorum* (Figs. 55-64) is confirming evidence that it was not a customary feature of defensive architecture. Furthermore, there is the question not only of when such an elaborate sculptural feature as the colonnade with arched openings came to be added as the upper story over imperial gateways, but also of whether it was not peculiar to the gateways of those cities which were the seat of imperial government in the provinces. The fact that many of the galleries on portals (Fig. 11) of the Augustan period are known to have been added later makes it possible that none of the arcades date back to the beginning of the Empire.[80] This presumption is supported by the numismatic evidence which shows the conventional crenellated parapet on the Augustan coin (Fig. 12) from Emerita in Spain and the first example of a crowning porticus on a coin of Bizya (Fig. 16), which dates from the beginning of Hadrian's reign.

The mere possibility that the innovation in gateway design did not take place until the close of the first century makes it possible to raise the related questions of whether the gallery with arched openings over gateways was a palatium symbol, and whether the motifs were taken over directly from the Palace of the Caesars for ideological reasons. After Domitian had built the *Domus Augustana* there was on the south side of the Palatine hill, overlooking the Circus Maximus, a concave wall, which it has been thought was crowned with a lofty gallery. From here the members of the *Domus divina* could walk and look down at the games in the Circus. If there was such a gallery of appearances, it would have been the natural instinct of the crowds in the Circus to have attributed royal and even celestial implications to this dominant and memorable feature of the Palatium, especially at a time when Domitian was endeavoring to introduce at Rome the Eastern custom of reverencing the imperial residence as a sacred and heavenly *templum*. Whether or not there was such an elevated porticus, which was looked upon as a mark of Olympian pre-eminence, we have in Martial's description of the *Domus Augustana*, as "elevated so high in the air that it approaches the sky," a reflection of the popular, and what was to become the customary, habit of seeing in the Palace of the Caesars a *Domus Dei*.

With the Palatine hill being what it is today, the indistinct outline and fragmentary ruins of its former magnificence, it may at first seem like unconfirmed speculation to suggest that once the *Domus Palatina* came to be thought of throughout the Empire as the ideal expression of imperial power it became a matter of state policy to make a crowning porticus, from which the Elect look down, a symbol of *Imperium Romanorum*. The presumption that the Romans took what had become a characteristic and distinguishing feature of palace architecture and made it epitomize in the public mind the authority which emanated from the Palatium is not entirely hypothetical when considered in relation to the numismatic evidence and the subsequent history of palace architecture. It has already been noted that at the beginning of the second century the gallery with arched openings first appears over the gateway of Bizya, which at

---

[80] Schultze, *Bonn. Jahrb.*, CXVIII, 1909, pp. 295, Taf. XIII (Aosta), Taf. XIII (Nîmes), 306-309, Tafs. XIV, XXI (Autun).

the time was the seat of government in Southern Thrace. It is equally significant that it was made an exaggeratedly marked feature over the city-gate of Anchialus (Figs. 19-24) only after that city had become the capital of Northern Thrace. The evidence that the motif had a special significance becomes more conclusive when it is realized that it never occurs on the other gateways of Thrace, and that on the coins of Asia Minor it only appears over the portal of Nicaea.[81] The possibility, then, that it was a palatium symbol intended to make evident a city's imperial importance would explain why in the course of the Empire the gallery was eventually added to the gateways of Gaul, and why superimposed palace colonnades were given so much prominence on the Porta Nigra at Treves, which was probably not built until after the Rhenish city had become the imperial residence and capital of the Western Empire.

The lack of extant architecture, which preserves the superstructure of any Roman palace, may make it impossible to trace an upper gallery, as a symbol of the Palatium, directly back to the Palace of the Caesars; but there is graphic evidence to indicate that a columnar arcade had a divine and celestial meaning in both the East and the West by the beginning of the Empire. In his discussion of the origin of the arched canon tables in Christian illuminations Nordenfalk pointed out that the arcade was an imperial form of architecture in the third century when the Christians took it over for the decoration of their martyria, but that in the minor arts it occurs as early as the first century on a Jewish ossurarium.[82] At the same time that it is necessary to account for the Christian interest in arcading, some explanation must be found for the way in which the arcade motif is so frequently used as a heavenly frame for deities and other figures on the *terra sigallata* vases of Gaul by the beginning of the Augustan period.[83] Since there must have been both an ideological reason and an architectural prototype back of this early use of the arcade to denote a heavenly setting, one may suspect that the arcade was a distinctive feature of royal residences before the construction of the *Domus Augustana*.

The fact that nothing remains from the second story of any Roman palace, unless the "Piliers de Tutelle" at Bordeaux with a richly decorated arcade over a Corinthian colonnade was a palace rather than a temple, makes it possible, if not probable, that colonnaded arched openings, arcaded galleries, and crowning arcades were from Hellenistic times located for privacy, light, and ventilation on the upper story of royal residences in all parts of the Empire.[84] Some indication of this can be seen on the Boscoreale frescoes in the Metropolitan Museum where, on the flanking panels, there are on the upper stories of the buildings either arched openings or columnar galleries as loggias, which perhaps preserve a Hellenistic tradition and were intended to represent either lofty palatia or ideal Roman villas.[85] Regardless of whether there

[81] Imhoof-Blumer, *Kleinasiatische Münzen*, II, 1920, p. 507, pls. LXXXVII/38, 39, LXXXVIII/12, 13, 15, 16.

[82] C. Nordenfalk, *Essays in Honor of George Swarzenski*, 1951, pp. 9-20.

[83] J. Déchelette, *Les Vases céramiques ornée de la Gaule Romaine*, 1904, I, pp. 36-37, figs. 20, 22.

[84] C. Julian, *Histoire de Bordeaux*, 1895, p. 30; R. Schultze, "Römische Architektur in Bonn," *Germania*, XVI, 1932, pp. 14-15.

[85] P. W. Lehmann (*Roman Wall Painting from Boscoreale*, 1935, pls. XII, XVII) has shown that these panels depict ruling-class Campagna villas, that upper galleries lighted by windows (p. 105) were

is any reason to trace the origin of the crowning gallery back to the Palatium at Rome, the whole history of late Roman, Byzantine, and mediaeval palatia shows that the elevated porticus and arcade were persistent features of a *Sacrum palatium* and, for that reason, acquired divine, celestial and royal implications.

By the fourth century the very emphasis which is given to the gleaming white arcade between flanking towers that crowns the façade on the mosaic of Carthage (Fig. 65) is evidence of this tradition, supporting the author's later contention that the building is not an ordinary villa, but an imperial palace in a pictorial panegyric.[86] By the time when the North African mosaic was executed the precedent for its castrum-type of palatium with an arcade in combination with a domical vestibule had been established by Diocletian at Salona. When Diocletian, the living Jove, constructed his palace overlooking the Adriatic the arcade was already so traditionally identified with the heavenly abode of a divine ruler that he had it sculpturally translated into a decorative arched corbel-tabel above the *Porta aurea* as the ceremonial entrance (Fig. 5), and had statues of the gods and perhaps of the royal family set into the openings of the arcade. The fact that it was an established mark of *Imperium*, with all the celestial implications customarily associated with a *Sacrum palatium*, is proved by the importance which is given to the motif on the "Palace of the Exarchate" at Ravenna (Fig. 6). In view of how little is known of antique palaces this evidence is important, as is the arcaded upper story of Theodoric's palace at Ravenna (Fig. 99) and the fact that the walls of the Byzantine palace of Tekfour Seray at Constantinople were enriched with purely decorative wall arcades.

Even though our knowledge of palace architecture during the Middle Ages has to be pieced together from fragmentary sources, all the evidence from the Byzantine East and mediaeval West is consistent in showing that a crowning arcade, from which the Elect looked down, was a long-established and persistent feature of royal residences. The palace of the King of Nineveh (Fig. 73), as depicted in the ninth century by the Byzantine illuminator of the Homilies of Gregory of Nazianzus, is a castrum-type palatium with an arcade over the portal and royal cupolas on the towers. When its arcade is compared with the gallery over the city-gate of Bizya (Fig. 28), the emphasis which is given in both representations to the little heads of the Elect looking down from the arched openings is an indication that the motif had some special significance on both palaces and gateways. On all the known mediaeval palaces, such as those at Wartburg, Wimpfen, Gelnhausen, and Münzenberg, Swoboda has shown that the arcade, or what he called the "porticus," was the consistent feature of the façades, where it gave distinction to the *salam regalem* and *solarium*.[87] The influence which this palatium motif had during the Carolingian period can be seen on the royal gate-house at Lorsch where the wall arcade in a triangular schematic way was

---

customary on the Roman *villa rustica* and that Augustus had an apartment (p. 106) at the top of his house on the Palatine.

[86] See pp. 70ff.

[87] K. M. Swoboda, *Römische und romanische*

Paläste, 1919, pp. 202-220 (Wartburg), 220 (Wimpfen), 221 (Gelnhausen), 222 (Münzenberg); he also points out the importance of the upper-story arcade on the early Venetian palaces.

made a decorative feature of the upper story to which the emperor was conducted when he was met by the chapter and honored in a ritual very similar to a Roman Adventus.[88]

The gate-houses of royal abbeys, we now know, were ceremonial structures, based upon imperial precedents, where both the Carolingian and Norman rulers were received as the "Royal Christus." This tradition by itself helps to explain why the arcaded upper story and the tower with a cupola, which are depicted on the "Porta Curie" (Fig. 7) in the twelfth century drawing of the monastery at Canterbury, were not only palace motifs but also had, as did everything taken over from the *Sacrum palatium*, very specific heavenly and royal implications. In the first place, the gable of the "Porta Curie" is surmounted by the royal orb as are the gables on the Palace of Herod (Fig. 71). Also, according to Willis, the upper room back of the royal arcade of the "Court Gate House" at Canterbury was called the "Paradise chamber" and sometimes referred to as the "Heaven chamber of the Gate House in connection with the Guest House."[89] There is further confirmation that the "Porta Curie" was the Royal Gate of the Abbey, that its arcaded "Paradise chamber" was a kind of royal oratory with heavenly implications, and that its tower crowned with a cupola was a royal insigne, in the way it is presented as adjacent to the "Nova aula" and to an outer gate-house which, according to the title on the drawing, was in the "murus civitatis." The reason for insisting that the entrance through the city walls was the King's Gate is that it will be demonstrated in a later section that its little cupola was a royal emblem which had been taken over from the imperial gateway symbolism of the late Roman palatium.[90]

The "Nova aula," therefore, in the Norman drawing, which has the royal lion and dragon over its gables, was not originally a "Hospitium" as Willis suggested, but was either the Abbot's palace or the royal "Guest Hall."[91] It has an arcaded upper story because throughout the Middle Ages abbey and episcopal palaces were not only used as royal residences when the king visited the various regions of his domain, but because it was the policy of the churchmen to take over the ceremonial and architectural features of the imperial tradition. Even more convincing evidence that a

[88] See p. 91. A. Fuchs, *Die Karolingischen Westwerke*, 1929, pp. 73-87; R. Krautheimer ("Carolingian Revival of Early Christian Architecture," *Art Bulletin*, XXIV, 1942, p. 35) compares the Torhalle at Lorsch to a Roman triumphal arch, such as those of Septimius Severus and Constantine, which had a ceremonial chamber in their attics. Excavations at Lorsch have uncovered the remains of a ceremonial gate-house in the enclosing walls of the monastery (F. Behn, *Das Münster*, III, 1950, pp. 336-340).

[89] R. O. Willis, *The Architectural History of the Conventual Buildings of the Monastery of Christ's Church*, 1869, p. 132.

[90] See pp. 60, 162, 189.

[91] Swoboda (*op.cit.*, pp. 262-263, Abb. 99) calls

it the Abbot's residence; Willis (*op.cit.*, pp. 15, 145), who was misled by its later use and the subsequent construction of an archbishop's palace, says its purpose was never recorded and suggests that it was a *Hospitium* for pilgrims; this is curious because he cites (p. 145) a record of 1290 which speaks of the "Great Hall next to the Court Gate" and quotes from the Statutes of 1298 that say "all doors to remain closed that lead from the Curia, or from the Palace." For evidence that it was customary by the twelfth century to use *curia* for the residence of a person with divine authority see Lehmann-Brockhaus, *Schriftquellen*, no. 185 (*Curia abbatis*), no. 2653 (*Curia imperialis*), nos. 597, 643, 1619 (*Curia episcopalis*).

crowning arcade was recognized as the distinguishing feature of a palatium, which throughout the Middle Ages was considered to be the seat of government and an architectural symbol of divine authority, are the buildings on the Bayeux tapestry. Although the Norman tapestry was not executed until after the middle of the twelfth century, its patterns for the design of the buildings undoubtedly followed long-established conventions. Hence it is of historical importance to find that William's PALATIUM (Fig. 9) is diagrammatically represented as a long hall crowned with an arcade and flanked by domical towers.[92] At the same time it is significant to find that the Palace of Edward the Confessor at Westminster (Fig. 10) has both a towered façade and an arcade over the portal.

Once it is recognized that the crowning arcade was traditionally a mark of heavenly authority, because it was the distinguishing feature of the *Sacrum palatium* and that the rulers and churchmen of the Middle Ages were motivated by their interest in *Renovatio Romanorum*, it is possible to account for the universal adoption of the arcade on the palaces and churches. As early as the beginning of the fourth century, when Treves was the capital of the Western Empire, the Constantinian basilica (Fig. 8), which was either the *Sedes Iustitiae* or an *Aula Palatina* not only had the symbolic towers of the castrum-palace at the four corners of its roof, but it had the royal arcade down the sides and around the apse. The reason for restoring its still extant towers with little cupolas and imagining a globe over the gable will be discussed later. Something of the prestige and symbolic significance of this Hall of Justice, or an imperial *auditorium sacrum*, becomes apparent when it is recalled that it was presumably one of the "royal works" which the panegyric to Constantine praised with much the same words that Martial used for the palace of Domitian, as "raised to such a height that they give promise of touching the sky and becoming neighbors of the stars."[93] Later the reverence which the Early Middle Ages had for Roman precedent can be seen in the way Theodoric copied his tomb at Ravenna, which was to be his eternal and heavenly home, from the famous mausoleum of Constantine with its elaborate arcaded gallery around the upper story.[94]

During the fifth and sixth centuries when Ravenna was the capital of the Ostrogothic Kingdom and then the center of Byzantine rule in Italy, the same desire which had led the Christians in Egypt to decorate their martyria with imperial arcades would

[92] H. Belloc (*The Book of the Bayeux Tapestry*, 1916, p. xix, panels 18-19) says, "the Palatium does not only mean a *place*, it also means an *institution*"; and "The convention of the Palatium, that capital institution of Europe, the seat of government in every land; in one aspect a building, in another a body of men, and throughout the West for a thousand years the continuator of Rome."

[93] For cupolas on corner towers see p. 79. D. Krencker, *Das römische Trier*, 1923, p. 42, Abb. 42, pl. VIII; A. Grenier, *Quatre villes romaines de Rhénanie*, 1925, p. 36, plan 38; K. Koethe, "Die Trier Basilika," *Trierer Zeitschrift*, XII, 1937, pp. 151-179; A. Boëthius ("Roman Architecture,"

Göteborgs Högskolas Årsskrift, XLVII, 1942, p. 23) considers it one of the buildings referred to by the panegyrist (*XII, Panegyrici latini*, VI, 22, 5) as *video circum . . . sedemque justitiae in tantam altitudinem suscitari, ut se sideribus et caelo digna et vicina promittant*; W. Reusch, "L'aula palatina à Trèves," *Mémorial d'un voyage d'études en Rhénanie*, Paris, 1953, pp. 145-153; and W. Seston ("La basilique de Trèves dans le tradition littéraire," *Mémorial*, pp. 211-215) cites evidence to show that it was an imperial audience hall, *auditorium sacrum*, comparable to a *consistorium*.

[94] A. M. Schneider, "Die Symbolik des Theodorichgraber im Ravenna," *Byz. Zeit.*, 1941, pp. 404ff.

account for the use of the wall arcade on the tomb of Galla Placidia, that saintly and royal daughter of Theodosius, and then on the clerestory and side aisles of Sant' Apollinare in Classe, as a means of making both the tomb and church a more royal and divine abode. If these assumptions are tenable then the incentive, which resulted in the widespread adoption of the wall arcade during the pre-Romanesque period, was the desire of the age to make the churches as impressive and heavenly-looking as the palaces. One is hesitant, of course, to insist too strongly upon ideational values after architectural features, like the arcade, had become established building conventions. Nevertheless, it could not have been solely habits of design in the creation of Romanesque architecture, especially in the Rhenish and Lombard regions, which account for the exaggerated importance of the arched corbel-table, wall arcade and arcaded galleries not only around the apses and crossing towers, but also along the raking cornices and across the façades. In the German domains this was the period when the Ottonian and Hohenstaufen masters of the Holy Roman Empire were insisting in their struggle with the Papacy that the Church, as an adjunct to the State, was under the Palatium. Hence, as patrons of architecture, they still thought in imperial terms of the façade at the entrance to the church as an expression of the emperor's divine relation to God, and were interested in reviving the forms of imperial architecture as a means of making their authority more manifest. It is probable, therefore, that they approved of the excessive use of the arcade motifs on the churches because they thought of them as palace symbols.[95]

At the same time the problem of interpretation is complicated because the churchmen of the period, who were systematically endeavoring to transfer all the imperial forms and ideas to the greater glorification of Christ and the enrichment of his Royal House, were equally interested in the symbolism of the arcade. It was presumably their desire to make the heavenly House of God more magnificent than an earthly palace which explains the peculiar emphasis that was given to the superimposed arcades on the façades of the Pisan and Tuscan churches. Even as we speculate about the intent of the churchmen and wonder to what extent the traditional palace symbolism had begun to fade into a decorative aesthetic by the end of the Romanesque period, the façades of the Gothic cathedrals, like those of Paris, Amiens, and Rheims, are evidence that back of their design was a gateway and palace concept. The proof that the Gothic churchmen and builders were still aware that a crowning arcade had celestial and royal implications over the "Royal Door" and between the towers of a triumphal "Porta coeli" is the way in which they made its symbolism more explicit by the sculptural introduction of a "King's Gallery."

3. The city-gate on the coins of Thrace and Asia Minor

Much of the evidence for the stages by which the city-gate motif became an imperial symbol is recorded on the Roman coins. The first numismatic use of towered walls

---

[95] Bandmann, op.cit., pp. 222-226; H. G. Evers, *Tod, Macht und Raum als Besichte an Architektur*, 1936; Von Fiedler, *Dom und Politik*, 1937.

to designate a city and perhaps to denote royal supremacy occurs on the coins of the sixth century when Ionia and Sidon were under Persian domination.[96] As late, however, as the Hellenistic age, when fortifications were essential to every Greek city and when the King's Gate had become the place where the elaborate Epiphany receptions of a city's gods and of the deified kings began, the idea of representing a city by its military architecture was still foreign enough to the Greeks so that city walls and gateways were never used on the coins until after the Roman conquest of the Near East.[97] Even during the Empire the gateway as such never occurs on the coins issued at Rome until Diocletian,[98] but it does occur with some frequency in the provinces, and especially in Thrace where it had long been customary to receive a ruler as a *Deus praesens*.

When it comes to interpreting the towered gateway on the earliest Roman examples, were it not for our knowledge that throughout the East ideas of heavenly and royal power had long been associated with the city-gate and that it was the place where the Hellenistic kings were customarily received as gods, there is nothing in the treatment to suggest a symbolic intent.[99] There are also other difficulties, such as why the motif should first occur in the West at the beginning of the Empire on the coins of *Colonia Augusta Emerita* (Fig. 12), the capital of the Spanish province of Lusitania.[100] This gateway, it will be noted, has the flat-roofed towers and crenellations which were customary on the contemporary city-gates of Italy and Gaul.[101] Keeping to the chronological order, there is again nothing to suggest more than a conventionalized *civitas* on the first Eastern example, which is an ordinary gateway with double towers (Fig. 14) on a coin of Titus (A.D. 78-81) from Caesarea Germanica in Bithynia.[102] The first indication that the motif may have commemorated an event and was a symbol of supremacy is the seated figure, denoting a conquered people, at the side of

[96] Babelon, *Les Perses achménénides, cat. monnaies grecques*, 1893, pls. v/18-20, xxix/21-23; B. V. Head, *Numismatica Orientalia, the Coinage of Lydia and Persia*, 1879, pp. 35-38, pl. ii/4, 5, 7-9, 13.

[97] Towered walls to signify a city occur frequently during the seventh and eighth centuries B.C. on the silver bowls of Cyprus (C. Densmore Curtis, "The Bernardini Tomb," *Mem. Amer. Ac. in Rome*, III, 1919, p. 38, pl. 20; E. Gierstad, *Opuscula Archaeologica*, IV, 1946, pp. 1-15, pl. VI); the patera from Amathous must depict a Syrian city because it has a row of domical huts in front of the towered wall (Perrot et Chipiez, III, fig. 547; A. Marquand, *A.J.A.*, III, 1887, p. 335).

[98] A coin of Marcus Aurelius (H. Stuart Jones, *Papers of the Brit. School at Rome*, III, 1905, p. 259, pl. xxix/6) shows the Emperor, preceded by a representative of the legions and a guard and followed by a Victory, approaching an arch. Jones and Sjöqvist (*Opuscula Archaeologica*, IV, 1946, p. 119) have identified the arch as the one Domitian built into the Porta Triumphalis; Kantorowicz, *Art Bulletin*, XXVI, 1944, p. 214, fig. 10.

[99] An early patera of Augustus, found at Fins d'Annecy, has on it a two-towered wall which seems to have a divine content because the whole patera was designed to show the heavenly nature and ancestry of Augustus as the son of Apollo; the towered wall, with Apollo and Neptune standing beside it, was meant to be either Troy or the stronghold of Olympus from which a deity like the Emperor has come (W. Deonna, *Revue archéologique*, XI, 1920, p. 12; M. Rostovtzeff, "Augustus," *University of Wisconsin Studies, No. 15*, 1922, pp. 134-147).

[100] H. Mattingly, *Coins of the Roman Empire in the British Museum*, I, 1923, p. 53, pl. 5/9-12; T. L. Donaldson, *Arch. Numismatica*, 1859, p. 320, no. 86.

[101] R. Schultze, *Bonn. Jahrb.*, CXVIII, 1909, pp. 280-352.

[102] W. Wroth, *Brit. Mu. Cat. Greek Coins, Pontus, Paphlagonia, Bithynia and Kingdom of Bosphorus*, 1889, p. 122, no. 1, pl. xxvi/9; W. H. Waddington, *Recueil général des monnaies grecques, d'Asie Mineure*, I, 1904, p. 281, pl. XLIV/1 (Germanicus Caesar), pl. XLIV/2 (Titus Caesar).

the towered portal on a coin of Sauromates I (Fig. 15) who ruled the Bosphorus Cimmerians (A.D. 94-124) under Roman suzerainty.[103]

It is a coin of Bizya (Fig. 16), the capital of the Astae and the seat of imperial government in southeastern Thrace, which raises the question of whether the towered city-gate motif in the eastern provinces was still considered a heavenly symbol and, because of its ceremonial distinction in the reception of a divine ruler, had become a numismatic convention with which to commemorate an event that partook of the nature of a Triumph and Epiphany.[104] The date of the coin makes it necessary to assign the event to that problematic period (A.D. 117-118) when Hadrian, following the death of Trajan, may have visited the city on his return from Antioch to Rome.[105] Whatever the occasion, which was important enough to have been celebrated by the issue of two similar variants, the symbolic conception of the city-gate motif is illustrated by the way in which it is presented as a *Porta Triumphalis* surmounted by a chariot, driven by a figure carrying the palm of victory, that rises heavenward over what was a "royal and celestial arcade." Even though it is not known whether the coin refers to an actual triumphal visitation, or only records the city's recognition of Hadrian's coming to power as a kind of Adventus, the chariot of apotheosis indicates how the people of Thrace, who had long thought of their rulers as immortals and were accustomed to welcome a king as the personification of a god, must have looked upon this gateway.

Two later coins of Bizya, minted for Philippus Senior (A.D. 244-249), furnish other details to strengthen the presumption that the city-gate motif was identified with emperor-worship and was used to commemorate either a visitation, or anniversary, which was comparable in popular ideology to a triumphal Coming.[106] The same figures are over the gateway on both coins, but on the Berlin example (Fig. 28) the portal is part of a bird's-eye view of the city, showing the forum with its double stoas, the temple with statues on columns, a building in the lower right corner which may be a royal bath, and little heads looking out through the openings in the arcade over the entrance. The elaborate sculptural treatment of the gateway may be a further indication that the coin memorialized an actual imperial visitation: in addition to the traditional scene of deification by apotheosis over the archway, the horseman at the left of the portal has been recognized as the Thracian hero-god,

---

[103] Wroth, *op.cit.*, p. 59, no. 16, pl. XIII/10; a sestertius from the Thracian Bosphorus (Crimea) belonging to Sauromates I has a towered gateway with a tree behind it and at one side a curious figure with flying draperies, which is called a prisoner chained to the tower (A. I. Zograf, *Antičnye Monety, Materialy i issledovanija po archeologii SSR*, vol. *16*, Moscow, 1951, pp. 201, 247, pl. XLVII/3); another from the same region attributed to Rhescuporis II (A.D. 68-92) has a city-gate with one tower and over the arched portal an equestrian statue (*op.cit.*, pp. 202, 247, pl. XLVII/8).

[104] B. V. Head, *Brit. Mu. Cat. Greek Coins,*

Thrace, p. 88, no. 3; Donaldson, *op.cit.*, p. 314, nos. 83, 84; A. Löbbecke, *Zeit. für Num.*, XXI, 1898, pl. VIII/6.

[105] Hadrian's movements in A.D. 117/18 are discussed by B. W. Henderson, *The Life and Principate of the Emperor Hadrian*, 1913, *appx.*, B; J. M. C. Toynbee, *The Hadrianic School*, 1934, p. 125.

[106] Berlin (Löbbecke, *Zeit. f. Num.*, XXI, 1898, p. 254, pl. VIII/5; G. MacDonald, *Coin Types*, 1905, p. 166, pl. VIII/10); Sofia (Löbbecke, pl. VIII/7; Imhoof-Blumer, *Journal international d'archéologie numismatique*, XI, 1908, p. 185, pl. XI/23.

with whom the emperor was presumably identified at the time of his reception; and on the opposite side the three figures may be Virtues or Charities, as they have been called, who were thought of as taking part metaphorically in the Adventus as attributes of the divine visitor, or they may represent a delegation coming forth for the reception.[107]

At an earlier date a comparable use of the city-gate as a triumphal entrance, where a sun-god is presented as the solar protector of the city, is seen on a coin of the Thracian city of Nicopolis (Fig. 27) which has the quadriga of Helios-Elagabalus (A.D. 218-222) soaring heavenward over the towered portal.[108] Frequently, however, no figures appear on the city-gates. Hence there is nothing, other than the traditional implications of the motif in the East, to indicate the content of the three-towered gateway (Fig. 17) on a coin of Caracalla (A.D. 211-217), issued at Trajanopolis,[109] until it is compared to a similar and earlier coin (Fig. 18) brought out under Septimius Severus (A.D. 193-211) at Isauria in Cilicia.[110] On the Asia Minor example the figure of Tyche carrying the cornucopia of plenty and seated within the portal may well refer to the emperor and the bounty which came from an imperial visitation. From the time of the Diodochi it had been customary in the Near East to associate a Tyche with the ruler and under the Romans the Fortuna Redux of the imperial family was identified with Tyche, while the Cult of the Caesars was celebrated in the Tychaia and shrines of Fortuna.[111] At Perge (Fig. 13) the way in which the old city-gate with its flanking round towers was made during the Empire into a ceremonial monument and sanctuary by the addition of a triumphal arch across the open end of the vaulted elliptical vestibule back of the portal suggests that it served, like the temple of Fortuna Redux in connection with the Porta Triumphalis at Rome (Fig. 4), as a kind of Tychaion for a triumphal reception and the worship of the protectress of the emperor

[107] Löbbecke, op.cit., p. 256; B. Pick, Zeit. f. Num., XXIII, 1891, p. 44; for female personifications see Imhoof-Blumer, op.cit., p. 185. A statue of Virtue with a golden crown of olive leaves rode beside Ptolemy Philadelphus in his great procession at Alexandria (Athenaeus, Deipnosophists, I, v, 33).

[108] B. Pick, Die antiken Münzen von Dacien und Moesien, I, 1898, no. 2003, pl. XX/13.

[109] R. S. Poole, Brit. Mu. Cat. Greek Coins, Thrace, 1877, p. 78, no. 11.

[110] G. F. Hill, Brit. Mu. Cat. Greek Coins, Lycaonia, Isauria and Cilicia, 1900, p. xxvii n. 5, pl. XL/2; Imhoof-Blumer, Kleinasiatische Münzen, II, 1902, p. 449, pl. XVII/12.

[111] Daremberg et Saglio, Dict. des Antiquites, II, 1266-1276; Roescher, Lexikon der Griech. und Röm. Mythologie, "Fortuna," 1524-1526; Pauly-Wissowa, Real-Encyclopädie, 2 Ser., VII², 1943, 1666, 1675. Earlier it was noted that Domitian's temple of Fortuna Redux in the Porticus Divorum is depicted on the stone map of Rome (Fig. 4) with the unique feature of a horseshoe-shaped apse. It is interesting to find a similar three-quarters round

apse on the sanctuary at Baalbek, which Krencker (Wiegand's Baalbek, II, pp. 90-110, 126) identified as a Tychaion, and on a small temple at Rahle, which Krencker (D. Krencker u. W. Zschietzschmann, Römische Tempel in Syrien, 1938, pp. 226, 280, pl. 95) suggested was probably used for the imperial cult. In fact, his assumption that the other apsidal sanctuaries in Syria, such as the one at Hössn Soleimann (op.cit., p. 99, pl. 41), were for the Cult of the Caesars may explain why at Rome the temples of Fortuna Redux and the Templum Urbis were apsidal. Since the horseshoe plan of the apses on the Syrian shrines where the Tyche, or Fortuna, of the Emperor was probably worshiped implies a domical vault, it is interesting to find at Perge (Fig. 13) that the apsidal sanctuary in combination with the triumphal arch is somewhat horseshoe in plan, and that the domical shrine of "Good Fortune" at Umm-iz-Zetun is inscribed "for the preservation and victory of our Lord Marcus Aurelius Probus Augustus" and that "the community of the village and of the god built the sacred kalubé" (H. C. Butler, Syria, II, A, p. 361; Smith, The Dome, pp. 70-71, fig. 120).

and the city.[112] Furthermore, an inscription found in the ruins of the structure says, "The Demos of Perge, Tiberius Claudius Caesar, Augustus, the Father of his Country."

At this point, in following the chronology of the city-gate motif, it is necessary to ask why the die-cutters of the Thracian coins were instructed to depart from the architectural standard of flat-roofed towers with crenellations, which were customary in both Italy and the East, and to introduce domes on the towers. The change is illustrated by a series of city-gate coins minted for Anchialus after it had become the seat of imperial government in Northern Thrace. The earliest (Fig. 19), belonging to Commodus (A.D. 180-192), is distinguished both by the tower roofs and by the exaggerated height of its royal arcade which, it has been noted, has only appeared over the gateways of provincial capitals and had an imperial significance.[113] The only earlier example is from the first century B.C. on a coin of Pella in Macedonia which had conical roofs on a structure that has been called a royal palace.[114]

Although it has been suggested that conical roofs were first introduced for climatic reasons in the northern provinces,[115] the subsequent examples of city-gates and defensive towers with conical roofs in both Roman and Early Christian art fail to conform to any reasonable geographic and environmental distribution.[116] Instead there is the likelihood that conical roofs were at first merely a diagrammatic way of indicating domes. Certainly, as will be discussed more fully in a later section, there is convincing evidence from both the Late Empire and the Middle Ages to prove that domes with their royal, cosmic, and celestial symbolism were imperial insignia on the coins of Thrace.[117]

One issue of Septimius Severus (Fig. 20) from Anchialus has only a city wall with what appear to be conical roofs on the towers, while the other (Fig. 21) has the city-gate, a crowning portico, a heroic deity and very emphatic domes.[118] The new domical type, once it is recognized that the cupolas referred to the celestial nature of the event and the cosmic authority of the emperor, may help to explain the heroic naked figure holding in one hand a lance, or scepter, and in the other a serpent. If, for no other reason, the size of the god shows that we are not dealing with just the sculptural decorations of an actual gateway. In a literal sense, the figure is a specific god: either Poseidon, as has been suggested because of the "sea-serpent," or more likely Hercules, a popular Thracian deity who was not uncommonly represented on coins

[112] K. Lanckoronski, *Städte Pamphyliens und Pisidiens*, I, 1890, p. 40, fig. 28.

[113] F. Münzer und M. L. Strack, *Die antiken Münzen von Thrakien*, II, 1912, p. 227, no. 439, Taf. VI/17.

[114] H. Gaebler, *Die antiken Münzen von Makedonia und Paionia*, III, 1935, p. 98, no. 25, pl. XIX/16; Imhoof-Blumer (*Monnaies grecques*, 1883, p. 88, no. 103) suggests that the fortress is the royal palace at Pella.

[115] The theory of R. Forrer ("Zur Bedachung

der spätrömischen Festungstürme in den Rheinländern," *Germania*, II, 1918, p. 73) has been contested by W. Kubitschek, "Zur Bedachung römischer Festungstürme," *Germania*, III, 1919, pp. 9-15.

[116] See p. 66.

[117] See pp. 69, 109, 128, 188.

[118] Münzer und Strack, *op.cit.*, p. 238, nos. 483/4 (fig. 9) pl. VI/34 and p. 239, no. 487 (fig. 10) pl. VI/33.

in a similar posture, grasping the Hydra in his hand.[119] Symbolically, however, it is suggested that the colossal deity towering over the portal was intended to refer, like the chariot of apotheosis on the Bizya coins and the figure of Constantine as Apollo over the gateway of his city of Treves (Fig. 50), to the emperor, who at the time of his visitation was welcomed as a *Deus praesens* and the personification of the city's protective god. If this is so, then it is difficult to believe that the Greek *delta*, which is so prominently displayed in the open portal and is so curiously emphasized on other Thracian coins, was only a mint mark and did not refer to the divine nature of the emperor in whose honor the coin was struck.[120]

That the domical shape on these coins had some expressive value, and that we are dealing with the representation of ideas rather than with the record of archaeological facts become more evident under Caracalla (A.D. 211-217) when all three variants issued at Anchialus have domical towers, but are strikingly different. One has no portal between the towers; the second (Fig. 23) has a very schematic treatment of the royal arcade and niches on the face of the towers which presumably carried statues of the emperor; and the third (Fig. 22) has an enthroned figure under a baldachin, or apsidal niche, on top of the gateway.[121] Finally, in the series of Anchialus the issue (Fig. 24) of Gordianus (A.D. 238-244) has the domes and a crowning arcade.[122] On the coin of Caracalla (Fig. 22) the formal method of presenting a ruler or deity under a canopy at the entrance to his city again suggests that these coins were related to a rite of welcome. It was customary in the East to set up the figure of the king in the gateway. Later it will be shown that the custom of honoring a ruler under a baldachin, or in an apsidal exedra, at the entrance to his palace and city was related to the Roman and Byzantine tradition of having domical vestibules at the entrance to palaces and to the mediaeval convention (Fig. 70) of denoting a royal and divine reception by means of a ciborium in combination with a city-gate. In the fourth chapter it will be shown that in the tradition of the Epiphany ritual, as it came down from the Hellenistic period, there was a divine Tent of Appearances which was set up either at the city-gate or the entrance to the royal palace so that the Kosmokrator,

[119] The labors of Hercules appear on the coins of Anchialus and on a coin of Callatis (Imhoof-Blumer, *Die antiken Münzen Nord-Griechlands*, I, 1898, p. 122, no. 354, Taf. XVII/27). Philippus Senior is represented as Hercules holding the Hydra in a similar posture. Another reason for identifying the figure over the gate as the emperor is because it was customary in Thrace to immortalize men as divinities and to identify the emperor with Hercules (J. Bayet, *Mélanges d'arch. et d'hist.*, XLVI, 1929, pp. 1-42).

[120] Although the *delta* and the *epsilon* on the Thracian coins have always been called mint-marks (B. Pick, *Die antiken Münzen von Dacien und Moesien*, pp. 129, 155, 189), it is difficult to understand why these letters were given so much prominence on the coins from Caracalla through Gordi-

anus unless they were also an abbreviation of a ruler-title. On a coin of Thomi the *delta* occurs directly over the *Adventus* figure of the emperor on horseback (Poole, *Brit. Mu. Cat. Coins of Thrace*, p. 60, no. 41) and on another issue it has a curiously prominent position over the triumphal chariot of Maximianus being led by a Nike (*op.cit.*, p. 60, no. 46).

[121] No portal (Münzer und Strack, *op.cit.*, II, no. 533, Taf. VII/11); rectangular door (*op.cit.*, no. 534, Taf. VII/12); and with baldachin (*op.cit.*, no. 537, Taf. VII/10).

[122] Münzer und Strack, II, p. 290, no. 681, Taf. VIII/27; a Russian coin from Anchialus, dated A.D. 198-217, has a large arcade over the portal and cupolas with the petal-like treatment on the towers (Zograf, p. 240, n. 103, pl. XXVI/7).

enthroned like a god in his shrine, could sit in solemn state while receiving the acclamations, adoration, and supplications of his subjects.

It remains to be seen whether the subsequent history of gateway ceremonials justifies any of these at present suppositional interpretations. A Thracian coin from Callatia (Fig. 25), issued under Geta (A.D. 209-211), strengthens the assumption that it was customary to represent the emperor as the protective god of a city, for it has a figure on the face of one of the towers, in this instance with a conical roof, which has been called a ruler because of his long scepter although the long garment suggests a Tyche.[123] The other city-gate coins of Thrace from Marcianopolis (Fig. 26) and Nicopolis (Fig. 29), both issued under Gordianus, furnish no new sculptural details except the symbolic orbs along the cornice and the curious petal-like treatment of the domes, which will be discussed later.[124] The use of the *epsilon*, either in the portal (Fig. 26) or over the gateway (Fig. 25), again raises a doubt as to whether this letter, like the *delta*, was merely a mint mark.[125]

Finally, there is more direct confirmation that the domical towered gateway in Thrace was recognized as the symbol of the celestial stronghold of a deified person. A coin (Fig. 30) which has been attributed to Decius (c. A.D. 250) and assigned to Philippopolis, bears the legend DIVUS MARCUS AURELIUS and shows the already apotheosized Augustus between the domical towers of a conventionalized city-gate.[126] As far as the popular import of the subject is concerned, it is relatively of little importance whether the coin was intended to present in numismatic abbreviation the fact that a commemorative statue was set up in the city-gate, or that the towered façade motif with domes referred only to the celestial home of the emperor. At this time ruler statues were received, looked upon, and adored as if they were real beings. In discussing the coin, Mattingly refers to "the ardent belief in immortality" among the Dacians which insured, as he says, "a special respect for the cult of the deified Emperor." The strongest reason for believing that the Thracians also had the idea that the towered façade symbolized an Olympian stronghold, a sacred palatium and a heavenly castrum may be seen when this Roman coin is compared with the same use of the domical gateway in Christian art to show the *Sacrum palatium* of "Charlemagne" with the Hand of God over the head of the Emperor (Fig. 158), the divine seat of authority in which the Evangelists write (Fig. 68), the heavenlike palatium of the Holy Roman Emperors (Figs. 83, 84), and the celestial *castrum-palatium* in which Christ is crowned with thorns.[127]

[123] Poole, *Brit. Mu. Cat. Greek Coins, Thrace,* p. 23, no. 11.

[124] Marcianopolis (Poole, *op.cit.,* p. 40, no. 89); Nicopolis (Donaldson, *op.cit.,* p. 310, no. 82); Imhoof-Blumer, *Die antiken Münzen Nord-Griechenlands,* p. 518, no. 2107, Taf. xx/16.

[125] The *epsilon* is given great prominence on the Thracian coins, especially those of Dionysopolis and Marcianopolis, from the time of Caracalla. It appears with various figures, usually divinities; but on a coin of Caracalla (Poole, *op.cit.,* p. 30, no.

20) it is alongside a triumphal arch and on another issue of the same emperor (Poole, p. 30, no. 19) it has an equally prominent position alongside a shrine in which the Emperor is enthroned as Zeus. Hence one wonders, numismatists to the contrary, if it could not have been an abbreviation of a royal title.

[126] H. Mattingly, *Roman Coins,* 1928, pp. 206-207, pl. LI/9.

[127] In the Salzburg Gospel Book in the Morgan Library, no. 781, fol. 83v (*Life*, April 2, 1945, p.

The evidence that the city-gate on the Thracian coins had an intended imperial and Olympian symbolism seems slight and dubious only when it is evaluated without any consideration of a) the long history of the gateway in the East as a form of heavenly distinction, b) the fact that it first occurs on the Eastern coins of those emperors who by the beginning of the third century were most interested in cultivating the ruler concepts of their Eastern subjects, and c) its very specific symbolic content on the coins of the fourth century when the Eastern ideas of emperor-worship had become the religion of the State. In the end, however, it is the persistent influence of the whole city-gate concept, with its overtones of heavenly and kingly meaning, on the coins, architecture and iconography of the Middle Ages which records with the greatest clarity the ideas which had come to be associated with the gateway in the Roman and Hellenistic East.

4. Portals with baldachins and cupolas on the coins of the Late Empire

A. THE PERIOD OF DIOCLETIAN (A.D. 284-305)

There are no other examples of the city-gate motif, either with or without domical towers, until after Diocletian had instituted his monetary reforms from his capital in Asia Minor. Then there appeared in all parts of the Empire four new types of portal, all with cupolas. The most traditional, and perhaps the earliest, shows a conventionalized city, seen in partial perspective (Figs 31-32), with the two emperors and their respective Caesars performing a ceremony in front of the towered gateway. The coins of this type have not been related to any particular event, although the four figures in front of the portal have been identified as the members of the divine Tetrarchy. Therefore their ceremonial act was probably a commemorative one which did not require the actual presence of the four rulers. All the examples are silver denars; while there are variations in the treatment of the city wall on the issues of the different mints, the towers, especially those flanking the portal, have domical roofs. These denars, issued for both Diocletian and Maximianus by most of the imperial mints, carry the legends PROVIDENTIAE AUGG, VICTORIAE AUGG, VICTORIAE SARMATICAE (all with variations in the spelling) and sometimes VIRTUS MILITUM.[128] The type was later used by Constantius Chlorus, Constantine as Caesar, and Maximinus Daza.[129]

The second type, which is a schematic representation of a fortified enclosure, like a military camp, places more emphasis on the surmounting domes. Instead of the flank-

---

59) Christ being crowned with thorns is seated between the flanking towers of a symbolic *castrum-palatium* which are roofed with corrugated cupolas to signify a celestial *skene*, and on the enclosing back wall, directly over the head of the enthroned Christ, is a cupola which was a palatium symbol of domination over Rome and the World that occurs over the palace on mediaeval ruler coins (Fig. 82) and on the Bayeux tapestry (Fig. 53).

[128] K. Pink, "Die Silberprägung der Diocletienischen Tetrarchie," *Num. Zeit.*, XXIII, 1930, p. 11, pl. 1/1, 2, 16; Cohen, *Description historique des monnaies*, VI, nos. 411-413, 427, 487-489 (Diocletian) and nos. 486, 548-552, 622-625 (Maximianus).

[129] Cohen, VII, p. 163, no. 207.

ing towers, this castrum type has three cupolas over the façade and four cupolas, two large and two small, over the back wall which is seen in partial perspective. On the coin minted at Rome (Fig. 34) the domes appear to be lanternlike cupolas, while on another (Fig. 33) from Ticinum, or Pavia, they very clearly resemble a royal ciborium. The type was used exclusively on the gold coins of Diocletian and Maximianus and carried the legends VIRTUS MILITUM or PROVIDENTIAE AUGG.[130] Inasmuch as they were all minted in Italy, and mostly at Rome, they show that the imperial implications of the cupola were by this time recognized in Italy. There is also the possibility that the type was brought out to commemorate Diocletian's *vicennalia*, or what was both the anniversary of his imperial Advent and his first Coming to Rome in A.D. 303, which would, therefore, relate it to the tradition of the Eastern Epiphany.

The third version, which is a further simplification, has only the castrum façade with three cupolas (Fig. 35). It usually bears the legend VIRTUS MILITUM, but sometimes has VICTORIAE AUGG or VICTORIAE SARMAT, and was issued for Diocletian and Maximianus by the Eastern mints of Nicomedia, Cyzica, Thessalonica, Serdica, and Antioch.[131] The fourth version, which seems to be another condensation of the castrum, has four cupolas and the same legends; it was usually brought out by the Eastern mints, but was also minted for Maximianus at Treves.[132] The large star, which appears over the portal on the coin of Diocletian (Fig. 36) from Nicomedia, and the double star on an issue of Maximianus (Fig. 37) at Treves, recall the stars which were a mark of deification on the coins of the Hellenistic kings, thereby suggesting another connection between the city-gate motif with its celestial symbolism and the ceremonial custom of welcoming a ruler with such titles as "Lord of all the Sun and Earth.[133] The fact that the cupolas are not structural domes, but are presented like ciboria with supporting uprights, and are sometimes stylized to resemble a *sphaera*, will prove important later in showing why these castrumlike portals on the coins of the Tetrarchy did not represent a specific city, but were a more universal and graphic presentation of the ideas stated in their legends.

B. THE CONSTANTINIAN PERIOD (A.D. 306-337)

Following the retirement of Diocletian, both the four-cupola (Figs. 38-39) and the three-cupola (Fig. 40) gateways were used occasionally by the various Emperors and their Caesars during the troubled period between A.D. 306, when Constantine began his struggle for supremacy, and his defeat of Licinius in A.D. 323. For the most part the gateway coins bear the legend VIRTUS MILITUM, although some issues have either

[130] K. Pink, *Num. Zeit.*, XXIV, 1931, Taf. I/11, 15; Cohen, VI, p. 473, no. 519 (Diocletian) and nos. 485, 626 (Maximianus); later examples (Cohen, VII, p. 125, nos. 221, 222).

[131] Pink, *Num. Zeit.*, XXIII, 1930, p. 13, Taf. I/3; Cohen, VI, nos. 485, 520 (Diocletian) and nos. 558, 627, 628, 630 (Maximianus); later examples: Cohen, VII, nos. 145-148 and Maurice, *Numisma-*

tique constantinienne, I, 1908, pl. X/5; II, pp. 578, 583-584, pl. XVII/8.

[132] Pink, *op.cit.*, p. 13, pl. I/4, 5; Cohen, VI, nos. 484, 492 (Diocletian) and nos. 547, 553, 631, 632 (Maximianus).

[133] G. Gerlach, *Griechischen Ehreninschriften*, 1908, p. 75.

PROVIDENTIAE AUGG or VIRTUS AUGG.[134] Finally, after Constantine had become the sole ruler, there appears a new version of the gateway between A.D. 324 and 326.

The new type is characterized by two cupolas (Figs. 42-45) and a large sun, thereby bringing the design back more nearly to the gateway tradition, only with cupolas instead of towers. It carries the legend PROVIDENTIAE AUGG and was issued, as small bronzes, in full sets by all the mints of the Empire for the Augustus and his sons, the Noble Caesars, Crispus, Constantinus, and Constantius.[135] The occasion of this empire-wide emission was either the advanced celebration of the *vicennalia* at Nicomedia in A.D. 325, or the combination *vicennalia* of Constantine and the *decennalia* of his Caesars in A.D. 326 at Rome. The religious nature of the event as a kind of Epiphany, taken in combination with the use of the symbolic castrum portal to present the idea of the supreme ruler as the heavenly source of *providentiae*, the marked emphasis upon the Sun of Heaven rising gloriously over the entrance and the way in which the cupolas are frequently stylized into globes, all combine to prove that the gateway motif was universally recognized as a symbol of celestial and cosmic power, and was used to commemorate an imperial anniversary.

The ascendant "Day Star" over the gateway is no longer merely a sign of deification, as it had been on the Hellenistic coins, but is the *Sol Domini imperii Romani* and pertains to the rising to power of the imperial Lord of Heaven and Earth. At the same time it may have referred to the *coelo demissus*, or *coelo receptus*, and undoubtedly had the same theophanic significance as the star over the Royal Gate on the coin of Diocletian (Fig. 36), the deities over the gateways on the Thracian coins (Figs. 21, 22) and the figure of Constantine himself rising heavenward over the "Famous Portal" on his Treves medallion (Fig. 50). This symbolism, which went back to the Hellenistic period when the Greek kings identified themselves with Helios the Kosmokrator in order to be accepted as the incarnation of Amon-Ra, Jupiter Heliopolitanus, and the other solar deities of the East, was consistent with Constantine's early interest in Apollo and his policy of associating himself with the Invincible Sun in the hope that both pagans and Christians might be united in an imperial cult.[136] Even after he became the protector of the New Faith and wished to disassociate himself from the Herculean and Jovian emperors who had persecuted the Christians, there is no indication that he abandoned the idea; for he allowed his person to be represented at Constantinople as Apollo, in a statue which bore the inscription "To Constantine all glorious as the Sun," and he made no effort to discourage his identification with the

[134] Four-cupolas (Cohen, VII, p. 313, no. 706; *Coll. Bement*, pl. 56/1490; Maurice, *op.cit.*, II, p. 174, pl. VI/12); three-cupolas (Cohen, VII, p. 312, no. 705; *Cat. Hamburger*, 1925, pl. 65/1826; Maurice, II, p. 578, pl. XVII/8).

[135] Representative examples: Constantine, mint of Treves (Maurice, I, p. 475, pl. XXIII/8), mint of Thessalonica (Maurice, II, p. 461, pl. XIV/8, 9); Crispus, mint of Tarragona (Maurice, II, p. 275, pl. VIII/13, 14); Constantine, mint of Lyon (Mau-

rice, II, p. 124, pl. IV/17).

[136] A. Alföldi, *The Conversion of Constantine*, 1948, pp. 5-11; M. H. Baynes, "Constantine the Great and the Christian Church," *Proc. Brit. Ac.*, XV, 1929-31; Boissier, *Fin du paganism*, II, pp. 219-327; Maurice, *op.cit.*, II, pp. xi-xiii (solar dynasty of the Flavians), p. xx (Cult of Apollo in Gaul); M. Toutain, *Cultes païens dans l'empire romain*, I, 1907, p. 317.

Sun, which continued to be popular with the majority of his subjects and with the Neoplatonists who were prominent in his court.[137]

Constantine's numismatic emphasis on the solar symbolism between A.D. 324 and 326, while important to the interpretation of the castrum and its cupolas, has little bearing on the controversy regarding the date and sincerity of the Emperor's conversion to Christianity. Neither Constantine, nor even his Christian subjects, could have been seriously troubled by what now seems like the delicate problem of maintaining his divinity and at the same time recognizing the omnipotence of God. Even after the transitional period when Constantine was politically and personally adjusting his relations with the Christian King of Heaven to the popular conception of the Augustus as a supreme and cosmic ruler, the issues did not become serious. Compromises were made, but throughout the history of the Byzantine Court the Basileus was looked upon as a *Divus* who shared with God the throne of supreme authority, who was always ritualistically presented as the living "image of Christ," and who in the palace liturgy continued to be compared with the Sun. Something of the original importance of the Constantinian sun symbolism is indicated by the established ceremonies of the Byzantine palace, which were adaptations of Roman Court rituals first introduced by Constantine, because they preserved in thinly veiled Christian formulas the traditional identification of the Emperor with the "Day Star" and reveal the way he was customarily received as the resplendent personification of the Son of God.[138]

Nevertheless, the presentation of the Emperor on the coins as the shining Golden Sun does mark an important stage in Constantine's adjustment to Christianity and hence in his use of pagan symbolism. Immediately after A.D. 326, with the exception of an emission struck at Arles (Fig. 46) and perhaps another at Treves,[139] sun, cupolas,

[137] Maurice, *op.cit.*, pp. xli ff.; Max Vogelstein, *Kaiseridee-Romidee und das Verhältnis von Staat und Kirche seit Constantin*, 1930.

[138] The Christian emperors continued to be identified with the imperial star or sun, which was an ancient astrological manifestation of a supreme ruler. Constantine was referred to as *Lux aurea mundi, Lux aurea seculi* and *Romula Lux* by Optatianus Porphyrius (Alföldi, *Conversion of Constantine*, p. 58 n. 4); Th. Preger, "Konstantinos Helios," *Hermes*, XXXVI, 1901, pp. 457-469. Eusebius calls him the "Sun of righteousness; the Light which far transcends all light" and repeatedly compares him to the "radiant sun" ("Oration in praise of Constantine," *Nicene and post-Nicene Fathers*, I, ch. i, iii). Corippus in his panegyric on Justinian (W. Jaeger, *Panegyrici veteres*, II, 1779, p. 487, I, 96f.) compares the *Domus iustini* to the glorious house of the Sun and says (I, 250) *Lux urbis et orbis, Iustiniane pater, dilectam deseris aulam!* The persistence at the Byzantine Court of the tradition of the *regale vexillum* (Grabar, *L'Empereur dans l'art byzantine*, p. 227) is seen in the use in the ceremonies of the refrain "The Star announces the Star" (A. Vogt, *Le Livre des cérémonies*, I, 1935, pp. 29, 31, 32; II, p. 123). In the

tenth century Liudprand in describing the reception of the Emperor Nicephorus by the populace wrote, "Singers began to cry out in adulation, 'Behold the morning star approaches; the day star rises; in his eyes the Sun's rays are reflected'" (F. A. Wright, *The Works of Luidprand of Cremona*, 1930, pp. 240-241). The persistence of the imperial sun symbolism at the Byzantine Court is also illustrated by the laudation of the Basileus as the Sun and the Augusta as the Moon in the celebration of the *Prokypsis* during the Christmas and Epiphany rituals (O. Treitinger, *Die oströmische Kaiser- und Reichsidee*, Jena, 1938, pp. 112-120, and L'Orange, *Studies on the Iconography of Cosmic Kingship in the Ancient World*, Oslo, 1953, p. 111) and by the solar significance of the elevation of a newly elected emperor on a shield and of his enthronement (L'Orange, *op.cit.*, pp. 103-113).

[139] In addition to the examples of the two-cupola castrum with the star and the legend PROVIDENTIAE, which was standard at all mints between A.D. 324-326, the mint of Arles brought out as part of a fifth emission a four-cupola castrum with the legends VIRTUS AUG, VIRTUS CAES and VIRTUS CRISPUS (Maurice, II, pp. 174-175, pl. VI/12, 13). Between A.D. 326-330 Arles also brought out a sixth emis-

and gateway disappear from all Constantinian coinage. Although the motifs were revived by some of the later Christian emperors and were officially readopted as symbols of heavenly authority on the coins of the Germanic and Latin kings,[140] this abrupt discontinuance of what had been a kind of Epiphany symbolism suggests that Constantine decided after the Council of Nicaea in A.D. 326 that such explicit celestial, cosmic, and sun symbolism was no longer appropriate to his position as a Christian monarch.

C. RHENISH COINS WITH DOMICAL TOWERS

There are two exceptional medallions of Gallic origin, one of uncertain date that may be pre-Constantinian and the other of Constantine, which commemorate imperial receptions and contribute more evidence that domical towers had an imperial significance. The one of lead (Fig. 49), found in the Saône near Lyon, is a trial strike of what was to have been, or was, the reverse of a commemorative gold medallion.[141] The inscriptions on the buildings identify the fortifications on the left as MOGANTIACUM, or Mainz, and the defensive enclosure at the end of the bridge, across the FL (uvius) RENUS, as the Roman CASTEL (lum). All the towers, including those which flank the entrance to the city and castrum, have domical roofs with spherical finials. The nimbed figures in the upper exergue are two deified rulers who are receiving either the submission of chieftains with their families, or the acclamations of all the inhabitants, men, women, and children. The event has usually been interpreted as an episode in some one of the imperial campaigns against the German tribes,[142] the most recent suggestion being that the scene symbolized the annexation made on the right bank of the Rhine in A.D. 288-289 by Diocletian and Maximianus.[143]

The customary explanation of the upper scene as the submission of a conquered German tribe, rather than the celebration of an Adventus by the populace, does not account for the emphasis given to the fortified city, its Castellum across the river, the figures on the bridge and the domical towers as a mark of imperial presence. If Mainz was first fortified and raised to the status of a *civitas* under Diocletian and Maximi-

sion including examples of the two-cupola castrum with the legends PROVIDENTIAE or VIRTUS MILITUM (Maurice, II, pp. 183-185, pl. VI/15, 20; I, p. 139, pl. XII/7). The examples of the four-cupola castrum after A.D. 326 Maurice says are false, but on the basis of the mint mark PTRE he assigns two coins with the two-cupola castrum to an eighth emission of Treves (I, pp. 475-476, pl. XXIII/12).

[140] Theodosius I (A.D. 378-395) issued at the mint of Thessalonica a castrum façade surmounted by two orbs and with the legend "The Glory of the State" (Mattingly, *Roman Coins*, p. 252, pl. LVIII/18); Magnus Maximus (A.D. 383-388) at Arles used the castrum with two cupolas, the star, and the legend "Hope of the Romans" (Mattingly, p. 252, pl. LXIV/17); and Valentinian II (A.D. 425-455) at Rome used the castrum surmounted by two orbs (Mattingly, pl. LXIV/19).

[141] Alföldi, *Zeitschrift für Numismatik*, XXXVI,

1926, pp. 161-174, pl. XI/4; Babelon, *Traité des monnaies-grecques et romains*, I, 1901, p. 947; Babelon-Blanchet, *Cat. des bronzes antiques de la Bibl. Nat.*, 1895, pp. 370-371; M. Berhardt, *Handbuch.*, 1926, p. 139; R. Forrer, *Germania*, II, 1918, p. 73; W. Fröhner, *Les médallions romains*, 1878, p. 259; K. Schumacher, *Germania*, I, 1917, p. 16, Abb. 6; W. Unverzagt, *Germania*, III, 1919, pp. 74-76; Babelon, *Aréthuse*, IV, 1927, p. 4.

[142] The proposed dates range from A.D. 286 to 368 and the event has been variously interpreted as Maximianus and Diocletian receiving supplications, Maximianus crossing the river, Constantinus Chlorus and Constantine visiting the city, and Valentianus with Gratianus crossing the river against barbarians.

[143] W. Seston, *Dioclétien et la Tétrarchie*, 1946, pp. 71-73.

anus, as Grenier insisted, then this unique medallion may have been designed to commemorate the event and record the city's joy at being honored by an imperial visitation.[144] Even if the exergue does refer to a victory, the scene on the bridge must depict the triumphal Adventus which took place at the entrance to the city. Certainly the group on the bridge, whether it represents an emperor preceded by Victories advancing toward the gateway of the city, as Blanchet suggested, or only depicts people waving their arms and carrying branches, pertains to a ceremonial reception.[145] This expression of rejoicing would explain the legend SAECULI FELICITAS which by the Late Empire had come to mean a renewal of Happy Times, even a Golden Age.[146]

Another indication of the intent of the medallion is seen in the nimbi, for by the end of the third century an Augustus was received as a "celestial being" and his Advent was comparable to the appearance of a god.[147] Throughout the Empire by this time the Epiphany of an emperor, his anniversaries, victories, and visitations were all occasions for ceremonies and festivals of a religious nature.[148] In Gaul the panegyrics record the fervor with which these imperial fetes were celebrated. To the ordinary man, who could not imagine anything more sublime than the coming of an Imperator and his appearance before his people as an enthroned god, it was no empty oratory that extolled the way in which the *Sacritissime Imperator* was received as a god in heaven (*in coelo deus*), praised as a triumphant Savior and assured by songs and acclamations of immortality and of the happiness which his coming brought to his subjects.[149] The day of his Advent remained sacred and often was made the beginning of a new calendar. Back of the extravagant eulogies of the panegyrists was the popular conviction, which persisted in the Middle Ages, that the honored city was itself to enjoy something of the distinction and blessings of heaven by becoming the residence of the *Deus praesens*.[150] This popular veneration of the Augustus as "an incarnate God" is also illustrated by another Gallic medallion.

This famous coin, which shows another Rhenish city with domical towers, was issued at Treves.[151] On the obverse is the head of Constantine wearing the Helios crown, while on the reverse (Fig. 50), which bears the legend AUGG GLORIA, is the Emperor, like the protective deities on the Thracian coins (Fig. 21) and the figure of Isis (Fig. 47) on a coin of Trajan,[152] rising heavenward like the sun over the towered and domical gateway of his residential city. Something of the commemorative nature of the event is indicated by the figures of conquered barbarians at either side of the closed portals facing the bridge over the Moselle River. The gateway, which is un-

[144] A. Grenier, *Manuel d'archéologie Gallo-romaine*, v, 1931, p. 404; *Quatre villes romaines de la Rhénanie*, 1925, p. 87.

[145] A. Blanchet, *Les Enceintes romaines de la Gaule*, 1907, pp. 125-127.

[146] G. M. Hanfmann, *The Seasons-Sarcophagus in Dumbarton Oaks*, 1951, p. 167.

[147] Seston, *op.cit.*, pp. 229, 240.

[148] Seston, pp. 222-224.

[149] Jaeger, *Panegyrici veteres*, I, 1179.

[150] See p. 152; Kantorowicz, *Art Bulletin*, XXVI,

1944, p. 210 and *Laudes Regiae*, p. 72.

[151] E. Babelon, "Un nouveau médallion en or de Constantine le Grand," *Mélanges Boisier*, 1913, pp. 49ff.; A. Baldwin, "Five Roman Gold Medallions," *Numismatic Notes and Monographs*, 1921, no. 6, pp. 37-63; Maurice, *op.cit.*, I, pp. 104, 476, pl. IX/6, XXIII/14; A. Blanchet, *Les Enceintes romaines de la Gaule*, pp. 88-93.

[152] S. W. Grose, *Cat. of the McClean Coll. of Greek Coins, Fitswilliam Museum*, III, 1929, p. 436, pl. 370/12.

doubtedly the "Famous, or Glorious, Portal" (*Porta Incluta*) on the northwest side of the city, was described during the Middle Ages in the *Gesta Treverorum* as "adorned with gold and precious stones so that at night ships might be illuminated as it were by the sun, the moon and the stars."[153] This extravagant figure of speech calls for some explanation, as does the fact that all the towers are so emphatically domical on this finely executed coin minted at Treves, which was the *summa urbs Gallorum* and a royal residence after A.D. 286.

The explanation depends to a large extent upon what event in the history of the city the medallion commemorated. Because Maurice was compelled by the logic of his method of reconstructing the chronology of Constantinian coinage to assign the medallion to an eighth emission, between A.D. 326 and 337, he was forced to associate it somewhat vaguely with the return of Constantine to his former capital around the close of A.D. 328 when he was compaigning along the Rhine.[154] This date has been questioned because the only event in the history of Treves which fully explains all the details and satisfactorily accounts for the minting of such an exceptional medallion was the *Natalia* of the city in A.D. 310.[155] The one reason for assigning the coin to a late date is its rare mint mark, PTRE, which occurs on four other coins presumably later than A.D. 326. Inasmuch, however, as everything else points to an early date—the pagan method of presenting the Emperor like a god over the city, the plural AUGG in the legend and the stylistic treatment of Constantine's head on the obverse—it seems equally logical to disregard the conventions of numismatic chronology and assume that an exceptional and imperial medallion would have had an exceptional mint mark, which may then have been reused at a later date on more ordinary coins.[156]

The *Natalia* of Treves in A.D. 310, when Constantine anticipated his *quinquennalia* anniversary so that his Jubilee and the birth of the city could be celebrated together, was an important event in the life of the Emperor and the city, as was recorded by the panegyric of Eumenes.[157] At this festival, which was the Roman equivalent of an Epiphany and somewhat reminiscent of the Egyptian Pharaoh's Heb-Sed jubilee, Constantine was joyously welcomed by the city as an *imperator in terris et in coelo deus* (VI, 4, 2), was called *Apollo tuum* (VI, 21, 47), and was told *quam circa tua, Constantine, vestigia urbes et templa consurgent* (VI, 22, 7), while at a later ceremony he was addressed as *Deus ille mundi creator et Dominus* (IX, 2, 4, 13).[158] Because the event was a kind of Adventus it is readily understood why the Emperor was presented on a commemorative medallion, all Glorious like the Sun, as a heavenly figure over the *Porta Incluta* of the imperial city where his Coming and Appearance took place.[159]

[153] Leibnitz, *Accessiones historicae*, 1698, v, 1, p. 124; Baldwin, *op.cit.*, pp. 53-55.
[154] Maurice, I, pp. 476-477.
[155] Baldwin, *op.cit.*, p. 41.
[156] The four other coins with PTRE and assigned to A.D. 326-330 (Hettner, *Westdeutsche Zeitschrist f. Geschichte u. Kunst*, VI, 1887, p. 143; Maurice, I, p. 474) are two of Constantine and Constantinus Caesar with a two-cupola castrum, another of Constantinus and a fourth of Fl. Helena Aug.

[157] During the Late Empire great emphasis was given in the provinces to the old Roman tradition of celebrating the imperial *Natales* along with the Birth of the City (see p. 73).
[158] W. Jaeger, *Panegyrici veteres*.
[159] Eusebius (*Vita Constantini*, Bk. IV, ch. xv) says, "His portrait also in full length was placed over the entrance gates of the palaces in some cities."

This "Famous Portal" must have been the Royal Gate where all the emperors normally entered the city when they came down the Moselle in boats. It was the beginning of the processional way leading to the palace and was the place where the emperors were received by the populace as the "Lord of the Sun, the Moon and the Stars" and greeted with such titles as *Lux aurea mundi* and *Lux urbis et orbis,* thereby explaining why the *Porta Incluta* was remembered during the Middle Ages as a place of supernatural illumination.

II · THE IMPERIAL TRADITION OF THE TOWERED FAÇADE, CASTRUM, SACRUM PALATIUM, WORLD SPHAERA, AND HEAVENLY BALDACHIN

1. The castrum portal

ANY consideration of Roman architectural symbolism cannot disregard the values which the Roman emperors attached to their numismatic designs as a means of cultivating ideas in the mind of an uneducated public accustomed to think in graphic images. This is demonstrated on the coins of Diocletian and Constantine by the way in which they made use of the castrum portal, surmounted by cupolas, ciboria, and orbs.

When Diocletian and his successors approved the use of the castrum portal with either cupolas or orbs, it was because the motifs were recognized throughout the Empire as having a specific meaning in relation to the legends PROVIDENTIAE AUGG or VIRTUS MILITUM. It was not, therefore, as it has been called, an ordinary Roman camp, or more specifically the *Castra Praetoria*, or a schematic representation of the particular city where a coin was minted. Of all the emperors, it was most unlikely that Diocletian would have been the first to identify himself in this way with the camp of the Praetorian Guard, for this particular castrum was peculiarly inappropriate to denote the virtues of a ruler who never resided at Rome and who cultivated by every means at his command the popular conviction that he was the incarnate Jove. It was Diocletian who reduced the Praetorian Guard to a garrison and Constantine who disbanded it, because its power to make and unmake emperors had proven such an intolerable threat to the stability of the realm and the position of the Augustus as a god on earth.

What, then, did the peoples of Asia Minor, Gaul, Thrace, and the other provinces see in the image of a fortified camp with cupolas? Certainly not the castrum of the troops at Rome who guarded the palace in a city which was no longer the imperial residence. In an abstract sense, perhaps, they saw it as Rome, because wherever the Emperor was there was *Roma* and the center of the *orbs Romanorum*. In another sense they may have realized that it implied *Imperium Romanorum*, as Pink suggested.[1] Actually, however, the combination of the castrum portal with the cupolas and globes was the palatium, because, by the time that Diocletian built his palace at Salona in the form of a military camp, the idea of the castrum was associated with the seat of government and hence symbolized the dwelling of the *Deus Patrius* who governed Rome and the World. Furthermore, it was the *Sacrum palatium*, the *Templum* and Olympian abode of a being who embodied the religion of the State. In the divine world

---

[1] K. Pink, *Num. Zeitschrift*, XXIII, 1930, p. 12; the legend "The Glory of the State" was used with the castrum portal on coins of Theodosius I (Mattingly, *Roman Coins*, pl. LVIII/18).

of the Tetrarchy where the Roman emperors in their theocratic absolutism were surrounded with all the pomp, ritual, and adoration of the East, both they and everything associated with them were sacred.[2]

It cannot be assumed, just because the gateway concept with its ceremonies and celestial ideology had its inception in the Orient, that there was anything peculiar to the East in the anagogical habits of thought which transformed the towered façade of the city-gate into an imperial and Christian symbol of a *Domus Dei*, and by the fourth century had come to see in the castrum portal an image of the seat of government, a *Sacrum palatium*, from which emanated the universal authority, wisdom, and military virtue of a divine ruler. Images and words, as vehicles of thought, have always been enriched with transferred and more generalized meanings. In the course of the Empire it was by a natural process of related images that *castrum*, in its most memorable and universal aspect as the stronghold of Roman rule, became synonymous with both *praetorium* and *palatium*, and thereby a means of representing the justice, wisdom, and virtue which came from the emperor.

Palatium, unlike *domus, aedes, aula,* and *villa* that were used for the royal residence, did not originally mean a dwelling, but came from the Palatine Hill, with the result that its use never entirely lost its early meaning of being a high place and citadel.[3] The literary apotheosis of *palatium* can be deduced from the words of Ovid, where he refers to the abode of the gods as *magni palatia coeli*, and later from Martial's praise of Domitian's palace, which he compares to a temple and describes as "so high in the air that it approaches the stars."[4] The habit of thinking of heaven in terms of a royal residence began in the East and persisted there. The Roman idea, however, of attributing celestial values to the place of the Caesars and of visualizing the heavenly stronghold in terms of the *Domus Palatina* became customary in Rome under Domitian, when his magnificent *Domus Augustana* was thought of as a sanctuary and there was a more general acceptance of the Augustus as a *Deus manifestus ac praesens*, who expected to be greeted by his people as "Our Lord and God."[5] Therefore, before the end of the Empire the *aedes imperatoriae* was called a *Sacrum palatium*, a usage and belief which not only persisted in Byzantium and the mediaeval West, but had a lasting influence upon architectural symbolism.[6] In the theocratic imperialism of both the Carolingian and Byzantine states the "Sacred Palace" was a concept which implied far more than a royal residence. Like the "Palatium" of the Roman emperors, it stood for the government and represented the divine authority invested in the person of a supreme ruler who was a "throne-sharer" with the King of Heaven.

[2] W. Seston, *Dioclétien et la Tétrarchie*, p. 227.

[3] W. A. Diepenbach, *"Palatium" im spätröm-ischen und fränkischen Zeit*, Diss., Mainz, 1921, pp. 31-33.

[4] Martial, *Epig.*, vii, 56; viii, 36; Ovid, *Metam.*, I, 175; K. Scott, *The Imperial Cult under the Flavians*, 1936, pp. 65-99.

[5] A. Alföldi, *Röm. Mittl.*, XLIX, 1934, pp. 31ff. and *ibid.*, L, 1935, pp. 46, 127; K. Ziegler, "palatium," Pauly-Wissowa, *R.-E.*, XVIII, 1949, pp. 66ff.;

Scott, *op.cit.*, p. 99; H. P. L'Orange, *Serta Eitremiana*, 1912, p. 12.

[6] L. Bréhier and P. Batiffol, *Les Survivances du culte impérial romain*, 1920, pp. 26, 419; Dessau, *Inscriptiones Latinae*, I, 186, no. 837; P. E. Schramm, *Kaiser, Rom und Renovatio*, 1929, pp. 225ff.; Diepenbach, *"Palatium,"* p. 9 n. 8 and p. 50. For bibliography on the "Sacred Palace" as a World House (Bandmann, *Mittelalterliche Architektur*, p. 126 nn. 21-23).

It is misleading to assume that this verbiage was nothing more than an empty euphuistic hyperbole. By the Late Empire everything associated with the Augustus was so sanctified that in the panegyrics the *Domus Augusti* was comparable to Olympus, *palatium coeli* was the equivalent of heaven, and the *divina palatia patris* of Justinian was described as like the radiant house of the Sun.[7] At the Court and in the literature the frequent references to the dwelling of the Caesars as a Heavenly Palace were little more than a laudatory convention in the eulogistic writings and orations, but at the same time they reflected popular convictions. To the common people of the Empire, who worshiped their rulers and thought of the imperial family in such terms as *Domus Augustana* and *Domus divina*, the image of a *Sacrum palatium* was the only means by which they could visualize an Olympian abode.[8] Furthermore, in order to understand why *palatium*, and the *castrum* as its graphic image, came to acquire, as Diepenbach has shown, the abstract sense of divine and "royal power," and in the Codices of Theodosius and Justinian was used in reference to the palace, court, person, and family of the emperor, it is essential to realize that the usage was essential to the concept of the State as centered in The Palace.[9]

Of even more importance to the development of both verbal and figurative imagery was the way in which the word for "military camp" acquired transferred and more generalized ideas to become analogous to *palatium*. Early in Roman usage *castrum*, we are told, took on the meaning of *colonia* and *civitas*.[10] Then, as the stronghold, citadel, and fortified *civitas*, in which was located the *praetorium* and the headquarters of the emperor when he was campaigning and residing in his provinces, castrum came to be thought of and seen throughout the Empire as a symbol of royal power. Because of the conceptual importance of the castrum before the end of the Empire, it and its *praetorium* became a synonym for *palatium*.[11] One reason for this correlation of words and ideas was that the emperors were spending so much of their time in the provinces, living in the citadel of the *praetor*. The other, and more basic reason, was that the *castrum* and *praetorium* were intuitive means of visualizing the headquarters and seat of authority which embodied the idea of *Principia* and was the place where either the person or *numen* of the emperor operated as the supreme power controlling the world.[12]

[7] W. Jaeger, *Panegyrici veteres*, II, Corippi, "In laudem Iustini Augusti," Bk. I, p. 487, line 97; p. 490, line 135; III, 210-244.

[8] de Ruggiero, *Dizionario epigrafico*, II, 1922, cols. 2062-2066; C. Julian, "Domus divina," *Bull. Epig.*, IV, 1884, pp. 25ff.; M. Movat, "Le domus divina et le divi," *Bull. Epig.*, V, 1885, pp. 221-224, 309-316; and 1886, pp. 31-36.

[9] Diepenbach, *op.cit.*, pp. 34-35.

[10] Furlanetto, *Lexicon*, II, 175; *Thesaurus Lat.*, III, 562.

[11] As early as Hadrian *castrum* was used with the meaning *"speciatim palatium imperatoris"* (*Thesaurus Lat.*, III, p. 561). At Dura-Europas *principia* was used in the inscriptions for palace

(M. I. Rostovtzeff, "The Palace of the Dux Ripae," *The Excavations at Dura-Europas*, III, 1952, pp. 85ff.). For the use of *praetorium* as the official residence of emperors and governors see: Rostovtzeff, *op.cit.*, pp. 85-92; Diepenbach, *op.cit.*, pp. 39-45; T. Mommsen, *Gesammelte Schriften*, 1905-1913, VI^c, pp. 128-133; M. Durry, *Les cohortes prétoriennes*, 1938, pp. 45-54. For the evolution of the word *castra* as applied to headquarters see: Domaszewski, *Die Rangordnung des römischen Heeres*, 1908, p. 101; Rostovtzeff, *Röm. Mittl.*, XIII, 1898, pp. 108-123; E. Stein, *Geschichte des spätrömischen Reiches*, I, 1928, p. 54; Alföldi, *Röm. Mittl.*, L, 1935, p. 96.

[12] Domaszewski, "Die Principia des römischen

Not only was *praetorium* used for imperial residences, country houses, and villas, but during the Late Empire and Middle Ages *praetoria regis*, like *palatium*, usually implied a royal castle, *castellum*, or *castrum*.[13] By the same process that palatium acquired the general meaning of "royal power," so praetorium came to be used as the equivalent of *Domus iudiciaries* and at times for the State itself, which was thought of as centered in the person, court, and justice of the rulers as the *Lex animata*.[14] Therefore, it is only necessary for the modern reader to imagine representing on a coin the architectural complexities of either a *palatium*, or *praetorium*, in order to realize why the castrum portal, with its ceremonial importance as the "Golden Gate," was by the time of Diocletian an ideal image with which to convey the conception of a *Domus Dei* from which came VIRTUS MILITUM and PROVIDENTIAE AUGG.

There were other ways by which the sacredness of the castrum became fixed in the popular imagination, as can be deduced from the coins of Marcus Aurelius and Septimius Severus. Under these emperors the empress, in addition to her titles of *Mater Deus*, *Mater Patriae* and *Mater Augustorum*, was designated as *Mater Castrorum*.[15] Although this title, which continued in use, referred to the revered position of the Augusta in the military cult of the army, nevertheless the association on the coins and inscriptions of "Castrorum" with the empress as a *Diva* placed the word in a sacred context. Furthermore, the late usage of *praetorium* and *militare in palatio* to refer to the Emperor's Court, and the way in which during the Middle Ages various forms of *castrum* were applied to dignitaries of the palace, makes one suspect that *Mater Castrorum*, which was used in the military calendar in connection with celebrating the Cult of the Living Empress, came to have the connotation in the provinces of mother of the government, court, and palace.[16]

This gradual formation of the castrum-palatium concept of the seat of government, taken in combination with the long history of the palace in the East as a fortified stronghold, explains the appearance of the castrum gateway on the coins of Diocletian and the use of the word *castrum* for palace in the Bible and literature of the Middle Ages.[17] In fact, the persistence of the castrum type of palace in both Byzantine art (Fig. 73) and Islamic architecture makes one suspect that Diocletian built his palace at Salona

---

Lagers," *Neue Heidelberger Jahrb.*, IX, 1899; T. Mommsen, "Praetorium," *Hermes*, XXXV, 1900, pp. 437-442. Another reason why *praetorium* came to have the meaning of *palatium* was because it was not uncommon for the Roman governor to have his residence and headquarters in an existing royal palace, as at Jerusalem where it was in the Palace of Herod and at Alexandria where it was for a time in the Ptolemaic Palace (K. Kraeling, "The Roman Standards at Jerusalem," *Harvard Theological Review*, XXXV, 1942, pp. 278-279).

[13] Diepenbach, pp. 22-23, 40 nn. 46, 47.

[14] *Ibid.*, p. 45.

[15] Alföldi, *Röm. Mittl.*, XLIX, p. 69; Dessau, III, 288, 294; Fink, Hoey, and Snyder, "The Feriale Duranum," *Yale Classical Studies*, VII, 1940, pp.

175, 189. Caligula adopted the title of *Castrorum filius* (Suetonius, *Galigula*, 22).

[16] In the military calendar *mater castrorum* went with the celebration of the Cult of the Living Empress (Fink, Hoey, and Snyder, *op.cit.*, p. 75). Diepenbach, *op.cit.*, pp. 37 (*in palatio militare*), 39, 42 (*militare in praetoria*); Du Cange, *Glossarium Lat.*, "Castrense," "Castrorum" (Palatium Principis), "Comes Castrensis."

[17] Vigouroux, *Dict. de la Bible*, IV, col. 1964; Du Cange, "Castrum"; O. Lehmann-Brockhaus, *Schriftquellen.*, II, 1938, p. 243. It is only the imperial meaning of the word as the royal seat of authority which explains why the Christian churchmen spoke of the *castra Dei* and used castrum for *ecclesiae* (*Thesaurus Lat.*, III, 563).

in the form of a military fortress not so much for protection in his retirement, but because it had come to be a recognized symbol of "the Glory of the State" and the authority which he personified.[18] The way in which the ideology of this *Sacrum palatium*, or heavenly castrum, had begun to influence architectural expression before the end of the fourth century can be seen in the Constantinian basilica at Treves (Fig. 8), which was constructed with towers at the four corners of its roof in order to identify it with the Seat of Justice and hence with the Emperor as the *Lex animata*. It was also during the fourth century at Treves (Fig. 76) that the Roman core of the building that eventually became the Cathedral, and was known as early as the ninth century as "the Palace of Helena," was rebuilt like a *praetoria regis* with a great tower over the central hall and the little towers of a castrum at the four corners.[19] That this form was taken over from the existing palace architecture and hence was related in origin to the similar construction of so many Byzantine churches is a premise which must be sustained in the subsequent chapters.

2. "Urbis et orbis" and "providentia"

The castrum, for much the same reasons that it had become the equivalent of palatium and praetorium, also stood for Rome and the State because, according to Herodian, "Where the Emperor is, there is Rome." This more universalized conception of The Palace accounts for the way in which the cupolas over the castrum on the coins of Diocletian and Constantine were so frequently transformed into globes. The motif politically meant *urbs et orbis*, for Rome in the person of the Imperator was the capital of the world, and the Emperor was the *Magnus parens orbis*, the *Pacator orbis, Restitutor orbis*, and *Lux urbis et orbis*.[20] In fact, the way in which the cupolas over the gateway to the *praetorium*, or *palatia patris*, were presented with global finials, or made into globes, is proof positive that the *ciborium* and *orbis* were established emblems of the emperor with much the same cosmic meaning.

Originally the globe, or *sphairos*, was an astronomical sphere developed by the Ionian philosophers.[21] By the fifth century B.C. it was considered by Empedocles and Xenophanes to be the ideal shape of the one perfect, unborn, and all-inclusive God.[22] In the course of the Hellenistic period its original significance was extended so that it became an attribute of Aphrodite Urania and the Muse Urania. After the Hellenistic kings adopted it as a symbol of their cosmic sovereignty and the Romans took it over as an imperial emblem, it acquired great political importance as an insigne of uni-

[18] See Diepenbach (pp. 50-62) for discussion of how the praetorium type of palace was at first provincial and in the course of the fourth century became standard.

[19] See p. 80.

[20] Alföldi, *Röm. Mittl.*, L, 1935, pp. 36, 88, 99, 118-120; Bréhier, "L'Origines des titres impérieux à Byzance," *Byz. Zeit.*, XV, 1906, p. 162.

[21] O. Brendel, "Symbolik der Kugel," *Röm. Mittl.*, LI, 1936, pp. 1-95; A. Schlachter, "Der Globus," *Stoichera*, VIII, 1927, pp. 1-118; Alföldi, *Röm. Mittl.*, L, 1935, pp. 118-120; as a symbol of a Kosmokrator: F. Cumont, *L'Égypte des astrologues*, Brussels, 1937, pp. 27-28; P. Hombert, "Sarapis Kosmokrator," *L'Antiquité classique*, XIV, 1946, pp. 319-329.

[22] Brendel, *op.cit.*, p. 31; W. Jaeger, *The Theology of the Early Greek Philosophers*, 1936, p. 140; Schlachter, *op.cit.*, pp. 9-15.

versal supremacy. By the time when the Roman emperors were regularly portrayed holding the orbis and wearing the sun-crown, there was a very conscious parallel between the imperial World-Ruler and the Helios-Kosmokrator, such as the figure on the Pompeian fresco who carries the sphairos and is depicted, like a Hellenistic king, with upturned eyes, wearing the divine nimbus and crowned with the rays of the Sun.[23]

The ideological association on the late Roman coins of the *sphairos* with the domical covering, or celestial canopy, undoubtedly had its origin in the Hellenistic East, presumably in Alexandria. There, as will be more fully discussed in the later sections, the tent of heaven was not only a cosmic world shelter, but it was also the baldachin which the Hellenistic rulers used as a manifestation of their divine nature.[24] A fresco of Herculaneum (Fig. 48) has the *sphaera* under a celestial *skene* that is flanked by griffins, which were solar beasts in Pharaonic Egypt.[25] The extent to which the Late Antique world was still interested in this Ptolemaic symbolism is illustrated by the Corbridge lanx (Fig. 51), which dates from the late fourth or early fifth century A.D.[26] On it Apollo is presented standing in his world ciborium, which is a tent, with the sun and moon over it, the *sphaera* on a pedestal before it and the griffin at his feet, all closely related to the way in which both a Hellenistic god-king and a Roman emperor wanted to be visualized as a supreme Sun-god.

It is now evident why the castrum portal was so appropriate to illustrate the *providentia* and *virtus militum* of the Master of Rome and the World. At first, in the early days of Roman culture, *providentia* was a human quality;[27] by the late Republic it had come to be considered a kind of foresight which, when manifested by either gods or men, helped to preserve the peace and happiness of the State; and during the first century of the Empire *providentia Augusti* was usually glorified as the imperial prescience which provided for a successor.[28] Later, however, during the fourth century when it was represented by the heavenly castrum, it was an imperial virtue comparable in many ways to the Divine Providence of the Christian God.[29] Although *providentia* was presented in different ways as the supreme quality equivalent to the omniscience of a divine Kosmokrator, it is to be noted that by the fourth century the orbis was an attribute of both the Virtue and the Augustus.[30]

It is, therefore, tempting to speculate as to whether the magistrates in charge of coinage at Constantine's Neoplatonic Court, who in depicting *providentia* had the domical ciborium turned into globes over the heavenly castrum, thought of the

[23] Brendel, Abb. 8; Schlachter, p. 106.
[24] See pp. 109, 112, 120-122.
[25] W. Zahn, *Ornamente aller klassischen Kunst-Epochen*, 1870, pl. 41; Lehmann, *Art Bulletin*, XXVII, 1945, fig. 67.
[26] Brendel, "The Corbridge Lanx," *Journal of Roman Studies*, XXXI, 1941, pp. 100ff., pls. VIII-XI; A. Dyroff, *Bonn. Jahrb.*, CXXXIII, 1928, pp. 155ff.; P. Gardner, *Jour. Hellenic Studies*, XXXV, 1915, pp. 198ff.
[27] A. D. Nock, "A Diis Electa," *Harvard Theological Review*, XXIII, 1930, p. 266.

[28] M. P. Charlesworth, "Providentia and Aeternitas," *Harvard Theological Review*, XXIX, 1936, pp. 107-132; H. Mattingly, "The Roman Virtues," *Harvard Theological Review*, XXX, 1937, pp. 103ff.
[29] Maurice, *Numismatique constantinienne*, II, 1911, pp. cxiv, 122-123; M. P. Charlesworth, "The Virtues of a Roman Emperor, Propaganda and the Creation of a Belief," *Proceedings of the British Academy*, XXIII, 1937, pp. 105-133.
[30] From the time of Hadrian the globe appears on the coins as an attribute of *Providentia* (Schlachter, *op.cit.*, p. 79).

sphairoslike cupolas as pertaining to the ideal god-image of unity, harmony, perfection, and intelligence which would appeal to both pagans and Christians. Even if they had no intent to universalize the conception of the emperor in terms of Xenophanes' god, who "was a sphere, and everywhere like unto himself," they and their age were fully aware that the gateway motif in combination with either the celestial ciborium or the universal orb represented that imperial and divine wisdom which governed Rome and the World.

Under their theocratic despotism the late Greeks and Romans wanted to see in their rulers all the virtues which meant so much to their happiness, peace, and prosperity. Hence, in their ceremonies they welcomed the ruler as the personification of Justice, Military Virtue, and Wisdom. In the Hellenistic Epiphanies the king's virtues were not only extolled in the panegyrics delivered in his presence at the city-gate, palace entrance, or vestibule of a sanctuary, but they were also represented by statues and personifications which were given prominence in the processions; and by the Late Empire *Virtus*, according to Maurice, had become an imperial title of divinity.[31] Another way of understanding the significance of the globe and cosmic *skene* on the Constantinian coins, where the emperor was identified with *providentia*, is to consider the representation of "Sapientia seated in the Temple" (Fig. 52) from a ninth century copy of the *Psychomachia* of Prudentius.[32] Prudentius lived at the time when the sons of Constantine ruled the Roman world. Therefore, the archetype of this miniature, in which the Virtue is presented seated upon an orb under a baldachin and the Templum is depicted as a castrum with many gateways, followed imperial iconography and shows how Prudentius and his age thought of the symbols on the coins. It also explains why the symbolism of the royal personification of the Virtues seated upon the world and under the canopy of heaven was transferred to Christ.

Clearly the cupola and globe were related emblems of royal power, which accounts for the fact that throughout the history of mediaeval (Figs. 7, 9, 53, 54, 83-97) and Renaissance architecture the cupola and dome were nearly always surmounted by a global finial. Only the ideational relation of the two motifs, the domical *tholus* and *sphairos*, and the fact that in the West the pointed spire had become an architectural substitute for the celestial cupola, explain the curious verbal usage of Durandus in the thirteenth century, who in describing the globe at the apex of the Gothic spire called it a *tholus*.[33]

---

[31] Athenaeus, *Deip.*, I, v, c. 33; Maurice, *op.cit.*, I, p. cxxix n. 2.

[32] *Psychomachia* of Leyden, Universität bibliothek, Cod. Burm. Q. 3, scene 89 (H. Woodruff, "The Illustrated Manuscripts of Prudentius," *Art Studies*, VII, 1929, p. 40, fig. 47); and Paris, Bibl. Nat., Ms. lat. 8085 (*op.cit.*, p. 40, fig. 64). The fact that these manuscripts were related to the royal abbey of Reims is further evidence that the rulers and churchmen knew the antique symbolism of the ciborium and globe when they used them on the coins and architecture.

[33] *The Symbolism of Churches and Church Ornament, a Translation of the first Book of Rationale Divinorum Officiorum*, J. M. Neale and B. Webb, 1893, p. 165, "The ball (*tholus*) upon which the cross is placed doth signify perfection by its roundness." Earlier Sicardus (Migne, ccxiii, 24) calls the ball at the top of a spire a "tholus" (J. Sauer, *Symbolik des Kirchengebäudes*, p. 143). Further evidence that a tholus, or domical shape, was traditionally thought of as referring to a

3. Imperial and heavenly domes over city-gates, palatia, and castrum portals

Now that it has been seen on the coins of Diocletian and Constantine that the baldachinlike cupolas over the portal of the castrum, or symbolic palatium, were emblems of the *Pater orbis*, it may be possible to answer the question of why, a century earlier, cupolas should have suddenly appeared on the towers of the Thracian city-gate coins under those emperors who were so receptive to all the Eastern ideas of a ruler being a divine Kosmokrator. Putting aside for the moment the contention, already advanced, that the domical shape in antiquity was commonly considered to be a heavenly form,[34] the clearest means of showing that the domes on the Thracian coins were imperial symbols is to work backward from the mediaeval survivals of the Roman tradition.

As late as the twelfth century the Latin kings of Jerusalem, in their desire to establish their prestige in the Near East, not only made the Gate of David, which was historically the King's Gate of Jerusalem, a royal emblem on their seals (Figs. 94-97), but they also revived the Late Antique use of cupolas over the tower of this sacred portal, which was also their residence.[35] That they were carrying on a Constantinian convention and saw in the cupolas a mark of divine authority is recorded in the way they had the cupolas stylized into globes (Fig. 97). Later it may be possible to show that the Latin kings did not derive this symbolism of the *skene-orbis* from only the Late Antique numismatics, but that the ciborialike cupolas were still in use as sculptural and decorative symbols of authority on the entrances to the imperial palaces at Constantinople. This is indicated by the survivals of their use over portals in late Islamic architecture which were influenced by the Turkish mastery of the East Roman and Byzantine Empires.[36]

Prior to the revival of imperial symbolism by the Latin kings of Jerusalem, the Ottonian and Hohenstaufen emperors had also made use of the ciborium and orb on their seals and coins. The way that these masters of the Holy Roman Empire used domes, as interchangeable with globes, on the gateway towers of the *aula Regia* (Figs. 82-92) to make manifest their divine authority over both Church and State, and even to represent a Heaven which they alone supported (Fig. 93), is evidence that the whole tradition of domical symbolism had been, and still was, of great importance as a means of illustrating the power of those who aspired to the authority of the Roman Augustus. The very fact that the cupolas are sometimes depicted on imperial and monastic coins as actual crowns is again proof of their royal meaning.[37] Against

worldly globe is the way the word *orbes* is inscribed under the dome on the tower over the gateway of the worldly city in the twelfth century *Hortus Deliciarum* of Herrad of Landsberg (A. Straub and G. Keller, *Hortus Deliciarum*, Strasbourg, 1901, p. 45, pl. LVI, fol. 215v).

[34] E. B. Smith, *The Dome*, 1950; L. Hautecoeur, *Mystique et architecture, symbolisme du cercle et de la coupole*, Paris, 1954.
[35] See p. 104.
[36] See p. 192.
[37] See p. 101.

the background of the numismatic evidence it is of historical significance that on the Bayeux tapestry the towers flanking the "PALATIUM" (Fig. 9) have *skene*like domes, that the palace of Edward the Confessor at Westminster (Fig. 10) has a towered façade with conical cupolas capped with the orbis finial, that two of the castles of William the Conqueror are distinguished by a central tower with a great dome, and that over the hall in which Harold is enthroned (Fig. 53) there are three little cupolas.[38] It is this persistent use of cupolas to designate an *aula Regia* on the Norman tapestry and earlier on the German coins of the eleventh century (Fig. 83) which proves that we are dealing with imperial symbolism and that the city portal with a cupola over its double archway on the Norman drawing (Fig. 7) of Canterbury is a Royal Gate.

Back of both the Norman palace conventions and the domical gateways on the coins of the German emperors was the precedent of the Carolingian tradition, which in turn was based upon a systematic policy of *Renovatio Romanorum*. In the ninth century illuminations of the Utrecht Psalter, which was presumably executed in the royal abbey of Reims under the supervision of the "palace clergy," the kingly and heavenly city of Sion is depicted as a castrum with cupolas on its corner towers and in the scene of the Lord's Advent (Fig. 54), which brings us back again to the ceremonial importance of the gateway, only the portal towers are crowned with domes.[39] The Coming of the Lord, it is to be noted, is pictured in terms of an *Adventus Augusti*: the Triumphator wears the divine nimbus, is preceded by his Cursor carrying his sword, and is greeted at the gateway by a delegation whose rolls undoubtedly represent the panegyrics which were to be delivered as an expression of the city's exultation, praise, and adoration. Throughout the Carolingian period towers are crowned with domes to indicate the celestial distinction of the House of God and the residence of either the "Royal Christus" or the actual Son of God. They symbolize the Palace of "Charlemagne" (Fig. 158) as the seat of divine authority, flank the heavenly gateway in which the Evangelists sit as the spokesmen of the Lord (Fig. 68) and deck the walls of cities honored by the presence of the King of Kings (Fig. 70).

The way in which the Byzantine artists consistently used the gateway and castrum motif of flanking towers with cupolas to denote a royal and divine residence is another indication that there was an imperial precedent back of this imagery in both the East and the West. The castrum-palace of the King of Nineveh (Fig. 73), for example, from the ninth century illuminations of the Homilies of Gregory of Nazianzus has the royal cupola on the four towers. Throughout the Menologium of Basil II either domical towers, or great baldachins (Fig. 125), appear on the palace architecture back of the Saints to show that the glory and grandeur of their divine abode was comparable to the sacrum palatium of an emperor. That the motif was specifically associated with the imperial palaces of Constantinople is best illustrated in the Skylitzes manu-

---

[38] H. Belloc, *The Book of the Bayeux Tapestry*, 1916, pp. 1 (Westminster Palace), 15 (Castle of William with central dome and flanking towers), 18-20 ("PALATIUM"), 27 (Stronghold of William with dome), 30-31 (Hall of Edward crowned with little cupolas), 34 (*Aula Regia* of Harold surmounted with little cupolas).

[39] E. T. DeWald, *The Utrecht Psalter*, Princeton.

script of the eleventh century by the representation of the famous Boucoleon palace (Fig. 159), which acquired its name after the old Hormisdas palace was rebuilt by Constantine Porphyrogenitus. When the evidence is traced back to the sixth century in the Christian East there is the mosaic of Khirbut Mukhayyat (Fig. 2) in Syria which pictures the church of St. Lot as a castrum-palace type of "Royal House" with towers at the four corners and with domes on the bulwarks flanking the processional entrance.

The evidence which is most convincing in tracing back the origins of the mediaeval palace tradition and in visualizing the dominant features of the Late Antique, or fourth century, *Sacrum palatium* is the mosaics of the church of St. George at Saloniki. No longer is it possible to assume that it was not until the sixth century that the Christians turned the domical mausoleum of the Emperor Galerius into a martyrium for their warrior saint. The excavations of Dyggve, while not yet published except in preliminary reports, have shown that the unfinished domical structure of Galerius, which was intended to be either a mausoleum or a temple for the worship of the divine Tetrarchy, was remade and decorated at the end of the fourth century as the palace-church of Theodosius the Great.[40] If this proves true, then the magnificent mosaics of the dome acquire a new importance in the history of Early Christian art from this early date. It is also of great significance, especially when it comes to tracing the symbolic implications of the towered façade, to learn from the excavations that this fourth century palace-church had a portal on the south side with a towered façade facing the ceremonial avenue, which led to the triumphal arch of Galerius at the crossroad in front of the entrance to the palace.

All that remains of the brilliantly colored mosaics which decorated the celestial hemisphere of the Theodosian chapel, a sanctuary that was almost equal to the Pantheon in size, is the lower band of architectural motifs back of the saints; but the cleaning of the dome has revealed indications of a middle zone of mosaics, probably depicting Prophets, and an upper circle preserving the preliminary outlines of a Triumphant Christ, which look as if it may have been adapted from the figure of Constantine trampling on the serpent, that was over the doorway of the Chalce at the entrance to the Imperial Palace at Constantinople. What is revealing in the existing mosaics (Fig. 74) is the way in which the symbolic conventions of the imperial palace architecture are used to depict the martyrs' future rewards in the sumptuously decorated halls of the celestial King of Kings. Around the base of the dome there are repeated, with many variations, all the characteristic and traditional features of the *Sacrum palatium*, such as the towered façade surmounted by either ciboria-cupolas or gables, the royal *fastigium*, the imperial apse, fountains of life and various types of baldachins, some of which have the striations of the domical *skene*. The fact that each one of the architectural units in this scene of the heavenly City

[40] E. Hébrard, "L'Arc de Galère et l'église de Sainte Georges à Salonique," *Bull. Corr. Hell.*, XLIV, 1920, pp. 5-40; E. Weigand, *Byz. Zeit.*, XXXIX, 1939, pp. 116-146; E. Dyggve, "Recherches sur le palais impérial de Thessalonique," *Studia Orien-*talia Ioanni Pedersen, pp. 59-70; Hjalmar Torp, "Quelques remarques sur les mosäiques de l'église Saint-Georges à Thessaloniques," *Hellenika*, Society of Macedonian Studies, 1954, pp. 489-498.

of God records the palace tradition, which went back in origin to the *aula Regia* of the Hellenistic kings, will become more apparent when the mosaic designs are compared with the Roman *scaena frons* and the frescos of the fourth Pompeian style (Fig. 113), both of which reflect the influence of the Alexandrian palaces. Were there still any doubt as to whether the cupolas on the Constantinian coins were conceptually ciboria, the richly patterned domical shapes which crown the towers of the Theodosian mosaics are proof that they were ceremonial insignia of a divine and cosmic Master of the World. Here they are clearly tent-canopies whose jeweled and richly embroidered reticulations resemble those of the baldachins of state under which the Byzantine Basileus was enthroned.

Other early examples of the towered façade are the buildings pictured in the Alexandrian World Chronicon, the archetype of which was executed at Alexandria around A.D. 400, but was based upon earlier "City Chronicles" of Alexandria and Constantinople.[41] Although Strzygowsky assumed that all the missing buildings had domical towers (Fig. 157), only one fragment of the Coptic papyrus shows these cupolas; the others depict buildings either with unroofed round towers or with gabled roofs. There is no doubt that the buildings were a pictorial means of designating certain provinces of Asia Minor. The fact, however, that they all have the royal *fastigium* between the flanking towers shows that they were not intended to be city gateways. Therefore they must have been a graphic method of symbolizing the *praetorium* as the seat of government in the provinces and are further evidence that the towered façade was an established convention for denoting the concept of the *Palatium*.

At this point it may strengthen the argument to disregard a strict chronology and consider whether the mosaics which frame the Councils in the Church of the Nativity at Bethlehem do not furnish proof that the towered façade with crowning cupolas was a palatium motif in East Christian art and hence was derived from the palace architecture of Constantinople. Two frames of the Antioch and Sardica Councils have survived, but the Ciampini drawings of the lost mosaics show similar frames for the Councils of Carthage, Gangra, and Laodicea.[42] The architectural elements of the Antioch panel (Fig. 75) consist of a central archway surmounted by a richly decorated dome which is flanked by towers with *skene*like cupolas that are curiously bulbous, or nearly global. For the purpose of this study the most important question is to decide whether the mosaics were intended to depict a palace symbolism or to represent the churches in which the Councils were held. Once the meaning of their architecture is understood it may be easier to settle the question of whether the mosaics were executed in A.D. 1169 at the order of the Emperor Manuel Comnenus, or were made around the beginning of the eighth century after the design of earlier models, as Stern has suggested.

[41] A. Bauer und J. Strzygowsky, *Eine Alexandrinische Weltchronik*, 1905, pp. 23, 120, Taf. II.

[42] H. Stern, "Les représentationes des conciles dans l'église de Nativité à Bethléem," *Byzantion*, XI, 1936, pp. 101-152; "Nouvelles Recherches sur les images des Conciles dans l'église de la Nativité à Bethléem," *Cahiers archéologiques*, III, 1948, pp. 82-105, pl. I.

There are several reasons why it is impossible to agree with Stern that the frames are conventionalized representations of the churches in which the various Councils met. Apart from the great palace-church at Antioch, we have no reason to believe that the churches of Gangra, Laodicea, and Sardica were domical. Also, to the best of our knowledge, the towered façade with cupolas was uncommon on both Early Christian and Byzantine churches. Furthermore, it cannot be assumed that all councils assembled in churches. Some met in the "Secretarium" of churches, some in episcopal residences, one in the "portico" of the "Great Church" at Constantinople, another at Bordeaux in the "castrum Modogarnomo" of the Church of St. Peter and many, we are told, convened in the imperial palaces.[43] Finally, it is architecturally impossible to explain these frames, especially those of Antioch and Gangra, as churches because the space back of the central dome over the arched opening is not a roofed building, but a court with the sloping roofs of its flanking halls showing at either side.

Each one of these objections takes on a positive value when the frames are seen as a conceptual representation of the imperial palace and hence as a symbolic means of making manifest in a double sense the universal authority of the emperor under whose divine auspices the gatherings took place, and the heavenly authority of the Councils. From the time of Constantine, when the first Oecumenical Council was held in his presence at his palace in Nicaea, all the Councils in the East were either called, or sanctioned, by the emperor as the recognized head of the Church. He it was, or his representative, who opened the meetings, sometimes presided and frequently controlled the deliberations of the contending factions. After the meetings it was the emperor who approved the decisions and issued the letters which made the decrees into laws of the empire. At the Council of Constantinople in A.D. 448, after the wishes of the emperor had been read from his "sacred letter," the assembled bishops enthusiastically concurred, saying in unison, "Long life to the Emperor! His faith is great! Long life to the pious, orthodox and high-priest Emperor!"[44] In Byzantium, therefore, where the affairs and creed of the Church were the responsibility of the Basileus, who was still the *Pontifex Maximus*, and recognized as "priest and king at

[43] C. J. Hefele, *Histoire des Conciles*, 1907: meetings in church *secretarium* at Carthage in 418 (II¹, p. 191), at Chalcedon in 451 (II², p. 656), at Arles in 455 (II², p. 886), in Palestine in 536 (II², p. 1154), at Mapsuesta in 550 (III¹, p. 38), of Santa Sophia at Constantinople in 553 (III¹, p. 68) and in 880 (IV¹, p. 603); in the *basilica de la regio secunda* at Carthage in 403 and 407 (II¹, pp. 154, 156); in the episcopal residence at Ephesus in 431 (II¹, pp. 321, 325, 330); in "portico" of the "Great Church" at Constantinople in 449 (II¹, p. 546); in the *castrum Modogarnomo* of the church of St. Peter at Bordeaux in the seventh century (III¹, p. 299). Those specifically known to have been held in the palace: Nicaea in 326 (I¹, p. 408 n. 2); Milan in 355 (I², p. 873); Great Synod of 753 in Hiéria Palace near Constantinople (III², p. 695), the Seventh Oecumenical Council of Nicaea in 787 first met in church of St. Sophia and was transferred to Con-

stantinople where the last session was held in the Magnaura Palace (III², p. 759), and the first two sessions of the Council of 880 held in the Chrysotriclinos (IV¹, p. 802).

In the West where the Carolingian emperors modeled their relations to the Church on Byzantine precedents, the Councils were called *sub nomine regis* and usually held in a *palatium*: in 755 under Pepin *in Verno palatio* (III², p. 934); in 772 under Charlemagne *in villa publica* of Nivhinga (III², p. 958); all those at Aachen in the Palace; in 792 when Charlemagne presided at Ratisbonne *ad palatium regis* (III², p. 1035); in 794 at Frankfurt *in aula sacri palatii* (III², p. 1046); in 817 at Aachen *in domo Aquisgrani palatii quae ad Lateranis dicitur* (IV¹, p. 25); and in 895 in the Royal Villa at Tribur on the Rhine (IV², p. 697).

[44] Hefele, *op.cit.*, II¹, p. 534.

the same time," one may ask how an artist, trained in the iconography of the Court, could have indicated that heresy was a crime against the State except by placing the altar of God within the portal of the *Sacrum palatium*?

Stern noted one of the reasons for seeing a palace symbolism in the mosaics when he compared the frames of the Bethlehem mosaics to the decorative panels of the ninth century in the Church of San Julian de los Prados at Santullano, although he failed to take into account the fact that the Spanish frescoes are in a palace-church and hence followed not so much Roman theater decorations as the long-established decorative conventions of Roman palaces.[45] The best evidence that we are dealing ideologically with palace forms in the Bethlehem mosaics is the representation of a Byzantine palace (Fig. 98) on the ivory casket in the Cathedral of Troyes, which was presumably executed in either the tenth or eleventh century and brought back from Constantinople after the Fourth Crusade.[46] The cover of this casket, which is stained a royal purple, depicts an emperor on either side riding away from a palace. There are little figures gesticulating on the battlements, and in the portal of the defensive walls there is a female figure, sometimes identified as the empress, who wears a crenellated headdress and carries a crown. The figure is undoubtedly a personification and presumably is either a Tyche, or Fortuna, responsible for the emperor's safe and victorious return. Because of the crowned personification and the gestures of the people on the walls, which he thought were gestures of supplication, Grabar suggested that the cover was intended to represent a conquered city and that on the prototype, from which the Troyes ivory was copied, the emperor must have been depicted in heraldic symmetry riding towards the city. Since the Troyes box was probably an imperial casket it is unnecessary to assume a copyist who made a mistake in reversing the figures. Actually the emperor on horseback, the female personification with the crown and the joyously gesticulating figures on the parapet are all consistent when the scene is accepted as the representation of a ceremony of departure, like a Roman *Profectio*, from the imperial palace.

Regardless, however, of whether the building stood for Constantinople or the capital of a conquered people, the Byzantine craftsman, in order to denote the royal importance of the city, depicted a palace within its defensive walls. In order to do this he chose to represent the most important ceremonial aspects of a complicated palace by means of a great domical vestibule, which is comparable to the *salutatorium* at the entrance to Diocletian's palace (Fig. 133), the domical Chalce (Fig. 130/B) at the entrance to the imperial palace at Constantinople and the "House of the Lord" (Fig. 132) in the Utrecht Psalter. Flanking this domical *pro aula* he showed the ends

---

[45] Fortunato de Selgas, *Bolentino de la Sociedad Espanola de Excursiones*, XXIV, 1916, p. 28; A. Goldschmidt, *Sizungsberichte der Preuss. Ak. der Wissenschaften, phil.-hist. Klasse*, 1926, p. 12; H. Schlunk, *Archivo espanol de arqueologia*, XXV, 1952, pp. 15-37.

[46] F. Volbach, G. Salles et G. Dutkuit, *Art byzan-tin, cent planches*, 1931, pls. 26-28; A. Grabar, *L'Empereur dans l'art byzantin*, pp. 50, 56, 57, **60**, 61, 131, 134, 144, 169, pl. x/1, 2; Pierce and Tyler, *Byzantine Art*, 1926, pls. 51, 54; A. Goldschmidt und K. Weitzmann, *Die Byzantinischen Elfenbeinskulpturen*, 1930, p. 63, no. 122ª, pl. LXIX.

of the apartments down either side of the central court in much the same way that they are represented on the Bethlehem mosaics. Also, he carved at either side of the royal entrance little conical cupolas with the customary global finials, which it has been seen were traditional features of a *Sacrum palatium* and comparable to the domical towers on the Antioch frame. In the Ciampini drawings of the lost frames of the Councils of Carthage, Laodicea, Gangra, and Sardica the windows of the royal apartments are round, as they are on the version of the Troyes casket published by Dalton in his *Byzantine Art and Archaeology*.[47]

Both the domical palace on the Byzantine ivory and the conceptual intent of the Antioch frame from Bethlehem to represent the Palatium, through which the will of God operated, become more significant when they are considered in relation to the Sixth Oecumenical Council called by Constantine IV (Pogonatur) in A.D. 680-681 and the "Second Council in Trullo" called by Justinian II in A.D. 692 at Constantinople. The two councils were convened by the emperors in an effort to harmonize the conflicting views of Eastern and Western churchmen on the nature of Christ, and both were assembled in the imperial palace. *Trullam*, or *trulla*, was a technical name for any domical edifice and the texts made it clear that "in Trullo" referred either to a domical hall in the imperial palace or to the Palatium as exemplified by a dome, for in the *Liber Pontificalis* it says, *in basilica quae Trullus appelatur, intra palatium*.[48] Therefore, at the time when the designs for the Bethlehem mosaics were made we know that Councils were associated with the imperial palace and that the sacred palace was pictorially visualized as a domical structure with entrance towers capped with symbolic *skene-sphairos* cupolas. Hence, we may assume that the decorations on the dome of the Antioch frame refer to the nature of Christ which the councils had been endeavoring to define. We may also suspect that at the imperial court, where this palace iconography originated, there would have been no objection to the people identifying the emblem of Christ with the emperor.

When it comes to dating the Bethlehem mosaics there are now additional reasons for believing that their designs originated around the beginning of the eighth century when the representation of Councils, as Stern has pointed out, are recorded as having decorated the imperial palace at Constantinople.[49] Since it is very difficult to believe that the actual mosaics could have been executed in the Church of the Nativity during the early years when the Arabs were masters of Palestine, it seems more reasonable to suppose that they were made in the twelfth century for Manuel Comnenus, from established palace designs, at the time when the Byzantine emperor was endeavoring to conciliate the Roman Church and the Latin kings of Jerusalem.[50]

[47] O. M. Dalton (*Byzantine Art and Archaeology*, 1911, p. 231, figs. 144-145) published a different version with round windows and no figures on the battlement, which is unlike any other photograph of the box.

[48] Hefele, *Histoire des Conciles*, III¹, p. 485 (Sixth Council), p. 560 (Second Council in Trullo).

[49] Stern, *Byzantion*, XI, 1936, p. 144; C. Diehl, *Manuel de l'art byzantin*, 1910, p. 529.

[50] B. Bagatti, *Gli antichi edifici sacri de Betlemme*, Jerusalem, 1952, pp. 79-93; O. M. Dalton, *Byzantine Art and Archaeology*, pp. 414-415; Dalton in R. W. Schultz, *The Church of the Nativity at Bethlehem*, London, 1910, pp. 31-51; C. Diehl, *Manuel d'art byzantin*, 1910, pp. 527-529; Vincent and Abel, *Bethléem*, 1914, pp. 154-156; Wiegand,

Regardless of their date, however, the frames of the Bethlehem mosaics fit consistently into a clearly defined pattern of persistent architectural symbolism.

In tracing back this pattern, in order to link up the domical towers with imperial Roman usage, it is necessary to ascertain to what extent and under what conditions cupolas were constructed on Roman fortifications. The most valuable evidence is the illustrations of the *Corpus Agrimensorum Romanorum*.[51] Its various texts, which describe the religious rites and practical considerations of city planning, were based upon early Roman sources, although the actual archetype did not antedate A.D. 450, and the drawings are thought to have been executed in the sixth century. The late date of the drawings raises the question of whether the illuminator in depicting the different types of Roman cities was following established traditions or was introducing features, such as domical towers, which were peculiar to his own age.

The large number of domical mausolea illustrated in the *Corpus* resemble in a general way the imperial type of sepulchral monument made popular by Diocletian and the domical "Aeternae memoriae" represented on the coins of the Constantinian period.[52] At the same time their curiously bulbous and pointed domes are the same as the gilded wooden ones which were used on the early churches of Syria and Palestine.[53] Therefore, it can be argued that the illuminations reproduce architectural features, such as the domical towers, which did not antedate the beginning of the fourth century. On the contrary, when the representations of domical towers in the *Corpus* are considered in relation to the Thracian city-gate coins there is a reason for believing that the use of cupolas in the Near East went back at least to the beginning of the third century. At the same time the illustrations as a whole show what we know from other sources, that Roman defensive towers were customarily and traditionally flat-roofed; and they support the evidence already reviewed that cupolas were uncommon and had a symbolic significance.

All the Italian cities pictured in the *Corpus* follow established usage in having flat-roofed towers: on the ancient Suessa in Campagna (Fig. 56) the towers are tall and crenellated[54]; on an unidentified "Colonia Claudia" (Fig. 55) they are massive and round[55]; and on the "Colonia Auxurnas" (Terracina) (Fig. 57) they are square like the towers on cities identified as Spello in Umbria, Mintorno, Brixentes, and Torino.[56] Only two cities are shown with pyramidal roofs on all the towers[57] and, except for the mediaeval drawings in the much later *Liber Diazografus*, there are only two cities (Fig. 59) with conical roofs.[58] This leaves five cities which depart from

Die Gebürtskirche in Bethlehem, 1911; de Vogüé, *Les Églises de la Terre Sainte*, 1860, pp. 93-106.

[51] Lachmann, *Gramatici veteres, du liber coloniarum*, 1848; C. Thulin, *Corpus Agrimensorum Romanorum*, 1913, and *Die Handschriften des Corpus Agrimensorum Romanorum*, 1911.

[52] Smith, *The Dome*, pp. 24-25, figs. 17-21.

[53] *Ibid.*, pp. 10-44.

[54] Thulin, fig. 35; Lachmann, fig. 36.

[55] Thulin, fig. 95; Lachmann, fig. 156.

[56] Thulin, p. 157, fig. 92; Lachmann, fig. 153; F.

Castagnoli, "Le 'formae' delle colonie romane e le minature dei codice dei gromatici," *Atti delle Reale acc. d'Italia, Mem. della classe di scienze morali e storice*, Ser. VII, IV, 1943, pp. 83-118: the cities identified are Mintorno (fig. 4), Spello (fig. 5), Terracina (fig. 6), Brixentes (fig. 8) and Torino (fig. 10).

[57] Thulin, figs. 39, 135; Lachmann, figs. 175, 196a.

[58] Thulin, figs. 94, 136a; Lachmann, figs. 155, 197.

the standard type in having domical towers. Two of these furnish no clues as to the purpose of their domes: the "Colonia" (Fig. 61) is exceptional in having only one domical tower in the middle of each side of the castrum[59]; and the "Colonia Julia" (Fig. 62) has curiously bulbous domes on all the towers.[60] The other "Colonia Julia" (Fig. 63), located in the mountains which are designated as MON TIBUSCON CLUSA, is more instructive because all the purely defensive towers at the four corners of the castrum are flat-roofed and square, while the gateway towers on three sides have pyramidal roofs, and only the *Porta Praetorium*, which was the imperial gate, has pointed domes on its flanking towers.[61]

This differentiation between the towers of a *civitas*, which was perhaps located on the Dacian frontier, helps to confirm the conclusion already derived from the mediaeval usage that the domes were not utilitarian, but had an expressive purpose. More conclusive evidence is furnished by the two other cities (Figs. 60, 64) that have inside their walls an imperial mausoleum or memorial crowned with a large cosmic dome, similar to the *aeternae memoriae* on the Constantinian coins.[62] These examples recall the mediaeval cities decked with domes (Figs. 70, 72) because of the presence in them of the King of Kings, and suggest that the domes were a mark of distinction to show that the cities had been honored by the eternal presence in them of a dead emperor. Once these domes are thought of in relation to the cupolas on the Constantinian coins, which as insignia of the *Pater orbis* were so commonly transformed into globes, it becomes apparent that their bulbous shape represented an effort to make manifest their celestial and global significance as a combination *skene-orbis*.[63]

At this point the investigation of the import of domes over Epiphany gateways, sacred palatia, the House of God and royal strongholds brings us back to the gold medallion (Fig. 50) issued in honor of Constantine by his imperial city of Treves, and the question of whether its cupolas with their global finials were intended to signify the royal importance of the city. It is no longer possible to disregard the numismatic evidence by assuming that domes were only exotic and decorative features peculiar to the Orient. Not only were they constructed during the early Middle Ages in the Rhineland, but at the time when Constantine had his capital at Treves they were not uncommon on the towers of the Gallic cities. It is even probable, as Forrer has argued, that they were used on the circular wooden and stone towers of the ancient fortifications of Alesia, Saverne and the *vicus* of Mayen.[64] In support of this

---

[59] Thulin, fig. 107; Lachmann, fig. 168.

[60] Thulin, fig. 97; Lachmann, fig. 158.

[61] Thulin, fig. 114; Lachmann, fig. 175. There was a *Tibiscon* on the Dacian frontier (A. Frobiger, *Handbuch der Alten Geographie*, III, p. 758.

[62] *Fig. 60* (Thulin, fig. 113; Lachmann, fig. 174) and *fig. 64* (Thulin, fig. 136).

[63] See pp. 107, 119.

[64] R. Forrer, *L'Alsace Romaine*, 1935, pp. 73-85. There was a domical tradition in Gaul going back in origin to the early native houses, or *mardelles*, which the Romans referred to as Celtic *turguria*

(A. Grenier, *Habitations gauloises*, 1906, pp. 23-45; *Manuel d'archéologie Gallo-Romaine*, VI², 1934, pp. 752-775). Long after the natives had adopted Roman house forms they continued to attach a heavenly significance to the domical shape of their ancestral huts: 1) they frequently gave a marked domical shape to their hut-urns and house-shaped grave-steles (M. A. Folloux, "Les urnes cinéraires," *Mém. lus à la Sorbonne*, 1869, pp. 93-104; E. Linckenheld, *Les stèles funéraires en forme du maison*, 1927, fig. 19, pls. III/5, 7 and IV/4, 5; *Bericht, Deutsches archäologische Inst. Römisch-*

contention recent excavations of Roman Strasbourg have uncovered a fresco showing a wall with a domical tower and a number of terra-cotta caps with orbis finials which are thought to have been the crowning feature of wooden domes on the ancient towers of the city.[65] Furthermore, the Gallic mosaic from Auriol (Fig. 58) shows that domes must have been customarily used on the towers of gateways in much the same way that they are presented on the medallions of Mainz (Fig. 49) and Treves (Fig. 50).

Clearly there was a domical tradition in Gaul and the Rhineland. Hence it no longer seems improbable that the Porta Nigra with its palace colonnading and the other, now destroyed, gateways of Treves once had golden domes on their towers, as the medallion of Constantine records.[66] In fact, numerous statuettes have been found in the excavations of Roman Treves which represent an enthroned mother goddess, either the Tyche of the city, or the Fortuna Redux of the imperial family, who wears on her head, not the conventional battlemented crown, but a city-gate with domical towers and arcades such as probably existed on the Porta Incluta as the Royal Gate.[67] There is, therefore, every reason to believe that domes and ceremonial canopies were used over the portal of a royal city and palace to proclaim the presence of the *Magnus parens orbis* and to make manifest his cosmic dimensions.

Because of this evidence it is no longer possible to dismiss as purely fanciful the mediaeval representations of gateways (Figs. 54, 63, 73), palaces (Figs. 74, 79, 83) and churches (Figs. 2, 79) with domical towers. There is nothing imaginative and inexplicable about these domical towers or, for example, about the cupolas which crown the "Porta aurea" on the seals of Ravenna as late as 1472, once they are seen in relation to the castrum cupolas on the Roman coins and recognized as imperial emblems which presumably persisted on the Byzantine palace architecture.[68] In the case of the Ravenna seals it is reasonably certain that the royal and heavenly cupolas must have been added to the original Roman gateway when the city became the capital of the Exarchate. The representational evidence that the West was influenced by the imperial architecture of Constantinople, as can be seen when the pictorial conventions of mediaeval architecture are compared with the Byzantine palace depicted on the Troyes ivory (Fig. 98), cannot be disregarded just because the Western builders in the course of the Middle Ages eventually substituted the more easily constructed celestial spire for the heavenly dome of the imperial palace tradition.

Germanische Komission, XVII, 1927, p. 149, fig. 17); 2) sometimes they depicted the dwelling of a local divinity as a domical hut-shrine (É. Esperandieu, *Recueil général des bas-reliefs etc. de la Gaule Romain*, VI, 1915, p. 37, no. 4568; VIII, 1922, p. 80, no. 6000; X, 1928, p. 174, no. 7534; C. Huelsen, *Germania*, III, 1919, pp. 65-71); and 3) they continued to build large circular temples which were probably roofed with wooden domes (K. Koethe, "Die Keltischen Rund-und-Vielecktempel der Kaiserzeit," *Bericht, Deutsches arch. Inst. Röm-Ger. Komission*, XXIII, 1933, pp. 1off.). Also, if the excavations at Gergovia are accepted, the royal strongholds of pre-Roman Gaul were constructed with the traditional round huts translated into domical, stone strong-points which were connected by stone walls, and are, therefore, the earliest example of the association of the domical shape with a royal stronghold (M. Busset, *Gergovia*, 1933; M. Gorce, *Vercingetorix*, 1935).

[65] Forrer, *op.cit.*, p. 110, fig. 30; Grenier, *Manuel . . .* , V, p. 538, fig. 203.

[66] Grenier, *op.cit.*, V, pp. 538-542.

[67] S. Loeschke, *Bonn. Jahrb.*, CXXVII, 1922, p. 316; F. Kutzbach, *Germania*, VIII, 1924, pp. 91-94.

[68] H. Kaehler, "Die Porta aurea in Ravenna," *Röm. Mittl.*, L, 1935, pp. 172-224, Abb. 1.

If it is granted on the basis of the mediaeval evidence and the Constantinian coins that domes by the beginning of the fourth century had an imperial significance on towers and over portals, then there are reasons for believing that they must have had a similar content when they suddenly appear on the city-gate towers of Anchialus at the time when the emperors were so frequently in Thrace defending the Danubian frontier. Once a domical symbolism is associated with the Thracian city-gate coins it strengthens the earlier contention that they were intended to commemorate imperial visitations or anniversaries. Furthermore, when the motifs on the Thracian coins are reviewed in relation to the history of the *skene-orbis* as royal emblems, there is no doubt that the globes over the portal of Nicopolis (Fig. 29) must refer to the emperor. Also, on the assumption that all the details on Roman coins were carefully supervised and designed as graphic propaganda, it is necessary to account, if possible, for the curious petal-like treatment of the dome, which only appears in the middle of the third century on the coins of Gordianus issued at Anchialus (Fig. 24), Marcianopolis (Fig. 26), and Nicopolis (Fig. 29).

It has already been noted that the bulbous domes on city walls and mausolea (Figs. 60, 64) were presumably the result of a desire to combine into one form the related implications of the ciborium and globe as celestial and cosmic symbols, which would account for the persistence of this type of dome on the architecture of the Near East. Later it will be seen that the corrugated and melonlike dome was a conscious effort in both Roman and mediaeval architecture to reproduce in more permanent form the celestial *skene*, which was customarily associated in the Helenistic East and on early Roman wall paintings with the *sphaera*.[69] Therefore, it might be argued that the domes on the coins of Gordianus show a schematic means of indicating that they were symbolically the tent of heaven. At the same time their decoration with what appears to be stylized petals, resembling the lotus rosettes which were used in Hellenistic and Roman art on ceilings and apses with celestial implications, suggests another derivation.[70]

This other possible derivation is indicated by the fact that the Latin and Greek words for *ciborium* and κιβώριον, which by the late Empire had come to be used for baldachins, aediculae, and eventually domes, had the early meaning of "cup" and were associated by classical writers with the *colocasia*, a kind of Egyptian lotus.[71] Inasmuch as ritualistic cups in Egypt were customarily decorated with lotus petals, one may suspect that there was a symbolic relation between the cup-shaped *ciborium* decorated with petals of the life-giving *colocasia* of Egypt. Some intimation of a persistent Nilotic symbolism may lie in the obscure reference in the Fourth Eclogue of Virgil to the *colocasia* and acanthus as Egyptian plants traditionally associated with the birth of the child-god, whose coming was destined to bring about a new Golden Age.[72] In discussing

[69] See p. 119.

[70] Smith, *The Dome*, pp. 58, 129, figs. 77, 142, 188, 197.

[71] J. Braun, *Der Christliche Altar*, 1924, pp. 189-193; Kraus, *Real-encyclopädie der Christlichen Alterthümer*, I, 1882; Daremberg and Saglio, *Dict. des antiquités*, I, 1887, p. 1171.

[72] Virgil, *Eclogues* (Loeb), line 20: "But for thee, Child, shall the earth untilled pour forth, as her first pretty gifts, straggling ivy with foxglove everywhere, and the Egyptian lotus (*colocasia*) blended with smiling acanthus."

this passage pertaining to the mystic Adventus of a new world ruler, Jeanmaire has suggested that the words of Virgil refer to the Messianic promise of a royal Epiphany and pertain to the ancient Egyptian idea that the Horus-sun, or Apollo-ruler, was born from the lotus.[73] Dubious as this may be, nevertheless, when taken in combination with the lotus and cup-shape connotations of *ciborium*, there is the possibility that the petal treatment of the ciboria on the Thracian towers was a symbolic reference to the conception of the divine emperor as a Sun-god. Otherwise the apparent petals were only a schematic way of indicating the striations of a *skene* cupola.

4. The "divina palatia patris"

On the Roman coins of the fourth century it has been seen that the castrum portal, surmounted by ciborium-cupolas, had become a recognized symbol of a *Sacrum palatium*, which not only represented the seat of government, but also stood for the State as the heavenly abode of the Divine Providence which in the person of the Imperator controlled the whole global universe. At the same time it has been noted that there was throughout the Middle Ages a tradition, following Roman precedent, which associated the dome as an imperial insigne not only with city-gate towers but also with the throne-room and reception vestibule of a divine ruler. Furthermore, by the beginning of the fourth century this conception of *castrum-palatium* with flanking towers, a crowning marble arcade that had celestial and royal implications and with a domical vestibule, or *salutatorium*, was already established in the palace of Diocletian at Salona as the architectural prototype of a *divina palatia patris*.

There are three representations of a palatium on Roman mosaics from North Africa which help to prove that the cupola-crowned castrum with a towered façade and arcade was an established palace convention in the fourth contury. On a mosaic from Carthage (Fig. 65), usually identified as a scene depicting the rich villa of "Julius Dominus," there is a border with various scenes pertaining to the bounty of the seasons and in the center a fortified castrum-palace with the traditional flanking towers, an imperial arcade emphasized in white tesserae and a lofty cupola over the entrance.[74] The customary interpretation of this imposing palatium as merely the villa of a "Lord Julius" disregards such important factors as the royal character of the structure, the fourth century significance of the dominant cupola, the relation of the mosaic as a whole to other allegorical representations of the seasons, or labors of the months, and what seems to be an erroneous restoration of the inscription which the servant in the center presents to the enthroned figure. The inscription, written

[73] H. Jeanmaire, *Le Messianisme de Virgile*, 1930, pp. 184-192. By the third century when Emperor-worship had become practically compulsory and emperors like Gallienus were being presented "as a source of fertility," "the Savior of the People" and a second Alexander the Great, this kind of imperial interest in lotus, Virgilian, and domical symbolism was a prelude to Christian mysticism (G. Mathew, "The Character of the Gallienic Renaissance," *J.R.S.*, XXXIII, 1943, p. 68).

[74] M. A. Merlin, "La Mosaïque du Seigneur Julius à Carthage," *Bull. archéol.*, 1921, pp. 95-114, pl. XII; Merlin, *Bull. archéol.*, 1920, pp. cii-civ, pl. XCVII; Merlin, *Anz.*, XLVI, 1931, p. 500, Abb. 14; Paribene, *Röm. Mittl.*, LV, 1940, p. 145, fig. 12.

in uncials, reads ? IV DOM, and has been restored as either IV (LIO) DOM (INO), OR IV (LIANO) DOM(INO). Inasmuch, however, as the first word does not begin with I, because that letter is preceded by a space only large enough for one more letter and in which there still appears to be a mutilated D, its fits in with the symbolic character of the mosaic to read the inscription as either [D]IV (O) DOM (INO) or [D]IV (INA) DOM (US).

The most compelling reason for not accepting the building as the residence of a wealthy individual with the title of "Dominus" is the fact that it is unlike any known private villas. Instead, it closely resembles the contemporary palace-castrum of Diocletian, even to the "royal arcade" over the *Porta aurea* (Fig. 5) and the dome, which in Diocletian's palace was on axis with the portal and over the ceremonial vestibule (Fig. 133). The large structure to the left of the central dome would then be the basilica of justice, while the smaller domes with smoke, or steam, coming out of their "omphalos" would be the imperial baths, instead of granaries as they have been called.[75] This building then is a *Sacrum palatium*, or *praetoria regis*, comparable to the castra on the coins of the fourth century, which gives more significance to the activities around the border.

In discussing these scenes both Doro Levi and more recently Hanfmann have interpreted them as representing the seasons of the year.[76] The way in which the scenes fail to conform to the usual method of personifying either the seasons or the labors of the months has been explained by both writers as a kind of "panoramic" method which resulted from the artist having followed a Hellenistic festival calendar, or a Roman rustic calendar, that described the activities of each season in several different ways. Whether the episodes in the border refer to the seasons, or to the more general prosperity of the country, a comparison of the mosaic with other Roman representations of the seasons gives another clue to the symbolism of the palace in the center. From Hellenistic times there was always the belief that a "Divine Reason" was in control of nature, and on Roman representations of the Seasons there is usually in the center a heavenly figure, such as Helios, Bacchus, Neptune, or even a *sphaera*, to show the divine source of the cosmic order.[77]

Once the mosaic is interpreted in imperial terms there is the probability that some of the episodes in the border, such as men traveling and going forth to hunt, may only refer to the happiness, safety, and enjoyment of a bountiful nature which was the result of peace and prosperity in the Empire. Regardless of whether the border is a "pano-

[75] According to Timarchos (*Athen*, xi, 501) the hot baths at Athens were round domical structures with an opening in the top called an "omphalos" (Schneider, "Laconicum," Pauly-Wissowa, *R.-E.*, 1924, XII, p. 347). This projecting boss, like an omphalos, at the top of a domical bath can be seen in the drawing of a *Lavacrum* in the *Corpus Agrimensorum Romanorum* (Lachmann, *Gromatici veteres*, p. 343, fig. 324).

[76] D. Levi, *Art Bulletin*, XXIII, 1941, p. 278, fig. 19; G. M. A. Hanfmann, *The Seasons-Sarcophagus in Dumbarton Oaks*, 1951, I, no. 546, pp. 222-223

n. 52; G.-C. Picard, *Mélanges d'archéol. et d'histoire*, LVIII, 1941-46, p. 96, refers to the mosaic as a glorification of *Felicitas temporum*.

[77] Hanfmann, *op.cit.*, pp. 107-109; P. Gauckler, *Inventaire des mosaïques de la Gaule et l'Afrique*, 1909-1911, I, no. 203 (Sphaera); II, no. 447 (Head of a God); III, no. 41 (Annus ?), no. 181 (Bacchus). The sculptures on the ceiling of the Roman Porte de Mars at Reims (de Laborde, *Les Monuments de la France*, 1816-36, I, pl. CXIII) have the labors of the months around a heavenly circle in the center of which is a seated deity.

ramic" view of the seasons, or pertains to the blessings which come to men from the imperial rule, the symbolism is a kind of pictorial panegyric. By the Late Empire the custom of identifying the emperor with the seasons and of presenting him as the "Creator" and "Moderator" of the seasons, ideas which had their origin in ancient Egypt, had become a popular means of extolling the godlike nature of the Augustus.[78] Hence the palatium at the center, like the castrum surmounted by cupolas on the coins of Diocletian, refers to the imperial source of divine *providentia*, and its cosmic dome, royal arcade, and towered façade identify it as a *divina palatia patris*. This does not mean, however, that the seated figure in the right foreground and his bejeweled lady on the opposite side are necessarily the *Pater orbis* and his *Mater Castrorum*. The informal way in which they are presented suggests that they are either the owners of the house where the mosaic eulogized the *Domus divina*, or they are intended to show how both rich and poor alike enjoy the blessing of peace, which men owe to the Palatium as exemplifying the government.

Another fourth century mosaic (Fig. 66) from Carthage has a somewhat similar and equally exceptional palace with a lofty dome, flanking towers and an arcade in the shape of a hemicycle, which is on an island in the middle of a marine scene.[79] In front of the island is the resplendent figure of Venus Anadyomene whose shell is blown upon by the winds from the four parts of the world. Were it not so evident that the dome by the fourth century was an imperial insigne and that during the Middle Ages the towered façade and central cupola were established features of a *Sacrum palatium*, one would naturally accept this mosaic as nothing more than a charming mythological scene in which the island palace indicated the birthplace of the goddess. Inasmuch, however, as the building is no ordinary villa, but is a pictorial condensation of the most significant characteristics of a fourth century imperial palatium, there is the possibility that the mosaic was intended to be a laudatory allegory in which the heavenly castrum is a figurative reference to the *Domus divina*.

Venus, "a ruler of heaven, earth and sea," in addition to being the ancestress of the

[78] Hanfmann, *op.cit.*, pp. 163-184. For the Egyptian origin of the ruler as the "Maker of the Seasons" see J. H. Wilson in H. and H. A. Frankfort, *The Intellectual Adventure of Ancient Man*, 1946, pp. 80-81. L'Orange (*Studies on the Iconography of Cosmic Kingship*, p. 33, fig. 15) cites a coin of Constantine holding the circle of the zodiac, or cosmic clipeus, as an *imago mundi* to illustrate the idea of the ruler as the controlling God of Fate who governs the seasons and all that pertains to them. The references in panegyrics and art to the divine emperor as in control of the seasons should not be thought of as forms of empty flattery in need of being traced back to a dim past. At the popular level throughout the Empire they reflected what was still an instinctive and traditional faith in the supernatural powers of kingship. From the earliest beginnings of kingship in the agricultural cultures of Asia, Africa, and Europe men had always be-

lieved in their ruler as a priest-king who set the calendar, regulated the seasonal rebirth of vegetation by his magic, and frequently took the part of the deity in the religious ceremonies of the New Year (F. M. Cranford, *The Unwritten Philosophy*, Cambridge, 1945; A. M. Hocart, *Kingship*, London, 1927, pp. 33-36; W. E. Soothill, *The Hall of Light, a Study of Early Chinese Kingship*, London, 1951, pp. xvi-xviii, 22-29). Beginning with Augustus, as Hocart has pointed out (p. 36), "When the Romans brought back divine kingship from the East they also brought with it a belief in the King's influence over the food supply and the general prosperity." Therefore, in the provinces of the Roman world the average man continued to think of the ruler, distant as he was, as the one being who kept the world from reverting to chaos and who was his assurance of peace, prosperity, and abundance.

[79] Gauckler, II, p. 226, no. 671.

Caesars, was in North Africa sometimes designated as *Venus Augusta*.[80] Her great popularity on the Carthaginian mosaics, it has been pointed out by Picard, was due to her identification with a local divinity, Celestes, who was sometimes called *Celestes Augusta* and glorified as the sovereign of the universe, the source of all happiness and fecundity.[81] Venus, then, in the words of Ovid, who "owns a kingdom second to no god," who "gives laws to heaven and earth and to her native sea, and by her inspiration keeps every species in being," was an ideal theme with which to praise the emperor as the "Moderator of the Winds" and indicate his descent from the Carthaginian Celestes.[82] In addition to having been "transferred to Rome" in order to become "the author of the race" and the divinity from whom great Caesar traced his descent,[83] Venus and her worship in the *Templum urbis* at Rome were closely associated with the conception of *Urbs Roma Aeterna* and the Emperor cult which were celebrated together in the *Natalis urbis*.[84] Therefore, by the fourth century when it was customary in the provinces to celebrate the *Natalis urbis* in combination with the imperial *Natalis*, this scene of natural bounty around the *divina palatia patris* may well have been a pictorial means of praising the Augustus and acquiring credit with Venus Celestes.[85]

The central motif on a third mosaic (Fig. 67) of the fourth century from Carthage is again a towered façade surmounted by a lofty tower crowned with a great domical baldachin.[86] While there is little in this crudely executed mosaic to relate the architectural symbolism to the glories of the emperor's rule, the exaggerated importance of the dome would seem to indicate that this scene, like the others from Carthage, is another version of an ideal life, a kind of hunter's paradise which can only be enjoyed in an age of peace and prosperity. Regardless of whether these mosaics are to be understood as pictorial panegyrics, the fact remains that the towered façade and domical tower had very specific associations with the *Sacrum palatium* in the fourth century and later, as part of the policy of *Renovatio Romanorum*, were used by the emperors of the Holy Roman Empire on their seals and coins (Figs. 82-93) to represent an imperial *Domus Dei* and its heavenly authority.

[80] J. Toutain, *Les Cultes païen dans l'empire romain*, III, 1920, p. 384; Ovid, *Fasti*, I, 39 (author of the race); IV, 120-130 (Caesar's ancestress); IV, 875 (transfer to Rome); IV, 877 (Vinnalia at Rome).

[81] A. Audollent, *Carthage romaine*, 1910, pp. 377, 378; G.-C. Picard, "Le couronnent de Vénus," *Mélanges d'archéol. et d'hist.*, LVIII, 1941-46, discusses popularity of Venus as a national deity (p. 70), her position as the source of prosperity (pp. 92-96), the prophylactic value attributed to her images (p. 70), and mosaic in question (p. 63).

[82] In the fourth century it was customary to compare the emperor to Jupiter as "The Moderator of the Winds" and to the Earth as "The Mother of the Harvests" (Hanfmann, *op.cit.*, p. 64). For the idea of the emperor as a *Mundi administrator* see M. Vogelstein, *Kaiseridee-Romidee*, 1920, p. 106.

[83] Ovid, *Fasti*, IV, 91-106.

[84] Fink, Hoey, and Snyder, "The Feriale Duranum," *Yale Classical Studies*, VII, 1940, pp. 108-112, 147.

[85] J. Gagé, *Annuaire de l'Inst. d. phil. et d'hist. orientales et slaves*, IV, 1936, pp. 155, 161, 163.

[86] B. Bernard, *Bull. archéol.*, 1906, p. 12, no. 34, pl. XXIV; Gauckler, *Comptes rendus de l'Ac. des Inscr.*, 1904, p. 697.

III · IMPERIAL ARCHITECTURAL SYMBOLISM
DURING THE MIDDLE AGES

1. The anagogical and political significance of
the towered façade in the West

THE Romans desired to make their public buildings and monuments through-out the Empire an impressive manifestation of the enduring supremacy of the State. This meant that the architecture associated with the ruler was intended to be seen in relation to the ceremonies as an expression of the divine and cosmic nature of the emperor who was the embodiment and personification of the State. The ideas, however, which gave content to the Roman architectural forms, making them a readily comprehensible means of imperial propaganda, cannot be reformulated without reference to their persistent importance during the Middle Ages, any more than the intent of Christian imagery can be explained without reference to its pagan antecedents. When the Christians shifted the emphasis from the resplendent glories and Messianic promises of a Roman imperator to the splendor and salvation of a heavenly King of Kings, they inevitably took over imperial concepts, ceremonies, rituals, emblems, vestments, art and architectural forms, in so far as they could be adapted to the Christian needs, because they were the only comprehensible means by which the spiritual import of their beliefs could be made apparent to a public ac-customed to visualize divinity in imperial terms. In the transition to the Middle Ages neither the triumph of Christianity nor the dissolution of the West Roman Empire under the impact of the northern invaders terminated the Antique pattern of ideas associated with the forms of Roman architecture. Instead, *Renovatio Romanorum* and the revival of everything expressive of the divine authority of the ruler as a *Restitutor orbis* and *Pacator orbis* became a conscious policy when the Carolingian emperors and their successors endeavored to recreate a universal and theocratic state.

During the slow rebuilding of Western Europe the churchmen and rulers were profoundly interested, sometimes for divergent reasons, in appropriating the universal concepts, architectural symbolism, ceremonies, and liturgy of Imperium Romanorum to their aims.[1] Throughout the Carolingian period the ecclesiastical and the royal patrons of the arts sought with a conscious purpose to revive as best they could the motifs of Roman architecture for the expression of both religious and political ideas. Motivated by their policy of *Imitatio imperialis*, both realized that the long estab-lished beliefs regarding the meaning of the castrum, palatium, city-gate, towered façade, cupola, baldachin, and orb, when thought of in relation to the implications of the Messianic-ruler tradition and the popular ideas associated with the ruler cere-

---

[1] E. H. Kantorowicz, *Laudes Regiae, a Study in Liturgical Acclamations and Mediaeval Ruler Worship*, Univ. of California Publications in History, 33, 1948.

monies, made these motifs a visible means of giving more significant content to the iconography of the Church and to the political claims of the rulers who embodied the State. Frequently in the course of the Middle Ages these two protagonists read changing, multiple, and at times conflicting meanings into the motifs because everything—architectural symbolism, insignia, and ceremonies of all kinds—took on a vital importance during the long and bitter struggle between the popes and northern rulers as to which had inherited *auctoritas imperialis* and were to be obeyed by all men as the *Magnus parens orbis*.

By the ninth century the Carolingian churchmen were fully aware that a castrum exemplified the seat of authority, that its towered portal crowned with imperial cupolas had stood for the *Sacrum palatium*, and that it still embodied the politically important idea of *urbs et orbis*. Therefore, when they had their illuminators depict a castrum portal with royal cupolas to help denote "The Coming of the Lord" (Fig. 54), it was not only because they were following Roman iconography but also because the towered gateway at the entrance to royal cities, palaces, and royal abbeys was the place where their own rulers were still received with the Adventus ceremony of the Roman emperors. Everyone, they knew, would see in the image of a triumphal gateway the idea of a *Porta coeli, Domus Dei* and *Civitas Dei* when they had their craftsmen present it, with great fidelity to Roman precedent, as the place where an Evangelist (Fig. 68) spoke in the name of God.[2] The sculptor of the ninth or tenth century ivory from Vienna (Fig. 69) was obviously instructed to depict every detail of a Gallo-Roman *porta*, even to the royal arcade, cupolas, and pendent crown of the city, in order to show that the Holy Gregorius had taken his seat, like a kingly personage, in the Royal Gate of Heaven.[3]

For the representation of Jerusalem (Fig. 72) and the cities in the Epiphany scenes from the life of Christ, such as the Nativity (Fig. 70), the Coming of the Magi, and the Flight into Egypt, the ivory carvers depicted an antique type of city, its towers decked with royal domes and its walls enriched with jewel patterns, so as to make manifest the glory and distinction which a city acquired from the presence in it of the Son of God, the heir of the heavenly *Pater orbis* and the future Master of the World.[4] Hence the Carolingian ivories are very specific evidence both as to the persistence of imperial architectural symbols and the Epiphany theme which they were still used to glorify.

In contrast to the iconography of the ivories it is not apparent, until the architecture is seen in relation to the ideas and aspiration of the Carolingian rulers, why the royal and ecclesiastic patrons of architecture made the towered façade a dominant feature

[2] A. Goldschmidt, *Die Elfenbeinskulpturen aus der Zeit der karolingischen und sächischen Kaiser*, II, 1918, no. 99, pl. xxx. A comparable use of the domical towered façade of a palatium as a heavenly symbol is seen in the Byzantine manuscript of Mt. Athos (*Ms. 43, Stauronika*) where the Evangelist Mark sits in front of the traditional semicircular exedra of a *porta regia* which is crowned with the royal arcade and flanked by domical towers (A. M. Friend, *Art Studies*, VII, 1929, fig. 11).

[3] Goldschmidt, *op.cit.*, I, no. 122, pl. LIV.

[4] The Nativity (Goldschmidt, I, nos. 109, 159, pls. XLIX, LXX; II, nos. 102, 103, pls. XXXI/b, XXXII/b); the Magi (I, no. 95, pl. XLII); the Doubting of Thomas (I, no. 45, pl. XXI; II, no. 103, pl. XXXII/d).

on so many of the monastic churches and cathedrals of northern Europe. At first, the Christian church in both the East and the West was a simple colonnaded hall without towers. What then brought about the change which by the beginning of the thirteenth century had made the cathedral a lofty and august monument, its façade like a towered "Gate of Heaven" with over its "Royal Door" a round window made resplendent in honor of the King of Heaven, and crowned with a celestial arcade often made more explicit by the addition of a "King's gallery"?

From the beginning of church architecture in northern Europe there was a growing interest in tower symbolism, even though the two patrons of architecture, the Church and the State, came to hold quite opposite views as to its implications. As early as the fifth century in the West the churchmen began to add towers, especially over the crossing, to the traditional basilican type of church, largely because of the significance of "turris" as it exemplified "templum" and pertained to Christ in the writings of the Church Fathers.[5] St. Martin's at Tours (A.D. 470-474) was constructed *in turre a parte orientis*, its "tower as a shield for the faint-hearted and a bulwark for the frightened," and in it were inscribed the words *vere templum dei est et porta coeli*.[6] While some of the early churches in the West are described as *in modum turris*[7] and Apollinaris Sidonius refers to a church at Lyon with "a bulwark of stone rising up high and strong at the west front," there is no specific evidence of there having been any churches with a two-towered façade before the end of the eighth century.[8] Even if the builders in some instances may have been influenced by the gateway symbolism of the Bible, the figurative imagery of St. Augustin's "City of God," and the precedent of the Syrian churches, it is nevertheless true that the towered façade was uncommon, if not unknown, in the West before it became an expression of political ideas in the Carolingian period.

It has been customary to assume that the transformation of the unpretentious meeting-place into a towered Gothic cathedral was the result of Christian mysticism made more real and beautiful by the imagination and skill of the mediaeval builders. This would at first seem to be true when we recall the statements of the early churchmen who wrote of the towers as the "Evangelists," read the references to the church as a "towered bulwark" (*superiora propugnacula*) and find that Durandus, Bishop of Mende and formerly a captain of papal forces, at the close of the thirteenth century

[5] M. l'Abbé Auber, *Histoire et théorie du symbolisme religieux*, 1884, III, pp. 116, 120; du Cange, *Glossarium Lat.*, "turres"; R. Egger, "Vom Ursprung der romanischen Chorturmkirche," *Wiener Jahreshefte*, XXXII, 1940, pp. 85-125; E. Knögel, "Schriftquellen zur Kunstgeschichte der Merowingerzeit," *Bonn. Jahrb.*, CXL, 1936, nos. 108, 241, 380, 384, 434 (*in modum turris quadrifidae*), 780, 902, 921-26, 1006; O. Lehmann-Brockhaus, *Die Kunst des Xth Jahrshunderts im Lichte der Schriftquellen*, 1935, pp. 29, 52 n. 3, 71 n. 86, 73 n. 107; Sauer, *Symbolik des Kirchengebäudes*, pp. 137, 140, 141; for "Tower" as equivalent of "Temple" see Chapter I n. 19, and R. H. Charles, *The Apocrypha and Pseudepigrapha of the Old Testament*, 1913, I, Enoch, 89[50].

[6] E. Le Blant, *Inscriptions chrétiennes de la Gaule*, I, no. 177; Egger, *op.cit.*, pp. 99-104; Knögel, *op.cit.*, no. 921.

[7] Knögel, *op.cit.*, no. 1006.

[8] Sidonius Apollinaris, *Ep.*, II, 10; Egger, *op.cit.*, p. 114; the towered façade of St. Martin at Autun, which J. Hubert (*L'art pré-romain*, 1938, p. 83) thinks may date from the sixth century, was probably the result of the rebuilding under Louis the Fat.

said, "The towers are the preachers and prelates of the Church, which are her bulwark and defense."[9] The first intimation that these statements do not tell the whole story and that back of the development of the towered façade in mediaeval architecture there were serious political issues, involving the relation of the Emperor to God and the Church, comes from the empirical evidence of the monuments. The distribution of churches shows that the towered façade first appeared on the royal abbey churches of the Carolingian kings, was persistently rejected during the Middle Ages in those regions under the control of the Papacy, continued to be important in the northern domains of the Holy Roman Empire and for a brief period was used in South Italy and Sicily at the time when the rulers came from the north and were in active opposition to the claims of the popes at Rome.[10]

The reasons why the towered façade was constructed at the west end of the Carolingian and so many of the Romanesque churches, as an architectural provision for the emperor's ceremonial participation in the church services and as an expression of his exalted position in the Church, have been obscured by the historical records. Throughout the Middle Ages the evidence is complicated by the fluctuating powers and policies of the successive rulers and popes, and by the changing allegiance of the abbots and bishops responsible for the various rebuildings of the churches. During the period when the struggle between the emperors and popes had become most bitter, and the political significance of the towered façade as a symbol of the palatium was of paramount importance, most of the references to architectural symbolism were written by churchmen often intent upon disregarding the controversial issues in their desire to present only the spiritual meanings attributed to the various parts of the House of God. Before the end of the century the political implications of the architectural forms were not only concealed, but ultimately forgotten, when the Church was successful in its determination to transfer all the imperial symbolism to the glorification of the Majesty of Christ.

Theoretically the innovation of elevating the heavenly towers of the *Aula Palatinis* at the entrance of the abbey churches, which were honored by being periodically visited by the king and his court, should have first become an expression of policy when Charlemagne completed the rebuilding of the royal abbey of St. Denis in A.D. 775. Already the founders of the Carolingian Empire were turning to Rome, Treves, Ravenna, and Constantinople for precedents by which to make it apparent that they were the heirs of Constantine and destined as the New David to reunite the

---

[9] G. Bandmann, *Mittelalterliche Architektur als Bedeutungsträger*, 1951, pp. 91-125; Durandus, *The Symbolism of Churches and Church Ornament* (trans. Weale and Webb), 1893, p. 22; Sauer, *op.cit.*, pp. 141-142; H. Sedlmayr, *Die Enstehung der Kathedrale*, 1950, pp. 95-143; M. L. Serbat, "Frons Ecclesiae," *Mémoires de la Soc. Nat. des Antiquaires de France*, 78, 1928-33, p. 213.

[10] In Central Italy the only examples of the towered façade are: the great imperial abbey at Farfa (P. Markthaler, *Rivista di archeologia cristiana*,

v, 1928, pp. 36-44; G. Croquison, *Rivista.*, xv, 1938, pp. 36-71), San Martino at Farfa (H. Thümmler, "Die Baukunst des 11 Jahrhunderts in Italien," *Römisches Jahrbuch für Kunstgeschichte*, III, 1939, pp. 205-207, Abb. 207), and the abbey of San Salvatore near Monte Amiata (Thümmler, p. 195, Abs. 193, 196). All these churches had relations with the North, especially the royal abbey at Farfa where the Carolingian kings resided before making their ceremonial entrance into Rome (see Ch. v n. 39).

peoples of the Roman world. At the time when St. Denis was being rebuilt by Abbot Fulrad under Pepin, royal prestige was already an issue of paramount importance, for in the Frankish Church the king had precedent over the pope.[11] It was at St. Denis that Pepin was anointed by Pope Stephen II, and it was in the narthex of this church, directly in front of the "Royal Door" that Pepin (d. 768) was entombed, not because he was a penitent "for the sins of his father," as the later records would have us believe, but because it was a place of honor at the triumphal gateway to the Celestial Jerusalem, and to his *capella regale* as an eternal abode.[12]

It is difficult to realize that questions of prestige and authority were involved in the design of churches at a time when there was such devout faith. At the imperial level, however, what was at stake was of equal importance with salvation, for it was vital to the whole feudal system with its loose organization and dependence upon allegiance, that all authority should have a divine source and be vested in a supreme head. Because no dividing line could be drawn between spiritual and secular power the Carolingian rulers strove to establish a theocratic state in which the king was *rex et sacerdos*, in exactly the same sense as it was expressed by Leo the Isaurian when he wrote to the Pope, "I am Emperor and priest of the faith."[13] Following the precedents of the Roman Augustus and Byzantine Basileus they, and most of their successors at the head of the Holy Roman Empire, insisted that they embodied *imperium* and *sacerdotium*. Because they were a *Deo coronatus* they believed, like the Venerable

---

[11] Kantorowicz, *Laudes Regiae*, pp. 46-55.

[12] The burial of Pepin the Short at the entrance to St. Denis was probably not an act of penance, but a mark of royal distinction. Whatever its symbolic implications were, it was the beginning of a mortuary tradition which was followed by his successors, by relatives of the Carolingian rulers, and by many high ecclesiastics. Pepin of Italy was entombed in the vestibule of San Zeno at Verona (E. aus'n Weerth, "Das Grab König Pippins von Italien zu Verona," *Bonn. Jahrb.*, LII, 1872, pp. 129-137); Count Egbert and his wife were buried in the towered Westwerk of the Abbey Church at Hersfeld (H. Wismann, *Grab und Grabmal Karls des Grossen*, Inaug. Diss., Heidelberg, 1933, p. 27); and Archbishop Angilbert, Charlemagne's son-in-law, was interred *in porticu ecclesiae* at Centula. There have been many theories as to where Charlemagne was first buried in his Palace Chapel at Aachen; but Wismann has advanced convincing arguments to show that he followed his father's precedent and was originally buried under "the place of his throne" in the apsidal vestibule of his Palace Chapel, which was dedicated to the Savior. He explains both the account of Otto III having opened the tomb, which says that the Emperor was found *in solio regio*, and the later legend that Charlemagne was discovered seated on his throne, by pointing out that in the description of the coronation of Otto I at Aachen *in solio regio* refers to the place of the king's throne, which was in the concave vestibule of the Palatine Chapel where he

sat when he was acclaimed by his followers in the atrium (Wismann, pp. 35-37). There is the possibility that Pepin the Short and Charlemagne, when they were buried at the entrance to their Palace Chapel, or symbolic palatium, were following a much earlier pagan custom of burying a king at the entrance to his palace, because it is recorded that the Lombard King Albion was buried at the steps of his royal residence to show that he was the "Keeper of the Palace" (Wismann, p. 23 n. 49).

[13] F. Kampers, "Rex et Sacerdos," *Historisches Jahrb.*, XLV, 1925, pp. 495-515; A. Dempf, *Sacrum Imperium*, 1929, pp. 154-157; G. H. Williams, "The Norman Anonymous of 1100 A.D.," *Harvard Theological Studies*, XVIII, 1951, pp. 156, 157; M. Vögelstein, *Kaiseridee und Romidee und das Verhältnes von Stadt und Kirche seit Constantine*, 1930, pp. 1-14; F. Kern, "Der Rex et Sacerdos in bildlicher Darstellung," *Festschrift für D. Schäfer*, Jena, 1915, pp. 1-5. The claims of the Carolingian and German emperors to the sacerdotal authority of the Roman Augustus and the Byzantine Basileus were not presumptive and without popular support. As Frazer first demonstrated in *The Golden Bough*, priestly duties were not only the traditional responsibility of the early Teutonic kings, but throughout the long history of kingship it was both the sacred function and nature of the ruler which were of primary importance to his people. Always it had been the king, either as the real or titular high priest, who enacted, controlled and embodied the religion of the country.

"Optat de Milève," who wrote, "It is not the State which is in the Church; it is the Church which is in the State; above the Emperor, there is only God."[14]

At the same time no one had forgotten, and least of all the Frankish emperors with their Caesar-Christus ideals, that Treves had been the former capital of the Empire and the city from which Constantine, their model, had gone forth to become the first Christian *Restitutor orbis*. Therefore, any explanation of the origin and purpose of the Carolingian "Westwerk" with its towered entrance must start with Treves and the imperial architectural symbolism of the fourth century.

A. THE IMPERIAL "WESTWERK"

At the time when Treves was an imperial city the *castrum*, as the stronghold of the *praetorium* and *palatium*, had come to embody the idea of the government in the same way that during the Middle Ages its derivative, the castle, stood for the feudal power. Also, by the Constantinian period the cupola and globe were symbols of imperial domination over *urbis et orbis*, with the result that on the fourth century coins of Treves the castrum portal surmounted by the *skene-orbis* was a graphic epitome of the State, representing the *Sacrum palatium* and making manifest the celestial and cosmic dimensions of the emperor who governed Rome and the world. Therefore, on the Constantinian "Basilica" (Fig. 8) of Treves, which was either a *Sedes Iustitiae* or possibly an actual *Aula Palatina* (Ch. I, n. 93) the little towers at the four corners were palace symbols and as such should be restored with cupolas, because it has been seen that *skene*like domes were used in the Rhenish region throughout the late Empire and Middle Ages on the towers of a royal castrum and palatium. At the same time its gable was probably surmounted by a global finial, because the *sphaera* was an imperial emblem and can be seen persisting as a gable feature over the *Porta curia* (Fig. 7) of Canterbury, on the royal *fastigium* above Christ in the Doubting of Thomas (Fig. 72), and above the gables of the palace of Herod (Fig. 71) on the Carolingian ivory.

At the end of the eighth century when the Carolingian rulers began to build their royal abbey churches with towered façades, they were not only influenced by the imperial buildings, like the "Basilica" at Treves, but they were also impressed by the Byzantine traditions at Constantinople, where the towered façade and the domical *salutatorium* with little cupolas at the corners were already characteristic features of the Byzantine Palatium. Hence, in the architectural imagery of the Middle Ages, at the time when the new aspirants to imperial authority were endeavoring to construct an architecture that would embody their ideas and express their admiration for everything Roman, the towered façade with its *skene*like cupolas surmounted by an orbis stood for The Palace, the government, and the emperor's heavenly authority over the State.

An important link between the Christian and Imperial architecture of Treves is the Cathedral (Fig. 76), the Roman core of which has been thought to have been a

---

[14] C. Diehl, *Études sur l'administration byzantine dans l'Exarchate à Ravenna*, 1888, p. 383.

Constantinian palace with a central tower, perhaps domical, and smaller towers at the four corners. Although recent excavations have proved that the original Constantinian structures under the present Cathedral and the adjacent Liebfrauen church were simple basilicas, parallel to one another, nevertheless, the palacelike structure, as restored by Krencker, dates from a rebuilding at the end of the fourth century.[15] Inasmuch as there was a baptistery (Fig. 77/A) between the two Constantinian basilicas, and the southern one was always a church, there is the probability that the northern basilica, as has been suggested, was either an imperial or episcopal residence, comparable to the Lateran palace and the episcopal provisions at Aquileja in the fourth century. This would explain why the north church, as early as the ninth century, was described as having been "the palace of Helena."[16] In A.D. 326 when the north basilica was built it had at the east end a large rectangular tribune, such as one might expect to find in an official audience hall. Later, under the Emperors Valentius and Gratian, this east end (Fig. 76) was rebuilt with an arrangement of massive walls, indicating that it had a large central tower and smaller towers at the corners. There is even the possibility that the corner towers of this castrumlike structure were originally crowned with the royal cupolas.

As yet the actual purpose of this building is not known. In the middle, elevated on a square bema approached by steps on three sides, was a circular foundation which originally had a peristyle of small columns and which is now thought by the excavators to have been a sacred "memoria." In view of the fact, however, that this so-called "memoria" was removed in the sixth century, when it is known that the structure had become the sanctuary of a church, and that its place was not sufficiently sacred so that it was kept as the location of the altar in the later Romanesque cathedral, there is the possibility of this towered hall with its circular tholus having been a throne room, royal mausoleum, or martyrium. If it was an imperial tomb structure, it was comparable to the circular and domical mausoleum of Constantine at the east end of the Church of the Holy Apostles; and if it was a martyrium, it was comparable to the Church of the Prophets, Apostles, and Martyrs at Gerasa which was built in the form of a *Sacrum palatium* with a domical tower over the *sacrarium* and towers at the four corners.[17] Regardless of whether it was a memorial, or either an imperial or episcopal residence, it was a palace type of structure which was a precedent for the later towered churches of the Rhineland.

[15] J. N. von Wilmowsky, *Der Dom zu Trier*, 1874; F. Oelmann, "Zur des römischen Kernes im Trier Dom," *Bonn. Jahrb.*, CXXVII, 1922, pp. 130-188; D. Krencker, *Das römische Trier*, 1923, p. 44, Abbs. 2-5, and *Arch. Jahrb.*, XLIX, 1934, pp. 88ff., Abb. 34; N. Irsch, *Der Dom zu Trier*, 1931; T. K. Kempf, *Das Münster*, I, 1942, pp. 129-140, III, 1950, pp. 52-53 and *Germania*, XXIX, 1951, pp. 47-50, Abbs. 1-5. At the time when the north basilica was rebuilt in the Carolingian period, prior to A.D. 882, there may have been flanking towers at the entrance to atrium (Kempf, *op.cit.*, Abb. 3); Kempf, "Les premiers résultats des fouilles de la Cathédrale de Trèves," *Mémorial d'un voyage d'études en Rhénanie*, 1953, pp. 153-162.

[16] Bandmann, *op.cit.*, pp. 171, 174 (Treves), 173 (Aquileja), 182-183 (Lateran). In the *Vita S. Helenae*, cap. 9, written in the second half of the ninth century by the monk Altmann, the church is referred to as the *Domus* of the mother of Constantine and as an episcopal seat (Oelmann, *op. cit.*, pp. 139, 188); and in the *Gesta Treverorum* of about A.D. 1100 is the statement that in A.D. 368 St. Agricius made the palace into a cathedral (Oelmann, p. 187).

[17] Smith, *The Dome*, p. 112, figs. 175, 177.

That there was a direct relation between an imperial *Domus Dei* and the towered churches of the Rhineland is indicated by another building at Treves (Fig. 131), which Krencker has called a late *praetorium-palatium* that was constructed out of a portion of the imperial baths. Its round towers at either side of the apse, where the emperor, or his representative, was enthroned, resemble the round towers on the Rhenish churches which flank both a western apse, where the emperor sat, and an eastern apse, where the altar and symbolic throne of Christ was located. Furthermore, the presumption that the two-towered motif, whether at the entrance to a city or on the façade of a palatium, had celestial connotations in Roman Treves is supported by the terra-cotta statuettes of the Fortuna of the imperial family, or the city's Tyche, which were always crowned with a city-gate that had domical towers.[18] In other words, we have to keep in mind the prestige of Treves when we consider the architecture of the Carolingian period, which was a monumental assertion that the founders of this new Empire were the successors of Constantine.

By A.D. 775 when Abbot Fulrad had completed the rebuilding of the monastic church of St. Denis, Charlemagne had already envisaged a universal state in which the king, like the Caesars, was a divine person, comparable to the Son of God, and with supreme authority. In formulating the theocratic absolutism of this emperor-dominated Church and State, Charlemagne had as his ideal a Christian counterpart of the Roman Augustus, who was to be presented ceremonially, ritualistically, and theologically in terms of a combined Caesar and "Royal Christus."[19] In developing this policy he was supported by his "Palace Clergy," for at the time when he dedicated the new abbey church at St. Denis Abbot Fulrad was the *Capellanus* at the head of his "Royal Chapel."

The Royal Chapel consisted of those ecclesiastics surrounding the king who were often nobles, sometimes relatives, always supporters of the Crown, and the group from which the bishops and abbots were appointed. As prelates they served as functionaries and advisers at the Court and agents of the king in the administration of government in the areas where their monasteries were located.[20] Because the Frankish and later the German Courts seldom had a permanent place of residence, but moved for administrative and ceremonial purposes from one royal city to another, the king, in following the *itinera regis per regna*, usually established the "Royal seat" in the monastic strongholds of his palace clergy, thereby making their ecclesiae his palace-churches and the palaces of their bishops and abbots his palatium.[21] It is, therefore, significant that the Carolingian "Westwerk," or advanced narthex, with its towered façade first became

---

[18] Kutzbach, *Germania*, VIII, 1924, p. 91.

[19] Dempf, *op.cit.*, p. 154; P. E. Schramm, *Der König von Frankreich*, 1939, I, p. 50; Williams, *op.cit.*, pp. 128, 156, 200.

[20] Bandmann, *op.cit.*, pp. 219-220; F. Folz, *Le souvenir et la légende de Charlemagne*, 1950, pp. 95-105; H. W. Klewitz, "Königtum, Hofkapelle und Domkapitel," *Archiv für Urkundenforschung*, XVI, 1939, pp. 102-156; M. A. Luchaire, *Histoire des institutions monarchiques de la France sous les*

premiers *Capétans*, I, pp. 187-203; M. Prou, *Hincmar, De ordine Palatii*, 1884, pp. 42-45.

[21] A. Fuchs, "Entstehung und Zweckbestimmung der Westwerke," *Sonderdruck aus Westfälische Zeitschrift*, c, 1950, p. 253; Kantorowicz, *Laudes Regiae*, p. 97; H. S. Rieckenberg, "Königsstrasse und Königsgut in Liudofingischer und Frühsalischen Zeit," *Archiv. für Urkundenforschung*, XVII, 1941, pp. 32-154.

a monumental feature of the royal abbey churches at the time when St. Denis was dedicated in A.D. 775, Lorsch was rebuilt in about A.D. 774, Centula constructed between A.D. 790-799, and Charlemagne's imperial chapel at Aachen was erected between A.D. 796-805. Also, for the purpose of showing that this new type of façade was taken over for political reasons from the Late Antique tradition of palace architecture, it is equally important to note that when Lorsch was rebuilt, its Westwerk, or *superior fabrica*, was called a *Castellum*.[22]

Theoretically, therefore, the new Royal Abbey Church of St. Denis, begun before Pepin's death in A.D. 768 and completed by Charlemagne in A.D. 775, should have been the first Carolingian monument to have an imperial Westwerk. Unfortunately, the difficult excavations under this much rebuilt structure have not satisfactorily solved the important question of whether it did have an advanced church with flanking towers.[23] Hence, we are still left with the statements of Abbot Suger in the twelfth century, who wrote: "we tore down a *certain addition* made by Charlemagne"; and "since in the front part, toward the north, at the entrance to the main doors, *the narrow vestibule was squeezed in on either side by twin towers* neither high nor very sturdy."[24] These statements suggest very strongly: first, that the small polygonal apse uncovered by Crosby at the entrance to the Carolingian church was Pepin's imperial crypt and certainly not an imperial loge, which would have been in the tribune; second, that the excavators may not have dug far enough to the west to get the full depth and façade of Charlemagne's "certain addition"; and, third, that the actual façade was like the entrance to the Westwerk at Centula and Aachen in having a "narrow" semicircular vestibule "squeezed in on either side" by relatively small, round towers.[25]

There is, however, one important piece of evidence which has been overlooked in the discussions of whether there was a Palatine Chapel in three floors at the west end of St. Denis. Around A.D. 827 Dungal wrote a poem describing the abbey in which one verse describes a window back of the throne of David, which Schlosser thought referred

---

[22] H. Walbe, "Vom Kloster Lorsch," *Zeitschrift des Deutschen Vereins für Kunstwissenschaft*, IV, 1937, p. 54; the church at St. Trond was referred to as *Castellum regium* (Lehmann-Brockhaus, *op. cit.*, I, no. 1988); and the church at Glatz was called *ad castrum* (*op.cit.*, I, no. 441).

[23] S. M. Crosby, *The Abbey of St. Denis*, I, 1942, pp. 118, 150-151; "Excavations in the Abbey Church of St. Denis 1948; the Façade of Fulrad's Church," *Proceedings of the American Philosophical Society*, 93, 1949, pp. 347ff.; Wismann, *op.cit.*, pp. 22ff. and 58, advances reasons why St. Denis had a towered porticus. Crosby, *L'Abbaye royale de Saint-Denis*, Paris, 1953, pp. 14-15, fig. 14 (model of façade which does not satisfy the requirements of a Westwerk), fig. 25 (plan of excavations).

[24] Crosby, *op.cit.*, p. 358; E. Panofsky, *Abbot Suger*, 1946, pp. 44, 88.

[25] In discussing his discovery in 1948 of the foundations of a small polygonal apse in front of the doorway, Crosby (*op.cit.*, p. 354) says the foundations "establish the fact that changes were made in the plan of the narthex evidently while it was under construction," thereby suggesting that it was after the tomb of Pepin was built that Charlemagne had the narthex enlarged into a Westwerk. The dimensions of the apsidal structure, 6m x 3.4m, are too small to have been a western apse, like those at Fulda (A.D. 819), St. Gaul, and the recently discovered one under the west end of Cologne Cathedral (O. Doppelfeld, *Das Münster*, II, 1948. pp. 1ff.). Therefore, "the new construction" mentioned in Charlemagne's Diploma of A.D. 775 and Suger's reference to "the addition made by Charlemagne" should mean an extension of the narthex to the west. If the Westwerk at St. Denis was like the imperial chapel at the entrance to the churches at Aachen and Centula, it is readily understood why the description of St. Denis, to which J. J. Morper (*Kunst-Chronik*, I, 1948, part 10, p. 11) refers so vaguely, does not mention a towered façade.

to a fresco decoration around a window in the actual palace.[26] Inasmuch as Dungal's sequence of verses follow a processional approach, leading from the atrium with its font through the Westwerk to the altar at the east end of the church, the verse about the window takes on a new significance when it is interpreted as referring to the elevated tribune with the throne of Charlemagne. It reads, "Lest the shrewd temptor enter the low throne (*grabatum*-couch) of David, this window shows the hand of God. The four Evangelists guard the whole Body, and the omnipotent spirit the interior." Then Dungal goes on to say, "that the great hand of God guards the church from the enemy, that the right hand of God on high guards Charlemagne, the exalted Augustus; that the lofty hand of God guards and protects his progeny."

Here is specific proof of a Westwerk once these verses are taken as referring to the Emperor seated on the throne of David, in front of the glowing hand of God and with the symbols of the four Evangelists about him, so that he appeared to all men beneath him in celestial glory as the guardian of the Gate of Heaven and the earthly counterpart of the *Majestas Domini*. When Charlemagne and his successors are pictured here at St. Denis elevated in three stages, as they were at Centula, and later at Corvey (Fig. 78), above the kings of the earth and acclamantes on the ground floor, we begin to see something of the ceremonial and dramatic staging which presumably influence the iconography of the illuminators in the atelier of St. Denis. In the Apocalypse of Treves, which is thought to have been executed at St. Denis either in the eighth or ninth century, the Anonymous is variously pictured on high, seated upon the global throne of the world with the Evangelists about him, and on the floors beneath him his reception in a grand alleluia by angels, kings, saints, and acclamantes.[27] Also the imagery of the Emperor silhouetted against a halo of light, thereby recalling the eulogy of Constantine in which Eusebius said, "whose throne is the arch of heaven, and the earth the footstool of his feet," may have influenced the new *Majestas Domini* in the Bible of St. Paul at Rome, which was probably executed at St. Denis at about the time when Charles the Bald was the secular Abbot, where Christ on the globe is pictured in front of a mandorla of light.[28] Certainly the conception of Christ seated on the globe was taken over directly from the imperial tradition in which the emperor as the personification of a Virtue was presented enthroned on an orb (Fig. 52).

Comparable to St. Denis, the abbey-church of St. Riquier at Centula, which had a tower of Christ over the crossing and round towers flanking the apse, was entered at the west end through an imposing structure that consisted of a lofty central tower and small, round towers at either side of a concave vestibule.[29] This Westwerk with its *turris occidentalis* was erected in honor of *Sancti Salvatoris* "to give Augustus Karoli

[26] Schlosser, *Schriftquellen zur Geschichte der Karolingischenkunst*, nos. 910, 911:
Ne David grabatum temptator callidus intret
Signetur domini ista fenestra manu.
Quadrus evvangelii defendat numerus omne
Corpus, et interius cunctipotens anima. (no. 910)
[27] Van der Meer, *Maiestas Domini, théophanies de l'Apocalypse dans l'art chrétien*, 1938: Apoca-

lypse of Treves, fol. 18v (fig. 24), fol. 15v (fig. 65), fol. 61 (fig. 67), fol. 67v (fig. 68), pp. 111, 284-288.
[28] *Op.cit.*, p. 334, fig. 78.
[29] A. Fuchs, *Westfälischen Zeitschrift*, c, 1950, p. 234 and *Die Karolingischen Westwerke*, Paderborn, 1929, pp. 10, 28-38; W. Effmann, *Centula*, 1912; W. O. Rave, *Centula*, 1937; E. Lehmann, *Der frühe Deutsche Kirchenbau*, 1938, p. 109, Abbs. 86,231 (section), 265 (façade).

imperial delight"; it was constructed in two stories, a low story at the entrance level and above it a great tower chapel in which on the west side was an elevated oratory for the king. Later, when Charlemagne built his domical Palace Chapel at Aachen, the portal structure, as at Centula, not only consisted of an apsidal niche vestibule between round towers, but was separately dedicated to St. Savior and had in the tribune over the entrance the Emperor's throne.[30] Since the new type of façade, dedicated to the Savior, was a ceremonial provision for the emperor as the *christus Domini*, as Fuchs has proved, and the towered façade was a palatium symbol, as I hope to prove, then there arises the question of whether the concave vestibule at Centula and Aachen, which was not uncommon on the later Rhenish churches, was not, like the eastern apse, another traditional palace feature.[31] Its concave shape recalls the *porta regia* of the Roman stage palace, the palace entrances pictured on the frescoes of the Fourth Pompeian style (Fig. 113), the vestibule of Nero's *Domus aurea*, the towered and concave portal which Dyggve has discovered at the entrance to the palace-church of Theodosius at Saloniki, the *"Sigma"* (Fig. 121) at the entrance to the *"Triconchos"* of the Byzantine palace at Constantinople, and the importance of the semicircular exedra at the entrance to so many Roman buildings.[32] Furthermore, the façade of the palace of the Exarchate at Ravenna (Fig. 6), with an apsidal place of appearances over the entrance, is evidence that it had continued to be a distinguishing feature of palace architecture which Charlemagne would have known and admired.

In reviewing the ceremonial and symbolic purposes of the towered Westwerk it is interesting, and also suggestive, to note that the new type of entrance was considered to be a separate structure which was always dedicated, quite apart from the church itself, to its own patron, who was most frequently St. Salvator. The examples dedicated to the Savior were Centula (790-799), Aachen (796-805), St. Alban at Mainz (805), Fulda (791-819), Werden (c. 804, or 843), Farfa (830-843), Fontanella (833), Frankfurt a.M. (843-876), and St. Nicasius at Reims (820-862).[33] Their architectural provisions and the way they were referred to in the documents have made it evident that all these massive advanced churches were a kind of palace chapel in which the emperor was ceremonially honored when he visited his royal abbeys.

Usually they were called a *regale sacellum* and *capella imperialis*, but sometimes they were designated as a *regia, locus regalis, thronus imperialis, oratorium, auditorio regali, coenaculum,* and *solarium.*[34] For the purposes of this study the best example of

---

[30] Bandmann, *op.cit.*, p. 105, fig. 3; A. Haupt, *Die Pfalzkapelle Kaiser Karls d. Gr. zu Aachen,* 1913; Lehmann, *op.cit.*, p. 106, Taf. 3, Abbs. 7, 84; H. Schiffers, *Karls d. Gr. Grab in der Vorhalle des Aachener Münster,* 1934; J. Buchkremer ("Untersachungen zum Karolingischen Bäu der Aachener Pfalzkapelle," *Zeitschrift für Kunstwissenschaft,* 1947, pp. 1-22) says there is some evidence in the absence of bonding that the round towers at either side of the vestibule were constructed after the walls of the polygonal church were erected.

[31] Bandmann, pp. 106-109.

[32] See p. 121.

[33] Centula (Schlosser, *Schriftquellen,* no. 782); St. Alban (Schlosser, nos. 183, 184); Fulda (Fuchs, *Westwerke,* p. 15; Lehmann, p. 113); Fontanella (Fuchs, *Westwerke,* p. 13); Farfa (Fuchs, *Westwerke,* p. 13); St. Nicasius at Reims (Fuchs, *Westwerke,* pp. 10-11); Frankfurt a.M. (Lehmann, p. 112); at Werden the Westwerk was dedicated to St. Peter and the church to the Savior (Fuchs, *Westwerke,* p. 15; Lehmann, p. 143).

[34] *Palatium regale* (Fuchs, *Zeitschrift,* p. 255; *Mon. Ger. SS.,* XI, p. 533, 16); *sacellum* (Fuchs, *Zeitschrift,* p. 256); *regia* (Fuchs, p. 258); *capella regia* (Fuchs, p. 261); *locus regalis* and *thronus*

what was sometimes referred to as a *Palatium regale,* or *capella regia,* is Fuchs' presentation of the Westwerk at Corvey, which was built in A.D. 873-885.[35] In section (Fig. 78) it consisted of a great central tower in two stories where the emperor was enthroned in the upper gallery so that he could look down into his private chapel; and on the façade (Fig. 80) it had flanking towers at either side of the projecting bay with its royal *fastigium* in which was located the imperial *oratorium.* The emperor sat in the upper gallery, his throne raised on a wooden dais in much the same way that Charlemagne's throne is raised in the gallery at Aachen, so that he would have a clear view of the altar and also so that he would be seen in majestic elevation against the light of his sun window. Probably on either side of the emperor in his elevated seat was the angelic choir, which was referred to at Corvey as the *chorum supremum.*

The builders made use of different devices and palace features to dramatize the ruler's exalted position in the Church with the result that there was considerable variation in the provisions for the emperor in the Rhenish churches. At Reichenau, for example, where the Westwerk was not constructed until the tenth century, the emperor's supramundane nature and peculiar relation to the Church was shown in theatrical fashion by the location of his chapel.[36] Here the *palatium regale* was a great royal apse with a single tower rising about it; and in it the *locus regalis* was so placed that its special window looking down into the apse came directly beneath the half dome, thereby making the emperor's position comparable to that of Christ in the eastern apse. There could have been no doubt in the minds of the people about either the heavenly and angelic import of the towered Westwerk, or the divine nature of the ruler whom they saw looking down from his western apse, much as the image of Christ was seen in the eastern apse, because over the emperor's royal chapel was the oratory of the Archangel Michael, the Guardian of the Gate of Heaven.

It is no longer possible to explain the square towers flanking the entrance and the round towers which rise up so high at both ends of the early churches, like Centula, and the later Romanesque cathedrals, like Worms, as merely bell-towers or a means of access to the upper galleries and chapels, because they were seen and thought of, regardless of their functions, as symbols of the palatium and heavenly castrum.[37] Even at the time when the churchmen were successfully endeavoring to present them as the Evangelists at the corners of the celestial ramparts, the twelfth century account of the

---

imperialis (Fuchs, *Westwerke,* p. 89); *capella imperialis* (Rieckenberg, *Archiv. f. Urkunderforschung,* XVII, 1941, p. 57); *auditorio regali* (Schlosser, no. 864). According to Fuchs (*Zeitschrift,* p. 254) *aedificium regium* refers to the place of receptions at the entrance to a monastery. At Persenberg a document of A.D. 1045 says, *Caesar* (Henricus III imp.) *sedit in colloquo eminentiori quodam vestibulo* (Lehmann-Brockhaus, *Schriftquellen,* no. 1079).

[35] Fuchs, *Westwerke,* pp. 17-27 and *Zeitschrift,* pp. 235, 252, figs. 5, 6; Effmann, *Die Kirche der Abtei Corvey,* 1929; Lehmann, *Kirchenbau,* p. 123, Abb. 91; R. Rensing, "Pfarrsystem und West-

werk in Corvey," *Westfälen Jahrb.,* XXV, 1940, pp. 51-58.

[36] O. Gruber, "Die Kirchenbauten des Reichenau," *Zeitschrift für Christlichen Kunst,* 33/34, 1920, p. 37-48; "Das Westwerk: Symbol und Baugestaltung Germanischen Christentums," *Zeitschrift des Deutschen Vereins für Kunstwissenschaft,* III, 1936, pp. 168-169; "Der Westwerk der Benediktinerkirche in Reichenau-Mittelzell, *Zeitschrift für altchristliche Kunst,* 1920, pp. 37-48; Lehmann, *op.cit.,* p. 136.

[37] Fuchs, *Westwerke,* pp. 49-59; P. O. Rave, *Der Emporenbau in romanische und frühgotischen Zeit,* 1924.

disaster which overtook the royal abbey church at Freising records how imperial ideas associated with towers persisted, for the account reads, *Ruit sedes cathedralis ac imperialis dignitas edificiorum. . .; ruit domus organorum et turris regalis cum dulcissimo sono campanarum; ruit ipsum palatium cum suis capellis depictis auro et argento.*[38]

It does not follow that all the various theories which have been suggested to account for the advanced church are necessarily false, because during the greater part of the year when the emperor was not in residence at a particular abbey, or visiting it temporarily for the celebration of a festival, the Westwerk was made use of in other ways than as a *capella imperialis.* The fact, however, that the Westwerk served as a kind of martyrium for relics and as a sacred place for burials does not mean, as Wismann attempted to prove, that it was nothing more than an imperial grave monument. What is important in explaining the mortuary functions of the Westwerk are not the earlier customs of placing reliquary oratories in the towers of Syrian churches and of using the narthex, or even a western apse, for burials *ad sanctus,* but the palace tradition of making the royal chapel a martyrium.[39] In the Great Palace at Constantinople there had been ever since the time of Constantine special chapels for the emperor, which were protected and sanctified by the presence of holy relics and called the "Guardian of the imperial house." The best evidence that the Carolingian rulers were following Byzantine precedent, and also considered relics as necessary guardians, is the derivation of the word "capella," that was applied to the Westwerk, from the "Cap," or cape, of St. Martin which was the very special relic of the Merovingian and French kings, being often taken with them into battle and on their travels.

In addition to its royal functions the advanced church served as a kind of parish chapel for many monasteries and was also a place of meeting and voting, being sometimes used for church councils. There is even some evidence by the Romanesque period, probably after a monastic establishment was no longer used as a royal resi-

[38] Lehmann-Brockhaus, *Schriftquellen zur Kunstgeschichte des 11 und 12 Jahrh.*, 1938, p. 88, no. 401. Freising was of sufficient importance during the Carolingian period to have been the seat of two church councils, one in A.D. 800 and a second in A.D. 803 (Hefele, *Histoire des Conciles*, III², pp. 1101, 1126).

[39] H. Wismann, *Grab und Grabmal Karls des Grossen*, 1933, Heidelberg, pp. 43-60. A. Grabar (*Martyrium*, 1946, I, pp. 562-570) points out the relation of the Palatine chapels in the West to the imperial oratories at Constantinople and quotes from a letter of the Bishop of Tulla (c. 840) who speaks of an imperial chapel in the Villa Gundum (Gondreville) as, "Villae Domus imperator . . . , iussit ut in fronte ipsius palatii solarii opus construerem, de quo in capellam veniretur" (Grabar, p. 576; Schlosser, p. 66, no. 233). A verse (*Monumenta Germanica, SS.*, XV, I, p. 222, lines 45-49), describing the early ninth century translation of the remains of St. Boniface from his tomb in the middle of the church to the new west end of the royal abbey at Fulda, reads: "Hoc namque occidua martyr tumulatus honore Altithroni regis comta iacet altus in ara, Absida quam super exstructa namque imminet ingens." G. von Bezold ("Zur Geschichte der romanischen Baukunst in der Erdiözese Mainz," *Marburger Jahrbuch für Kunstwissenschaft*, VIII, 1936, p. 6), not being aware of the royal significance of the western apse at Fulda, translated it, "Denn in diesen westlichen Hochaltar liegt der Märtyrer mit hohen Königlichen Ehren bestaltet. Die Apsis, welche darüber erbaut ist, erhebt sich gewaltig." If it is read, "For in the western end, adorned in honor of the high-throned king, the martyr's entombment lies high up, in the altar, over which the apse is built up, for it (the towered superstructure) rises up mightily," then we have evidence that the king was enthroned high up in the apsidal Westwerk at Fulda, as he was later at Reichenau, and that the martyr's relics were guardians of his special chapel.

dence, that the upper chamber of the advanced church became the episcopal quarters. Prior to about A.D. 1220, when the double choir went out of use, it naturally served as the place for the emperor's choir, because it was traditional, especially at the Byzantine Court, to receive the emperor even in his palace with organ music and choral singing.[40] At Centula and Reims the baptistery was on the ground floor, while the presence of upper oratories in honor of the Baptist at Corvey and Hersfeld can be explained by the royal associations of the Baptist, as the Precursor of Christ, with the emperor, and the traditional significance of baptism as a royal rite.[41]

The reference to the royal upper floor in the Westwerk at Fontanella (833) and Seligenstadt (828-840) as a *coenaculum* raises an interesting question.[42] While this word, which primarily meant "dining-room," was most frequently used during the Middle Ages for an "upper floor," its application to a *capella regia* may have had a ceremonial and Christological significance. The most famous Christian *coenaculum* was the domical oratory on the upper floor of the Mother Church at Sion in which it was believed that Christ partook of the Last Supper with his Apostles. In the Byzantine palace ritual it was customary for the emperor, as the "earthly Christ," to celebrate the Last Supper by enacting the part of Christ with twelve guests in the "Triclinium of the Nineteen Beds." It was also an established part of the ceremonies at the Byzantine palace-churches for the *Christos-Basileus*, after listening to the services in his parakyptikon located in the tribune over the western entrance, to be conducted to a *triclinium* for a ceremonial repast.[43] Therefore, if the imperial liturgy in the Carolingian royal abbey-churches was similar to the Byzantine ritual, it is possible that the *coenaculum* in the Westwerk not only refers to the place where the emperor partook of the Communion, but also implies the theocratic distinction of the Carolingian emperor as the personification of the Son of God, the "Royal Christus."

The intent of the Carolingian builders to show that the gateway and towered façade had a heavenly meaning is made evident by the importance which was given to the cult of St. Michael, the Guardian of the Gate of Heaven and the Captain of the Heavenly Hosts, and the location of his oratory either over the gate-house of a monastery or in the upper gallery of the Westwerk.[44] Because of the Archangel's pre-eminence at the

---

[40] Bandmann, *op.cit.*, pp. 227-229; at Centula the 300 monks were divided into three choirs, located in the east choir, the nave and St. Salvator at the west end (Fuchs, *Westwerke*, p. 44).

[41] Fuchs, *Westwerke*, pp. 12, 14, 15, 39-40, 41; Bandmann, *op.cit.*, p. 208.

[42]) At Fontanella, "a parte occidentali . . . constructo desuper coenaculo . . ." and "Hunc vero triumphum . . . rex in superiore coenaculo" (Fuchs, *Westwerke*, p. 13; Lehmann-Brockhaus, *Die Kunst des X Jahrb.*, p. 68 n. 70; Schlosser, p. 290, no. 870); under Abbot Wido (A.D. 753-787) a document tells of the *auditorio regali* (Schlosser, no. 864).

b) At Seligenstadt, "In coenaculo quod porticum basilicae est" (Fuchs, *Westwerke*, p. 13; G. Weise, *Untersuchungen zur beschichte der Archi-*

tektur und Plastik der früheren Mittelalters, 1916, p. 105 n. 2).

c) In the Westwerk of St. Stephen at Auxerre, a "ligneum coenaculum" on the upper floor (Lehmann-Brockhaus, *Die Kunst des X Jahrb.*, p. 67 nn. 68, 69; p. 68 n. 70).

d) At Reims over the south gate, known as the "Porta Basilicaris" which was at the entrance to the "Via Cesarea," there was the palace of Archbishop Rigoberto (d. 749) with the windows of its *coenaculum* opening on the monastery of St. Remi (Schlosser, p. 247, no. 764; J. Leflon, *Histoire de l'église de Reims*, 1942, pp. 64, 69).

[43] See p. 171.

[44] Fuchs, *Zeitschrift*, pp. 231, 235, 241. In the gate-house at Centula (Fuchs, *Westwerke*, p. 7); at Glanfeuil (Fuchs, *op.cit.*, p. 6); in the *Porta*

entrance to so many of the Carolingian churches, Gruber advanced the suggestion that the Westwerk was a symbolic representation of Heaven as pictured in the "Celestial Hierarchy" of Dionysius the Areopagite, the manuscript of which had been given to the Abbey of St. Denis.[45] While it is possible that the churchmen may have cultivated this symbolic concept of the façade at a later date, it is most unlikely that the writings of the Areopagite were translated and known in time to have influenced the building of Centula and the other early abbey churches. Instead there is every reason to believe that the honor accorded to the Archangel was part of the Carolingian Emperor-cult, for Michael, in addition to being the Psychopompos, was not only a Prince of Heaven, who in Early Christian art was presented like an Imperator carrying the orbis and ruler's scepter, but throughout the Middle Ages was figuratively identified with the emperor, whom the papacy at Rome desired to recognize only as the Marshal of the Church and the Guardian of the *porta coeli*.[46]

The use of *solarium* to refer to the *capella regalis* in the Westwerk of the Servatius church of the abbey of Fontanella, and also at Lyon and York, raises the much larger issue of whether the designation of the king's place of honor as a "sun-room" did not have a special significance, derived from the imperial palace tradition which had persisted at the Byzantine Court, of identifying the emperor with the "radiant Sun" and of comparing his dwelling with the Golden House of the Sun.[47] In the Carolingian litany the emperor was *Lux et vita nostra*, and at the time of the coronation of Otto I his throne in the vestibule of the Westwerk of the Aachen Palatine Chapel was called a *solium regale*, or royal sun throne.[48] There is also the account of the Synod of Frankfurt in A.D. 1027 which says, "Novus vero noster imperator (Konrad II) in occidentali parte chori eminentiori solio sub thronizatus assedit. . . ."[49] At Jerusalem the Gate

---

Basilicaris at Reims (Fuchs, p. 6; Schlosser, no. 764); in atrium towers of St. Emmeran at Regensberg (Fuchs, p. 7); Nazarius basilica at Lorsch (Fuchs, p. 7); oratory of St. Michael in St. Alban of Mainz (Schlosser, no. 186); altar to St. Michael on upper floor of Westwerk of Petersberg by Fulda in A.D. 836 (Schlosser, no. 375).

[45] O. Gruber, "Das Westwerk," *Zeitschrift des Deutschen Vereins f. Kunstwissenschaft*, III, 1936, pp. 149-173; also see Fuchs (*Zeitschrift*, pp. 230-235) and Bandmann (*op.cit.*, p. 209).

[46] R. Holtzmann, "Der Kaiser als Marschall des Papstes," *Schriften der Strassburger Wissenschaftlichen Gesellschaft in Heidelberg*, no. 8, 1928. C. Diehl (*Études sur l'administration dans l'Exarchate à Ravenna*, 188, pp. 264-265) refers to the spread of the cult of the Archangel from Constantinople to Rome and Ravenna and says it was particularly strong among the Lombards, who considered Michael to be the protector of the nation, thereby suggesting a parallel with the emperor; R. Janin, "Les sanctuaires byzantins de Saint Michel," *Échos d'Orient*, XXX, 1934, pp. 28-52; L'Orange (*Studies on the Iconography of Cosmic Kingship*, p. 113) in describing the ceremonial

Prokypsis of Michael Palaeologus discusses the comparison of the Byzantine emperor to the Archangel.

[47] At Fontanella the early basilica of A.D. 742-747 had a *solarium* to which one ascended (Schlosser, no. 860); at Conques the *solarium* was connected with the oratory of St. Michael (Lehmann-Brockhaus, *Die Kunst des x*[th] *Jahrsh.*, p. 28 n. 96); Lyon (Fuchs, *Zeitschrift*, p. 252); York (Fuchs, *Zeitschrift*, p. 254; Schlosser, no. 709). In the mediaeval palaces the royal room was on the second story, arcaded and called either a *solarium* or *salam regalem* (Swoboda, *Römische und romanische Paläste*, pp. 238, 255-258). Under "solarium" Du Cange (*Glossarium Lat.*, VI, p. 302) says, "ni fallor, Sozain, vel Souzoein estage dictum tabulatum superius," which seems to imply that at one time the sun-room was associated with the Suzerain.

[48] Wismann, *op.cit.*, p. 36; there is also the reference (Ch. III n. 39) to the "imperial house" of the royal "Villa Gundum" as "in fronte ipsius palatii solari."

[49] O. Lehmann-Brockhaus, *Schriftquellen zur Kunstgeschichte des 11 und 12 Jahrsh.*, I, no. 394.

of David, which was the actual residence of the Latin kings, is described by the Pilgrim of A.D. 1172 as, "It stands . . . together with the newly built *solar* chamber and palace which adjoins it."[50]

Once a royal sun connotation is seen in the designation of the emperor's oratory as a *solarium*, then there is the possibility that the source of light back of the imperial throne, such as the window of St. Denis, and at Corvey (Fig. 80) which is distinctly elevated, was thought of as a sun-window framing the ruler, as the *christus Domini*, in a mandorla of light.[51] Furthermore, the history of the oculus and the appearance of a round window in A.D. 1180 back of Frederick I in his Westwerk of Sint Servaas at Maastricht (Fig. 123) suggest that round windows, such as are seen on the palace frames of the Councils in the church at Bethlehem (Fig. 75), were taken over from the imperial palace architecture of Constantinople.

The evidence that the towered façade was at first a symbol of the palatium brings us back to the question of why so many of the imperial chapels at the entrance to the Carolingian royal abbeys were dedicated to St. Salvator. At the time when the palace clergy of the Carolingian rulers were building a Westwerk at the entrance to their churches it was a policy to present the emperor in both imperial and Biblical terms as a Messiah, the New David destined to reunite the peoples of God, who was comparable to the Savior. It was not uncommon for the emperor to be designated "the Savior of the World" and in the protocol of 877 he was called "Salvator mundi."[52] Among the advanced churches erected in the name of the Savior it is interesting to note that at the imperial abbey of Farfa, which the Carolingian emperors used as a place of residence before entering Rome, between A.D. 830 and 843 Abbot Sicardo con-

[50] "Theodoric's Description of the Holy Places," *Palestine Pilgrims Text Society*, v, 1891, p. 6.

[51] There seems to be no specific evidence of any sun symbolism having been openly attributed to the west window back of the Carolingian emperor seated in the tribune of his Westwerk. That it was tacitly recognized is indicated by the solar implications of praising the rulers as *Lux et vita nostra*, calling them *Luminaria mundi* and by the revival of Byzantine sun symbolism under the Ottonian and Hohenstaufen emperors (see p. 102). During the twelfth century it may, therefore, have influenced both the introduction of the wheel window and Frederick II's interest in the circular window. In A.D. 1179, just prior to his reconstruction of Sint Servaas with a circular window back of his imperial loge, Frederick helped to rebuild the church at Fossanova, which has over the door an oculus with a crown above it and the inscription, "Fredericus I · imperator semper · Augustus · hoc opus fieri fecit" (A. Frothingham, *A.J.A.*, VI, 1890, pp. 17-23).

Also, if there was a window with the Hand of God and the Evangelist symbols back of Charlemagne's throne in the Westwerk of St. Denis, which was intended to be seen as an imperial *Majestas Domini* with the Emperor silhouetted against the light, then it is possible that Suger had in mind the Carolingian tradition when he introduced a wheel window type of *Majestas Domini* in the façade of St. Denis. That there may have been latent, but serious, controversial issues involved in the development of this type of window and in the eventual association of the western "Glory window" with only Christ is suggested by the first use of the Wheel of Fortune window at St. Étienne at Beauvais in A.D. 1120-1140 and later in the way Christ as the world Judge is placed above the windows of San Zeno and the Cathedral of Trent. This possibility becomes more apparent when it is realized that it was the anti-imperial churchmen, who were against any identification of the emperor or king with the *Majestas Domini*, that had the king depicted at the mercy of changing fate in their new wheel windows. While these men were following, as has been pointed out, Boëthius' (Bk. IV, 6, 21) description of Fortuna as impermanent Fate, they also were undoubtedly endeavoring to discredit the other tradition of Fortuna as the special protectress of the emperor and as an imperial attribute of a world ruler whose Providentia and Sapientia were solely responsible for the good fortune of the State.

[52] P. E. Schramm, *Der König von Frankreich*, I, 1939, p. 40 n. 4, p. 45 n. 1.

structed its towered Westwerk as an "oratory" *in honorem Domini Salvatoris, adiunctum ecclesia Sanctae Marie,* thereby recalling the palace church at Aachen, and that in the same region north of Rome there is in the church of San Salvatore Maggiore the eleventh century fresco portrait of the nimbed Emperor Henry II accompanied by his wife and figures bearing a rotulus and crown.[53]

There is, therefore, a strong presumption that the towered *palatium regalis*, dedicated to St. Savior at the entrance to the Carolingian abbey-churches, was intended to be seen as a monumental expression of the Saviorlike nature of the ruler.[54] The papal opposition to this popular association of the emperor with the Savior is intimated by the way that the great "Basilica Salvatoris" at Rome, which was built by the first Christian emperor in connection with the Lateran Palace and was known throughout the Middle Ages as "Constantine's church," was rededicated in A.D. 896 to John the Baptist and its distinction of being "the Mother and the First Church of the City and the World" was eventually transferred to St. Peter's. Another indication of this opposition is the history of Theodoric's palace-church at Ravenna, originally dedicated to the Savior, which was reconsecrated first as S. Martino in coelo aurea and finally as S. Apollinare Nuovo.

In reconstructing the symbolic and political intent of the mediaeval builders it must be recalled that the litany of the "Carolingian Emperor-church" is evidence that "It was the prerogative of the Frankish King and an honor intended for him alone to have his abode in the most prominent place." What Kantorowicz wrote about the king's supreme position would apply figuratively to his towered narthex, dedicated to St. Savior, with its angelic choir and chapel of St. Michael. "The King's place," he wrote, "is in the 'royal box' which he shares with his angelic and super-angelic

[53] G. Croquison, *Rivista di archeologia cristiana,* XV, 1938, pp. 37-71; P. Markthaler, "Abbazia imperiale di Farfa," *Rivista,* V, 1928, pp. 83, 86 (a document of A.D. 1060 after the rebuilding of the church of Farfa, records the consecration of the two altars of the *beatae Mariae dominae nostrae et domini Dei Salvatoris mundi.* The portrait of Henry II (Markthaler, fig. 40).

[54] At first one is reluctant to attach any significance to the fact that it was very common during the early Middle Ages to dedicate churches to the Savior (A. Ostendorf, "Das Salvator-Patrocinium, seine Anfänge und seine Ausbreitung im Mittelalterlichen im Deutschland," *Westfälischen Zeitschrift,* C, 1950, pp. 357-376). Then one begins to realize that in Constantinople, Rome, and the Carolingian domains there was a persistent form of the imperial cult, which the Church either tolerated or so redirected that it was eventually forgotten, but which for a long time was implied without any explicit recognition, in the association of the Savior with the emperor. In Constantinople the oratory of St. Constantine opened on the steps of the column in the Forum on which the emperor was represented as late as A.D. 1105 as a Sun-god, and throughout much of the Byzantine period it was customary for the Court to visit this oratory on certain feast days and at the time of triumphal entries for the emperor to stop at this shrine and receive the acclamations from the steps of the column (J. Ebersolt, *Sanctuaires de Byzance,* 1921, pp. 71-74 and *Constantinople, Recueil d'études, d'archéologie et d'histoire,* 1951, pp. 71-74). At Rome there was an "oratory of St. Caesarius" in the *Sacrum palatium* on the Palatine to which the statue of a new Byzantine emperor was conducted in a kind of Adventus ceremony (see p. 150) and Krautheimer (*Art Bulletin,* XXIV, 1942, p. 33 n. 190) has pointed out that the oratory of *San Salvatore de arcu Trasi* was either alongside the Arch of Constantine or in its attic chamber. The presumption that the dedication of so many Carolingian advanced churches to the Savior was influenced by the parallel between Christ and the Emperor as the "christus Domini," or "Royal Christ," does not invalidate Fuchs' (*Westwerke,* p. 45) and Krautheimer's (*op.cit.,* pp. 35-36) suggestion that Charlemagne by dedicating his Palace Chapel at Aachen to the Savior and calling his palace "the Lateran" was endeavoring to show that his *Sacrum palatium* was comparable to the Lateran at Rome.

patrons, whereas the Pope with his apostles occupied the 'stalls' on the ground floor."[55] To continue to paraphrase Kantorowicz, it can be said that the architectural symbolism, like the royal acclamations and intercessions addressed to the Frankish king, was intended "to symbolize the King's *character angelicus*—nay make him, almost *ipso facto*, the human counterpart of Christ enthroned in celestial majesty."

What made the towered façade a dramatic expression of the emperor's Christlike domination were the ceremonies which took place at the entrance to the royal abbey churches. On the feast days it was presumably the ruler who enacted the part of Christ. At the time of the coronation of Otto I we are told how the Emperor was enthroned in the vestibule of Charlemagne's Chapel at Aachen, which was like a *porta regia*, where he was acclaimed by the throng of nobles and officers in the atrium in front of him; then later led into the church for the ceremony; and finally conducted up to his throne in the imperial loge over the entrance, where he could be seen by everyone in all his exalted and divine majesty.[56] The records also make it clear that the mediaeval emperors were always welcomed at the gateways of their monasteries and the portals of their churches in a ritual which followed the precedent of the Roman Adventus.

The way in which the mediaeval man was accustomed to think of a royal visitation in terms of an imperial ceremony can be seen in the "Advent of the Lord" (Fig. 54) from the Utrecht Psalter. The Lord is here presented as a triumphant imperator, preceded by his *cursor* carrying his sword, who is met at the domical gateway by representatives of the honored city and by a group holding scrolls with the panegyrics of praise. Much the same kind of receptions undoubtedly took place at an abbey gate-house, or at the so-called "Torhalle" of Lorsch which dates back to the ninth century and stood like a triumphal arch over the processional way leading from the gateway to the Westwerk.[57] At the time of his Coming the ruler was triumphantly

[55] Kantorowicz, "Ivories and Litanies," *Journal of the Warburg and Courtauld Institutes*, 1942, pp. 56-81. In an excellent review of A. Fuchs' "Entstehung und Zweckbestimmung der Westwerke," W. Lotz (*Kunstchronik*, v, 1952, pp. 65-70) has pointed out the significance of Kantorowicz's study of the litanies in relation to the symbolic interpretation of the Westwerk, and says that it was not until the close of the fourteenth century that the old function of the Westwerk, as the place of the emperor, was forgotten.

[56] H. Wismann, *Grab und Grabmal Karls des Grossen*, pp. 36-37; *Mon. Ger.*, III, 437.

[57] Kantorowicz, *Laudes Regiae*, p. 72; Fuchs (*Westwerke*, p. 81 n. 7) says at Lorsch the emperor spent the night in the ecclesia awaiting the start of the solemn procession and the next morning made his Adventus; at Corvey the emperor was received with acclamations (Fuchs, *Zeitschrift*, p. 260). Regarding the so-called gate-house at Lorsch, both Fuchs (*Westwerke*, pp. 73-85) and Krautheimer (*Art Bulletin*, XXIV, 1942, pp. 32-34) compare it to a triumphal arch and suggest that

its upper story, which recalls the chamber in the attic of some of the Roman triumphal arches, was for the ceremonial reception of the ruler. At Bamberg there was a *capellam quoque super portam* (Lehmann-Brockhaus, *Schriftquellen*, no. 129). Earlier it was pointed out that the "Heaven chamber" on the upper floor of the Porta Curia at Canterbury was probably the royal oratory (see p. 35). In a manuscript of the Bibl. Nat. in Paris (*Ms. fr. 10440*, fol. 45) there is a seventeenth century drawing of a destroyed Carolingian triumphal arch which not only illustrates the interest of the early Middle Ages in appropriating late Roman triumphal iconography, but also suggests that it may have been customary to construct a kind of triumphal arch over the processional way leading from the gateway either to the Westwerk of a royal abbey church, as at Lorsch, or to the palace (B. de Montesquiou-Fezensac, "L'Arc de Triomphe d'Einhardus," *Cahiers archéologiques*, IV, 1949, pp. 79-103). While the arch was a Christian monument commemorating the Triumph of Christ, and perhaps referring to the conversion of the Saxons, "received like Christ" by the whole chapter and conducted to his royal chamber, which was sometimes an oratory of St. Michael. At Canterbury (Fig. 7) it has already been noted that this special oratory in the *Porta curia*, with its royal arcade, its cupola and its *fastigium* surmounted by a global finial, was known as the "Paradise chamber" or "Heaven chamber."

At the time of visitations, coronations and feast days the Carolingian and Germanic kings, like the Roman Augustus at the city-gate and the Byzantine Basileus at the vestibule of his palace churches, were received with music, singing, and acclamations as they were conducted in solemn fashion to this place of honor and appearances in the tribune over the portal. That these official comings were thought of as an Adventus may be deduced from the letter written by the Bishop of Lyon to Charlemagne in A.D. 813, for it says, "Also I erected a *domus*, in two stories with a *solarium* and furnished properly for you, in order that your *adventus* may be in that part (of the church).[58]

The fact that the Church after the Carolingian period began to challenge more vigorously the claims and prerogatives of the northern monarch did not change for a long time the political ideas underlying the architectural symbolism. It was not until the end of the thirteenth century, after the papacy was victorious in its critical struggle with Frederick II, that it was finally successful in transferring all the façade symbolism from the royal majesty of the *christus Domini* to Christ as the *Majestas Domini*.[59] During the Romanesque period it was not solely in the Rhineland that political implications were associated with the towered façade. This was presumably true in Normandy, which would explain the not always successful efforts of the Norman kings to impose the towered façade upon their churches in Sicily and South Italy. What was involved is made evident by "The Anonymous of A.D. 1100," which is our best evidence that the Norman dukes and kings insisted, even more emphatically than the Carolingian emperors, that *"Rex sanctus est," "Rex sacerdos est," "Rex*

---

many of the figures, such as the two horsemen trampling on the serpent, who are thought to symbolize the Eastern and Western emperors, were taken over from the imperial iconography of the Constantinian period.

[58] "Aliam quoque domus cum solario aedificavi et duplicavi; et hanc propter vos paravi, ut si in illis partibus vester esset adventus, in ea suscipi possetis." (Schlosser, no. 709)

[59] There are two late twelfth century ivories of the "School of Cologne," one at Darmstadt and the other in Brussels, which appear to record the transference of all the imperial significance of the German Westwerk to the Glory of Christ (Goldschmidt, *Die Elfenbeinskulpturen aus der Römanischen Zeit*, III, 1923, no. 52/2, pl. XV and no. 53/a). Of the two the Brussels ivory is the most interesting because it is shaped like a church, except that it has at both ends a portal surmounted by a Westwerk with three towers, the flanking

towers being crowned with cupolas and large global finials. In one portal is the Virgin and Child and in the other is Christ seated under a domical baldachin, much as one might imagine Otto I enthroned in the entrance of the Palatine Chapel at Aachen when he was acclaimed by his followers, with the four symbols of the Evangelists given great prominence above him on the façade of the Westwerk. If I am correct in believing that at St. Denis (see p. 83) the emperor was seen as the personification of the *Majestas Domini*, when he sat on his throne over the portal and in front of the window with the Hand of God in it and the Evangelist symbols around it, then these two ivories, which are similar, are a counter assertion that the Westwerk belongs only to Christ and that the towers are not palatium features, but stand for the Evangelists, or, as Durandus wrote, for "the preachers and prelates."

messias est," that by the grace of God he is the *"christus Domini,"* and hence that the Palatium is over the Church.[60]

Proof, therefore, that the towered façade was a symbol of the Palatium in regions under Norman rule are the buildings of the Bayeux tapestry, which although not executed until after the middle of the twelfth century undoubtedly followed established precedents. Throughout the tapestry all the royal residences are distinguished in one way or another by flanking towers whose domical, or conical, roofs have the striations of the celestial *skene*: the palace of Edward the Confessor at Westminster (Fig. 10) has a towered façade; at either side of the PALATIUM of William the Conqueror (Fig. 9) there are domical towers; and over the throne-room of Harold (Fig. 53) there are little imperial cupolas. Furthermore, on the tapestry the ordinary church at Bosham is presented as towerless, but the royal abbey church of St. Peter (Fig. 79), in which King Edward is buried, has both a towered façade and an exaggeratedly large and *skene*like dome over its lofty western tower.

Neither the documents nor the architecture make it clear whether or not the Carolingian kings, German emperors and Norman rulers sat in their churches under either a baldachin or a structural dome in the way the Byzantine Basileus was enthroned in the tribune of his palace-churches. If we can judge, however, by Sint Servaas at Maastricht the ceremonial provisions for the emperor were similar in both the Byzantine and Holy Roman Empires. Maastricht was an imperial residential city until the thirteenth century and Sint Servaas was a royal church from the time of Charlemagne.[61] After its destruction by the Normans it was rebuilt around A.D. 900 and then again about 1039; but it was in A.D. 1180 that its massive Westwerk was reconstructed by Frederick I with flanking towers at either side of its great central tower in which there was a dome over the *palatium regale* and an apsidal bay in the center of the tribune gallery.

One has only to look at the reconstruction of Sint Servaas (Fig. 123) as it was to see how the exalted and godlike appearance of the Barbarossa was made apparent when he was enthroned in front of the circular sun-window in the apsidal chapel of the gallery, while the chanting of his angel choir coming down from the lofty tribune under its heavenly dome and in front of the cruciform window of Christ was like "the choirs beyond the vault of heaven," which Eusebius speaks of in his "Oration in praise of Constantine." The German emperor and his people were undoubtedly fully aware of the celestial implications of the ancient ceremonial tradition which presented the ruler as a heavenly being praised by singers. During the celebration of the Feast of Charlemagne, whose canonization and cult had been instituted by Frederick I as a means of affirming the royal dogma of the Staufen, the *Antiennes* in the Office at Aachen referred to the "Angelici chori . . . inter chorus angelorum coronatus" and

[60] G. H. Williams, *Harvard Theological Studies,* XVIII, 1951, pp. 165-194.

[61] W. Rave, "Sint Servaas zu Maastricht und die Westwerkfrage," *Westfälen Jahrb.,* XXII, 1937, pp. 49-75, Abb. 1 (façade), 2 (plan), 3 (restoration of interior), 9 (section); Fuchs, *Zeitschrift,* p. 274.

the *Hymn* reiterated the old imperial doctrine, "O Rex orbis triumphator, terrae regnum imperator."[62]

It requires more than the history of the advanced church in the West to understand why the architectural provisions of Sint Servaas, as Rave has written, were "a monumental expression of all the worldly and spiritual might that was united in the hands of the great Lord of the First Reich." Actually it is necessary to go back to Aachen and realize not only that the development of the towered façade in the West was a continuation of an imperial tradition, but that there was a direct relation between the Carolingian Westwerk and the palace architecture of Constantinople. That we are dealing with imperial forms and customs, which began to be established in the time of Constantine, becomes more apparent when it is realized: first, that the Palatine Chapels in the West were the result of a conscious desire on the part of Charlemagne and his successors to appropriate the palace ritual and architectural precedents of the Byzantine Court; second, that the towered gateway façade with cupolas was a long established symbol of the *Sacrum palatium* in Byzantium; and, third, that there was an exact parallel between the Western emperor, elevated in his chapel under an angelic tower over the Royal Door of his abbey churches, and the Byzantine Basileus seated under his domical parakyptikon in the tribune over the entrance to his palace-churches.

Already Grabar has shown that when Charlemagne built his Palace Chapel in honor of the Virgin, and at the entrance constructed a Westwerk dedicated to the Savior with a concave *porta regia* flanked by round towers and in it a tribune for the imperial throne, he had in mind some one of the buildings in the Great Palace at Constantinople, perhaps the very special imperial chapel called the "Virgin of the Lighthouse" which was built sometime before A.D. 768 by the iconoclastic Emperor Constantine Kopronymos.[63] While little is known about the plan of the Virgin of the Lighthouse, it is significant that Western travelers referred to the eighth century sanctuary, whose name implies that it was distinguished by towers, as *Capella imperatoris* or "Sainte Chapelle des Empereurs" and that at the Byzantine Court it was called "The Guardian of the Imperial House." The question of whether the Carolingian building was based upon some early Byzantine imperial structure has been

[62] R. Folz, *Études sur le culte liturgique de Charlemagne dans les églises de l'empire*, Strasbourg, 1951, pp. 53-66. That at Sint Servaas the angelic choir, bearing lights like the stars of heaven, went up into the dome over the imperial throne in the Westwerk to sing their acclamations in honor of the Barbarossa, and that the whole Western tradition of a royal choir to chant the Laudes Regiae was either influenced by, or derived from, the choral singing of the palace ceremonies, which was probably first taken over into the services of the palace-churches at Constantinople, are indicated by the "chanted" office which is described in *Ms. Athens 2061* as having been customary in the great church of Hagia Sophia at Saloniki. In a

study of this manuscript, to be published in the next volume of the "Dumbarton Oaks Papers," Professor Oliver Strunk of Princeton University says that for the Vespers held in Hagia Sophia on the evening of September 14, "the psaltists, bearing lights, are described as going up into the dome (i.e., the gallery around the base of the dome which was accessible from the outside by steps on the roof), and it is from there that they sing their (imperial) acclamations."

[63] Grabar, *Martyrium*, I, pp. 565-567, 570ff.; Ebersolt, *Constantinople*, 1951, p. 29; R. Janin, *Les Églises et les monastères*, Paris, 1953, pp. 241-245.

settled by the excavations of Dyggve, which have shown that St. George at Saloniki was the palace chapel of Theodosius and like Charlemagne's Palatine Chapel had round towers flanking the entrance to its domical rotunda.

The way in which Charlemagne and his age visualized the palace as a sacred seat of government in terms of a towered façade is illustrated by a seventeenth century drawing of a Carolingian book illumination (Fig. 158) in which "Charlemagne," according to the inscription, is pictured seated in his palace between two court officials, the "Primicerium et Secundicerium."[64] It is the Hand of God over the head of the Emperor which emphasizes the sacred nature of the structure and the way in which the Emperor was looked upon as the "Chosen of God." In order to fit the architecture of this miniature into the Late Antique tradition and understand why the motif of domical towers had become the mark of a royal and divine residence, it is only necessary to compare it with the towered castrum, symbolizing the *palatium coeli* of the DIVUS MARCUS AURELIUS, on the third century Thracian coin (Fig. 30) and the symbolic representation of the imperial government from the World Chronicle (Fig. 157) of Alexandria.

It is again the graphic evidence which records that Charlemagne in adopting the towered façade on his buildings and seals (Fig. 81) was directly influenced by the contemporary palace architecture of the Byzantine emperors, even though this conclusion means that more importance must be attached to towers in imaginatively restoring the destroyed palaces of Constantinople. It has already been noted on the fourth century mosaics of St. George at Saloniki (Fig. 74) that flanking towers with baldachins were palatium motifs intended to depict the glories of the House of God. By the ninth century we must assume that the artist of the Homilies of Gregory of Nazianzus was following an established convention, which was comprehensible in terms of contemporary architecture, when he painted the Palace of the King of Nineveh (Fig. 73) as a castrum with domical towers. It has also been insisted that on the mosaics at Bethlehem (Fig. 75) the towered frames of the councils were meant to signify that the meetings were held either in the palace or under the authority of the *Sacrum palatium*. For the purpose, therefore, of establishing a direct link between Charlemagne's architectural ideas and Constantinople it is only necessary to compare the representation of the famous Boucoleon Palace (Fig. 159) from the History of John Skylitzes with the miniature of Charlemagne."[65]

Once it is recognized that Charlemagne was endeavoring to revive a Late Antique, or Constantinian, tradition as it had survived at Constantinople, then it seems most unlikely that St. Vitale was the prototype of his Palatine Chapel. Instead there is the probability that both the church at Ravenna and the sanctuary at Aachen were some-

---

[64] This engraving of 1610, which was published by P. E. Schramm (*Die deutschen Kaiser und Königer im Bildern Ihren Zeit*, 1928, p. 40, Abb. 10ᶜ), instead of being copied from a lost manuscript and depicting Charlemagne, as it says, was probably copied from a representation of Louis the Fat in an unspecified Carolingian manuscript in the Bibl. Nat. in Paris that has been published by L. Salvatorelli, *L'Italia mediovale*, Milan, 1939, p. 451, fig. 294.

[65] L. de Beylié, *L'Habitation byzantin*, 1902, p. 136.

what parallel examples of the influence of early Byzantine palace forms upon church architecture.[66] Since St. Vitale was the palace chapel of the Exarchate there is a strong presumption that the round structures, which once flanked the narthex, giving access by circular stairwells to the tribune, and are still at either side of the apse, were originally built up as towers to show the imperial distinction of the church, but were later either removed or turned into reliquary chapels when Ravenna came under the control of the Roman Church. It is, however, the palace-church at Preslau (Fig. 163) which furnishes the most conclusive evidence that the basic form of Charlemagne's Chapel and the Carolingian use of the towered façade as a palatium motif must have been taken over from some one of the buildings of the Great Palace at Constantinople.

The church at Preslau was located within the walled stronghold of the palace which was in the center of the city. It was built around the beginning of the tenth century at the time when Preslau was the residence of the Bulgarian emperor and when the architecture, art, and everything connected with the Bulgarian capital was being modeled after the precedents of the Byzantine Court.[67] Since the building was presumably designed and constructed by Byzantine craftsmen, it is not surprising that its domical naos surrounded by apsidal niches should recall both St. Vitale at Ravenna and the Chrysotriclinos (Fig. 122) at Constantinople. What is more important in explaining the sources from which Charlemagne derived his architectural ideas is the deep narthex of this church which was like a Carolingian Westwerk not only in the way it had a tribune for the ruler at the gallery level, but also in the fact that its façade was flanked by great circular towers. The court in front of the church had a fountain and was entered through a massive gateway, the plan of which suggests that it either had a domical vestibule or was like the triumphal arch on the interior. That the towered façade and tribune both at Preslau and at the entrance to the Carolingian royal abbeys were features of the palace tradition, intended to make evident the "supreme dignity of a universal souverain," will become more apparent in a later chapter of this study when they are seen in relation to the ceremonial provisions for the Byzantine Basileus in the palace-churches.

B. PALATIUM AND GATEWAY SYMBOLISM ON RULER COINS AND SEALS

The graphic key to the mediaeval architectural symbolism is the coins and seals of the Carolingian, Ottonian, and Hohenstaufen emperors on which the whole Antique pattern of motifs—towered gateway, palace-castrum, cupolas, globes, baldachins and

[66] Although no one has suggested that the round chapels flanking the apse of St. Vitale may have originally been towers, it has always been known that there were round towers, flanking the narthex, which gave access to the galleries (R. Bartoccini, *Felix Ravenna*, XXXVIII, 1931, pp. 71-101; LI, 1932, pp. 133-165; G. Jonescu, *Felix Ravenna*, LIII, 1934, pp. 37-57). While O. G. von Simson (*Sacred Fortress*, Chicago, 1948, pp. 35-37) and others have pointed out that St. Vitale was built and decorated as an expression of the "grandiose theodicy of Jus-

tinian's imperium" and a pictorial assertion of his sanctity as both emperor and a "Christ-like high priest," I do not recall any insistence upon the obvious presumption that St. Vitale was the palace-church of the Exarchate.

[67] Grabar, *op.cit.*, pp. 247-248, 567; K. Miatev, *Byz. Zeit.*, XXX, 1929-30, pp. 561ff.; for the Byzantine influence at the Bulgarian Court see J. Ebersolt, *Constantinople*, p. 6 and A. Rambaud, *Études sur l'histoire byzantine*, Paris, 1912, p. 284.

stars—were revived as a visible assertion of the rulers' claims to the divine and universal heritage of the Roman Augustus. Customarily the coins of Charlemagne bore on the reverse a crude representation of a gabled and columnar building, which has been variously interpreted as the Church, St. Peter's at Rome, the *Templum urbis*, and the Palatium. It is most improbable that it stood for St. Peter's where Charlemagne's unannounced and not entirely welcomed coronation by the Pope took place, because the one church in which he would have been interested was "Constantine's church," St. Savior of the Lateran, which was later rededicated to the Baptist. It seems most likely that Charlemagne chose the templelike structure because it was a traditional Roman form which expressed his imperial policy without antagonizing the Pope. To oversimplify a forthcoming study of these coins by J. Gaehde, there is convincing evidence to show that the building had the explicit meaning of the *Templum urbis* and at the same time the implicit meaning of Palatium in the conceptual sense that the Imperial Palace was a *templum* and the residence of a godlike sovereign who governed the Empire.

For his seal (Fig. 81), however, which he had struck shortly after his coronation in A.D. 800 he took the legend RENOVATIO ROMAN-IMP, the towered gateway with the title ROMA beneath it and over this Roman symbol of a castrum-palatium a cross in place of the *regale vexillam*, which had been so prominent on the similar Constantian coins (Fig. 42) of Treves.[68] The idea of *Renovatio Imperii*, which had been of great political importance during the troubled years of the Late Empire, had again acquired a far-reaching appeal at the beginning of the Carolingian period.[69] This concept on Roman coins was always represented by a gabled temple, the *Templum urbis*, because the faith in renewal of the Majesty of Rome was based upon the belief in *Roma aeterna*, which was a tenet of the old religion pertaining to the *Natalis* of the city and celebrated in combination with the emperor-cult in the Temple of Venus and Rome.[70] Following the conversion of Constantine, the triumph of Christianity, and the growing pre-eminence of the Church of Rome, this pagan doctrine of *Renovatio* had come to mean a rebirth and a new era in which *Aurea Roma*, now the city of the Apostles Peter and Paul, was the earthly City of God and the capital of the *orbis Christianus*. At the same time "Roma" still had the conceptual significance of being the dwelling place of the Imperator, for Charlemagne in his palatium insisted that Aachen was a "Roma secunda" and re-enunciated the pagan doctrine that, "Where the head of the world is, this place shall be called Rome."[71]

It was not solely because he had placed the *Templum urbis* on his coins that he did

[68] P. E. Schramm, *Deutschen Kaiser und Könige in Bildern ihren Zeit*, I, 1928, p. 33. Abb. 7/6.

[69] Schramm, "Kaiser, Rom und Renovatio," *Studien der Bibliothek Warburg*, XVII, 1929; Bandmann, *op.cit.*, p. 53.

[70] J. Gagé, "Le 'templum urbis' et les origines de l'idée de renovatio," *Annuaire de l'inst. de phil. et d'hist. orientales et slaves*, IV, 1936, pp. 151-186; "Saeculum Novum," *Transactions of the International Numismatic Congress, 1936*, London, 1938, pp. 179-186.

[71] Kantorowicz, *Laudes Regiae*, p. 63; the concept of Aachen as a "Roma Secunda" is voiced in a poem of A.D. 799 referring to Charlemagne as the "Rex Pater Europae" and to Leo III as "Summus Leo Pater in orbe" (*M.G.H.*, *Poetae*, I, pp. 366-379) and in the poem of Modoinus (*Ibid.*, p. 386).

not follow Roman precedent in illustrating RENOVATIO and ROMA. The new Christian Emperor, whose coming to power was intended to be received with the salvational promise of an ancient Epiphany, knew that the towered gateway had been a symbol of the *Sacrum palatium* on the Constantinian coins and was universally recognized as the place ceremonially associated with the triumphal Advent of a *Restitutor orbis, Pacator orbis* and *Pater orbis*. The motif of the towered gateway, with the exceptions of its use by Pepin, the King of Italy, on the coins of Pavia and by Ludwig I in the ninth century, does not reappear during the Carolingian period, partly because the *Templum* had come to represent the Palatium and largely because the Carolingian rulers in their dealings with the papacy in Italy did not for the most part endeavor to precipitate issues by the symbolism on their coins.[72]

It was not until the eleventh century, beginning with Conrad II and Henry III and continuing during the critical period down to the middle of the thirteenth century when the conflicting claims of emperors and popes to *Sacerdos et Imperator* swayed the mediaeval world, that the motif, again in combination with celestial domes and their symbolically equivalent globes, became an important means of asserting political and religious policies on the royal seals and coins throughout northern Europe. The Roman numismatic symbolism appears to have been at first revived on the imperial seals and then transferred to the episcopal coins before being adopted on the imperial coins. It is not always clear as to the exact meanings which the emperors and bishops intended to be read into their deliberate exploitation of Roman palatium motifs. Not only was the mediaeval mind accustomed to read more than one meaning into its graphic imagery, but also in the case of this particular kind of propaganda the interrelationship of the ideas involved allowed of different interpretations.

The Palatium, it has been seen, was a concept rather than a specific building, which implied a universal and divine power that came from God and was made manifest in the person of the ruler. Therefore, such imperial symbolism as the towered portal, jeweled walls, royal arcade, and domical structure within the bulwarks could denote an *aula Regia*, a royal city, the powers a Bishop derived from the Crown, the Church, and also *Aurea Roma* in either its specific or universal sense. For the same reasons that they had stood for *Providentia* and *Virtus militum* on the coins of the fourth century, the palatium motifs, regardless of whether they were intended to represent the Sacred Palace, the Royal House of God, or the *Porta coeli* as guarded by the Archangel Michael and the Emperor, were at the same time a means of picturing Heaven, for it made little difference to their celestial meaning if they were seen as the *Divus Burg* of God's earthly Vicar, as the Church of Christ, or as the stronghold of God's Celestial City. A cursory review of the numismatic evidence shows that, even when the particular meaning may be obscure, the iconography usually pertained to the controversial distinctions between the *Imperator coelestis* and the *Imperator terranum*,

---

[72] A. Blanchet and A. Dieudonné, *Manuel de numismatique français*, I, 1913, p. 341; E. Gabriel, *Les Monnaies de France sous le race Carolingienne,* II, 1884, p. 39; H. E. Cappe, *Die Münzen der deutschen Kaiser und Könige des Mittelalters,* I, 1884-1850, no. 33, pl. XX/327.

which involved the all-important issue of whether the northern ruler, rather than the Pope, was like his Roman predecessors and Byzantine contemporaries in being God's representative and hence the personification of the "Father of the World."

Before the significance of the buildings with domical towers, which look like churches on both the episcopal and imperial coins, can be understood it is necessary to keep in mind the conceptual relation of the Palatium to the Westwerk of the churches, the desire of the "Palace clergy" to show on their episcopal coins the distinction of their royal abbeys as imperial seats, and the larger problem of representing the authority of the Palatium over the Church. As long as the basic issue in the struggle between the crown and papacy involved the question of whether the emperor derived his divine authority direct from God or whether the king was "liegeman to the pope" and "by him is granted the crown," as it was stated in an inscription on the Lateran Palace, it was essential for men to see in the palace a sacred edifice, comparable to a church, in which the emperor was inspired by the Hand of God. The fundamental idea, therefore, underlying the numismatic symbolism was the traditional Roman, Byzantine, and Carolingian concept of the Palatium as a *Templum* through which worked the will of God. Even as late as the twelfth century this tradition is still voiced in Rahewin's continuation of "The Deeds of Frederick Barbarossa" where he is describing a typical military camp.[73] Having told how it was laid out in the Roman manner and divided "into accurately measured quarters" by means of streets and gates, he goes on to write, "In the center is the tent of the duke or prince, very much like a temple."

On the bulla of Conrad II and Henry III, dating between A.D. 1033-1038 and inscribed AUREA ROMA, it has already been pointed out by Bandmann that the jeweled walls, the flanking towers crowned with cupolas, and the gabled hall with its tower were meant to represent the *aula Regia*, which in turn stood for imperial rule over the Holy Roman Empire and the protection responsible for the new glories of AUREA ROMA.[74] Later Henry III, after he had become sole ruler and was dealing firmly with the Church, issued a coin (Fig. 82) at Duisberg which bears the inscription DIVS BURG and depicts a gabled building with an entrance tower, little cupolas on the roof and a star above it.[75] Although these cupolas in combination with the sun recall the *skene* baldachins over the palace-castrum on the Constantinian coins (Figs. 41, 44), one might hesitate to identify this divine stronghold as a *palatium regale*, instead of as a church, if it had not been seen that similar cupolas were used throughout the Middle Ages

[73] Otto of Frising, *The Deeds of Frederick Barbarossa* (trans. C. C. Mierow), 1953, Book III, 1, p. 233.

[74] Bandmann, *op.cit.*, pp. 101-102, pl. IV/3; it bears the legend *Roma caput mundi regit orbis frena rotundi.*

[75] Cappe, *op.cit.*, I, no. 479, pl. XIX/309; H. Dannenberg, *Die deutschen Münzen der Sächsischen und Fränkischen Kaiserzeit*, II, 1894, p. 584, pl. LXX/1514. The convention of placing little domes, or towers with cupolas, over the gable of a build-

ing to show that it was a royal structure was common in Ottonian manuscripts; in the Book of Pericopes of Henry III (A. Goldschmidt, *German Illumination*, II, 1928, fig. 52) the domical towers of a royal castrum are grouped together on the gable to show that the "Preparation of the Manuscript" took place in the Royal Scriptorium; and in the *Codex Aureus* from Madrid (*op.cit.*, fig. 58) the same grouping of domical towers is seen on the Royal Abbey in which the Virgin is enthroned with Henry III and his wife.

in both the East and the West to designate a kingly and divine residence. They occur over the royal house of God on the mosaics of Saloniki (Fig. 74) and in the Menologium of Basil II (Fig. 125), over the Byzantine Emperor enthroned in his palace (Figs. 162, 164), over the throne-room of Harold (Fig. 53) on the Bayeux tapestry, and were customarily used to designate both a royal residence and royal abbey in German illuminations.

First used as a new type by Henry III on his coins of Arnstadt,[76] but illustrated here by an issue (Fig. 84) of Henry IV (A.D. 1056-1106) the royal *fastigium* and flanking domical towers which frame the head of the Emperor were intended to represent the *Sacrum palatium.*[77] Even if it had not already been seen in the World Chronicle of Alexandria (Fig. 157), on the imperial Thracian coins (Figs. 20-30) and in the Byzantine illuminations (Fig. 159) that a towered gateway with cupolas denoted a seat of government, the conceptual intent of the German coin is made apparent by a scene of a Carolingian emperor in his palace. The mediaeval illumination (Fig. 158), which is preserved in this seventeenth century engraving, pictures "Charlemagne" seated with two court officials, his *Primicerium* and *Secundicerium*, between the two domical towers and within the enclosing wall of his palace.[78] The Hand of God over his head is in itself proof that the towered façade with its cupolas represented the *Sacrum palatium.*

In fact the symbolic indication of the presence of God in the Carolingian palace recalls the "Portico of the Hand of God" which was at the entrance to the Augusteus, the great Hall of Appearances that Constantine built in his palace at Constantinople. Other variations of this iconography are: a coin of Conrad III (A.D. 1138-1152), which has the Hand of God and a star over the royal head flanked by towers;[79] a coin of Henry VI (A.D. 1190-1197), picturing the crusading monarch on horseback between two domical towers;[80] and a still later coin of the Markgraf von Brandenburg (A.D. 1200), which has Otto armed with a great sword standing between domical towers.[81] In view of this sequence it is possible to insist that the towered façade still had much the same divine and heavenly implications that it had as a frame for the DIVUS MARCUS AURELIUS (Fig. 30) on the Thracian coin, and also that the motif on the coin of Henry IV signified that the Emperor in the seat of government spoke for God, as did the Evangelist who sits in the Gate of Heaven (Fig. 68) on the Carolingian ivory.

Since the western façade of the imperial churches was itself a palatium symbol, it is not surprising that the particular building denoting the *aula Regia* on the metal bulla of Henry IV (Fig. 83) was copied directly from the earlier coins of Archbishop Sigwin (A.D. 1079-1089) of Cologne.[82] It was the distinction of "Sancta Cologna" that its archbishop, who was traditionally a member of the "Palace clergy," had the privilege of crowning the emperor. Therefore, Sigwin's intent in using this palatium

---

[76] Dannenberg, *op.cit.*, II, p. 665, pl. XXXIII/1664.
[77] Cappe, *op.cit.*, I, no. 585, pl. XIX/311; another of Henry IV from Halberstadt (Dannenberg, II, p. 623, pl. LXXV/1565).
[78] See Ch. III n. 64.

[79] Cappe, II, no. 3, pl. II/3.
[80] *Ibid.*, no. 130, pl. IX/73.
[81] *Ibid.*, no. 165, pl. XIV/126.
[82] Bandmann, *op.cit.*, p. 101, pl. V/4.

motif is indicated by the way in which he had the flanking towers on his coins crowned, not with cupolas, but with actual crowns surmounted by the usual global finial.[83] The feature of the building on the bulla of Henry which is most important to a study of imperial ceremonies in relation to gateway symbolism is the cupola, or baldachin, that is given so much emphasis over the portal. This ciboriumlike covering over the gateway, which seems to have been peculiar to the coins issued at Cologne, was again used with some modifications by Archbishop Frederick I (A.D. 1100-1131) on his episcopal coins,[84] by the Emperor Frederick I (Fig. 87) who copied it with several variations in the details,[85] and by the Emperor Frederick II.[86] It has already been noted that in the East a tent of appearances, or canopy of distinction, was carried over a god-image at the time of his seasonal coming to a city and was erected over a king when he was enthroned at a palace and city-gate. In the subsequent chapters it will be seen that a domical ciborium was a heavenly covering over a divine king in the Hellenistic Epiphanies, and that domical vestibules were used at the entrance to Roman and Byzantine palaces for royal receptions which resembled the Hellenistic Epiphany and Roman Adventus. For the present it will suffice to indicate that the domical portals on the German coins belong to a common palace tradition, which had survived in the mediaeval West and East, if we compare the palace entrance on the bulla of Henry IV with the imperial parakyptikon over the portal of the Byzantine palace-church of St. Savior Pantokrator (Fig. 140) at Constantinople.

The conscious complexity of this numismatic use of traditional emblems is illustrated first by the coins of Frederick I,[87] and then by an example of Henry VI (Fig. 89), which have the *regale vexillum* either over or in the entrance, and which also present above the domical gateway a large umbrellalike dome rising heavenward over the towered stronghold.[88] At this time an *umbella*, which was traditionally a mark of distinction over a divine ruler in the East and thought to have been an insigne of Constantine, was a figurative term, the equivalent of *coelum*, that was sometimes applied to the ciborium over the mystical throne of Christ.[89] At the same time the "Day Star," which was given so much importance on the Constantinian coins, had continued to be associated with the Basileus in the Byzantine ceremonies and still referred to the emperor as the *Lux mundi*, is another example of how every numismatic detail had a studied purpose, because coinage was still the most effective form of political propaganda.

The underlying political content of this numismatic symbolism is most clearly

[83] Dannenberg, *op.cit.*, p. 171, pl. 17/407; W. Hävernich, *Die Münzen von Köln*, I, 1935, pl. II/390, b, c, d. Crowns also appear on a denar of Archbishop Hermann II (E. Lehr, *Numismatique de l'Alsace*, 1887, pl. II/390,b) and on some royal coins (Cappe, *op.cit.*, I, no. 603, pl. VIII/123 and no. 642, pl. II/145).

[84] Hävernich, *op.cit.*, pl. XII/455b, 431a, 432, 433a.

[85] Cappe, *op.cit.*, I, no. 634, pl. IX/140; Hävernich, pl. 48/544, 546, 547, 560.

[86] C. J. Gotz, *Deutschlands Kaiser-Münzen des Mittelalters*, 1827, pl. XXXVII/447.

[87] Cappe, *op.cit.*, I, no. 634, pl. IX/140 and Hävernich, *op.cit.*, Taf. 48/544, 546; a coin of Archbishop Frederick I (Hävernich, *op.cit.*, Taf. 12/455b).

[88] Cappe, *op.cit.*, I, no. 656, pl. XIX/313; also Frederick II (Gotz, *op.cit.*, pl. XXXVII/447).

[89] For use of *umbella* and *coelum* for a ciborium (J. Braun, *Der Christliche Altar*, II, 1924, p. 207).

illustrated by the way the designers were obviously instructed to make use of every possible change in the treatment of the crowning cupolas on the palatium towers. Ever since the third century gateway cupolas had been a mark of imperial presence, and by the time of Diocletian the *skene-sphairos* over the castrum-palatium gateway referred to the politically important concept of *urbs et orbis*. The reason the German die-cutters followed Constantinian precedent in making the cupolas either bulbous or global was in part to show the celestial nature and terrestrial power of the emperor, but primarily to revive the Roman contention that the Palatium stood for imperial domination over the City and the World. Sometimes, it has been noted, they even made the cupolas into specific crowns on the coins of the emperor, but more especially on those of the archbishops of Cologne who recognized in the emperor a "Summus episcopus." All these variations in the treatment of the cupolas mean that some explanation, other than the fancy of the designer, must be found for the way in which the four towers of the royal castrum on a coin of Henry III look like candles giving forth light, and on the coin of Henry VI (Fig. 89) the towers guarding the entrance to the stronghold of earthly and heavenly authority appear to be beacons.[90]

Back of this iconographic variation was the imperial tradition of the sun and moon as symbols of universal rule. Earlier during the Middle Ages the Frankish emperors were referred to as *Luminaria mundi*, just as Christ was the *Lux mundi*, Constantine was called *Lux aurea mundi* and Justinian was praised as the *Lux urbis et orbis*. During the eleventh century the Western emperors made a vigorous effort to revive the imperial sun symbolism as a figurative and graphic means of asserting their now disputed claims to being comparable to a Roman kosmokrator. This new interest was probably initiated at the Ottonian Court by Theophano, the daughter of the Byzantine Emperor Romanus I, and was at first encouraged by her son Otto III, whose use of the legend RENOVATIO IMPERII ROMANI on his seals exemplifies his efforts to reinstitute imperial ceremonies at Rome.[91] Before the end of the Romanesque period Otto's successors officially recognized and gave artistic expression to the conception that "Solus imperator est," as it was bluntly stated in the *Libellus de Cerimoniis aule imperatoris*.[92] Not only did the German kings wear the traditional cosmic mantle of a world ruler, but on his coins Henry III had himself presented like Constantine wearing the Helios crown of a *Divus Augustus*.[93]

[90] Henry III (Cappe, I, no. 483, pl. XVII/283).

[91] For the imperial sun symbolism and the designation of the emperors as *Luminaria mundi*: Schramm, *Die deutschen Kaiser*, I, pp. 125ff.; P. Kampers, *Von Verdegange der abendländischen Kaisermystick*, pp. 2-9, 12-27. A miniature in *Cod. Vat. lat. 4939* pictures Otto III in traditional sun chariot being blessed by a bishop (A. Brendell, *Die Antike*, XII, 1936, p. 280, Taf. 15); L'Orange in his *Studies on the Iconography of Cosmic Kingship*, p. 113, fig. 22, compares the illumination to the sun symbolism at the Byzantine Court; according to F. Kern (*Kingship and Law*, p. 67)

Peter of Elboli called Henry VI "resounding Jupiter, the Sun-god."

[92] The *Libellus de ceremoniis* was part of the *Graphia aurea Urbis Romae* (Schramm, *Kaiser, Rom und Renovatio*, II, p. 102). In his analysis Schramm (*op.cit.*, I, pp. 194-215) shows that although the work was written at Rome about A.D. 1155 it was based upon much earlier sources compiled at Rome about A.D. 1030.

[93] Schramm, *Die deutschen Kaiser*, p. 116, Abb. 91/o-p; and Cappe, *op.cit.*, I, pl. v/81 and no. 512, pl. XXII/372.

The old imperial sun symbolism, which Constantine had preserved and so success-fully made a manifestation of a Christian emperor that it had persisted for centuries at the Byzantine Court, had continued to be a means of insisting that a supernatural and mystic power came from anointment and went with the Crown. It still expressed that transfiguring idea of kingship, as an all-pervading and guiding illumination, which Eusebius had voiced in his "Oration" when he described Constantine as, "supreme and pre-eminent Ruler of the Universe, He shares the glory of His Father's Kingdom, for he is that Light, which, transcending above the universe, encircles the Father's Person," directing, "in imitation of God himself, the administration of the world's affairs." Hence, before the end of the twelfth century, its revival in the West made the numismatic convention of presenting the towers over the palatium as celestial lights a conscious reference to the bitterly contended issue of whether it was the Emperor or the Pope who reflected the full radiance of God.

The counter claim that the sun and moon were the two luminaries of the Church Universal had been voiced as early as the ninth century; and at that time expressed the papal policy, which was to be continued throughout the Middle Ages, of ap-propriating for the Pope and Church everything that had formerly been used to show the universal supremacy of the Roman Imperator.[94] Finally it was Innocent III who, in his effort to combat the imperial claims to all that was implied by *Luminaria mundi*, took a simile of Gregory VII for his famous decretal in which he announced that, "God has set into the firmament of Heaven, that is the Universal Church, two lights that are the two great dignitaries, the pontifical and royal authorities," and then went on to draw the anti-imperial conclusion that, "as the Sun, which presides over the day is greater than the Moon, which presides over the night, so is the Pontiff greater than the King."[95]

This papal effort to dim the emperor's Roman heritage of celestial glory and counter what had been his distinction in the Carolingian litany of being *Lux et vita nostra*, while consistent with Innocent's policy of *Imitatio imperialis*, could not be ignored by the northern rulers. The opposing claim that the lights, like domes and globes, were traditional symbols of imperial authority over *urbs et orbis* can be seen on the coins of Otto IV (Figs. 90, 91) in the way that the towers are presented as radiant luminaries, "Lights and protectors of the Empire," as the emperors were called.[96]

[94] Schramm, *Kaiser, Rom und Renovatio*, I, pp. 124-125 and II, p. 64.

[95] Decretal of Innocent III (A. J. Carlyle, *A History of Mediaeval Political Theory*, II, 1909, p. 215). Bryce (*The Holy Roman Empire*, 1889, p. 109) says in reference to Psalm 72, "They shall fear thee as long as the sun and moon endure," that "the moon being, of course, since Gregory VII, the Holy Roman Empire, as the sun, or greater-light, is the Popedom": he quotes from a letter of Gregory to William the Conqueror (p. 154), "God hath disposed the sun and moon, lights that outshine all other" and "provided in the apostolic and royal dignities the means of ruling it"; he refers (p. 359) to the famous simile of Greg-ory VII in which the Pope compares the Empire and the Popedom to the "two lights in the firma-ment of the church militant," the rays of the moon, or Empire, being borrowed and feeble, while the sun, or Papacy, shines with unquenchable bril-liancy; and earlier (p. 275 n. 1) he says that the analogy between the lights of heaven and the po-tentates on earth "seem to have originated with Gregory VII."

[96] Fig. 90 (Cappe, *op.cit.*, II, no. 565, pl. xxv/265) and Fig. 91 (Cappe, II, no. 568, pl. xxv/288). For Otto IV's interest in sun and moon symbolism see Kampers, *op.cit.*, pp. 2-9.

When these two coins are compared with another of Otto IV (Fig. 92), which is in-scribed OTTO ROMANORUM REX AUG and has a large sun in the portal, it becomes apparent that this age thought of lights, globes, cupolas, and crowns on the towers as royal emblems with much the same cosmic and universal significance.[97] At the same time this means of identifying the German Emperor with the lights "in the firmament of Heaven" suggests that the two stars flanking the gateway on the coin of Frederick I (Fig. 87) had the same implication; and they also indicate a parallel between Fred-erick's coin and the coin of Maximianus (Fig. 37), minted at Treves, which has two imperial stars over the castrum portal.

During the twelfth century the gateway motif, whose celestial symbolism originated in the Orient, was taken back to the East by the Crusaders and given prominence on the seals (Figs. 94-97) of the Latin Kings of Jerusalem.[98] The new masters of Sion chose for their dominant emblem the Gate of David for several reasons: first, because it had stood since Old Testament days for the earthly and heavenly Jerusalem; second, because it had always been synonymous with the seat of government and was again the citadel and royal residence of the Latin Kings; and, third, because it exemplified the old Frankish doctrine that the Christian king was a "Novus David," like the Biblical king who had been the "Son," the "Chosen of God," and the "Messiah" destined to reunite the people under his rule.[99] At either side of the King's Gate, they presented the Holy Sepulchre and the Templum Domini in heraldic symmetry, somewhat like the cupolas on the Constantinian coins. Up until the reign of Baldwin V (A.D. 1183-1185) they always placed the Templum on the right. Then they shifted the position of the two domes in relation to the gateway, and so emphasized the oculus of the Holy Sepulchre that it resembled a crescent moon in contrast to the Cross of Christ over the headquarters of the Knights Templars.

As yet no political or ideological explanation has been advanced to account for the shift of the Templum from the right to the left of the King's Gate and for the obvious play upon sun and moon symbolism, which had already been given marked prominence upon the earlier seals (Fig. 96), like the one of Baldwin II as Lord of Ramah.[100] One is tempted to see on the seals a reference to the sun and moon analogy as it pertained to the relative importance of the two lights in the firmament of the Universal Church. This inference would explain the marked distortion of the two domes on the royal seal (Fig. 97) of Jean de Brienne (A.D. 1210-1212), who was far from being a supporter of papal authority, and suggests that the way in which the dome of the Temple of the

[97] Cappe, II, no. 567, pl. xxv/287.

[98] Fig. 72 (de Vogüé, *Les Églises de la Terre Sainte*, p. 452; Schlumberger, *Sigillographie de l'orient Latin*, nos. 9, 10); Fig. 73 (Schlumberger, pl. xvi/5).

[99] Kantorowicz, *Laudes Regiae*, pp. 56-62. By identifying themselves with the Old Testament king the mediaeval rulers had Biblical precedent for their ideas of kingship, because the Davidic king, in addition to being the "Anointed" of Jah-weh and the "Messiah," was also the life force of his people in that he was the "Son" of the national deity (A. R. Johnson, "The Role of the King in the Jerusalem Cultus," *The Labyrinth*, 1935, pp. 78-80). For the history of the Tower of David see C. N. Johns, "The Citadel, Jerusalem," *The Quarterly of the Dept. of Antiq. in Jerusalem*, xv, 1950, pp. 163-167.

[100] Schlumberger, *op.cit.*, pl. xix/3.

Lord is made to resemble a globe was intended to refer to the Templars' claim to military command "of the earth and Jerusalem"; but there still remains the disquieting question of why the Holy Sepulchre by means of the crescent shape of its oculus should have been associated with the minor luminary.[101] Even if we are hesitant to accept these inferences, the Crusader seals prove the survival of imperial Roman symbolism in the way the designers at first used royal cupolas over the Tower of David and then on the later seals stylized them into globes.

Returning to the numismatic evidence on the coins of the Western emperors, the political and religious ideas, which gave so much content to the gateway and palatium motifs with their orbis domes, lights, and baldachins, become more apparent when the Hohenstaufen emperors began to bring the issues out into the open. Of all the masters of the Holy Roman Empire they were the boldest in asserting by means of their seals and coins that the *orbis Christianus* came within the *orbis Romanorum* and that their numismatic emblems were a graphic manifestation, as they had been on the Roman coins, that the Palatium had domination over the City and the World. Taken alone the coin of Henry VI (Fig. 88) does not make it clear whether the exaggeratedly large orbis over the dome in the center refers to the Universal Church within the ramparts, or to the Emperor's own Christlike and imperial supremacy over the world.[102] There is no question, however, about the intent of the symbolism and the whole theocratic conception of the ruler as the *Imago Dei*, who "was sent from Heaven," on the bulla (Fig. 85) of Frederick I.[103] Instead of any cupola, which might be considered to be the ciborium of Christ, it presents the Emperor himself inside the ramparts of the City of God, its towers crowned with great bulbous and globelike domes. It is also Frederick I who is shown on his coins (Fig. 86) wearing the divine nimbus and enthroned like the Son of God beneath the Heavenly City, which is like a *Sacrum palatium* with towers that emanate light.[104]

Frederick's aspiration and determination to revive the imperial prestige of his Carolingian and Roman predecessors is reflected in the poem of Rahewin in which he is addressed as the *christus Domini*, the "New Charlemagne," and which reads, "Hail, master of the world, our Caesar, we salute you, whose domination is sweet to the world."[105] Later it was his grandson, Frederick II, who made it apparent to all men that, "What God is in Heaven, that is what the Emperor is on earth."[106] Therefore, the way in which this great Emperor, whom many called the "Antichrist," is portrayed on his coins (Fig. 93) supporting with his own hands the canopy of the heavenly Palatium reveals what had been uppermost in the minds of so many of the northern monarchs ever since they had revived the Roman symbolism.[107]

[101] *Ibid.*, pl. 1/3.

[102] Cappe, I, no. 655, pl. XVI/259.

[103] O. Posse, *Siegel der deutschen Kaiser und Könige*, Dresden, 1909, I, pl. 21/3, 4. For emperor as *Imago Dei* see Schramm, *Kaiser, Rom und Renovatio*, pp. 225-280.

[104] Cappe, I, no. 636, pl. IX/141.

[105] R. Folz, *Le Souvenir et la legende de Charle-* magne, 1950, p. 200. According to F. Kern (*Kingship and Law in the Middle Ages*, p. 67) the poet Godfrey of Viterbo, addressing Henry VI, chanted, "Thou art a god among a race of gods."

[106] Kantorowicz, *Frederick the Second* (Eng. trans.), 1913, p. 230.

[107] Cappe, I, no. 712, pl. IX/146.

Frederick II, who organized his state as an *Imperialis ecclesia* and more nearly than any other mediaeval ruler attained to the stature of a *Divus Augustus*, built at Capua his now destroyed Triumphal Arch, which some have thought terminated one age and ushered in another.[108] It is also the most fitting monument in the West with which to close a chapter on gateway symbolism. Only the long history of the gateway tradition and its ceremonial importance in relation to an Epiphany, the Advent of a Messiah and the reception of a Victor explain why the "Triumphator of Capua" did not copy the more customary type of Roman arch, but instead chose to build a commemorative portal with "two towers of astounding size, beauty and strength." Back of its royal arcade, that originally decorated the façade, and "between the towers, where there is the entry, high above the archway is a royal chamber (*Regium cubiculum*) adorned with marble statues and antique figures."[109]

The whole conception of this monument, including the "Royal chamber," was based upon imperial precedent, even though the most recent study of the arch dismisses Campano's evidence by saying that a *regium cubiculum* was inappropriate and must refer only to the apsidal niche in which the statue of the Emperor was placed.[110] It may have been either a commemorative chamber, like the one in the triumphal archway of Castel Nuovo at Naples with the statue of King Alfonso in it, or relatively small, like the space back of the apsidal niche of appearance over the portal of the Palace of the Exarchate (Fig. 6), but it was not inappropriate. Quite the opposite, when we recall the arcaded gallery over the Roman city-gates, the small ceremonial chamber in the Roman triumphal arches, the royal oratory over the archway at Lorsch, the "Heaven chamber" in the Porta Curia at Canterbury, Frederick's predecessors sitting over the portal in the symbolic towered façade of their Rhenish churches, the imperial chamber in the tribune of the Byzantine palace-churches, and the Abbasid and Fatimite Caliphs seated during reception ceremonies in the *majlis* over their city and palace gateways.

If a place of honor was traditional over a royal portal, then there was a *regium cubiculum* in the gateway at Capua, because Frederick was undoubtedly thinking of it in terms of the ceremonial receptions of a triumphant and deified Imperator. The archway with its towers and decorations was intended to embody the political and religious issues of the Middle Ages, expressing the antique concept of Triumph and Ruler-worship which had persisted in spite of Christianity. In describing it the *Gesta Romanorum* says in words that were a kind of mediaeval "double talk": "the Emperor Frederick constructed a curious marble gate at the entrance to Capua. It stood above a fountain of running water; the Emperor is our Lord Jesus Christ. The gateway is the Holy Church through which it is necessary to enter the Kingdom of Heaven."[111]

[108] Kantorowicz, *op.cit.*, pp. 524-527, 531-533.

[109] C. Shearer, *The Renaissance of Architecture in Southern Italy*, 1935, pp. 17, 158.

[110] C. A. Willemsen, *Kaiser Friedrichs II, Tri-* *umphator zu Capua*, Wiesbaden, 1935, pp. 30, and 88 n. 99.

[111] "De Regno Celesti," *Gesta Romanorum* (ed. H. Osterley), 1872, ch. 54, p. 349.

IV · THE IMPERIAL CIBORIUM

THROUGHOUT this study cupolas and domical ciboria, as interchangeable motifs, have repeatedly appeared in relation to city and palace gateways. This association raises a series of questions: first, as to the origin of the imperial baldachin; second, as to its emblematic significance in various types of ceremonies pertaining to the public appearances and reception of a divine ruler; and, third, why it should occur so persistently in combination with a gateway. It has already been noted that the cupolas over the gateway of the symbolic castrum portal, or Sacred palatium, on the coins of Diocletian (Figs. 33-34) at the beginning of the fourth century were conceptually ciboria, not only because of their presentation on the coins as light, open, and tentlike canopies, but also because of the way they continued to imitate the reticulations of fabrics on the mosaic of Saloniki (Fig. 74) and preserved the character of baldachins in Byzantine illuminations (Fig. 125).

That these ciboria-cupolas were emblems of the *Pater orbis* and intended to present the heavenly and cosmic nature of both the *Domus Dei* and its royal occupant is shown by the way in which they were transformed into globes on the coins of Diocletian and Constantine (Figs. 35-46), the coins and seals of the German rulers (Figs. 85-92) and on the seals of the Latin Kings of Jerusalem (Fig. 97). In fact, the whole history of the cupola surmounted by a globelike finial proves that the motif always stood for *urbis et orbis*, and hence for domination over Rome and the World, down to the time when it was made the crowning feature on the new St. Peter's.

Once the original content of this imperial symbolism is established further consideration must be given to the way in which the ciborium form was associated for over nine hundred years with city and palace gateways, and to the related question of why in the rituals, art, and ceremonies of the Middle Ages it was so commonly used in connection with ceremonies and scenes which had the traditional and salvational implications of an Epiphany. Before these issues can be resolved it is necessary to reinvestigate the origins and various uses of both the divine and royal baldachin.

The royal ciborium (Figs. 100, 101), with its rich embroideries studded with golden stars, its celestial eagles, and inlays of brilliant jewels, became, as we know, the impressive Canopy of State over the emperor at both the Byzantine and Germanic Courts. Even though it is necessary to admit that there is no incontrovertible evidence of the use of an imperial throne-tabernacle before the sixth century, it can be seen in the representation of the throne of Theodosius (Fig. 100) that we are dealing with the same combination of related emblems as occurred on the coins of Diocletian and Constantine. This becomes more apparent when the throne of Theodosius, with orbis finials on its uprights, is compared with the sixth century representation of a Byzantine throne in the *Corpus Agrimensorum Romanorum* where the uprights of the throne are capped with little cupolas, instead of globes.[1] It is also important in establishing the tent origin and *skene* concept of the royal ciborium to note on the

---

[1] Codex Palatinus, C. Thulin, *Handschriften des Corpus Agrimensorum Romanorum*, Taf. VI.

ivory from the Museo Nazionale at Florence (Fig. 101) that the baldachin over the Empress, who is now thought to be the wife of Maurice (A.D. 582-602) instead of Amalasuntha, has the global finial, the striations of a *skene* and the cusped edges which were used on Roman coins to denote the starry nature of the canopy of heaven.[2]

Any study of the baldachin and its details is confronted by the fact that there are no literary references to a Byzantine throne-baldachin before the sixth century, which has given rise to the assumption that it could not have been an established feature of the Roman palace ceremonies, but was adopted by the Byzantine rulers from the East. In spite of these prevailing conclusions some explanation must be found for the obvious relation of the imperial baldachin to the ciboria on the coins of Diocletian (Figs. 33, 34) and some consideration given to all the evidence which shows that the Byzantine Court had a profound and political interest in following Imperial precedents. The most recent theory as to the origin of the baldachin is that it was taken over from the "throne-tabernacle" of the Persian Kings.[3] So far none of the explanations regarding its origin and adoption satisfy all the evidence. If, as Alföldi has suggested, the royal ciborium was originally an Iranian throne-tabernacle, then it is necessary to account for the fact that the Achaemenid kings sat under flat canopies and that the Sassanian and later Persian kings were not enthroned under a tent-tabernacle in the audience halls of their palaces.

Another weakness of the Persian theory is that it seems to disregard the many other early Eastern traditions of a sacred tent, and hence does not relate the adoption of the royal baldachin with the long and complicated history of the divine ciborium. Furthermore, there still remains the problem of whether this suppositional "throne-tabernacle" was taken over from the Persians by the successors of Alexander the Great in their Hellenistic palaces, or by the late Roman emperors, such as Diocletian, or possibly by the early Byzantine emperors. Underlying this question is the larger issue of whether the ruler concepts and ceremonials of Diocletian's hieratic court at Nicomedia, where the solemn conventions of ruler-worship resembled the forms surrounding the Sassanian "King of Kings," were primarily derived from the Persians, for whom Diocletian had little fondness, or represented a long development and adaptation of the ancient Egyptian palace rituals which had come down to the Romans by way of the Ptolemaic kings.[4]

The problem, therefore, is to ascertain if possible, first, whether the Roman em-

---

[2] A. Grabar, *L'Empereur dans l'art byzantin*, 1936, pp. 12-13, pl. v; inasmuch as it is the contention of this study that the royal baldachin was traditionally associated with the appearances and receptions of a triumphant ruler, it is significant to find Grabar insisting that the empress on the Bargello ivory wears the robes of a Triumphator.

[3] Alföldi, "Die Geschichte des Throntabernakels," *La Nouvelle Clio*, x, 1950, pp. 537-566, and *Röm. Mittl.*, L, 1935, pp. 127-130; *Ursprung und Anwendung des Baldachins*, Amsterdam, 1939, by the ex-Kaiser Wilhelm II, is only interesting

because of the author; L. Hautecoeur, *Mystique et architecture*, pp. 129-141.

[4] J. Maurice, "Les pharaons romains," *Byzantion*, XII, 1937, pp. 103ff.; L. Bréhier, "La conception du pouvoir impérial en Orient," *Revue historique*, xcv, 1907, pp. 75-79. Among the many imperial rites which can be traced back to Egypt it is interesting to find that the celebration of the *natales imperatorum* was an annual festival at Rome, but that in Egypt the birth of the king was honored every month (*op.cit.*, p. 76).

perors took over the baldachin idea from the Hellenistic East; second, at what time during the Empire they may have adopted this oriental emblem of divinity; and, third, with what kind of ceremonies was the royal baldachin at first associated. From the outset a clear distinction must be made between the early use of the divine and celestial ciborium as an imperial emblem, customarily associated with ceremonies of reception, and what may have been its later elevation, possibly at the Byzantine Court, into a throne-tabernacle. Arguing only from the numismatic evidence already reviewed, the very fact that the ciboria-cupolas occur so commonly during the fourth century on coins issued by all the mints of the Empire is by itself a strong indication that the ciborium was already recognized in both the East and the West as an imperial symbol. It can also be argued that if the domical shape over the palace-castrum on the coins of Diocletian was a royal insigne and a mark of universal authority, comparable in concept to the baldachinlike cupolas over the Sacred Palace on the fourth century mosaics of Carthage (Figs. 65-67), then it follows that the domical towers on the Thracian coins of the third century (Figs. 20-30), and especially the baldachin over an enthroned figure between the towers on the coin of Caracalla (Fig. 22), had a similar meaning.

The tentative presumption, then, that by the beginning of the third century the ciborium, and the related cupola, had been taken over from the ceremonial heritage of the Hellenistic East is consistent with the orientalizing policy and religious aspirations of Septimius Severus and Caracalla. Both father and son would have been interested in appropriating any established insignia which would have enhanced their claims to divinity and world power, for Septimius Severus sought in every way to make the imperial family the center of the religion, while Caracalla was obsessed with the belief that he was the reincarnation of Alexander the Great. Both were influenced by Julia Domna, the wife of Septimius Severus, who, it will be recalled, was a Syrian and daughter of the ruling priest of Emessa, where the supreme sky-god was worshiped in the form of a domical baetyl that was presented on the coins as if it were a royal person under a divine umbrella.[5] Since the sacred and domical tent, like the portable umbrella, was traditionally used in the Near East for the appearances of a god or king, it is readily understood why Septimius Severus and his family would have attached symbolic importance to its domical shape on their Eastern coins. In fact, the development of domical symbolism at this time becomes more understandable when it is realized that a similar divine tent of appearances was traditionally used over an Eastern ruler when he was received as a Sun-god in the various Epiphany and Triumphal ceremonies which had come to be accorded to the Roman emperors on their campaigns and travels in the East.

It now remains to be seen whether it can be demonstrated from the available evidence that the domical baldachin was originally an essential feature of the Hellenistic Royal Epiphany and that it went back to several similar ceremonial traditions, but mainly to the Egyptian and Mesopotamian customs of setting up a king's throne, like a god's image, out-of-doors under a symbolic festival-tent for his public adoration at

---

[5] Smith, *The Dome*, pp. 72-73, figs. 126-128.

the entrance to his cities and palaces. Again, as it was with the symbolism of the towered façade, it is the persistent pattern of ideas during both Antiquity and the Middle Ages which reveals with cumulative consistency an explanation for the association of the domical canopy of reception, and the derivative domical vestibule, with the religious welcome of a godlike ruler at a city and palace gateway. Once it is recognized that the ciborium form went with the Epiphany tradition, then it is possible to see why its use in the various Adventus and Triumphal ceremonies influenced the palace architecture of Rome and Byzantium, helps to explain the appearance of the parakyptikon and domical vestibule in Byzantine palace-churches, and accounts for the baldachin over the gateway in the architectural iconography of the Middle Ages.

Through its whole history the royal ciborium, which in origin was a sacred tent, was linked up with the *skene* and domical concepts. No single study can hope to advance an explanation for its inception and development which will bridge all the gaps in the evidence and present in a neat historical sequence a complicated evolution that unquestionably involves the numerous sacred tent traditions of the East and many of the domical beliefs which were part of the Roman heritage. By the time of the Roman Empire the expressive significance of the ciborium was influenced by the ·domical ideology which, for various reasons, had come to associate the domical shape as a celestial symbol with such various types of buildings at (a) the heroön, funerary tholus, tomb, and memorial, (b) the shrine, aedicula, tempietto, and temple, and (c) the place of royal appearances, the palace vestibule, city-gate, cosmic triclinium, and throne-room.

To illustrate the complexity of the problem, one of the tent traditions, which contributed to the popularity of the *skene* motif and was a factor in the eventual adoption of the domical triclinium in Roman palaces, went back to Alexander the Great when he took over the Achaemenid "Tent of Heaven" as his military dwelling, throne covering, and banqueting pavilion, where he and his guests could feast like the gods.[6]

[6] Every warlike Eastern monarch spent much of his time during his continuous campaigns and hunting expeditions living in a sumptuous military tent, which was one of the reasons why the *skene* came to be associated with a victorious world-ruler. The large, round tents which the Achaemenid kings, such as Xerxes used for great festivals (Esther 1:5, 6) and during his attempt to conquer Greece (O. Broneer, "The Tent of Xerxes," *University of California Pub. in Classical Archaeology*, I, pp. 305ff.), were noted for their magnificence. The tent of Darius captured by Alexander is described as "worthy of admiration for its size and height" (Plutarch, *Alexander*, xx, 8). According to Hesychius the Persians' "royal tents and courts of round awnings were called Heaven." From the time when Alexander the Great "took his seat for the first time under the golden canopy (οὐρανίσκον) of the royal throne" of the Persians (Plutarch, *Alexander*, xxxvii, 4) and used their *ouraniskos* on his campaigns for the reception of envoys (Q. Curtius, *History of Alexander*, IX, 7, 15) and as a banqueting pavilion with 100 feasting couches and a throne in the midst (Aelian, *Var. hist.*, VIII, 7; IX, 3), the royal and heavenly *skene* was associated with the memory of Alexander (Plutarch, *Eumenes*, XIII, 3-4) and became a symbol of power in the Hellenistic and Roman world (Daremberg et Saglio, *Dictionnaire des antiquités*, V, "tentorium," p. 117), with the result that when Pliny (xxxiv, 8) described the statues from the tent of Alexander he referred to it as a *tabernaculum*. Whether the Achaemenid tent was taken over from the Assyrians or introduced from Central Asia is not clear, because on the Assyrian reliefs round and dome like tents appear to have been used for ritualistic purposes, while the king's tent in most instances seems to have been a rectangular and uncovered pavilion with an apse like canopy at one end (A. L. Layard, *Monuments of Nineveh*, 1853, I, pl. 77; II, pls. 24, 50; P. E. Botta, *Monuments de Nineveh*, 1849-50, pl. 146).

At that time he established one of the precedents not only for incorporating a sacred meal into the palace ceremonies of the classical ruler-cult, but also for associating a royal and oecumenical banquet with a domical tent of symbolic, cosmic dimensions. There was, however, nothing peculiarly Persian in either the feast or the domical covering. All the religions of Antiquity had heavenly feasts in which the participants were exalted by dining in the company of the gods: the *theokenia* was an ancient religious rite in Greece; by the fourth century B.C. the Greek rite of the *lectisternes* had been adopted at Rome; and in Egypt, where the successors of Alexander the Great carried on the Nilotic traditions, the religious banquet was as much a part of the sacred palace ritual and ruler-worship as it was an established feature in the temple ceremonies.[7]

Also at the time when Alexander the Great and his successors were endeavoring to immortalize themselves in the minds of their Eastern subjects by feasting like the gods in the Achaemenid royal tent, they were fully aware of the relation of this type of banquet to the Greek Hero Cult, for the Greek heroön was itself a circular structure, traditionally a tholus, or *skias* ("parasol"), which was presumably covered on the interior with a replica of the heavenly *skene* and in which the celebrants feasted with their illustrious ancestors and semidivine heroes.[8] Even at Rome more than one religious tradition contributed to the gradual adaptation of the sacred meal to the ritual of emperor-worship. It was the young Octavius who anticipated it when he enacted the role of Apollo in an Olympian repast which imitated the *lectisternium* of the Twelve Gods.[9] By the time of Domitian the old Republican *Jovis coenatio* was celebrated by the Emperor, probably in the role of Jupiter, in the rectangular and apsidal triclinium of the *Domus Augustana*. It is, therefore, most unlikely that Nero, when he introduced a spectacular domical banqueting hall into his *Domus aurea*, was imitating either the Achaemenid *ouraniskos*, or a Parthian throne-room, although the memory of Alexander's "Tent of Heaven" was presumably one of the contributing factors.

It is even more unlikely that the Persian feasting and military tent was the prototype of the royal ciborium. From what is known of its use and appearance it must have been a large, round pavilion with vertical sides and a domical covering in which there was an opening, like an oculus, in the top. It was related to the portable tents of the Scythians, the *kabitka* of the Asiatic nomads, the imperial tent-wagons used for centuries in the Chinese palace processional ceremonies, the military tent of the Chinese

[7] A. B. Cook, *Zeus*, II, 1925, p. 1170; Daremberg et Saglio, *Dict.*, III, pp. 1006-1012; W. Warde Fowler, *The Religious Experience of the Romans*, 1911, pp. 263ff., 268, 318ff.; A. Frickenhaus, "Griechische Bankethauser," *Jahrb. d. K. Arch. Inst.*, XXXII, 1917, pp. 114-130; C. Pascal, *Rivista di filol.*, XXII, 1893; Paulys-Wissowa, *R.-E.*, XII, 1924, pp. 1108-1115; F. Robiou, *Revue archéol.*, XV, 1867, p. 403.

[8] J. N. Svoronos (*Journal international d'archéologie numismatique*, IV, 1901, pp. 5-34) advances evidence to show that the Greek heroä were dom-

ical; M. Rostovtzeff ("L'Empereur Tibère et le culte impérial," *Revue historique*, CLXIII, 1930, p. 14) says that the imperial custom of banqueting on beds in a celestial rotunda under a "tholus of wood" was influenced by the Greek Cult of Heroes. F. Robert (*Thymélè*, 1939) traces the development of the heroön but minimizes the evidence that it was domical.

[9] F. Altheim, *A History of Roman Religion* (trans. H. Mattingly), 1938, p. 367.

emperors, which from ancient times was the symbolic abode of the "Son of Heaven" when he was in the field with his army, the ceremonial "yurts" of the Mongol rulers and the portable audience tents (Fig. 103) of the late Chinese emperors.[10] The ciborium, on the contrary, in all its various uses and forms as a shrine over a divine statue, a baldachin over an equally divine ruler, an insigne of authority on Roman coins and a celestial tabernacle over Christian heroes, saints, and the mystical throne of Christ, was a light, open canopy on four posts.

1. The Origin of the Ciborium

Since every ancient Eastern culture with a nomadic heritage had some tradition of both a sacred and royal tent, it is impossible to trace the origin of the ciborium back to any one country. It was in Egypt, however, that the ritualistic use of a royal tent, as a place of appearances, was of the greatest antiquity in the religious cult of the Horus-king. From the beginning of the Old Empire it was used in the ceremonies during which the Egyptian Sun-god was adored by his court and subjects. Inasmuch as the Pharaonic forms were continued by the Ptolemaic kings and hence had a very direct influence upon the rituals of emperor-worship during the Roman Empire, it would have to be assumed, even if there were no evidence, that there was some Hellenistic link between the imperial baldachin and the symbolic canopies over the Egyptian Pharaohs.

From earliest times the Egyptian king, who was adored as the "Son of the Sun" and identified with the "Master of the Sky," made his various ceremonial appearances under three types of religious shelters: the primitive *zadou* sanctuary of bundled reeds and matting, the golden pavilion at his "Window of Appearances," and the *heb-sed* tent with its four posts and curved canopy which somewhat resembled the later ciborium.[11] The *zadou* was the covering under which the king was presented as a god in one of the palace-temple ceremonies.[12] The *heb-sed* was used for his Jubilee which, somewhat like a religious Epiphany, celebrated the renewal of his divine life. At the time of this festival the king, after a rite of purification, went to the festival hall, or platform in the court, and took his seat in a prescribed order under each of the two tent canopies which signifies his relations to Upper and Lower Egypt.[13] Since this festival was celebrated throughout "the entire earth," it also consisted of the presentation and adoration of statues of the king, each under the celestial *heb-sed* canopy, in all parts of the Empire.[14] What is of even greater significance for this history of the ciborium is a papyrus of the Middle Kingdom which shows how Senwosret, when he visited his cities in a ceremonial fashion, which recalls the later Epiphany and Adventus reception of the Hellenistic kings and Roman emperors, made his public

[10] Smith, *The Dome*, p. 81; an excellent eighteenth century engraving showing the ceremonial use of "yurts" in article by S. Cammann, *Art Bulletin*, XXXIII, 1951, fig. 7.

[11] A. Moret, *Du caractère religieux de la royauté*

pharonique, 1902, pp. 91, 295; Smith, *Egyptian Architecture*, 1938, pp. 71-75, pls. I/4, XVII/4-6.

[12] Moret, *op.cit.*, pp. 80, 295.

[13] *Ibid.*, pp. 238-252.

[14] *Ibid.*, pp. 253-255.

appearances as the living Horus under a baldachin that resembled the *heb-sed* tent.[15]

Although the Egyptian *heb-sed* tent in the ceremonial traditions of the ruler-cult was the oldest and most direct antecedent of the royal baldachin, still it did not have the domical canopy which characterized the divine and imperial ciboria of the later periods. By the time of the Hellenistic kings and the Roman Empire, when domical symbolism had become so important, there were throughout the East other types of sacred tent shelters: in the Assyrian Empire the statues of the gods made their public appearances and seasonal entrance to a city under a canopy; the ancient Semites venerated their ancestral "Shepherd Tent of the World"; the Hebrew tribes had their *ephods*, which were tent sanctuaries of great antiquity; and the pre-Islamic Arabs used a portable and domical *qubba* tabernacle, which they set up alongside a chieftain's tent as the shelter of their gods whom they worshiped in the form of a stone baetyl.[16]

In view of what is known about the antiquity and ceremonial importance of the king's tent in Egypt and the similarity of the Assyrian ritualistic tent to the imperial ciborium, it is difficult to believe from any evidence at our disposal that the royal ciborium concept can be traced back, as Alföldi has suggested, to a hypothetical Iranian throne-tabernacle. By the fifth century B.C. when the Achaemenid kings had become masters of the Assyrian and Egyptian Empires, the reliefs from their palaces and the so-called Treasury at Persepolis show that Darius and Xerxes were enthroned for certain kinds of ceremonies under a high, four-posted baldachin.[17] It is to be noted that these sculptural representations present the Persian baldachin, like the much earlier Assyrian divine covering, with a flat canopy hung with fringes. Before attempting to evaluate this limited Persian evidence in relation to the history of the ciborium, it must be asked whether a symbolic covering was customary in the ancient East for all types of royal ceremonies and especially whether it was used when a monarch was enthroned on the dais of his own palace audience-hall?

Such evidence as there is for the use of a royal ceremonial shelter at the Achaemenid Court leads to the conclusion, as do so many other aspects of Persian culture, that the Iranian rulers borrowed freely from the older civilizations which they had conquered. On some occasions the Persian king, like his Assyrian predecessors, appeared in public under a parasol, which was itself a symbol of divine authority. Although the evidence is not very conclusive, it may be presumed that the Achaemenid kings, like all Eastern rulers, must have sat in state under a covering, which served both as a protection from the sun and as an emblem of power, when they granted public audiences in the open courts of their palaces, reviewed their troops from the terraces and platforms, watched battles and received reports and gifts in the open court of the Tribute Building, as Darius is depicted at Persepolis. All the representational and written evidence, however, would seem to indicate that with the exception of the

[15] F. K. Sethe, *Der Dramatische Ramesseum-papyrus, ein Spiel zur Thronbesteigung des Königs,* 1928.

[16] Smith, *The Dome,* pp. 61-94.

[17] E. F. Schmidt, "The Treasury of Persepolis," *The Oriental Institute, Chicago University Com.,* No. 21, 1939, p. 31, figs. 14, 16; A. U. Pope, *A Survey of Persian Art,* IV, 1938, pls. 84, 88.

Egyptian Pharaohs the Eastern monarchs were not customarily enthroned under a sky-canopy when they appeared in their official palace throne-room where the dais, wall-niche, and ceiling decorations of the hall were sufficient to show that they were superior to ordinary men.[18] Later it will be seen that this tentative conclusion will help to explain the history of the royal baldachin in the Roman Empire.

Certainly, if we can rely on the Persian literary sources, the Sassanian kings were not enthroned in their palaces under a baldachin, because the references are very specific about the great crowns having been suspended just over the head of a ruler by a long chain hung from the cupola, arch or vault of the audience hall.[19] There are a few Sassanian coins, executed "under strong Hellenistic influence," which depict a deity under a ciborium;[20] but apart from the references to the legendary and controversial Throne of Khusrau II, none of the accounts, which describe in some detail the Sassanian thrones and crowns, mention a baldachin, while in the later Persian miniatures the king does not appear under a throne tabernacle.[21] Considering the

[18] On the evidence of tomb paintings U. Hölscher ("Erscheinungsfenster und Erscheinungsbalkon in königlichen Palast," *Zeitschrift für Ägyptische Sprache*, 67, 1931, pp. 43-44) insists that a "Thronhimmel" or baldachin stood over the Pharaoh in the audience hall of his palaces. Some Eastern texts are ambiguous on this question: in the Ugaritic poem of Baal and Anath (J. B. Pritchard, *Ancient Near Eastern Texts*, 1950) it reads, he "enters the pavilion of the King" and then goes on to describe the dais, footstool, mat and couch; in the "Legend of King Keret" (*op.cit.*, p. 144) after telling how the King had gone up to the top of the towers, it says, "He entered the shade of a pavilion," and then later (p. 146) speaks of a pavilion in the house of Keret.

[19] Firdausi (*The Sháhnáma of Firdausi*, ed. by A. G. and E. Warner, 1909, II, p. 242) says, "When Siyáwush sat on the ivory throne, and hung the crown above it," then of Shapor II (*op.cit.*, VI, p. 328) he writes, "The nobles came with golden girdles and hung over it (the throne) the crown of gold"; and in his account of the palace of Madá'-in (Ctesiphon) built by Kusrau Parwiz (VIII, pp. 403-404) he relates, "A ring of gold cast for the purpose hung from the ceiling of the cupola, and from the ring a chain of ruddy gold with jeweled links. Whene'er the King of Kings ascended to his throne of ivory they used to hang the crown upon the chain." In another description of "the palace of Madá'in, known as Îwânou Kisrâ, which has no equal in the world," al-Tha'âlibî (*Histoire des rois des Perses*, trans. H. Zotenberg, 1890, p. 698) writes, "A chain of gold, 70 arm's lengths long, was suspended from the ceiling of the palace, and the crown was attached to this chain, so that it touched the head of the King without being tight and without weighing down upon him." Also Ibn Hishám (*Biography of the Prophet*, ed. Wüstenfeld; E. G. Browne, *A Literary History of Persia*, I, 1920, p. 128) tells how Chosroes of the Immortal

Soul "used to sit in his audience hall where was his crown, like unto a mighty cask, according to what they say, set with rubies, emeralds and pearls, with gold and silver, suspended by a chain of gold from the top of an arch in his audience hall; and his neck could not support the crown, but he was veiled by draperies till he had taken his seat in this audience hall, and had settled himself in his place, whereupon the draperies were withdrawn."

That it was not considered customary to have the king enthroned under a baldachin is again indicated by Firdausi (*op. cit.*, III, 18, p. 329) when he tells how Kai Khusrau held a feast in the garden with his Palladins to welcome Rustam and describes how his "throne set beneath a bower" was shaded by an artificial tree of gold, silver, and jewels. Curiously the only reference to domical canopies seems to pertain to a kind of ceremonial welcome, that was comparable to an Adventus, which was accorded to Kai Khusrau (Firdausi, *op.cit.*, IV, 40, p. 357), for the poem says:

They decorated all the towns. . . .
All the nobles went to meet Khusrau,
The great men and chieftains of Iran.
They put up cupolas on way and waste;
The world seemed all brocade of gold.

[20] The few Sassanian coins which have an enthroned deity under a ciborium show strong Hellenistic influences according to Herzfeld, *Iran in the Ancient East*, 1941, pp. 298, 319, figs. 391, 409.

[21] It is a question of just how reliable are the accounts of the throne of Khusra II by Firdausi (*op.cit.*, VIII, pp. 391-396) and al-Tha'âlibî (*op.cit.*, p. 700) written around the beginning of the eleventh century. If all the various accounts are accepted, it was a magnificent structure of fabulous dimensions, consisting of a richly decorated throne of ivory and teakwood and a celestial baldachin of gold and lapis lazuli where stars, planets, signs of the zodiac and climates moved mechanically in a natural order, which gave forth thunder, shed

veneration which the Sassanians had for everything pertaining to the greatness of the Achaemenid kings, it, therefore, seems unlikely that the domical throne-tabernacle was of Iranian origin.

It is still not clear, outside of Egypt, to what extent the tent-tabernacle, which was usually taken over from the ancestral shelter of the tribal gods, was used over a ruler. Since every early culture seems to have associated a sky symbolism and cosmic concept with the sacral tent, there is a strong presumption that the divine covering was only adopted as a throne-tabernacle when a ruler was identified with heaven and presented to his people as a god. It is also likely that throughout the East, with the exception of Egypt, the royal tent-shelter was only used for those ceremonies in which a ruler made a public appearance. Inasmuch as there was in both Antiquity and the Middle Ages a close parallel between divine and royal ceremonies, each borrowing from the other at different stages in the development of the temple and palace rituals, it is important to find at Assur that the canopy, under which the statue of the Assyrian god made its public appearances, was set up, not over his throne, but just inside the

---

rain, and was purported to have been a reconstruction of an ancient Iranian throne-tabernacle. There are three interpretations of the literary evidence. P. Ackermann (Pope, *Survey of Persian Art*, I, 1938, pp. 775-778, 878) insists without qualifications that it is a record of an actual throne built by Khusra in imitation of the throne-tabernacle of the Achaemenid kings and that the structure is pictured on the bronze salver (figs. 160, 161, pl. 237) in the Staatliche Museen in Berlin. L'Orange (*Studies on the Iconography of Cosmic Kingship in the Ancient World*, 1953, pp. 18-27) also believes that "this throne of Khusra is only a renovation of the old Achaemenid throne destroyed by Alexander." The domical building on the Berlin dish, which A. Pope (*Art Bulletin*, xv, 1933, p. 10) called "a Sassanian Garden Palace," will be discussed later as a post-Sassanian creation of the tenth century (p. 194), which has no relation to the Takt-i-Tāqdēs.

Working from a passage in the Byzantine text of Cedrenus, Herzfeld ("Der Thron des Khosro," *Jahrb. d. Preuss. Kunstlg.*, XLI, 1920, pp. 1-24, 103-147) endeavored to prove that it was not a throne, but a clocklike structure, similar to a Greek *horloge* at Ghaza, which Khusra had in his palace (Firdausi says hippodrome) near Ganzah, where it was destroyed by Heraclius. The third view, advanced by F. Saxl ("Früher Christentum und späte Heidentum in künstlerischen Ausdrucksformen," *Wiener Jahrb. für Kunstgeschichte*, II, 1923, pp. 102-121) is that the legend of the throne was a composite myth based upon Oriental, Hellenistic, and Late Antique traditions of the ruler as a divine Kosmokrator who was a "Brother of the Sun, Moon and Stars," and hence a literary conceit. A. Christensen (*L'Iran sous les Sassanids*, 2nd ed., 1944, pp. 466-469) in describing the throne is non-

committal about its reality, purpose, and origin.

Since Khusra had been given asylum by the Emperor Maurice and had married a Byzantine princess, there is the possibility that he had a mechanical throne constructed by Greek craftsmen, for the accounts say that it was built by workmen from Rum and China, so that his palace could compete in magnificence with the mechanical wonders seen at the Byzantine Court. Even though the "Throne of Solomon" in Constantinople may not have been constructed before the ninth century, it is possible that the legend of the Takt-i-Tāqdēs was a literary myth that grew in the telling and so came to be based upon the throne in the Magnaura Palace, which had birds that sang, lions that roared, and scented rain that fell when the throne under its celestial baldachin mechanically rose higher and higher above the heads of the astounded audience (G. Brett, "The Automat in the Byzantine 'Throne of Solomon,'" *Speculum*, XXIX, 1954, pp. 477-487; Ebersolt, *Le grand palais*, pp. 68-69; F. M. Feldhaus, *Die Technik der Antike und der Mittelalters*, 1931, p. 247; F. A. Wright, *The Works of Luidprand of Cremona*, pp. 207-208; *De ceremoniis* [Bonn], II, 15, p. 569). Regardless of the actuality of the throne, which was never seen by any of the authors, before either the conception and execution of the Takt-i-Tāqdēs can be considered in any sense Persian, some evidence must be advanced to show that there were Achaemenid craftsmen capable of constructing such an ingenious wonder; for we are told that even the Sassanians were dependent for their scientific knowledge on Greeks and Romans. Also, if historical sequence means anything some precedence must be given to the mechanical, astronomical domes in Varro's villa and Nero's Golden House, which must have been contrived by Greek craftsmen.

doorway of his temple chamber and in front of the tunnel-vaulted sanctuary where the god was enthroned on a dais.[22] This portable, Assyrian ritualistic tent, which was flat on top like the coverings over the later Persian Kings at Persepolis, was removed from its floor sockets and carried over the god-image when it made its ceremonial excursions and Epiphany entrances into the city at such times as the Festival of the New Year.

There were, however, within the Assyrian Empire many different cultural traditions with the result that, while the most ancient sacred canopies appear to have been flat on top, others were domical in shape and a few may have been hooped like the early Mesopotamian cosmic house.[23] All that can be asserted with any confidence is that the Assyrian ceremonial tabernacle, such as the one depicted on the doors of Balawat (Fig. 102) in which Shalmanessar (859-825 B.C.) pours libations, and the royal tent of Ashurnasirpal (Fig. 104) on a relief from Nineveh, closely resemble the later imperial Byzantine ciborium.[24] From the fact that the Assyrian kings are sometimes depicted under an arch, which was a convention on Roman coins for a celestial ciborium, it may be deduced that they, like the gods, also appeared in public under a sacred covering.[25] Hence, in spite of the limited evidence, it is reasonably certain that the Mesopotamian *tentoria* of richly woven fabrics, which were supported on four posts with pine-cone finials and sacrificial horns, had a celestial significance over both gods and god-kings and were used, like the Egyptian ritualistic tents, for certain types of ceremonies in which a god-king and world master made his public appearances. In the ceremonies of the New Year Festival at Babylon we are told by S. H. Hooke (*Babylonian and Assyrian Religion*, p. 49) that the god appeared under "The 'golden heaven,' which . . . was a baldachin or canopy of gold or cloth of gold upon which the planets were represented." When the people welcomed the return of the god responsible for the renewed fertility of the land, the way in which it was customary in both the Mesopotamian and Egyptian rituals pertaining to the Spring Festivals for the priest-king to enact the part of "the vegetation deity" may explain how the heavenly canopy came to be associated with the appearance and ceremonial reception of a divine ruler.

In tracing back the history of the ciborium and its persistent association with a city and palace gateway, it is essential to keep in mind the importance of the gateway in the public and ceremonial life of a community. It is also necessary

---

[22] W. Andrae, *Das Wiedererstandene Assur*, 1938, pp. 35, 111-112, Abbs. 21, 51. In the Babylonian ritual used for the consecration and installation of a new or restored statue of a god the text says: "Take the hand of the god and lead him in and then repeat the incantation 'My king in thy goodness of heart' (till you come) up to the shrine. Set the god on his seat, and then repeat at his (seat) the incantation 'Place that is the *qisikku* of heaven' (and) the incantation 'Ornament of the exalted chapel.' *At the side of the shrine put up a canopy* . . ." (S. H. Hooke, *Babylonian and Assyrian Re-*

ligion, London, 1953, p. 119).

[23] Although all the early representations of a sacred canopy have a flat top, as Andrae restored them in his picture of Assur, an Assyrian relief from Nineveh depicts soldiers carrying a statue, or figure, under a baldachin which appears to have a hoop-roof (H. R. Hall, *Assyrian Sculptures in the British Museum*, 1938, pl. x).

[24] Balawat (Perrot et Chipiez, *Histoire de l'art*, II, 1884, p. 203, fig. 68); Nineveh (*ibid.*, p. 201, fig. 67).

[25] *Ibid.*, figs. 69, 312.

to realize that it was customary throughout the Near East to set up a covering as a place of honor, appearances, and receptions at the entrance to a city. In fact, it can be inferred from the later evidence that there was a canopy of distinction over the Mesopotamian king "Ur-Engur, God of Heaven and Earth," when he sat like the shining sun "as Counsellor" at the gate, known as "Thy God is a Great God."[26] A poem from Ras-Shamra says, "Thereupon Daniel, the man of Rephaim . . . rose and took his seat in front of the gate, beneath an *'adr* that is in (on) the threshing floor."[27] It has already been pointed out that the "goren," or threshing floor, in front of the city-gate in the Near East was a sacred locality and a place of public and religious rites.[28] It is also to be noted that the *'adr* under which Daniel sat in judgment was undoubtedly a ceremonial covering. It may indeed have been a rustic pavilion similar to the ciboria which are later depicted over the enthroned Christ and Virgin on the Christian ivories from the Syro-Palestinian region.[29] This *'adr* in the Ugaritic text is now thought to have been related to the *adru* in the Assyrian records, which was presumably a ritualistic canopy used during the New Year festivals for the public reception, or Epiphany, of a city's god.[30]

The imprint which this tradition left on men's imagery is reflected in the Jewish legend of "The Creation of the World," where it tells of Paradise with "its two gates of carbuncle" and says, "each (person) has a canopy according to his merits."[31] Therefore, in view of this evidence, when one visualizes the various public ceremonies described in the Old Testament, it begins to be apparent that there must have been a canopy of supreme merit, for example, over the Kings of Israel and Judah when they "sat each on his throne, having put on their robes, in the void place in the entrance of the gate" (I Kings 22:10). The subsequent history of the canopy of honor begins to acquire a traditional significance when it is realized that the peoples of the Near East, long before the establishment of the Hellenistic kingdoms, had been accustomed for generations to seeing their rulers, either their native kings or their Egyptian, Assyrian and Persian conquerors, enthroned like deities either in a military tent or under a ceremonial canopy of appearances. Taken in relation with the use of the *heb-sed* tent in the recorded royal ceremonies of Ancient Egypt, which was presumably continued by the Ptolemaic kings, this is a basic reason for believing that similar baldachins must have been adopted by the Greek kings for the Epiphany ritual in which they were welcomed as a Sun-god, received as a "Savior" and adored by the populace as the "Lord King."

[26] See p. 12.

[27] Sidney Smith, *Palestinian Exploration Quart.*, 1946, p. 6.

[28] *Ibid.*, 1952, pp. 42-45; J. Gray, *ibid.*, 1953, pp. 118-121. It should be added that Daniel recalls Ur-Engur, first, because he also was a divine king and, second, because from his seat in front of the city-gate "he judges the cause of the widow, he administers justice to the orphan" (C. Virolleaud, *Le Légende phénicienne de Danel*, i, pp. 91, 139).

[29] Smith, *The Dome*, pp. 67-70; the rustic type of ciborium, which is used on the Syro-Palestinian ivories over the enthroned Virgin and Child (fig. 114), the enthroned Christ (fig. 115), over Daniel (fig. 116) and the Holy Sepulchre (fig. 117), and the Tyche shrines (figs. 111, 112) on the Syrian coins were undoubtedly Christian and Roman versions of the old Syrian *'adr*.

[30] S. Smith, *Pal. Ex. Quart.*, 1946, p. 10.

[31] L. Ginsberg, *The Legends of the Jews*, i, 1942, p. 20.

Just as it is necessary to trace back the *'adr* over Daniel in the Ugaritic text to the *adru*, or religious canopy, over the Assyrian deities at the time of their ceremonial visitations, so is it necessary to understand to what extent a ciborium was a mark of divinity throughout the Near East before it can be fully realized why the ciborium became a prescribed provision for the Hellenistic Royal Epiphany, which in turn was to have a lasting influence upon Roman, Byzantine, and mediaeval royal receptions at city and palace gateways. In all parts of the Roman East there were many types of sacred tents, all going back in origin to ancestral shelters of a nomadic past, which had long been revered as festival tents, inner sanctuaries, portable shrines and the altar coverings of the various sky-gods. Such was their continuous use and veneration throughout the Empire that they were frequently represented on the Roman coins from Asia Minor, Syria, Palestine, and Egypt. The sacred dwelling on a coin from Lycia (Fig. 106) is a primitive tent of a round, bulbous, and global shape.[32] For the most part these tabernacles, such as the shrine of a goddess of Pisidia (Fig. 107), the holy of holies over Egyptian deities at Alexandria (Fig. 108), the sanctuary of the Tyches and sky-gods of Syria (Fig. 109), and the great baldachin over the Altar of Zeus at Pergamum (Fig. 110) were all ciboriumlike shelters whose domical canopies had a recognized celestial meaning.[33] Some of them are obviously portable coverings with poles under them so that they could be carried in the festival processions, taken out to the city-gate to meet a god-king and be used on the feast day for the Epiphany of the deity.[34]

So deeply had the old concepts of a sacred tent as the world abode of a god permeated the imaginative thought of the Near East that people visualized the universe in the shape of an ancestral shelter, with the result that throughout Antiquity and the Early Christian period the cosmological idea of Heaven as a *skene* was common in literature, art, and astronomical beliefs.[35] This meant that all the imagery of the cosmic tent, which had become widespread by Hellenistic times, remained common for centuries. An Etruscan mirror (Fig. 105), attributed to the third century B.C., depicts the sky-shelter, or *heroön*, of the legendary heroes Meleager and the Dioscurides,[36] while a silver lanx (Fig. 51) of the Late Empire shows Apollo, the Sun-god, standing in his world tent with the griffin at his feet and the *sphairos* on a pedestal.[37] Alexandria must have been the most important disseminating center of this *skene* imagery, for all the evidence indicates that it was there that the canopy symbol was taken over

[32] Drachm of Trajan (H. Mattingly, *Roman Coins*, 1928, pl. XLIX/5).

[33] Smith, *The Dome*, pp. 68-69, see also Fig. 107, a coin of Gordianus, Antioch in Pisidia (Imhoof-Blumer, *Kleinasiatische Münzen*, II, no. 25, pl. XII/20); Fig. 108, a coin of Alexandria (*Coll. Dattari*, pl. XXXIX/1132); Fig. 109, a coin of J. Domna, Damascus (*Brit. Mu. Cat. Greek Coins, Galatia*, no. 11, pl. XXXIV/9); Fig. 110, a coin of Septimius Severus, Pergamum (*Brit. Mu. Cat. Greek Coins, Mysia*, no. 315, pl. XXX/7).

[34] The round saplings by means of which a shrine was carried in the processions can be seen on the portable shrine of the Tyche of Tyre on a coin of Trebonianus Gallus (*Brit. Mu. Cat. Greek Coins, Phoenicia*, no. 437, pl. XXXIV/3) and of the Tyche of Antioch (*Brit. Mu. Cat. Greek Coins, Galatia*, no. 656, pl. XXVI/5).

[35] Smith, *The Dome*, pp. 35, 87, 109-110; L. Lehmann, *Art Bulletin*, XXVII, 1945, pp. 1-27.

[36] E. Gerhardt, *Etruskische Spiegel*, IV, 1867, pl. 355; Lehmann, *op.cit.*, p. 11, fig. 26.

[37] O. Brendel, *Journal of Roman Studies*, XXXI, 1941, pp. 100ff., pls. VIII-XI.

into the decorative arts of the palace where it was stylized into a domical, or conical, tent pattern with cusped edges and radiating lines, which in the past has been frequently misinterpreted as either a "fan-pattern," or confused with the shell decoration.[38]

The only example discovered in the deeply buried ruins of ancient Alexandria is from the ceiling of the "Ipsium tomb" which has the Egyptian griffins, as sun symbols, around the edge of the painted canopy of heaven.[39] Nevertheless, its Alexandrian origin must be assumed from its frequent appearance in the decorations of the second and fourth Pompeian styles and on the domes and ceiling of the Golden House of Nero, who had a passionate admiration for everything Alexandrian because of his desire to emulate Alexander the Great and the Ptolemaic kings. It was not only used in the decoration of Pompeian niches and apses, as in the Forum Baths, but, because it was an established convention for denoting the heavenly import of domes and apses, it became, as Lehmann has shown, a traditional feature on both Imperial and Christian vaults.[40] The early association of the *skene* baldachin with the *sphairos* and griffins, as illustrated by a fresco from Herculaneum (Fig. 48), is further evidence of its derivation from the palace decorations of Alexandria where the cosmic tent and globe were insignia of a Sun-king's domination over heaven and earth.[41] Also the presumption that the *skene-sphairos* was a royal Hellenistic motif helps to explain the importance of the cupola and globe as interchangeable motifs on the imperial Roman coins of the fourth century.

The persistent interest in this form of celestial and cosmic symbolism can be seen in the use of the sky tent, beginning with Nero, as a customary decoration on Roman and later Christian domes.[42] It is also illustrated on the late Roman mosaics of North Africa in the way the *skene* motif surrounds the deity in control of the Seasons.[43] It was the Hellenistic concept of a heavenly canopy, or cosmic dwelling, which accounts for the construction of Roman and Byzantine domes with melonlike corrugations, for the way in which the cupolas on Early Christian martyria are always depicted with the convex gores of the celestial tent, and for the continued use of cupolas with tent striations during the Middle Ages on palaces (Fig. 73) and churches (Fig. 79). The treatment of the dome over the *Domus Dei* on the Utrecht Psalter (Fig. 132) with cusped edges and convex gores is the clearest evidence that the Middle Ages still

---

[38] Lehmann, *op.cit.*, p. 20 n. 176.

[39] R. Pagenstecher, *Nekropolis*, 1919, p. 194, fig. 119.

[40] K. Ronczewski, *Gewölbeschmuck in römischen Altertum*, 1903, pl. 26; Lehmann, *op.cit.*, p. 13, fig. 35; for other examples of the *skene* pattern see Lehmann, figs. 25, 36, 54, 62.

[41] Casa del Argo ed Io (Zahn, *Ornamente aller klassischen Kunst-Epochen*, pl. 41). It is significant that this combination of *sphairos* and *skene*, globe and tent, world and sky, should be so common in Pompeian decorations: in the House of Diomedes (Niccolini, *Pompeii*, no. 96) a kind of tree-of-life upright supports a globe on which stands an eagle, which in turn is under a baldachin with a dome on the interior and a *fastigium* on the exterior; and on another fresco (Niccolini, no. 177) an arabesque tree-of-life supports a sphere, which in turn is under a *skene* baldachin.

[42] *Domus aurea* (Lehmann, figs. 27, 28, 37); Hadrian's villa (Lehmann, fig. 29); Palatine (Lehmann, fig. 62).

[43] Hippone (Gauckler, *Inventaire des mosaïque*, no. 41; Lehmann, p. 9, fig. 18); Lambèsi (Gauckler, no. 181).

thought of the heavenly *skene* as the symbolic covering over a divine Kosmokrator. Furthermore, the Hellenistic combination of the *skene* and *sphairos* as related emblems of cosmic rule explains why the baldachin with a global finial came to denote imperial authority over *urbis et orbis* on the coins of Diocletian, why cupolas and globes became interchangeable motifs on the imperial Roman and German coins, why the cupolas on the city towers of the *Corpus Agrimensorum Romanorum* (Figs. 61-64) were made bulbous to resemble globes, and why even as late as the Renaissance the cupola surmounted by an orb was used over St. Peter's to express in imperial terms the Church's heavenly authority over Rome and the World.

2. The Roman adoption of the sacred and royal ciborium

It is, however, the repeated use of the tent pattern and baldachin in the "Fourth Style" of Pompeian wall painting which is our best evidence that much of the *skene* symbolism must have come into the Roman world from Alexandria, and that the royal ciborium was an important feature in the palace ceremonies of the Hellenistic East. The problem of tracing the stages by which the Romans adopted from the East the sacred and royal tent canopy is greatly clarified once it is recognized how much influence the palace ceremonies, symbolism, and architecture of Hellenistic Egypt had upon everything pertaining to the ruler concepts at Rome. Since nothing remains of the Hellenistic palaces it is equally essential to realize that the treatment of the *scaenae frons* of the Hellenistic and Roman theaters must have been based upon the conventions of the palace tradition and is, therefore, a valuable record of palace architecture.

Back of the whole development of the Hellenistic and Roman stage, which the fourth Pompeian style appears to reflect, was the palace. While we are told that the Fourth Style of wall painting was derived from a mode of stage scenery which originated at Alexandria, too little consideration has been given to the question of what inspired the scenery and why the style became so popular as wall decoration. Actually what made the Fourth Style so popular at the beginning of the Empire was not so much the fact of its having been based upon the tragic scenery of the Hellenistic theater, as that tragic scenery itself presented all the architectural elements, royal symbolism, sumptuous and ceremonial provisions of the Hellenistic palaces. Throughout the history of architecture it was usually the palace which established the precedents for the elaborate modes of wall decoration. Well before the end of the Republic, when the Roman masters of Egypt had become so impressed by the fitting magnificence of the Ptolemaic royal halls, and certainly after the adoption of Alexandrian palace decorations in Nero's Golden House and on the Palatine, it was an admiration for everything pertaining to the Greek kings which gave rise to the popularity of the second and fourth Pompeian styles of painting. From the beginning of theater architecture it was the king's house which was the traditional and appropriate setting for the Greek tragedies. It was for this reason, and because theaters had come to represent the munificence of rulers, that the Roman *scaenae frons* turned into a monumental version of the tragic stage, which Vitruvius (v, 6, 9) said was "designed with columns, pediments (*fastigii*) and statues and other *regalibus rebus*."

Among the "other royal elements" of the "Fourth Pompeian Style," the appearance of palace façades with a semicircular *Porta regia*, in which Hellenistic rulers in the guise of gods, victors, and heroes are presented under a baldachin, must be a pictorial and stage reflection of the ceremonial settings at the Alexandrian Court. Only a Roman interest in the magnificent richness of kingly architecture and in the sacrosanct formality of its rituals accounts for the use of all the royal conventions on the walls of such different buildings as the Stabian Baths, the palaestra of the "House of the Gladiators" and the Casa di Apollo.[44] The scene from the Casa di Apollo (Fig. 113) depicts a Sun-god, wearing a nimbus, carrying a ruler's scepter and enthroned like a deified Hellenistic king under a circular baldachin, which in turn is set into the semicircular bay of the *Porta regia* and in front of a door leading into a domical vestibule.[45]

The Casa di Apollo and other examples, where a ruler in the guise of Helios, Hercules, or a Victor makes a public appearance at the entrance to an *aula regia*, while heralds sound the fanfare of welcome on trumpets, were not the fanciful creation of a decorator's imagination. Rather are they a record of palace ceremonies and the architectural provisions for them which must have been traditional in the palaces of Alexandria. Some intimation of exactly when these Hellenistic palace forms began to influence the development of the Roman stage, resulting in the introduction of a columnar reception vestibule in front of the *Porta regia* of the *scaenae frons*, is suggested by the references to Augustus having set up in the theater of Marcellus four columns *in regia theatri* and also having had the statue of Pompey honored *in regiam*.[46]

[44] In his study of the fourth Pompeian style, G. von Cube ("Die Römische 'scenae frons' in den Pompejanischen Wandbildern 4.Stiles," *Beiträge zur Bauwissenschaft*, Berlin, 1906) has pointed out how the Pompeian representations of an "Aula regis" (Royal House) with a baldachin in the semicircular niche of a *Porta regia* bear out the statements of Vitruvius and Pollux (p. 15) that tragic scenery was based upon palace architecture. In the Stabian Baths (v. Cube, pp. 38f., Taf. VIII; Niccolini, *Pompeii*, I, no. 69) there is a round and domical baldachin in the semicircular vestibule of the "Aula regis" in which stands a figure of Hercules, whom the Hellenistic kings frequently impersonated; in the triclinium of the house, Reg. I, ins. 3, no. 25 (v. Cube, pp. 21f., Taf. II) the baldachin of the palace façade, which von Cube restored (fig. 2) as a domical vestibule, has over it both the domical tent pattern and the royal fastigium, while on top of these motifs, as on the attic of a triumphal arch, is the quadriga of victory and apotheosis; and on the fresco from the palestra of the "House of the Gladiator" (v. Cube, p. 28, Taf. IV) there is a large, rectangular vestibule of appearances and salutations in front of the "Porta hospitalis" and in it stands a Helios figure wearing a nimbus, carrying a palm of victory, and accompanied by a Nike, while at the side a herald sounds a trumpet, all essential features of Hellenistic royal ceremonies.

[45] P. Herrmann, *Denkmäler der Malerei des Altertums*, Ser. I, 1904-1931, p. 198, fig. 57. Another fresco (v. Cube, *op.cit.*, p. 33, Taf. VI) from the Casa di Apollo depicts a palace façade with Apollo standing in a royal "Window of Appearances," which must reflect the old Egyptian palace tradition of the Pharaoh, as the incarnate Sun-god, standing in a window balcony looking down upon the court of his palace or temple.

[46] Augustus placed four remarkable columns from the House of Scaurus *in regis theatri* of the theater of Marcellus (Platner and Ashby, *A Topographical Dictionary of Rome*, 1929, p. 513); and in 32 B.C. he took the statue of Pompey from the Curia and set it up *in regiam* in the theater of Pompey (p. 516). Later it became customary to place a statue of the emperor in the apsidal niche over the *Porta regia* of the *scaenae frons*.

The two provisions which are implied by these references, of having a pavilion, or vestibule, of welcome in front of the Royal Door and of setting up an honorific statue at the entrance to a palace, were ideas first customary in the East which will be seen persisting in the palace of the Byzantine emperors.

Although the theater with its conventions of tragic scenery undoubtedly accustomed the Roman public to the appearance of gods and kings under a ciborium, or a gabled vestibule of reception, at the entrance to their stage palaces, it could have had only an indirect influence upon the eventual imperial adoption of the royal ciborium. In Alexandria, however, where we are told that the tragic stage scenery originated, there was the old Egyptian tradition of the royal *heb-sed* baldachin. It was the covering set up over the living Sun-god, or his statue, at the time of the Pharaoh's Jubilee Festival, which was a kind of royal Epiphany, and it was also the ceremonial canopy under which the Horus-king was received when he visited his city as a god. It would, therefore, seem to follow from the evidence of the second and fourth styles of Pompeian painting that the *skene* baldachin, or Tent of Appearances, was always an important feature in the public festivals, epiphanies and hieratic rituals of the Ptolemaic kings. Hence, it is to be deduced that among the factors which eventually led to the adoption of the baldachin in the Roman palace ceremonies were the imperial admiration for Hellenistic precedent, the influence of the royal Epiphanies which were accorded to the Roman emperors during their campaigns and travels in the Near East, and the recognition of the Augustus as a *Divus*, who at the time of his Adventus and public appearances in his Eastern cities was received and adored as the image of a god under his celestial tent-canopy.

Before attempting to sustain these deductions it is already apparent that much of their validity depends upon whether the architectural elements of Roman wall decoration, and their survivals in the art of the Middle Ages, should be thought of only as stage scenery, or as a reflection of palace architecture. It has been pointed out that in many instances the architectural features back of the Evangelists in mediaeval book illuminations appear to have been based upon the conventions of the Hellenistic and Roman stage.[47] That this is true does not mean, however, that the Christians were interested in the stage; quite the contrary, as we know. Nor does it mean, as has sometimes been assumed, that the theatrical architectural features in Byzantine art (Fig. 74) were executed and thought of as stage-settings. Instead, the importance which the Christians attached to imitating antique forms of architecture came from their desire to appropriate everything pertaining to the *Sacrum palatium*, as they had come to know it, in order to present the magnificence of the heavenly House of God and the stately glories of their own "King of Kings." To the extent that they were directly influenced by Roman wall decorations and the *scaenae frons* of the theater, it was only because they saw in them a palace tradition.

There was in the Hellenistic East a close relation between the two types of cover-

[47] A. M. Friend, *Art Studies*, v, 1927, pp. 144-146.

ing under which a god-image and a god-king appeared in public. In attempting to deduce from the meager evidence some intimation of the way in which the Eastern ceremonial provisions were introduced in the various rituals of emperor-worship, a differentiation must be made between the divine ciborium and the royal baldachin, and the order in which they were at first adopted by the Romans. Certainly by the beginning of the Empire the domical and ciboriumlike shrine was known in Rome and used as a sacred form for the aedicula of Mars Ultor (Fig. 111) on the coins of Augustus, where the divinity was intended to refer to the Emperor as the Avenger of Caesar.[48] It was also used by the time of Domitian over fire altars and presumably figured in the triumphal ceremonies within the *Porticus Divorum*.[49] At this time, however, there is no evidence that the emperors presented themselves publicly under the heavenly ciborium, except in art.

This is curious because many of them, beginning most obviously with Nero, endeavored to introduce at Rome the forms of ruler-worship which all the emperors accepted as a matter of course when traveling through their Eastern provinces. Apparently there was a limit to which any emperor dared go in adopting the ruler concepts of the Orient, for certainly Nero's ambitions to be recognized as a second Alexander the Great and to be identified with the Sun-god were not enthusiastically accepted. Nevertheless, underlying his vanities and extravagant obsessions, which to many Romans were as objectionable as his vices, there was a shrewd realization that his Eastern subjects, conditioned by centuries of king-worship, wanted to see a supernatural being in the Master of Rome and the World. Regardless of his motives Nero, it can be shown, was exceptionally interested in making use of domical symbolism. Even though he probably never went further at Rome than to have himself presented on his coins under a ciborium and to have his statue enshrined for public adoration, he nonetheless anticipated what was later to become an imperial policy.

When he built his magnificent *Domus aurea* and in it had constructed a great banqueting hall, where he could dine with his guests like a Kosmokrator beneath a domical heaven which "went round day and night like the world," he was the first to introduce into Roman architecture the domical triclinium as the place where the old religious rite of the *Jovis coenatio* could be made a part of the emperor-cult. It does not follow, however, that he was in any way influenced by the ceremonial and domical forms of those far-distant enemies of Rome, the Parthian kings, as L'Orange

[48] Coin of Augustus (H. Mattingly, *Coins of the Roman Empire in the British Museum*, I, no. 315, pl. 5/20; other variants of the domical shrine, pls. 8/2-6, 11-14, 17/12.

[49] See p. 26. While there is no evidence of an honorific covering or ciborium having been set up over the imperial throne at Rome, the Flavian coins record a symbolic tradition which may have influenced the eventual adoption of the Eastern baldachin as a throne tabernacle (A. L. Abaecherli, "Imperial symbols on certain Flavian coins," *Classical Philology*, xxx, 1935, pp. 131-140, pl. I). At the time of a *lecisternium* and for various public

festivals it was customary to set up in a banqueting hall, theater, circus, and court, empty chairs or thrones each surmounted by a symbol to indicate the presence of a divinity. A triangular symbol on a throne, derived from the *fastigium imperatoris*, signified a *Divus*; and an arched shape over a throne denoted a *Diva*. It has been suggested that this curved form, which on the coins looks somewhat like a ciborium over an empty throne, was derived from the hooped canopy that covered the *carpentum* or sacred processional wagon of the empress.

has suggested.[50] The notion of a mechanical dome recalls Varro's tholus in his sumptuous villa, which must have been the work of Hellenistic Greek craftsmen.[51] Nero's idea of an imperial feast in a triclinium of cosmic shape involved, in addition to the Roman tradition of a sacred meal, elements of the Greek Cult of Heroes with its heroön and heavenly repast, possible features of the synthetic cult of Sarapis and the ceremonies in the Hellenistic Serapheum at Alexandria with its cosmological dome, and some memory of Alexander's "Tent of Heaven." It was from Hellenistic celestial maps that he presumably took the heavenly images with which he had his Golden House decorated.[52] With his passion for everything Alexandrian, which went so far that he thought seriously of transferring the capital of the Empire to the Egyptian city,[53] Nero was consciously reviving at Rome the palace forms of Alexandria, when he systematically made use of the Alexandrian tent pattern on the ceilings of his *Domus aurea*.[54]

His interest in the *skene* symbolism and his desire to be apotheosized as a Hellenistic Sun-god were made manifest by the *velum* which he had stretched over the theater of Marcellus for the ceremonies following the coronation of Mithradates. "The canopies," it is recorded, "stretched overhead to keep off the sun, were of purple and embroidered in their center appeared Nero driving a chariot with golden star gleaming all about him."[55] At first it might seem as if there were no limits to what he was prepared to do in his effort to introduce Hellenistic and Eastern forms of ruler-worship, for during the coronation of Mithradates the Parthian king proclaimed, as he knelt before Nero in the Forum, "And I come to thee, my god, to worship thee as I do Mithras."[56] Neither this willingness to be identified with the Persian Sun-god, nor his representations on the coins as the Hellenistic Apollo type of an inspired and divine world-ruler,[57] are any assurance that Nero himself at this time appeared under a ciborium, because, if he had, Suetonius would have recorded such an audacious innovation.[58]

What is important to the history of the ciborium is the evidence that Nero was fully aware of the divine implications of the domical shape and was personally interested in the royal ciborium because it had belonged to the palace ceremonies of the Hellenistic kings at Alexandria in the days when the Ptolemies were adored as the embodiment of Helios-Apollo and the Egyptian Horus. In fact, among the decorations of his Golden House, according to an eighteenth century drawing (Fig. 117),

[50] H. P. L'Orange, *Serta Eitremiana*, 1942, and *Studies on the Iconography of Cosmic Kingship in the Ancient World*, 1953, pp. 28-34.

[51] Varro, *Rerum Rusticarum*, Bk. III, 2, 4, 5; Boëthius, "Nero's House," *Eranos*, XLIV, 1946, pp. 442-459; what is important regarding Varro's mechanical heaven is not whether it was an "architectural whim," as L'Orange says (*op.cit.*, p. 30 n. 1), but whether the idea and technical knowledge necessary to construct a moving dome originated in Persia or in the Hellenistic East.

[52] Hanfmann, *The Seasons-Sarcophagus in Dumbarton Oaks*, pp. 126 n. 130; p. 164 n. 134.

[53] G. L. Lafaye, *Histoire du culte des divinités d'Alexandrie*, 1884, pp. 58-60.

[54] Lehmann, *Art Bulletin*, XXVII, 1945, p. 12, figs. 27, 28.

[55] Dio Cassius, *Roman History* (Loeb), VIII, 1925, Bk. XLIII, 6.

[56] Dio Cassius, Bk. XLII.

[57] H. P. L'Orange, *Apotheosis in Ancient Portraiture*, Oslo, 1947, pp. 57-63; J. M. C. Toynbee, "Ruler-Apotheosis in Ancient Rome," *The Numismatic Chronicle*, 1946, pp. 126-149.

[58] Suetonius, *The Lives of the Caesars* (Loeb), IV, Bk. XIII.

was the fresco of a nimbed Helios, very similar to the radiant Sun-king from the Casa di Apollo (Fig. 113), who was enthroned under a domical baldachin and surrounded by the Seasons as he listened to the petition of Phaeton.[59] Nero, we may be sure, considered himself to be the Roman counterpart of this Hellenistic Master of the Universe and "Controller of the Seasons."

What his aspirations were is indicated as early as A.D. 59 when he constructed the Macellum (Fig. 112) and had it commemorated on his coins.[60] This building, which was a kind of monumentalized baldachin, or Hellenistic tholus, like shrines outlined in the ruins of Pompeii and Pozzuoli, was erected in the market place presumably for the public adoration of his enshrined statue in the guise of a deity.[61] Other evidence of Nero's early interest in the domical canopy as a mark of divine honor, and a further proof that his domical ideas were derived from the Hellenistic East, is the coin (Fig. 116) which, following the death of his daughter at the age of four months, he had issued in A.D. 63 by one of his Eastern mints.[62] On the obverse is the legend DIVA CLAUD (IA) NER (O) F and the figure of a woman, either his wife or his idealized and deified daughter Claudia, in a domical aedicula and on the reverse DIVA POPPAEA AUG.

Further evidence that Nero knew of the Eastern use of the royal ciborium, and was entertaining the idea of appropriating it, appears in A.D. 68, probably after his return from Greece where he had undoubtedly been received with all the traditional honors of the Hellenistic Epiphany. In that year he brought out a new type of AD LOCUTIO coin (Fig. 114) which, instead of following precedent in having the Emperor address the troops from an uncovered platform, shows in front of him the posts of a pavilion and in back the cusped edge of a *skene* around the top of the coin.[63] This schematic treatment, after the manner in which the tent pattern was depicted on the ceilings of his palace, was intentionally a very guarded reference to the *skene* as a divine covering; and hence has been either ignored or tentatively interpreted as a domical structure in the background. One would hardly dare to suggest that it was meant to indicate a baldachin of appearances were it not for the variant (Fig. 115) which Nero had struck by the mint at Lugdunum with a domical covering of thatch, in place of the tent, so that the implied symbolism might be more apparent to his Gallic subjects.[64]

This numismatic evidence, combined with the examples of the ciborium from the Pompeian frescoes and the use of the tent pattern in the decoration of Roman vaults

[59] Hanfmann, *op.cit.*, fig. 82; C. Robert, *Die antiken Sarcophagus-reliefs*, III, p. 407.

[60] Coin of Nero, Fig. 112, Vatican Lib., Rome (Rivoira, *Architettura romana*, pp. 79-80); other variants: Mattingly, *Coins of the Roman Empire in the Brit. Mu.*, I, p. clxxix, p. 236, nos. 191ff., pl. 43/5-7; E. A. Sydenham, *Coinage of Nero*, 1920, pp. 106-108. Bibliography on the Macellum: Dio Cassius, Bk. LXII, 18; Varro, *Apud non*, c. 6 n. 2; Platner and Ashby, *A Topographical Dictionary of Rome*, p. 323; Donaldson, *Architectura Numismatica*, p. 267, no. 72; A. M. Colini, "Storia e topografia del Celio nell'antichita," *Atti della Pontificia Acc. romana de archeologia*, Ser. III, VIII, 1944,

pp. 56-57; Wulzinger, "Die Marcellum Dupondieu des Nero," *Num. Int. Monatschrift*, 1933; J. M. C. Toynbee, *Numismatic Chronicle*, 1946, pp. 126-148.

[61] Pompeii (Mau, *Pompeii*, p. 85); Pozzuoli (Maiuri, *I Campi flagrei*, p. 21).

[62] Cohen, I, p. 315.

[63] Mattingly, *Coins of the Roman Empire*, I, p. 218, no. 122, pl. 41/5; Sydenham, *Coinage of Nero*, p. 122, pl. IV/57; P. G. Hamberg, *Studies in Roman Imperial Art*, 1945, pp. 135-149.

[64] Mattingly, *op.cit.*, I, nos. 303, 304, pl. 45/18; *Coll. Bement*, 1924, pl. 18/639.

125

at this time, is incontrovertible proof that the tent-ciborium was already an established feature of the ruler-cult in the Hellenistic world and had begun to interest those Roman emperors who were most desirous of being accepted as a god. Still it is most unlikely that Nero made any public appearances, while in Rome, under the cosmic Tent of Appearances; for there is no intimation that he so honored himself when he returned from Greece and had a new entrance broken through the old walls of Rome so that he could enjoy a fitting triumphal entrance as both an Olympic victor and glorified Apollo.

Following the death of Nero and the reaction to his many excesses, which resulted in the partial destruction of his Golden House, it was Domitian who revived his policy of orientalizing the Roman Court and succeeded in elevating himself to the stature of a *Dominus et Deus*. Like Nero, he exhibited an interest in the domical covering. In the construction of his *Domus Augustana* as the new Palace of the Caesars on the Palatine he had his architect Rabirius erect at least two domical halls (Fig. 135) in connection with the vestibule; and it was probably in one of these halls, referred to by Martial as "Caesar's tholus" (*Ep.* II, 59), that the Lord of the Oecumene feasted with his guests in the center of the cosmos.[65] The fact that Domitian encouraged the Roman writers to associate him and the other deified Flavians with the stars explains Martial's reference to the *astra polumque* (*Ep.* VII, 59): it is thought that he meant by "the stars and the pole," or *skene* and tent-pole, the sky symbolism of the domical triclinium which continued the tradition of Alexander's "Tent of Heaven" and Nero's banqueting tholus.

This *skene* symbolism, it has been noted, was probably peculiar to the palace conventions of Alexandria. It was also principally from the traditions of Pharaonic Egypt that the Roman emperors derived the conception of a ruler being "the son, successor, and heir of the gods"; and it was Domitian who adopted the divine titles of the Ptolemaic kings, even using in Egypt the formula the "Horus-ra of gold which his father has raised (to the throne)" in his effort to elevate himself into a *Divus* and thus to be identified with the religion of the State.[66] In view, therefore, of Domitian's theophanic policy and his desire to have his palace considered a *templum*, as was true of an Egyptian Pharaoh, it is easy to imagine him enthroned like the Horus-Ra of Egypt beneath a cosmic ciborium in the ceremonies of his Sacred Palace.[67] Once again, however, there is no evidence to intimate that he went further at Rome than to have his statue set up for adoration under a heavenlike canopy. On the coins (Fig. 118), where he is presented enthroned under a conical baldachin and guarded by soldiers, the scale of the figures leaves little doubt that it was a colossal statue, probably in the vestibule or forecourt, of his palatium, which was so honored.[68]

[65] L'Orange (*Studies on the Iconography of Cosmic Kingship*, pp. 30-31) discusses the concept of the ruler as "the Axis and Pole of the World" and Domitian's banqueting hall, where Statius (*Silvae*, 4, 2) says it was like "resting with Jupiter in the midst of the stars"; Lehmann, *op.cit.*, p. 22.

[66] A. Moret, *Du caractère religieux de la rayauté pharonique*, pp. 5, 23.

[67] Scott, *The Imperial Cult under the Flavians*, pp. 65-71; F. Sauter, *Der römische Kaiserkult bei Martial und Statius*, 1934, pp. 137-153.

[68] Coin of Domitian, mint of Rome (Mattingly,

Later, on the coins of Antoninus Pius (Fig. 119), it is once more not the person, but the statue, of the Emperor that is enshrined.[69] Here the starlike cusps along the outer edge of the arch were a decorative and numismatic means to indicate that the canopy was the arch of heaven, a convention which can be seen later on the Byzantine royal baldachin (Fig. 101).[70] So far, then, the coins have only recorded a significant relation between the appearance of the divine ciborium over an imperial image and those emperors most interested in manifesting their divinity. At the end of the second century on the coins of Commodus (Fig. 120) the figure of the double-faced Ianus standing under a ciborium is further proof that the baldachin was officially associated by this time with the adoration of the image of the Emperor as a god.[71] It is the Emperor himself who is presented as the personification of the ancient sky-god and solar deity of the Romans, the master of heaven always identified with the arch, for on other coins Commodus is portrayed as the double-faced god with his own head combined with that of Ianus, who was his alter ego and the counterpart of Jupiter.[72]

The absence of any evidence of the baldachin having been used as a "throne tabernacle" in the Roman palaces and the fact that the coin of Commodus at the end of the second century is the last example prior to the empire-wide appearance of the ciboriumlike cupolas on the coins of Diocletian are negative factors of historical significance. Before attempting to evaluate the gaps in the evidence it should be recalled that even in the Ancient East there was no proof of the baldachin having been used as a "throne tabernacle" when a ruler was seated in his own palace *sacrarium*. Instead, everything has suggested that a ritualistic Tent of Appearances was customary only when a divine king gave public audiences in the court of his palace, when either he, or his statue, was enshrined for the celebration of a public festival and when he, or his statue, was received with adoration and acclamations at the portal of a city and palace.

Against this historical background the very limitations of the Roman evidence lead to certain conclusions. Inasmuch as elaborate ceremonial honors were accorded by the Hellenistic cities to both the Republican generals and the later emperors, with the result that the royal Epiphany of the Greek kings became the Roman Adventus, it has been suggested that from the time of Augustus the emperors were accustomed to being received as gods in the East and enshrined for adoration under the sacred ciborium. During the first two centuries of the Empire there was still enough opposition at Rome to the oriental forms of ruler-worship so that the emperors did not venture further than to set up their own statues in public for adoration under a

---

Coins of the Roman Empire, II, p. 407, pl. 80/12; Alföldi, *Röm. Mittl.*, L, 1935, p. 129, Taf. 14/1; Mattingly (*op.cit.*, p. 388n) has voiced some doubts about this type of coin.

[69] Coin of Antoninus, Staatl. Münzensamml., Vienna (Alföldi, *op.cit.*, p. 129, Taf. 14/3).

[70] For similar astral decorations along the edge of an arch see Cook, *Zeus*, II, p. 362, figs. 255, 256, 259, 260. These star-tipped cusps occur also on the frescoes of the Fourth Pompeian Style (Niccolini, *Pompeii*, n. 138).

[71] Coin of Commodus (F. Gnecchi, *I Medaglioni romani*, II, 1920, p. 62, no. 94, pl. 84/5); Cook, *Zeus*, II, figs. 261-263; another version with a frontal ciborium (Mattingly, *op.cit.*, IV, 1940, p. 803, no. 568, pl. 106/5).

[72] Cook, *Zeus*, II, pp. 307-384, figs. 272-284; Gnecchi, *op.cit.*, nos. 92, 131, pls. 84/4, 87/1.

heavenly baldachin. By the end of the second century, however, beginning with either Commodus or Septimius Severus, the celestial *skene* had become so commonly associated with the "appearance" of the emperors in their Thracian cities that its form was recognized as an imperial emblem and its domical shape was depicted on the towers of the city-gate coins to commemorate either a visitation or anniversary.

It is only the assumptions that the emperors adopted the baldachin in the Eastern provinces for certain kinds of ceremonies and that gradually the cupola form of *skene* became identified with imperial receptions at a city and palace gateway which account for the emphatic and widespread use of the ciborium, cupola, and globe, as related insignia, on the coins of Diocletian and Constantine. In other words, by the fourth century, when coins with baldachins over the portal were issued by all the mints of the Empire, the ciborium, in combination with the orb, had become universally recognized as an emblem of the *Magnus parens orbis*. Furthermore, we are forced to the conclusion that the reason why there are no literary descriptions and no representations, prior to the sixth century, of the living Augustus enthroned under a baldachin was because it was not until the close of the Empire that the ciborium was taken out of its traditional use as a canopy of receptions and appearances, and adopted as a throne tabernacle.

Exactly when the sacred *skene* became so customarily associated with the official appearances of an enthroned ruler that it was elevated into a Baldachin of State is still conjectural. The prominence given to the royal ciborium on the coins at the beginning of the fourth century suggests that the change may have taken place in Diocletian's hieratic Court at Nicomedia. This presumption is supported by the evidence from the Imperial Cult room at Luxor, which was built in honor of Diocletian and his Tetrarchy in the old sanctuary of Amenophis III at the time when the Temple of Amon was in the center of a Roman castrum; for there was a ciborium in the Tychaion of this sanctuary, where we may assume that the Emperor was worshiped by the army in much the same way that he was adored by the court in his palace *sacrarium* at Nicomedia.[73] The late third or early fourth century date would also account for the prominence given to the various types of imperial baldachins in the various representations of a *Sacrum palatium* on the mosaics of St. George at Saloniki, which are

[73] U. Monneret de Villard, "The Temple of the Imperial Cult at Luxor," *Archaeologia*, xcv, 1953, pp. 85-105. At the close of the third century the legion stationed at Luxor constructed the castrum around the ancient Temple of Amon and in it made a chapel for the imperial cult. At the intersections of the crossroads on either side of the temple were found four column bases recording that one tetrastyle was dedicated about A.D. 300 to Diocletian, Maximian Hercules, Constantius Chlorus and Galerius and that the other was dedicated in 308-309 to the two Augusti, Licinius and Galerius, and their two Caesars. These tetrastyles in honor of the Tetrarchy presumably had domical coverings and were used, like the tetrapylons at the intersections of the roads in front of the palaces at Antioch and Constantinople, for ceremonial and processional receptions. The *sacellum* for the imperial cult, which was built into the sanctuary of Amenophis III and processionally approached through the forecourt and hypostyle hall, had a royal apsidal niche with a ciborium of four columns in front of it and its walls were painted with a processional scene in honor of Diocletian as Jupiter and Maximian, whose figure was later erased. It is purely conjectural as to whether the ciborium covered a sacrificial altar, a statue of Diocletian, or a figure of his Genius, which would have been identified with the imperial Tyche or Fortuna.

now attributed to Theodosius, and accords with the later pictorial evidence of there having been a domical throne-tabernacle of Theodosius (Fig. 100) in the Imperial Palace.

The lack of any specific proof as to when a formal throne-tabernacle was adopted by the Roman emperors in the East does not negate the other evidence that the Roman palace liturgy and architecture were both influenced at an early date by the Hellentistic ritual of setting up, or constructing in a more monumental form, a domical covering for the receptions and public appearances of a ruler at the entrance of cities and royal residences. Everything we know about the use of a domical vestibule in palace architecture shows very clearly that it was a ceremonial feature, like the tetrapylon in front of the palace entrance, which had resulted from the translation, for ideological reasons, of the symbolic ciborium concept into more permanent construction.

Before it can be demonstrated that the domical vestibule in Roman palaces was ceremonially comparable to the ciborium in the *Porta regia* of the Hellenistic palaces, and was a provision for a palace rite of welcome which had preserved many characteristics of the Hellenistic Royal Epiphany, it is necessary to work backward from the Byzantine palaces and their recorded ceremonies. In this way it may be possible to demonstrate that a celestial *skene*, either as a portable tent or domical vault, was a prescribed provision for a royal *parousia* in Antiquity, which explains: (1) the presence of the domical vestibule in Roman palace architecture, (2) why a ritualistic covering during the Middle Ages continued to be used over both Princes of the Church and State in Advent ceremonies, (3) why the baldachin appears so consistently over a city-gate in scenes with the implications of an Epiphany, (4) why eventually Byzantine monasteries built domical vestibules for the reception of their guests, and (5) why the royal baldachin was either set up, or constructed as a domical parakyptikon in the tribune, directly over the "Imperial Door," of the Byzantine palace-churches.

V · DOMICAL VESTIBULES AND HALLS IN ROMAN

AND BYZANTINE PALACES

IT IS very difficult for the matter-of-fact modern reader to comprehend the ceremonial and symbolic purpose of the domical vestibules and halls in the Roman
and Byzantine palaces. Over the centuries the popular ideas regarding kingship,
quite regardless of the weaknesses and mortality of individual monarchs, had come
to invest the Crown and "the Purple" with mystic powers; and the palace architecture
had developed into a ceremonial and dramatic stage-set intended to present the emperor as an awe-inspiring and heavenly world ruler, who was to be seen enshrined
above ordinary mortals in what was figuratively thought of as a cosmic dwelling. But
how are we to visualize the original splendor and ritualistic functions of the ruined
palaces, today stripped of their decorations and for the most part reduced to little
more than the bare outlines of their foundations? The ground plans, and even their
pictorial restorations, with their vast conglomerations of gateways, vestibules, courts,
anterooms and great halls, seem empty and purposeless without the formalities of
daily life, the carefully staged services, processions, receptions, and all the pageantry for
which they were designed. Throughout Antiquity, and down to the erection of Ver-
sailles for the French "Sun-King," the organization of space in a royal residence was
seldom controlled by considerations of comfort and privacy, but rather by precedent
and a desire to dramatize the ruler's exalted role as a godlike being.

We may believe that elaborate rituals of Hellenistic and Eastern origin governed
the architectural provisions surrounding the emperors from the time when Domitian,
inspired by Ptolemaic precedents, transformed the Palatine at Rome into a sacred
edifice; but how are we to give any reality to this tradition when so little is known
about the buildings and the ceremonies? All the evidence tends to get out of focus
unless it is recognized that there was a lasting veneration for Rome and all the forms
of Roman prestige, which resulted in the continuation of the Hellenistic and Roman
palace concepts by the Byzantine, mediaeval, and Islamic rulers. If there was a persistent palace tradition, modified of course by Christianity, by Western feudalism,
and by the Oriental heritage of Islam, then it is possible to approach the problem by
starting with the accounts of the palaces at Constantinople and the ritual as recorded
in the "Books of Ceremonies" of Constantine Porphyrogenitus, in order to see if there
were consistently persistent architectural features, ceremonial provisions, and symbolic
ideas in this tradition.

1. The Great Palace at Constantinople

From the time when "New Rome" was made the capital by Constantine the Great
and down to the tenth century, when the palace ceremonies were transcribed, both
the palace architecture and liturgies of the Byzantine Court adhered with great pride

to Roman precedent, even though the forms and rites were gradually enriched with new Eastern features and adjusted to the Christian faith.[1] Much of the studied solemnity, adulation, veiled secrecy, prescribed silence and religious mysticism surrounding the East Roman emperors were less the result of Byzantine contacts with the East than of the systematic orientalizing of the Imperial Court before the capital was shifted to Constantinople. Therefore, if it can be assumed that a rigid conservatism governed imperial architecture it should be possible to trace back the symbolic significance of the domical vestibule from the evidence of the Byzantine palace versions of ceremonies which were related in origin to the Hellenistic Epiphany and Roman Adventus.

At Constantinople the innumerable receptions of the emperor in the different parts of the palace were prescribed functions in the never-ending formalities of the Byzantine Court, where the Basileus was still invested with all the sanctity, theocratic power and hieratic distinction of a Roman Augustus. Many of these receptions took place at gateways and vestibules which are described as domical, and were first constructed by Constantine, who had not been brought up in the East but trained in his father's palace at Treves. In nearly every instance this Byzantine ritual of ingress and egress at the palace vestibules consisted of acclamations by the representatives of the political factions of the city, paeans of praise, music, singing, and all the formal features which had been part of the Royal Epiphany, and since Hellenistic times had characterized the *parousia* of a World-ruler, Savior and Triumphant Lord. It was at all times a religious ritual and the closest parallels we have today are the festivals and solemn ceremonies of the Church, which were influenced by it.

Unfortunately nothing remains standing of any of the principal buildings of the Great Palace. It is, therefore, necessary to establish the broad outlines of the palace ritual in relation to plans which have been reconstructed from documentary evidence. Since recent detailed studies of the documents, some of which have not yet been published, have changed the location of many parts of the palace and shown that they were frequently rebuilt, it is impossible to rely with any confidence upon the restorations of Ebersolt and Vogt.[2] The plan of Ebersolt, however, has been used in this study with many misgivings, not because it is the most accurate, but because it is so obviously diagrammatic and presents the ceremonial stations to be discussed in an axial and processional sequence.

The first domical structure of ceremonial importance in the processional approach to the palace was the Milion, which Ebersolt's plan (Fig. 130/A) locates as a gateway,

[1] L. Bréhier, *Les Institutions de l'empire byzantium*, II, 1949, pp. 53, 65-68, 88 and "Les Empereurs byzantins dans leur vies privée," *Revue hist.*, CLXXXVIII-IX, 1940, pp. 193-217; Ebersolt, *Mélanges d'hist. et d'arch.*, 1917, pp. 50-69; Piganiol, *Byzantion*, XI, 1926, p. 383; A. Rambaud, *Études sur l'histoire byzantine*, 1912, p. 207; O. Treitinger, *Die oströmische Kaiser-und Reichsidee*, Jena, 1938.

[2] C. J. Labarte, *Le Palais impérial de Constantinople*, 1861; Antoniadi, *Hagia Sophia*, I, 1907, p. 45, pl. 16; Ebersolt, *Le grand palais de Constantinople*, 1910, plan; A. Vogt, *Constantin Porphyrogénète, le livre des cérémonies, Commentaire*, I, 1935, plan and restoration. For archaeological evidence see: Mamboury und Wiegand, *Die Kaiserpaläste von Konstantinopel*, 1934; A. M. Schneider, *Byzanz, Vorarbeiten zur iconographie und archäologie der Stadt*, Berlin, 1936.

or monumental baldachin, at the entrance to the Augusteon, the great court that lay between the Palace and Hagia Sophia. It is now reasonably certain that the Milion was not a gateway, but a tetrapylon located at the intersection of the two avenues, one running either through or parallel to the Augusteon and the other the colonnaded Mese which came from the Forum and, after passing through the Milion and continuing in between the Palace and the Augusteon, terminated at the Chalce (Fig. 130/B) as the formal entrance of the Palatium.[3] The Milion was probably a pre-Constantinian structure, perhaps dating back to the time of Septimius Severus. It was a traditional provision in the ceremonial approach to an imperial residence, because in form and location it was like the tetrapylon at Antioch and the Arch of Galerius at Saloniki, both of which were at the intersection of the crossroads in front of the entrance to an Imperial Palace.[4] When one recalls the ceremonial scenes on the Arch of Galerius and the evidence that it was originally covered with a dome, one may suspect that the Roman tetrapylon at the approach to a palace, or imperial sanctuary, was itself a monumentalized version of a Hellenistic reception pavilion, or ciborium.

The interior of the Milion, which at a later date was decorated with mosaics depicting the six first Church Councils, was domical and on the exterior had statues of Constantine and Helena holding the cross, and perhaps the figure of a Tyche. The significance of this monumentalized baldachin in the tradition of royal ceremonies is the way it was used as a place of honor where the Basileus was received by representatives of the people when he was returning to the palace, usually on feast days after he had visited some church in the city. On some occasions the emperor and empress, having arrived on horseback, dismounted at the Milion where they were received, as if their coming was still celebrated like an Adventus or Epiphany, first by delegates of the Blue and White factions and then by those of the Greens and Reds.[5]

The Imperial Palace was divided into a succession of sections and at each successive part there was a domical vestibule, pavilion, or tribunal platform on which a throne was covered with a baldachin, where the various rites of welcome and appearances were religiously enacted. The principal entrance, where the most important ceremonies took place, was the Chalce, a monumental *vestibulum regiae*, which was at the end of the Mese, facing either the Augusteon or a smaller court between the Palace and Hagia Sophia. The next ceremonial station was the Lychnoi (Fig. 130/C) which was presumably a domical pavilion in front of the great assembly hall, known as the Consistorion. Further on other ceremonies of a formal and dramatic character

[3] Ebersolt, *op.cit.*, pp. 15-16; R. Janin, *Constantinople Byzantine*, 1950, pp. 104-105, 363-364; Mamboury, *Byzantion*, XI, 1936, p. 253; Mordtmann, *Revue de l'art chrétien*, XLI, 1891, p. 24; Vogt, *op.cit., Commentaire*, I, p. 86.

[4] G. Downey, "The Palace of Diocletian at Antioch," *Annales archéologiques de Syrie*, III, 1953, pp. 106-116; C. R. Morey, *The Mosaics of Antioch*, 1938, p. 16 (plan), 17; Evagrius, *Hist. eccl.*, II, 12. There was presumably a similar tetrapylon at the intersection of the roads in front of the palace of

Philippus Arabs at Philippolis-Sherbā (H. C. Butler, *Architecture and the Other Arts*, fig. 130). These monumental baldachinlike structures, which were usually domical on the interior like the Milion, had a ceremonial purpose and probably went back in origin to columnar canopies of reception, as is indicated by the columnar bases at the crossroads in front of the entrances to the imperial shrine in the castrum at Luxor (see Ch. IV, n. 73).

[5] Vogt, *Texte*, I, p. 25.

were enacted in the Onopodion (Fig. 130/E), which was a stagelike tribunal, probably with a domical pavilion, at the entrance to the Augusteus.[6] Also at the time of special festivals it was customary for the Basileus to receive the salutations of the Court and the acclamations of the representatives of the political factions while seated in a domical phiale.

Before attempting to describe the Chalce, it is essential to keep in mind that its domical hall was a traditional provision for a sacrosanct royal drama which had its origin in a revered and glorified past. In the imperial liturgy every event in the private and public life of the Basileus was so ordered that no one could forget that he was the Kosmicos Autocrator, the Oecumenical Master of the World, the High Priest or Pontifex Maximus of the Church, the Isapostolos (resembling the Apostles) and the Christos-Basileus.[7] At each of the many receptions which took place at the various stations in the palace all the standardized greetings with which the emperor was acclaimed suggest a venerated usage and a derivation from the *parousia* of the Hellenistic kings. On some occasions he was greeted as, "Soldier incomparable, Defender of the World," "Lord who loves Justice" and "Ruler, we invoke you for the happiness of our city"; but most frequently he was addressed with the words, "Many years to you, Autocrat of the Romans."[8]

It is the survival of so many aspects of the pagan emperor-cult which implies a similar continuity in the ceremonial provisions and in the symbolic ideas associated with them. At the same time that the court and clergy explained the inconsistencies between their Christian faith and the pagan survivals of the ruler ritual by insisting that they "worshiped only the purple," the fact remains that in the Byzantine palace liturgy the Basileus, like the Augustus of the Romans, was treated in a pontifical manner as "the image of God." Even the ancient custom of the pagan Epiphanies, in which the ruler

[6] The Lychnoi, according to J. B. Bury ("The Great Palace," *Byz. Zeit.*, XXI, 1912, p. 213) was the same as the "Tholos of Heptalychnos." The Onopodion, according to Vogt (*Commentaire*, I, pp. 27-28), was the great ceremonial vestibule of the Daphne Palace; but according to R. Guilland ("Autour du livre des cérémonies: L'Augusteus, Le Main d'Or et L'Onopodion," *Revue des études byzantines*, VI, 1948, pp. 167-180) it was a small open court in front of the raised tribunal at the entrance to the Augusteus. While it is not clear from the texts whether the Onopodion was a domical vestibule or a stagelike tribunal, on which was the throne covered by a baldachin, it was probably an open-air platform with a domical canopy not unlike the domical pavilion in front of the inner gate of the Turkish palace of Topkapu Saray at Constantinople (see p. 204).

[7] A. Rambaud, *Études sur l'histoire byzantine*, pp. 177-184. Anyone who is not a specialist in Byzantine history is hesitant to say under what circumstances "Christos-Basileus" meant only an emperor who lived and ruled "in Christ," or one who was comparable to the Son of God, like the Carolingian "Royal Christ" in the West, because the subtleties of his divine status in the *Corpus politicum mysticum* make it difficult to recognize accurately the various theological, ceremonial, and popular distinctions which were made at different times in the Basileus' relations to Christ. At the same time that he was "the living image and soul of Christ, expressing by his works and words, the truth" (A. Vogt, *Basil I*, Paris, 1908, p. 255), he was also a *Divus* (Bréhier, *op.cit.*, II, pp. 61-62) whose complicated relation to God is voiced in a letter of the Archbishop of Bulgaria, who called John Comnenus, "powerful Basileus crowned by God and god of the universe (Bréhier, p. 55); he was also the "Representative of Christ," the "Imitator of Christ" and the "Image of Christ" who was, therefore, "the earthly Christ" (Treitinger, *op.cit.*, pp. 33-53).

[8] Vogt, *Texte*, II, 29, 91. In these acclamations there was at times the implication that the Basileus was the Son of God, as when in the Hippodrome (*op.cit.*, II, 124) the people shouted, "He who loves not our Emperor will be lost, like Judas."

133

had been identified with the solar deity, was so little changed that the emperor, gleaming with gold and precious jewels, was still referred to in the traditional acclamations and standardized phrases as comparable to the Sun. Both in the palace and when he moved through the city there occurred over and over again such refrains as, "The Star announces the Sun" and "Behold the Morning Star approaches; the Day Star rises." At the time of the emperor's fourth reception, which took place in the Chalce during the celebration of the Feast of the Nativity, the singers chanted, "The Star arises and shines over the grotto in order to indicate to the Magi the Master of the Sun."[9]

At the moment when the Basileus arrived at the Hippodrome and took his seat in the imperial balcony the people chanted "$ανατολή$" (The Sun rises), and then at the beginning of the games shouted "$ἀνάτειλον$."[10] At other times his Roman and Hellenistic heritage as a heavenly being was proclaimed by such public salutations as "Ouranios," "Oh Power on High" and "Your Divine Royalty is welcome."[11] All these acclamations and chanted greetings in the hieratic conservatism of the Byzantine Court must have conformed to ancient formulas. Therefore, the way in which they consistently went with the public appearances of the emperor under a heavenly baldachin, or with his formal receptions under a monumentalized *skene* at the entrance to the *Sacrum palatium* is confirming evidence that the domical place of greeting was also traditional and that the domical vestibules in the earlier Roman palaces had a similar ritualistic function.

There were many domical structures in the vast imperial residence at Constantinople, but it was the Chalce and the Chrysotriclinos which best exemplify the ceremonial and symbolic significance of the dome in the long history of the palace tradition. The Chalce, which was the monumental entrance of the *Magnum Palatium*, was known as the "House of Bronze" because of its great door and the gilded bronze tiles on its dome. Originally, at the time when it was first constructed by Constantine as the royal portal in the defensive walls of the imperial citadel, it presumably had only a small domical vestibule, comparable to the square entrance hall inside the Golden Gate of Diocletian's palace at Salona.[12] Even at this time its importance as a triumphant entrance is indicated by the account of the painted scene over the portal, which depicted Constantine and his two sons as Christian Victors transfixing with the Cross the serpent under their feet.[13] Before the end of the fifth century the

[9] Vogt, *Texte*, I, 29, 31, 32, 43, 46; II, 91.

[10] S. Antoniadis, *Place de la liturgie dans la tradition des lettres grecques*, 1939, p. 196.

[11] Vogt, *Texte*, I, 43; II, 123. G. Millet ("Les noms des auriges dans les acclamations de l'hippodrome," *Recueil de N. P. Kondakov*, 1926, pp. 279-295) says that many of the acclamations in the hippodrome were conventional names for the colors of the factions and that "ouranios," the color of the emperor's habit, had its origin in the Hymn to Victory of Alexander, who as the "rising sun" had struggled in the stadium at Olympia, "making

all the other stars pale."

[12] I am indebted for much of my information on the Chalce and the related parts of the palace to C. A. Mango, who has allowed me to make use of his excellent, unpublished "Recherches sur le palais impérial de Constantinople: La Chalcé et ses abords," 1953. Instead of locating the Chalce facing the Augusteon, as do both Ebersolt and Vogt, he believes that it was at the end of the Mese facing west.

[13] Eusebius, *Vita Constantini*, III, 3, 78; A. Grabar, *L'Empereur dans l'art byzantin*, p. 44.

Constantinian structure was replaced by a magnificent building erected by the architect Etherius for Anastasius, perhaps to celebrate the Emperor's victory over the Isaurians. Following the disastrous fire which was the result of the political riots in A.D. 532 the Chalce was rebuilt by Justinian; and, according to Procopius, was a rectangular structure, extending north and south, with piers supporting the central dome and the vaulted chambers at either side.[14] The next important alteration in the form of the Chalce took place in the tenth century when Romanus I Lecapenus added to it an Imperial Chapel, dedicated to the Savior.[15]

At the end of the Mese and in front of the Great Door of the Chalce was a raised and balustraded platform, somewhat like a stage, on which was an organ of gold and a throne of gold, the throne undoubtedly covered by a baldachin, so that many of the reception ceremonies could take place in the presence of the people assembled in the court.[16] Over the Bronze Door, except for the period of the Iconoclastic Controversies, was a mosaic image of the Savior; and in front of the door was a circular slab of royal porphyry set into the pavement where the imperial "Christos-Basileus" stood like a living omphalos beneath the image of his heavenly prototype. Numerous statues, mostly of emperors, decorated the niches of the Chalce and stood upon the tribunal, which the documents refer to as if it were a sacred chancel. Within the ceremonial rotunda of the Chalce the mosaics of the dome, which suggest a parallel to the iconographic decorations of the Byzantine church, had in the center, according to Procopius, Justinian and Theodora surrounded by Senators "who rejoice and smile as they bestow on the Emperor honors equal to those of God" and then in a lower register scenes of Belisarius and his army celebrating the Emperor's victories.

This marble hall with its mosaics and statues was an impressive place of receptions, comparable in many ways both to the naos of a church and to the domical *salutatorium* at the entrance to Diocletian's palace. Here God's representative on earth stood under the celestial vault of heaven to receive the acclamations of representatives of the political factions of the city. There were two organs and singers so that the ritualistic Coming of the imperial "Star" could be celebrated like a Hellenistic Epiphany by means of joyous music, songs, assurances of immortality and the praises of his adoring subjects.[17] At the death of the Basileus it was under the golden dome of this "prothura" that his body was laid out in state to receive the formal farewells, the last kiss of the dignitaries and clergy, before its final egress from the palace and its procession to the tomb.[18]

It is necessary to raise several controversial issues regarding Byzantine architecture before it is possible to consider the appearance of the Chalce and decide whether the

[14] Procopius, *Buildings* (Loeb), I, 1940, x, 16-25.

[15] Banduri, *Imperium Orientale Antiq. Const.*, I, 1711, pp. 3, 7-9; 95, 146; Ebersolt, *op.cit.*, pp. 19-24; Vogt, *Commentaire*, I, p. 56. For the ninth century account by the Arab Haroun-ibn-Yahya: M. Izeddin, *Revue des études islamique*, 1941-46, p. 48; A. A. Vasiliev, *Byzance et les arabes*, Brussels, II, 1950, p. 365.

[16] The tradition of a stagelike platform in front of a palace entrance persisted in the Fatimite palaces at Cairo (see p. 202) and the Moghul palace of India (Figs. 170, 171).

[17] Vogt, *Commentaire*, I, pp. 56-67.

[18] Vogt, *Texte*, II, 84 and *Commentaire*, II, 96; Ebersolt, *Constantinople*, 1951, p. 17.

structure pictured in the scene of the Death of Romanus Lecapenus (Fig. 160) from the Skylitzes manuscript, which has a central dome partially concealed by the buttressing at its haunch and four corner cupolas, was intended to be the Chalce. The first issue is whether on the basis of the evidence already reviewed in the previous chapters we are justified in believing that symbolic castrum towers, cupolas, sculptured baldachins, globes, and arcades above gateways were all part of the palace tradition which the Byzantine architects inherited. The second and more specific issue is whether the domical structure with corner cupolas, such as is pictured in the Skylitzes manuscript, should be thought of as only a type of Byzantine church, or as originally characteristic of the *Sacrum palatium* before it was adopted for the Royal House of God.

Back of both of these issues is the much larger question of whether all our preconceptions regarding the appearance of imperial palaces are not in need of reexamination. For a long time architectural historians, trained to think of Roman palaces only in terms of extant gabled temples and colonnades, accustomed to the somewhat Neoclassic and Beaux Arts restorations of the ruined palaces, and in part convinced by the *Orient oder Rom* controversy as to whether all domical construction was not an intrusion from the East, have tended to stress the differences between early Byzantine and late Roman architecture. As a result little attention has been given to the persistent features of the palace tradition from Hellenistic times down to the Turkish period at Istanbul, and still less consideration has been given to the possibility that there is evidence even in the plans of the ruined Roman palaces to indicate that they had towers, cupolas, and domical vestibules which were the prototypes of similar features on the palaces of Byzantium and Islam.

Regarding the appearance of the Chalce, the most obvious assumption is that the towered façade with cupolas must have been a dominant and symbolic feature of the entrance to the Grand Palace at Constantinople. In addition to the third century B.C. evidence on the Thracian coins (Figs. 19-30) that domical towers flanked the triumphal entrance to the provincial seat of government, it has been seen that towers with either cupolas or baldachins characterize the *Sacrum palatium* on the mosaics of Saloniki (Fig. 74) and Bethlehem (Fig. 75), in the Homilies of Gregory of Nazianzus (Fig. 73), and appear over the royal stronghold on the Byzantine casket (Fig. 98) and on the façade of the Boucoleon Palace (Fig. 159) from the Skylitzes manuscript. That there were towers at either side of the Chalce can be deduced from the ceremonial references to the emperor having gone up by a staircase both to the Chapel of the Savior and to the upper gallery over an arcade, or colonnade, which connected the Chalce with the Sacred Well at the southeast corner of Hagia Sophia.[19] Pictorial

[19] According to Mango there was a private imperial passage (*Stenakion*) over an arcade, or colonnade, leading from the "Iron Door" of the Chalce to the galleries of St. Sophia. A circular tower at the corner of the Chalce would have provided the necessary stairwell for the emperor to ascend to the passage. Also, according to Mango, the reliquary Chapel of the Savior, which Romanus I added onto the Chalce, was on an upper story, entered by an "escalier en colimacon," and "audessus l'arc de la Chalcé." Long porticos connecting a royal residence with its palace-church were

evidence of this private gallery is preserved in the scene from the eleventh century manuscript of the Skylitzes (Fig. 165) which depicts the Empress Theodora leaving Hagia Sophia and going to the palace to speak to the people.[20] Her window or balcony of appearances, which has shutters and is marked like the royal castrum on the coins of Diocletian by four little cupolas over it, undoubtedly looked down upon the public space in front of the Chalce, this means that the diagrammatic structure with towers back of the people was intended to refer to the Chalce or to the gateway at the end of the Mese which opened into the inner court in front of the Chalce.

The four little cupolas over the window from which the Empress speaks to the people, like the three cupolas above the battlements in the scene of the enthroned Basil I (Fig. 162) and the two cupolas surmounting the arch over the Emperor Leo (Fig. 164), which recall the imperial insignia over the palace entrance on the coins of Diocletian (Figs. 33-38), are proof that sculptured ciboria had continued to be palace emblems ever since the beginning of the fourth century.[21] The fact that they were so important in the architectural iconography of Byzantium as to appear over the triumphal arch of Basil (Fig. 167), when taken in combination with their use as symbols of divine authority over the *aula Regia* on the German seals and coins (Fig. 82) and to designate the sacredness of the Palatium of William the Conqueror (Fig. 9) and the Throne-room of Harold (Fig. 53), is incontrovertible evidence that sculptured baldachins belonged to the palace tradition. Their persistence and significance in this tradition will become more apparent when it is realized that they continued to be used by the Turks at Constantinople (Figs. 174, 175) and as a result of Turkish architects going to India may have been introduced into the palace architecture (Figs. 171-173) of the Great Moghuls.[22]

What then was the prototype of the cosmic type of sacred edifice with the imperial cupolas of the palatium-castrum at the four corners of the heavenly *skene* over the *salutatorium*, which we are accustomed to think of as a late form of palace-church (Fig. 156) in Byzantine architecture? Was it first introduced in the ninth century when Basil I erected the Nea as a new type of palace sanctuary, or was it at a much earlier date a traditional form of the *Sacrum palatium*? If my restoration is acceptable, as early as the fifth century the Church of Prophets, Apostles, and Martyrs at Gerasa had a central and corner towers crowned with cupolas which, like other martyria, reflects the desire of the Christians to make the dwelling of their saints as heavenly as an imperial palace.[23] In the sixth century the so-called "Grave church" at Resafa, which had stone cupolas at the corners and a wooden dome over the center, may have

---

[20] Skylitzes ms., Madrid, Bibl. Nat. 5, 3 n. 2, 220v; L. M. Beylié, *L'Habitation byzantine*, 1902, p. 114.

[21] Fig. 162, Skylitzes ms., fol. 105v; Fig. 164, fol. 113r; Fig. 167, fol. 183r.

[22] See p. 195.

[23] Smith, *The Dome*, p. 112, figs. 175, 177; Crowfoot, *Early Churches in Palestine*, p. 85, fig. 8.

also common in the West: at Aachen (Fictenau, *Byzance und die Pfalz zu Aachen*, Graz, 1951, pp. 23ff.; J. Buchkremer, "Die karolingische Porticus der Aachen Pfalz," *Bonn. Jahrb.*, CXLIX, 1949, pp. 212-238); Ingelheim (C. Clemen, "Les Fouilles du palais carolingien à Ingelheim," *Revue de l'art chrétien*, LXI, 1911, pp. 131-134); and perhaps at Santullano and Palermo.

been a pre-Islamic Arab assembly hall, copied from Byzantine palace architecture.[24] Furthermore, it has been seen that the "Palace of Helena" (Fig. 76), which was rebuilt at the close of the fourth century at the east end of what became the Cathedral at Treves, may originally have had wooden cupolas over the central hall and on the towers at the corners.

It is, therefore, the contention of this study that the prototype of all these sacred edifices was the *Sacrum palatium* at Constantinople, and still earlier the *salutatorium* at the entrance to Diocletian's palace. Certainly by the ninth century, when Basil erected the "New Church" with its five cupolas, the *pentyrigion* constructed for Theophilus before A.D. 842 is evidence that five towers were already recognized as a traditional and sacred type of structure.[25] Like the many church reliquary boxes which imitated palace or church architecture, the *pentyrigion* was a large reliquary cabinet made, according to Grabar, in imitation of a palace with five towers, or cupolas. It was located in the throne-room of the Magnaura Palace, but on certain occasions was removed to the Chrysotriclinos, and was used to exhibit precious objects, such as the nuptial wreath when the imperial marriage was celebrated. The only question seems to be whether it was the Chalce or the Chrysotriclinos which established the direct precedent for this type of structure in Byzantine architecture.

Without keeping in mind the whole interrelated patterns of symbolic forms which had come to be associated with the palace, it would be dubious to argue from the eleventh century illuminations of the Skylitzes manuscript, which are schematically conceptual rather than descriptively accurate, that the building in the scene of the Death of Romanus Lecapenus (Fig. 160) is the Chalce and that the Chalce was the archetype at Constantinople of the five-cupola type of structure.[26] It is true that the same type of building is used in the manuscript for the burial of the Patriarch Stephen, because by the eleventh century it was characteristic of both a palatium and palace-church.[27] Also it can be argued that it is not the Chalce because Romanus Lecapenus died on the island of Prote and was buried in the Myrelaion.[28] Nevertheless, in spite of these objections to identifying the building as the Chalce, it is still possible to insist that the custom of holding the farewell ceremonies for a dead emperor in the vestibule of the palace was the kind of a convention which would have conceptually and artistically persisted, regardless of fact. The clearest indication that the building with the five cupolas denotes the Chalce is the scene (Fig. 161) from the same manuscript which pictures Romanus Lecapenus receiving and kissing the sacred veil with the imprint of the image of Christ.[29] Here the same type of building must be the Chalce because at the left it has the domical Chapel of the Savior which Romanus added onto the Chalce and in which he enshrined the famous relief.

[24] Sauvaget, "Les Ghassides et Sergiopolis," *Byzantion*, XIV, 1939, pp. 115ff.; Smith, *The Dome*, pp. 112-113; H. Spanner and S. Guyer, *Rusafa*, 1926, pp. 42, 66, Taf. 31.

[25] J. B. Bury, *A History of the Eastern Roman Empire*, 1912, p. 134; A. Grabar, *Münchner Jahrbuch der bildenden Kunst*, 1951, p. 51; Vogt,

op.cit., *Commentaire*, I, p. 103.

[26] Skylitzes ms., fol. 133v.

[27] Fol. 127r.

[28] S. Runciman, *The Emperor Romanus Lecapenus*, 1929, p. 236.

[29] Fol. 131r.

At the same time that the Chalce, like the gateways of the Mesopotamian and Egyptian palaces, was the one memorable feature known to the public and most likely to have symbolized the whole sacred edifice, it is equally probable that the Chryso-triclinos, built by Justin II between A.D. 565-568, was another archetype for the subsequent towered and domical halls of appearances in which either God or the Emperor was adored. Like the earlier palace-church of St. Vitale at Ravenna and the later palace-church at Preslau (Fig. 162), the Chrysotriclinos (Fig. 122), which was the official throne-room of the Basileus where he held his most solemn receptions and took part in the state banquets, had apsidal exedras on each side of its octagonal interior. The imperial throne, comparable to the altar in St. Vitale, was located in the eastern apse under the half dome decorated with the image of Christ.[30] Its central dome was pierced with sixteen windows and constructed in panels, which were prob-ably concave, or alternatively flat and concave like the dome on the palace-church of SS. Sergius and Bacchus, in order to represent the traditional shape of the heavenly *skene*. Also like St. Vitale, it must have had a gallery which gave access to the adjacent royal apartments on the second story of the palace. That there were towers, with staircases giving access to the gallery, either at all four corners or at either side of the entrance can be argued by analogy with the palace-church at Preslau (Fig. 163) and St. Vitale, which originally had towers flanking the narthex and perhaps the apse. Some confirmation of this conclusion is furnished by the Skylitzes manuscript (Fig. 166) in the scene of the Queen of Georgia being led before Romanus III who is seated in the Chrysotriclinos.[31] Although the illumination leaves much to be desired in the way of architectural accuracy, it depicts corner cupolas, one of which is clearly on a tower, and domes with the striations and cusping of a *skene*.

It is the long history of domical symbolism, but more specifically the persistent association of domical vestibules and cupolas over the entrance of the Byzantine palace with imperial receptions and appearances which were of Hellenistic and Roman origin, that justifies tracing back the tradition and insisting that the domical vestibules of the Roman palaces served the same purpose and had the same symbolic meaning. The parallel between the Byzantine ceremonies and the Roman rites of welcome is best illustrated by the Triumph of Theophilus in A.D. 831.[32] The event began outside the city at his Palace of Hieria, near Chalcedon, where he was awaited by the Empress and the principal officials of the city. Here he was met at some distance outside the palace gateway by the senators who did obeisance before him; and on the seventh day after his arrival Theophilus and his Court moved to the Palace of St. Mamas where he waited for another three days. On the tenth day he sailed up the Golden Horn to the Blachernae Palace on the outskirts of the city; after disembarking he rode around the city walls to the Golden Gate and was there received in a tent pavilion pitched in the meadow before the ceremonial gateway of the city.

[30] Ebersolt, *Le grand palais*, pp. 80-82.
[31] Fol. 206r; Beylié, *op.cit.*, p. 123.

[32] Bury, *op.cit.*, pp. 127-128; A. A. Vasiliev, *Byz-ance et les Arabes*, I, pp. 105-109.

Meantime the city had been arrayed in festive garb, decorated "like a bridal chamber" with purple hangings and silver ornaments. At the triumphal gate he dismounted and made three obeisances to the East before crossing the threshold. He was then presented with the crown and acclaimed a Victor by the Demes. All along the colonnaded Mese, which ran from the Golden Gate to the Augusteon, the people strewed flowers before him as he rode at the head of the procession on his white charger. When he reached the Milion in front of the gate of the Augusteon all the senators who had not taken part in the campaign dismounted and walked in front of him as he rode to the Sacred Well of Hagia Sophia. Although there is no record of what took place in this chapel, we may suspect that it was analogous in the Christian rites to the way that the Roman Triumphator was symbolically cleansed in the Lavacrum of the Porta Triumphalis at Rome. Following the services in Hagia Sophia the Emperor walked across the Augusteon to the "Bronze Gate," which was the Chalce. On the platform in front of this ceremonial entrance to the palace, we are told that there was a pulpit flanked by a throne of gold and a golden organ, known as the "Prime Miracle," and between the throne and the pulpit was a cross of gold. When the Emperor was seated under his celestial ciborium the Demes shouted, "There is one Holy." After this acclamation Theophilus rode to the Hippodrome where the grand finale of the triumphal procession took place.

2. Theodoric's palace at Ravenna

The fifth century palace at Ravenna, which Theodoric must have modeled in part after the Imperial Palace at Constantinople where he was educated, had a *Porta prima, Chalci, Prima porta palatii* and a *Tribunali triclinii*.[33] Apart from the account of Angellus and the mosaic (Fig. 99) in Sant' Apollinare Nuovo little is known about the residence of the Ostrogothic king. The mosaic was originally intended to represent a palace ceremony at the time when Sant' Apollinare was an Arian palace-church, dedicated to the Savior.[34] In the sixth century, when it was rededicated in the orthodox faith to San Martino *in coelo aurea*, Angellus made many changes in the mosaic, removing the triumphant figure of Theodoric on horseback from the tympanum of the palace façade, and the figures that were in the openings of the arcade. At the right the towered gateway, marked CIVITAS RAVENN, may refer to the Chalce as the portal of the palace, because Angellus wrote, "in fronte Regiae, quae dicitur Ad Chalci istius civitatis ubi prima porta palatii fuit."[35] The presumption that this gateway with its two towers crowned with conical roofs imitated Constantine's Chalce at Constantinople is strengthened when it is realized that the figure in white over the doorway, who

[33] E. Dyggve, *Ravennatum Palatium Sacrum*, 1941; C. Ricci, *Guida di Ravenna*, pp. 111-125; F. v. Reber, *Abhandlungen d. Bayerischen Ak. d. Wissenschaften*, XIX, 1891, pp. 713-795; W. Esselin, *Theoderich der Grosse*, Munich, 1949, pp. 259ff.

[34] G. Bovini, "Osservazioni sur frontone del 'Palatium' di Theodorico figurato nel mosaico di S. Apollinare Nuovo di Ravenna," *Festschrift für Rudolf Egger*, Klagenfurt, 1952, pp. 206-211; R. Bartoccini, *Felix Ravenna*, 1942, pp. 168-170.

[35] Agnellus, *Liber Pontif, Eccl. Ravennatus*, M.G.H. Schrit., rer. Long. et Ital. (ed. Holder-Egger, 1878), p. 337; Dyggve, *op.cit.*, pp. 45f.

holds a cross and tramples under foot a serpent, is not a saint, but Constantine with his two sons.[36]

It is impossible to agree with Dyggve that the mosaic pictures a schematic and expanded view of an atrium, such as was customary in front of a Christian church, and not one side of a large palace court with rooms and corridors back of the arcade of the upper story. The triumphal motifs of wreaths and victories which decorate the spandrils show that the elevated arcade had royal implications, either as the private quarters of the king, or as a processional gallery such as connected the Chalce at Constantinople with Hagia Sophia. Although domical structures appear in the background the entrance of the Palatium is an ordinary tribunal porch with a *fastigium*, which was itself a traditional symbol of divine and royal distinction on the vestibules of Roman palaces and temples; but at Galeata in the province of Forli the ruins of Theodoric's palace, which was probably a hunting residence, indicate that it may have had a towered façade and domical throne room.[37] It is not to be thought that the entrance to Theodoric's palace was intended to be comparable to the imperial portals at Constantinople because the Ostrogothic king was always careful not to compete with the Byzantine Basileus.

3. Diocletian's palace at Salona

The sacred castrum-palatium which Diocletian built at Salona almost two centuries earlier than the Ostrogothic palace is referred to in the accounts of the Imperial Palace at Constantinople as if it were looked upon as the revered and ideal archetype of a *Sacrum palatium*. It has already been shown that it was built in the form of a citadel, or military camp, not so much because it was intended to be a protection for the living Jove in his retirement, but because the castrum had come to exemplify the concept of the Palatium as the center of that divine authority which governed the Empire. Inside its "Golden Gate" (Fig. 5), which was crowned with the celestial and imperial arcade and had statues of the emperor and the other gods in its niches, there was a square vestibule.[38] That this square space, which in itself implies a domical vault, was originally covered with a celestial cupola is to be deduced from the Chalce at Constantinople and the fact that it can be shown that royal receptions at the entrance of a palace usually

[36] *Vita Constantini*, III, 3.78; A. Grabar, *L'Empereur dans l'art byzantin*, p. 44; for similar scenes on the Constantian coins see Maurice, *Numismatique Constantinienne*, II, pp. 414, 507, pl. XII/18.

[37] The *fastigium*, or triangular pediment, was from Republican times a recognized mark of an exalted, royal, and divine distinction: it was one of the royal elements prescribed by Vitruvius (V, 6.9) for tragic scenery; a *fastigium in domo* was an honor bestowed on Caesar (Alföldi, *Röm. Mittl.*, L, 1935, pp. 132-135; Boëthius, *Eranos*, XLIV, p. 455; Dessau, *Insc. Lat.*, II, 1902, 3593, 3975, 5446; *Thesaurus Linguae Latinae*, VI, pp. 1320ff). The small palace of Theodoric at Galeata in the province of Forli was entered through a colonnaded porch, which had at either end square structures whose shape and interior staircases indicate that they were towers, and its central throne-room with an apse is also square, implying that it was covered with either a wooden or masonry dome (G. Jocopi, "Galeata [Forli]," *Mon. Scavi Antiq.*, 1943, pp. 204-217; S. Fuchs, *Bericht Jhr. d. Deutsch. Arch. Inst. Anz.*, LVII, 1942, cols. 259-277, Abb. 3; P. Lévêque, *R. archéol.*, XXVIII, 1947, pp. 58-61).

[38] Dyggve, *op.cit.*, p. 45, fig. 2; E. Hébrard et J. Zeiller, *Mélanges d'arch. et d'hist.*, XXXI, 1911, pp. 247-275; *Spalato, le palais de Dioclétien*, 1912; M. Niemann, *Der Palast Diokletiens*, 1910; G. Stratimirovic, *Bull. di Archaeologia e Storia Dalmata*, 1911; F. Weilbach, "Diocletians Palads i Spolato," *Studier Fra Sprogog Oldtidsforskning*, no. 13, 1917.

141

took place under domical coverings as early as the Hellenistic period and as late as the Turkish dominations of the Near East.

From the *Porta aurea* the processional way led directly to the domical hall at the entrance to the palaces proper. This rotunda (Fig. 133) with its massive dome was the *salutatorium*, where the divine Diocletian was welcomed, acclaimed and adored in much the same way that the Utrecht Psalter (Fig. 132) pictures the "servants of the Lord" lifting up their hands "in the sanctuary" of the palatial House of God.[39] The approach to the triple-arched tribunal porch leading into the rotunda was not an un-roofed basilica and "tribunalium," like an atrium, but the customary colonnaded avenue, covered with canopies, that in so many Roman cities led from the ceremonial city-gate to either the *palatium* or *praetorium*.[40]

Since Diocletian's palace must have copied the now destroyed imperial residences at Antioch and Nicomedia and undoubtedly influenced the construction of the Great Palace at Constantinople, it is highly probable that its monumental vestibule, in addition to being covered with a great gilded dome, had on it domical towers, or sculptural baldachins, at the four corners.[41] This supposition is not entirely hypothetical because there are still staircases at either side of the rotunda going up to the roof, which recall the Hellenistic palaces and Roman temples of the Near East with staircases giving access to towers at the four corners.[42] Furthermore, this assumption is not unlikely if it is granted that towers had a heavenly significance in the East and were used from early times down to the Islamic period for ceremonial purposes.[43] Finally, there is the question of why sculptured ciboria should have first appeared on the coins of Diocletian (Figs. 31-38) if they were not already recognized symbols of power on the early fourth century palaces?

[39] That the "House of the Lord" and the similar other royal residences in the Utrecht Psalter were derived from existing Carolingian palace architecture, and that there was a persistent palace tradition based upon late Antique precedents, such as the palace of Diocletian, is indicated by the mediaeval accounts of the Carolingian palace at Farfa, outside of Rome (Schlosser, "II, Die Palastbeschreibung aus Farfa und der Profanbau des frühen Mittelalters," *Sitzungsberichte d. K. Ak. der Wissenschaften*, Vienna, CXXIII, 1891, pp. 41-64, Taf. I). According to Schlosser's compilation of evidence from the documents, this palace had: a *pro aulium*, or *prima porta*; then a columnar *salutatorium*, which he imagines to have been a large court, but which on the evidence of Diocletian's palace, the Chalce at Constantinople and the palaces in the Utrecht Psalter was presumably covered with a *skene*like wooden dome sheathed in gilded metal; a *consistorium* for audiences that Schlosser assumes was circular for no reason except that he used the Hellenistic palace at Palatizia as a model; a tri-apsidal triclinium, called a *trichorum*; and also a large bath, a gymnasium and a hippodrome.

[40] Dyggve's arguments are not convincing for calling the colonnaded street in front of the dom-ical vestibule an unroofed basilica and "tribunalium," like an atrium. Although a colonnade, or *porticus*, was from Hellenistic times a distinguishing feature of a royal residence and continued to be used on one or more sides of the court of a *Domus regalis*, it does not follow that by the fourth century all palaces were entered through a colonnaded court or atrium, and there seems to be no justification for associating the columns of a traditional processional way with a *basilica impetrale*.

[41] A. Grabar (*Martyrium*, I, pp. 216-219) has pointed out that the Imperial Palace at Antioch with its division into quarters, its open galleries, its tetrapylon, and its axial intersection of streets must have been the prototype of Diocletian's palace and that its basic architectural characteristics went back to Hellenistic models.

[42] Hellenistic palaces (see p. 14) and Roman temples (see p. 13).

[43] There was in the Ancient East (see p. 114 n. 18) the persistent custom of going up to the top of towers on palaces and temples, which were symbols of the dwelling place of the most high and the place from which the presence and divine will of either an earthly or spiritual master was proclaimed.

4. Other fourth century palaces

This restoration would make the façade of Diocletian's palace conform to the castrum concept already seen in the design of the royal "Basilica" at Treves (Fig. 8), which
may have been a palatium, and the so-called "Palace of Helena" (Fig. 76), which probably had a central dome and cupolas on the four corner towers. Also at Treves during
the last phase of its imperial architecture the Constantinian baths were remade into
what Krencker has identified as a "praetorium-palatium."[44] Here again, as in the palace
of Diocletian, the Hall of State was entered through a great domical vestibule (Fig.
131). Opposite to this ceremonial entrance was the main apse with round towers at
either side, in much the same way that round towers flank the eastern apse and the
apsidal Westwerk on so many of the later Rhenish churches.

The most important recent addition to our scanty knowledge of fourth century
palace architecture is the complex of buildings (Fig. 134) excavated at Piazza Armerina, near Enna, in Central Sicily. It was at first thought to have been a private villa of
the late fourth or fifth century; but the ceremonial provisions and the iconography of
the many mosaic pavements indicate, as L'Orange and Dyggve have suggested, that
it was a royal residence, probably a hunting villa, of Maximianus Herculius, the Western colleague of Diocletian.[45] Since the publication of the plan the excavations have
uncovered more parts with fine mosaics and evidence of the defensive walls that one
would expect to find around a palace. Thus it is possible to trace back with more cer-
tainty some of the architectural features of the Roman-Byzantine palace tradition in
relation to the ceremonies. It is first of all significant for the purpose of this study to
find in the plan every indication that the entrance to the palace at Piazza Armerina had
a towered gateway into which appears to have been built a kind of triumphal archway
decorated with niches for statues.

The court back of this portal was surrounded by an elevated colonnade from which
the staff of the palace could look down at the fountain in the center when there was a
royal entry. All this is curiously like the Porta Triumphalis at Rome, the adoption of a
fountain-of-life in the atrium of St. Peter's between the triumphal gateway and the
Christian *Domus Dei*, and the subsequent use of domical phiales for the reception of
the emperor in Byzantine palace-churches and monasteries. At the left of the entrance
court was a latrine and back of it was a domical structure (No. 4), probably a bath,
entered from a long vestibule with apsidal ends and decorated, according to verbal reports, with scenes on its mosaic pavement taken from the circus. To the right of the
forecourt, the sequence of parts and their lavish mosaic pavements show that the villa
of Maximianus was laid out according to a formal and procession plan. A flight of steps

[44] D. Krencker and E. Krüger, *Das Trier Kaiserthermen*, 1929, pp. 161ff., Abb. 206.

[45] G. V. Gentili, "Piazza Armerina," *Notizie
degli scavi*, IV, 1951, pp. 291-325; H. P. L'Orange
and E. Dyggve, "È un Palazzo di Massimiano Ercu-
leo che gli scavi di Piazza Armerina portano alle
luce," *Symbolae Osloenses*, 1952, pp. 114-128;

Santo Mazzarino, "Sull'otium di Massimiano Er-
culio dopo l'abdicazione," *Atti della Accademia
Nazionale dei Lancei*, VIII, 1953, pp. 417-421; Gentili, *La villa Romana di Piazza Armerina*, Rome,
1951. B. Neutsch, "Archäologische Grabungen und
Funde," *Jahrb. d. D. Arch. Inst.*, LXIX, 1954, cols.
553-598, Abb. 42 (plan), Abb. 44 (view of fountain).

led up to a narthex with apsidal ends, that are characteristic of Roman vestibules, which in turn opened into a rectangular hall (No. 5). This room has been called a "tablino" and "sacerdos," because of the figures of palace officials and singers depicted in the pavement, thereby suggesting that its "religious ritual" was similar to the Adventuslike receptions of the Byzantine emperors in the vestibule of their palaces. Just beyond this hall the little apsidal aedicula (No. 6) may have been either the place where the emperor sat to receive the salutations of his court, or a shrine for his statue in the heavenly guise of Hercules. At the east side of the great court (No. 7) staircases gave access to a long vestibule off from which opened the rooms of the main palace that are now being excavated. Recent excavations have uncovered in the middle of the great court the foundations of a long and presumably ceremonial fountain, consisting of semicircular ends and a circular center which may have been covered with a domical structure like an imperial phiale in the Byzantine palace and palace-churches.

South of the large court was the emperor's *paradisus* in front of a triapsidal hall, presumably a *tribunale-triclinii*, which was similar to the *praetorium-palatium* at Treves (Fig. 131) and the famous "Triconchos" (Fig. 121) of the Byzantine palace at Constantinople. It was square at the center, about 12 meters on a side, thereby indicating that its light walls supported a gilded wooden dome, for which there is ample evidence in the fourth century.[46] The imperial symbolism of the domical audience and banqueting hall is graphically recorded in the mosaic pavements of its three semicircular exedras. According to L'Orange, the mosaics in the medial and eastern apse, which would have been the throne sanctuary, commemorate the relation of Maximianus and Diocletian in the government of the Empire by depicting a gigantomachia in which Hercules comes to the aid of Jove. The northern apse continues the imperial theme by presenting the coronation, or apotheosis, of Hercules, while the southern apse is decorated with a scene of Dionysus, who as early as Anthony's triumph at Alexandria was identified with a Roman ruler.

This triapsidal hall was entered from an elliptical court which had a fountain in the center and was surrounded by a balustraded ambulatory with mosaic pavements. In many ways the court resembles the great circular garden space in front of the Triconchos (Fig. 121) of the Imperial Palace at Constantinople. Granted that the Byzantine palace architecture tended to follow established precedent, then there must have been a ceremonial covering over the fountain of immortality at Piazza Armerina, because at Constantinople the fountain in the court was a symbolic pine cone under a "mystical phiale" which figured prominently in the imperial ritual. The apsidal exedra on the opposite side of Maximianus's court is not comparable to the semicircular vestibule, called the "Apse," through which one entered the "Court of the Phiale" at the Byzantine palace. Instead, it was more like the "Sigma" at the entrance to the Triconchos, the vestibule at the end of the Pergamine basilica (Fig. 136) and a similar structure in Hadrian's palace villa (Fig. 138/C), which in the case of the "Sigma" was a place where the Basileus was received and sometimes enthroned. It, therefore, seems

[46] Smith, *The Dome*, Ch. II.

144

reasonably certain that this open apse was not merely a decorative "nymphaeum," but was a ceremonial structure where for certain festivals Maximianus could either dine with Jove and the other gods or be received with acclamations by his adoring Court.

5. Hadrian's villa at Tivoli

The domical vestibules in the palaces of Byzantium, the Adriatic and the Rhineland raise the issue of whether they were innovations first introduced from the East by Diocletian, or were ceremonial provisions which went back at least to the time of Hadrian and presumably had their origin in the much admired Hellenistic palaces. At Tivoli the Little Palace (Fig. 137) probably had an outer vestibule, circular and hence domical, at *A*; and it certainly had a monumental domical hall at *B* which resembles the main entrance to Diocletian's palace, even to the extent of suggesting in its ruined plan that it may have had a towered façade over the entrance.[47] The most spectacular structure in the Little Palace must have been the central-type building with the re-entrant apses, marked *C*, at the northeast corner of the court. What was it, if it was not a domical triclinium where Hadrian enacted in a dramatic fashion the *Jovis coenatio* after the tradition of Nero's banqueting tholos and Alexander's "Tent of Heaven," and in much the same way that the Byzantine emperors took the part of Christ in their "Triclinium of the Nineteen Beds" and held their state banquets in the Chrysotriclinos with its *skene* dome? Those who are accustomed to think of Hadrian as a practical administrator and scholar may object to the assumption that away from Rome, in the seclusion of his own estate, he surrounded himself with all the formal ceremonies of a divine ruler. Does it follow, because the Roman historians treat him with so much respect as an admirable and cultivated man, that Hadrian was merely an antiquarian who built solely for the pleasure of looking at his vast architectural creations? Either he insisted upon the palace rituals and the whole Graeco-Oriental tradition of personal glorification, which his buildings embodied, or both Tivoli and the Emperor were the exception to the history of palace architecture and royal behavior.

Contrary to almost everything written about his villa, there still seems to be no justification for thinking of the buildings at Tivoli as little more than a series of private museums, just because we know so little about Roman palace ceremonies. The architectural provisions of the Great Palace (Fig. 138), known as the Piazza d'Oro, are sufficiently similar to those at Constantinople to prove that elaborate receptions and spectacles, comparable to those which were so important in the Byzantine palace ritual, must have taken place in the various domical halls and vestibules. At *A*, in the middle of the south side of the court and directly on axis with the central hall on the opposite side, was a domical entrance, covered with a *skene* vault, which recalls the Chalce at Constantinople.[48] The round foundations of the smaller entrances at either side of the

---

[47] W. Winnefeld, "Die Villa des Hadrian bei Tivoli," *Jahrb. d. K. d. Arch. Inst., Ergänzungsheft*, III, 1895, pp. iii ff., pl. x; H. Kähler, *Hadrian und seine Villa bei Tivoli*, 1950, p. 73, Tafs. 11-14.

[48] Winnefeld, *op.cit.*, p. 60, pl. VI, Kähler, *op.cit.*, p. 132, Taf. 15-16. Recent excavations at Tiv-

main vestibule suggest that it too was flanked by domical towers. Why was it not, like the Chalce, the place where Hadrian was received by his ministers and the court singers and acclaimed as the divine Kosmokrator that he enjoyed being when in the Near East? Furthermore, the main hall of the Great Palace, marked *B*, might well be the prototype for the Chrysotriclinos at Constantinople in that it was an octagon with apsidal bays and, like the gateway vestibule, was vaulted with a gored dome, the melonlike corrugations of which can be explained as a masonry version of the cosmic *skene*. It is even within the limits of structural possibility, as Kähler partially realized in his restoration, that there were towers, marked *a* on the plan, at the four corners of this domical Hall of State.

The other large structure connected with the court is the exedra, marked *C*, which is restored with semicircular ends that may have been towers. Like the similar exedra of Domitian on the Palatine, the one in the court of Maximianus at Piazza Armerina and the one constructed during the Renaissance by Ligorio in the Belvedere of the Vatican, it is very doubtful whether any of these apsidal structures were originally only decorative nymphaea. From the time when the semicircular *Porta regia* appears in the palace decorations of the fourth Pompeian style (Fig. 113) and in the *scaena frons* of the Roman theater, and then down to the time of its ceremonial use at the entrance of the Triconchos (Fig. 121) at Constantinople and its use as a vestibule of the Palace Chapel at Aachen, where Otto I was acclaimed Emperor, there seems to be consistent evidence of its association with palaces as a place of royal appearances. Taken alone it is impossible in an isolated villa, such as Tivoli, to prove that any one of the many buildings had a specific ritualistic purpose. It is only when the Tivoli exedra is considered in relation to the history of the *Porta regia*, and compared to the so-called "Red Hall" at Pergamum (Fig. 136), that its heavenly symbolism and ceremonial purpose becomes apparent.

It is not known whether the partially excavated rectangular hall at Pergamum with its semicircular end, which was uncovered in the city below the acropolis, was a palace, praetorium, or basilica of justice.[49] The Hall itself, which is thought to have been an imperial building of the time of Trajan, is about 200 meters long and was divided into aisles by two rows of columns. At the end opposite to the entrance it has a door opening onto the exterior tribunal platform in the semicircular exedra, which is over sixteen meters in diameter. In the masonry shoulders of the hemicycle are large staircases, which by analogy with the similar stairs in the Roman temples of Syria and in the corners of Diocletian's palace vestibule must have gone up to the roof and possibly been covered with domical towers, or stone baldachins. Of even more significance are the circular rooms, or towers, on either side, whose massive walls imply domical vaults. If this heavenly apse, where the Emperor, or his representative, made a dramatic public

---

oli have shown that the domical tower, the "Torrone," on the Via Tiburtina was a fourth century vestibule which had replaced a rectangular vestibule at the entrance to what had been either a

large villa or a royal palace (*Jahrb. d. D. Arch. Inst.*, LVI, 1941, cols. 734-748, Abbs. 4-6).

[49] Krencker and Krüger, *Das Trier Kaiserthermen*, p. 173, fig. 233.

appearance, is restored with little towers at the corners of the exedra and the great flanking domes rose above the wall on either side, one is immediately startled by the resemblance to the façade of the much later Islamic mosques and palaces.

In view of what we know about Hadrian there is no reason why we should disregard the architectural evidence at Tivoli and assume that it would have been out of character for him to have modeled his palace ceremonies, as he did his buildings, on Hellenistic Greek precedents. That he was interested in palace rituals, and all the personal adulation which went with them, only seems unlikely when we persist in regarding him only as a scholarly art collector, resembling an eighteenth century gentleman in his desire to enrich his private estate with copies of everything seen and admired on his travels. What about his excessive vanity, his deification of his beloved Antinous, and his readiness to encourage all forms of personal glorification when in the East? He it was who had his many Adventus receptions commemorated on his coins and contributed so generously to the building of temples for a Hadrianic cult in the Eastern cities, as at Smyrna where he was worshiped as the Olympian Zeus with the title of "Savior of the whole human race."[50] Why then should his palace villa not be explained in terms of the Hellenistic East? Without the solemn formalities of a court ritual, which presented him as a manifest god, his architectural creations at Tivoli would have been as empty, meaningless, and tiresome to him as they are to the casual visitor who wanders aimlessly from one unused structure to another.

6. Palaces prior to Hadrian

There should be included among the palaces with either a domical vestibule or banqueting hall the so-called Nymphaeum of the "Horti Sallustiani" at Rome, which is now thought to have been part of a palace dating probably from the period of Hadrian.[51] The rotunda is forty-three feet in diameter and was covered with a gored and *skene* type of dome, similar to the domical vaults at Tivoli. It was entered from the west and had to the east a rectangular hall which suggests a throne-room opening onto either a *salutatorium* or *triclinium*. Prior to Hadrian, however, the existing remains furnish very little evidence to show where his architectural ideas originated, although it is to be inferred from the way in which he copied the famous structures of Alexandria in his villa that he was emulating the Hellenistic kings.

Theoretically the *Domus Augustana* of Domitian at Rome should have been the revered archetype of all subsequent imperial residences. Unfortunately, after the centuries of neglect and vandalism which turned the Palatine into a stock pile of marble to be demolished by the builders of the Renaissance, even the plan of the Palace of the Caesars is in part hypothetical and any restoration of its vast ruins must remain to a large extent conjectural. On the south side, where it overlooked the Circus Maximus, it has been thought that the concave retaining wall of the Palatine hill was formerly

[50] C. J. Cadoux, *Ancient Smyrna*, 1938, pp. 257-259.

[51] Rivoira, *Archittetura romana*, 1927, pp. 121-122, fig. 104; J. Lindos, "Il Palazzo degli Orti Sallustiani," *Opuscula archaeologica*, I, 1935, pp. 196-227.

crowned with a lofty porticus, which was connected with the royal quarters by a doorway in the center. Here, in this private and shaded gallery which seemed to be "elevated so high that it approached the sky," the vast crowds in the Circus below would have seen the members of the *Domus divina* looking down from their sacred residence, as from the top of a very real Olympus. If there was this porticus, reserved for those who were comparable to the gods, and if it was flanked by towers, as the fragmentary remains of the retaining wall have sometimes been restored, it would be much easier to understand why the Roman world came to think of towers and a colonnaded upper story with arched openings as the most memorable and characteristic features of a Sacred Palace.[52] But, with the evidence what it is, this is only speculation.

For the purposes of this study there is only the certain evidence that there were domical halls at either side of the vestibule (Fig. 135) which opened onto the peristyle court of the *Domus Augustana*. It is, therefore, to be assumed that the domical shape had a symbolic significance in relation to the ceremonies, as it had in the Golden House of Nero, especially since it is believed that one of these domical halls was "Caesar's tholus," where the Lord of the Oecumene feasted with his guests under a symbolic heaven and where, according to Statius, it was like "resting with Jupiter in the midst of the stars."[53] Also, if we can judge by the ceiling decorations in Nero's palace and later in Hadrian's villa, it is not unlikely that even the groin vaults over the public halls of the imperial residence were painted with circular *skene* patterns in order to make apparent the cosmic and celestial implications of the sacred residence.

Excavation on the northwest side of the Palace of the Flavians, where the great halls of state were located, have shown that the entrance to the colonnaded court between the Throne Room, the *aula regia*, and the *Triclinium* was through a circular vestibule, which was probably domical.[54] In view of this limited evidence, including the little which is known about the palace ceremonies, it seems unlikely that the domical vestibule had the same ritualistic importance under Domitian which it had later in the palaces at Tivoli, Salona, Treves and Constantinople. Even if it is granted that the

[52] The best known restoration of the exedra with a porticus and towers is the one by Deglane in 1886 (G. Seure, *Monuments antiques, publication de l'Institut de France*, II, pls. 123-124); it may have been influenced by the more fanciful restoration of Fr. Biancini, *Del Palazzo dei Cesari*, Verona, 1738, Tav. XIV; for a discussion of the restorations by the architects of the Academy of France see H. Deglane, "Le Palais des Cesars au mont Palatine," *Gaz. arch.*, XIII, 1888, pp. 211-224, pls. 21-30; R. Lanciani (*The Ruins and Excavations of Ancient Rome*, London, 1897, p. 143) merely says there was a state balcony on the "Pulvinar" from which the emperors could watch the games in the Circus; G. Lugli (*Roma antica*, Rome, 1946, pp. 509-512) is noncommittal.

[53] The remains of these domical halls are described in all the books on the Palatine; both Lehmann (*Art Bulletin*, XXVII, 1945, p. 22) and L'Orange (*Studies on the Iconography of Cosmic King-*

ship in the Ancient World, p. 31 n. 1) discuss the symbolic significance of the tholus where Domitian held his banquets; Statius, *Silvae*, 4, 2.

[54] No ceremonial significance has been attached to this vestibule, although it appears in all the plans (Deglane, *op.cit.*, pl. 23; Lanciani, *op.cit.*, p. 162, fig. 60; and Lugli, *op.cit.*, p. 491, Tav. VIII-21, E); J. Bühlmann ("Der Palast der Flavier auf dem Palatin in Rom," *Zeitschrift für Geschichte der Architektur*, I, 1907-08, pp. 113-134, Abbs. 1-3) seems to be the only person to have emphasized its domical vault in a restoration. While the plan and restorations of the Palatine by Fr. Biancini (*Del Palazzo dei Cesari*) are wholly imaginative, it is interesting to note, perhaps as an indication of a tradition, how much importance an early eighteenth century artist gave to innumerable circular vestibules, flanking towers, *skene* cupolas, and sculptural baldachins.

initial adoption of domical symbolism was probably due to Nero's and Domitian's admiration of the palace architecture and ceremonies of the Ptolemaic kings, it must be deduced that the subsequent use and growing importance of the domical vestibule was the result of imperial contacts with the East and the gradual orientalizing of the Roman Court by means of a ritualistic drama which was intended to present the emperor as a sacred person.

Since nothing remains of the Alexandrian palaces, there is only the traditions of the East, the Royal Epiphanies, the Alexandrian tombs with domical vestibules and the evidence of the fourth Pompeian style to indicate that the domical vestibule, like the domical Tent of Appearances, was a symbolic and ceremonial feature of palace architecture in the Hellenistic East.[55] The ruins of the small royal palace at Palatizia in Macedonia, which antedate the Empire, raise more questions regarding Greek palaces than they clarify.[56] It was entered through an Ionic propylaea which terminated in a square vestibule at the entrance to the interior court. To the left of this vestibule, but entered from the court, was a circular hall 11.25 meters in diameter with massive walls that must have carried a domical vault. Opposite this rotunda, which has been called a throne-room because of the dais found in it, was a rectangular room which has theoretically been restored as a *hestiatorion* with tables for a sacred banquet. The possibility that the functions of these two halls should be reversed depends upon whether the circular and probably domical hall is considered to have been a kind of heroön, comparable to Alexander's banqueting tent, or was in some way related to the earlier Greek *prytaneum*.

Even though it is necessary to presuppose Hellenistic prototypes for the domical provisions of the Roman palaces, it was only by gradual stages, and without too obvious a break with Roman precedents, that the successive emperors took over the Eastern customs of being received as a divine person and adored either under a ciborium or in a domical vestibule. From early times at Rome the *vestibulum*, whether at the entrance to a temple, public building, or the residence of an important personage, had its own ceremonial tradition.[57] There the nobles received the *salutio* of their clients; there in the public buildings were placed divine images, trophies, and honorific insignia; and even before the Empire it was in the vestibule of the Palatine that the rulers of Rome appeared in order to receive the acclamations of the people. According to Gellius, "a great multitude, of all ranks, were in the vestibule of the Palatine palace

[55] In Egypt royal and upper-class tombs and mortuary chapels were always influenced by palace architecture. Hence the appearance in the first century B.C. of a new type of rock-cut tomb with a domical vestibule or chapel presupposes an earlier palace tradition of a domical entrance hall where the official family paid their honors to the master of the house; examples are at Sidi Gabbari (R. Delbrueck, *Hellenistische Bauten im Latium*, II, 1907-1912, pp. 79, 102), the catacombs of Mex, known as the "Baths of Cleopatra" (R. Pagenstecher, *Nekropolis*, pp. 134f., pl. I), the tomb at Taposiris Magna (*op.cit.*, p. 54, pl. III), the one of

the first half of the third century near Hadra (*op.cit.*, pp. 84, 153) and the second century catacomb of Kom esh-Shuqâfa, which has a large domical rotunda with a triclinium, chapels, and burial chambers opening from it. The influence of this type of Alexandrian tomb can be seen at Tall Hinnon in Palestine (Smith, *The Dome*, pp. 57-59, figs. 75-81).

[56] Heuzey and Daumet, *Mission archéologique de Macédoine*, 1876, p. 175, pl. 14; *Bull. Corr. Hell.*, LXIII, 1939, p. 317.

[57] Daremberg and Saglio, *Dictionnaire*, V, "Vestibulum," pp. 763-764.

expecting the salute of Caesar."[58] Accustomed as they were to divine images and imperial salutations in the *vestibulum* of the palace, it was not long before the Roman public accepted the statues of their emperors, when set up in the entrances of temples and palaces, as cult images; but it was some time before the Romans were prepared to adore without criticism the person of the emperor as a god.

Certainly there was opposition to Caligula's efforts to be worshiped, especially when he remade the Temple of Castor and Pollux into a vestibule to the Palatine palace and there frequently presented himself between the Dioscuridi, like the Triumphator in the gallery of the Porta Marzia (Fig. 3), "in order to be adored by all comers" and addressed as Jupiter Latiaris.[59] It may have been the tragic way that Caligula "learned by experience that he was not a god" which persuaded Nero to restrain his theophanic ambitions and to be satisfied with a colossal statue in the concave vestibule, or *Porta regia*, of his Golden House. During the first two centuries of the Empire, when the Roman custom of images in a vestibulum was being adjusted to the new Cult of the Caesars, the behavior of Caligula, the coins of Nero (Figs. 112, 114-116) and the way in which Domitian (Fig. 118) and Antoninus Pius (Fig. 119) had their statues presented under baldachins on their coins implies that the habit of setting up an imperial cult image at the entrance to a palace was a transitional stage at Rome leading to the adoption of the palace ritual in which the divine Augustus was himself adored in the *salutatorium* of his *palatium-templum*. It is, therefore, only a question of whether the second stage of this Easternization of the palace ritual took place when Hadrian made his palace retreat a replica of everything which he had admired in the Hellenistic East.

By the Late Empire the tradition of worshiping both the person and the image of the emperor at the entrance to his palace was fully established, for in addition to the evidence of the Chalce at Constantinople we are told that at Antioch the statue of Maximianus was honored *in vestibulo regiae*.[60] Here again we must rely upon later evidence and the assumption that mediaeval conventions were based upon established usage. During the period when Italy was ostensibly ruled from Constantinople it was customary for every newly elected Byzantine emperor to send his statue to Rome. There, according to the records, "the imperial image, received in a grand ceremony by the clergy and Roman populace" was conducted through the city and "placed in the oratory of St. Caesarius in the sacrum palatium."[61] This account proves that imperial images were welcomed with all the formalities of an Adventus and shows how the Christian reception of relics followed imperial rites. At the same time the name and location of the chapel of St. Caesarius in the Sacred Palace, like the oratory of

[58] Gellius, IV,1.1; K. Ziegler, Paulys-Wissowa, R.-E., XVIII, pt. 2, vol. 2, 1949, "palatium," p. 55.

[59] Suetonius, *Caligula*, xxii; Dio's *Roman History*, lix, 28; for *adorare imagines* in imperial cult (Alföldi, *Röm. Mittl.*, XLIX, 1934, pp. 61-72).

[60] Ammianus Marcellinus, xxv, 10, 2; Schlachter, *Der Globus*, p. 75.

[61] C. Diehl, *Études sur l'administration byzantine dans l'Exarchate de Ravenna (568-751 A.D.)*, 1888, p. 186; L. Duchesne, "La chapelle impériale du Palatin," *Bull. Crist.*, VI, 1885, pp. 417-424; *N. Bull. di arch. crist.*, 1900, pp. 17-28; Duchesne, *Liber pontificalis*, I, pp. 371, 377 n. 2; II, pp. 114, 136 n. 23, 386; A. Bartoli, *N. Bull. di arch. crist.*, 1907, pp. 191-204.

San Salvatore de arcu Trasi which was either alongside the Arch of Constantine or in its attic chamber, may reflect another successful effort of the Roman church to transform a mediaeval survival of emperor-worship into a Christian rite.[62]

Again the receptions of ruler images and relics reflect the influence which the traditional forms of the Epiphany, Adventus, and Triumph had upon the Middle Ages. Before illustrating in the next chapter how the mediaeval use of the ciborium in the formal receptions of kings and prelates at the entrance to palaces, cities and monasteries was based upon much earlier rites of welcome, it is necessary to realize how directly the royal and ecclesiastic ceremonies in the West were influenced by the Adventus ceremony with which the Byzantine Emperor and his Exarch were received at Rome. During the Middle Ages, when a ruler came to Rome, the Pope, clergy, and people went forth to meet him, six miles outside the city, and led him to the Imperial Palace.[63] Along the way the people prostrated themselves and greeted him with music and acclamations as the procession moved through the city. After visiting the great basilicas of the city he went up to the *Capitoleum aureum* where in the Roman tradition he received the homage of his subjects.

[62] Caesarius, whose oratory was the domestic chapel of the emperor in the Palatine Palace was not, according to Duchesne, the Roman saint (*N. Bull. di arch. crist.*, 1900, p. 22). One may, therefore, suspect the imperial origin of the name, especially since the feast of this S. Caesario was celebrated on April 21, which was the traditional anniversary of the pagan festival of the *Natalis urbis* when the founding of the city and the birthday of the emperor were customarily celebrated together.

[63] Diehl, *op.cit.*, p. 186; the account is thought to have been based upon the reception of Constantine (*Lib. pontif.*, 135) and customary adventus receptions recorded in the *Graphia Aurea Urbis Romae*.

VI · THE CIBORIUM AND DOMICAL VESTIBULE

IN THE MIDDLE AGES

THE persistent association of the ciborium and domical vestibule with gateways in the architecture and iconography of the Middle Ages is further evidence of an imperial precedent. Both the imagery and symbolic thinking of the mediaeval man was directly influenced by the ceremonies; and the ceremonies, it must be realized, carried on the Adventus, Epiphany, and Triumphal rites of meeting a ruler as a divine person at the city-gate, welcoming him with music and panegyrics, and conducting him through the city where he was adored by his joyous subjects. The Adventus ceremony not only persisted at Rome and Ravenna, but was taken over by the Western rulers, adopted by the Prelates of the Church, and followed by the monastic orders for the reception of distinguished guests. By the eighth century when Zacharius, Bishop of Rome, visited Ravenna we are told that, "his voyage was a triumphal march"; and in A.D. 774 Charlemagne was received at Rome with an Adventus ceremony similar to the receptions accorded to the Exarch of Ravenna.[1]

How closely the popular beliefs conformed to Roman precedent is revealed by the many poems entitled *In Adventum regis*, which had been handed down from the ninth and tenth centuries.[2] The *In adventu regis* of Metz, written in the tenth century, relates that in Charles the Bald "a new Constantine has irradiated this world," that there is universal rejoicing whenever he makes an "appearance," and that the city of Metz exults when "The Prince of Peace arrives at your *gate*, to bring forever blissful joy."[3] It is easily understood why an age of pageantry and hieratic formalities would have continued the Roman ceremonies intended to dramatize a ruler's godlike nature and heavenly authority. It is more difficult for the modern reader to comprehend why the mediaeval man continued to see a Messianic promise of peace, prosperity, and happiness in the triumphal Coming of his earthly Lord, and why as a Christian he believed that his city would enjoy a heavenly distinction from the presence in it of a ruler whom he was accustomed to equate with the Son of God. Actually there had been little change in the popular beliefs since the Roman Augustus honored the cities of his Empire with his presence, except that in the mediaeval world every terrestrial city had come to be thought of as another Jerusalem at the Advent of the Anointed, who on the occasion of his royal visitation was ritualistically, at least, identified with Christ. According to Kantorowicz, "the liturgical celebration of an Adventus reflects, or even stages, the Christian prototype of the Messianic entries, that is, the Lord's triumphant Entry as King into Jerusalem on Palm Sunday."[4]

The influence which the pagan Epiphany and Adventus had upon religious thought

[1] C. Diehl, *Études sur l'administration byzantine dans l'Exarchate de Ravenna*, p. 336 (Zacharius), p. 225 (Charlemagne); Kantorowicz, *Art Bulletin*, XXVI, 1944, p. 211 n. 23.

[2] Kantorowicz, *op.cit.*, pp. 209-211.

[3] A. Prost, *Mémoires de la Société nationale des antiquaires de France*, XXXVII, 1876, pp. 209, 212 (Prost associates the Adventus with Charlemagne); Kantorowicz, *op.cit.*, p. 209.

[4] Kantorowicz, *op.cit.*, p. 210.

at the time when Christian ideas were being formulated is illustrated by the literal way the Roman Church at an early date took over into its *Ordo commendationis animae*, as Kantorowicz has pointed out, the Adventus imagery as a means of glorifying death in terms of an imperial reception to be accorded to the triumphant soul at its entrance into the City of God.[5] There was nothing exceptional in this kind of transferred imagery. The custom of visualizing a journey into the other world and of presenting the opening of the gates of the afterlife in terms of a palace ritual went back to a remote past and had their inception in the eschatology of Babylon and Egypt.[6]

All the stages of an Imperial Adventus, as a means of picturing the soul's welcome at the gate of heaven, are presented in a Gnostic fresco (Fig. 124) of the third century from the hypogeum of Aurelius Felicissimus at Rome.[7] What has not been noted by commentators on the Gnostic scene is the lightly indicated and partly obliterated canopy over the symbolic Rider on the White Horse. Obviously the artist in painting his condensed version of a royal *apantesis* realized that the pavilion of reception at the city-gate was essential to the event, but not wishing to separate it from the recipient of divine honors he compromised by placing it over the galloping horseman. This canopy of honor is specific evidence that a celestial covering was a prescribed provision in the royal ceremonies on which the Gnostic promise of spiritual apotheosis was based.

It is the art rather than the documents which shows the importance of the ciborium of reception during the Middle Ages. The documents are no more satisfactory in regard to the use and shape of the canopies than were the references to the pagan Adventus. In the ninth century at the time of his triumphal entry into Constantinople, Theophilus was received in a tent pavilion set up for the occasion in front of the Golden Gate.[8] There is also a Byzantine illumination from the Skylitzes manuscript (Fig. 144) which depicts the Emperor Theophilus, nimbed, mounted on a white horse, and accompanied by members of his court being received at the church of St. Mary Blachernae.[9] That the domical ciborium in front of the church, whether intended to be a tent or phiale, was the imperial place of reception is made apparent by the "Book of Ceremonies," which tells how the official visitations of the Basileus to a palace-church on a feast day were celebrated like an Adventus and Epiphany.

The references, however, to the Adventus receptions of the German emperors at Rome and to their coronation processions, which in so many ways followed the precedents of a Roman Triumph, are unsatisfactory regarding the canopy of honor.[10]

[5] Kantorowicz, *op.cit.*, p. 207.

[6] J. Kroll, "Gott und Hölle, der Mythos vom Descensuskämpfe," *Studien den Bibl. Warburg*, XX, 1932.

[7] A. Wilpert, "Le Pitture del'ipogee di Aurelio Felicissimo presso il viale Manzoni in Roma," *Atti di Pontificia Acc. Romana di Archaeologia Memoriae*, Ser. III, 1924, pl. XXII; Kantorowicz, *op.cit.*, p. 215, fig. 26; C. Cecchelli, *Monumenti Christiano-*

eretici di Roma, 1944, pp. 26-46, pls. XII-XIII.

[8] *Const. Porph. di Cer.*, 504; B. Meyer-Plath und A. M. Schneider, *Die Landmauer von Konstantinople*, II, 1934, p. 63.

[9] See Ch. VII n. 35.

[10] E. Eichmann, "Studien zur Geschichte der abendländischen Kaiserkrönung II, zur Topographie der Kaiserkrönung," *Hist. Jahrb.*, XLV, 1925, pp. 21-50.

By the fourteenth century, when the records are more specific and the miniatures picture actual royal receptions, we find that a heavenly canopy was carried over the emperor in the procession. When Charles V of France in A.D. 1377 welcomed the Emperor to his "imperial city" of Cambrai, we are told how he rode forth at the head of a cortege of burghers and clergy to meet the Emperor outside the city.[11] Then, as the event was pictured, the Emperor, followed by his son, the King of the Romans, walked under a flat canopy carried by four bishops when he made his processional entry into the city.[12] At this time the Adventus covering, a "riche ceil," in both shape and use recalls the ritualistic shelter under which the Assyrian god-image made its entrance into Assur and the royal baldachin over the Achaemenid kings when they were enthroned out-of-doors for public audiences.[13] It was also like the golden canopy (*panno aurea*) which was carried over the English King at the time of his coronation, when he rode bare-headed through the streets of London in a ceremony of welcome that was not unlike a Roman Adventus and Triumph.[14] This carrying of the canopy by the Four Barons was an established feature of the English coronation as early as 1189 and in the twelfth century is described as an "ancient custom"; but there seems to be no evidence as to whether the flat canopy was peculiar to the "coronations and solemn feasts" in England or was a provision brought back by the Crusaders from the Orient.[15] It is clear, however, that during the Middle Ages the participants in a royal Adventus honored their secular lord as the likeness of the Lord of Heaven.[16]

Since there was more than one kind of celestial covering it does not follow that it was a domical ciborium referred to in the fifteenth century records of the Master of Ceremonies at the Papal Court which, at the time of the Pope's visit to Bologna, tell of *two canopies* having been brought forth to the city-gate, one for the Pope and the other for the Blessed Sacraments symbolizing the presence of Christ.[17] What is of historical importance in this late reference to a processional and ceremonial tent of welcome is the fact that it illustrates the papal policy of *imitatio imperialis*, which had resulted in the archbishops of Rome adopting the forms and insignia of the Roman emperors in order to appear before the public as the *Pater urbis et orbis*.

During the centuries when the popes and emperors were endeavoring by every visible and dialectical means to strengthen their relative prestige and universal authority, it is the art, rather than the documents, that reveal the traditional symbolic importance of the domical ciborium in the receptions of emperors, kings and princes of the Church and illustrates the influence of the ruler liturgy upon the dramatization and presentation of the life of Christ. During the Carolingian period, when the

[11] R. Delachenal, *Chronique des Règnes de Jean II et de Charles V, Les Grandes Chroniques de France*, II, 1916, pp. 197ff.

[12] Delachenal, *op.cit.*, IV, 1920, pl. XXXIV; pl. XX shows King John entering Paris on horseback but covered by a canopy; Kantorowicz, *op.cit.*, fig. 45.

[13] See p. 116.

[14] I. G. W. Legg, *English Coronation Records*, 1901, pp. xxi, xxiv, xxvi, 49, 51, 58, 62, 85, 100, 108, 198, 207, 222; A. Taylor, *The Glory of Regality*, 1820, pp. 139, 165f., 172.

[15] P. E. Schramm, *A History of the English Coronation*, London, 1937, p. 69.

[16] Kantorowicz, *op.cit.*, p. 208 n. 9.

[17] E. Bishop, *Liturgica historica*, 1918, p. 438.

Western rulers, motivated by their ideas of *Renovatio Romanorum* and *imitatio Christi*, were systematically making claims to the pre-eminence of the Roman emperors, it is those scenes of the life of Christ, which were envisaged and actually *enacted* as an Epiphany, that show the conceptual importance of the domical baldachin at, or over, a city and palace gateway. An explanation, perhaps, for the renewed emphasis upon the ciborium, and the other means of presenting the scenes of the First Appearance of Christ in the more specific terms of a Victorious King and Savior, is to be found in the way the rulers at both the Byzantine and Western Courts were accustomed to take the part of Christ in the dramatization of the Christian feasts, and in the influence of the *sancti palatii ritus* upon the iconography.

The feasts which were presented in art, and presumably enacted by the ruler in the palace-church ceremonies, as an Adventus and Epiphany were: the Nativity in which the emphasis was upon the adoration of the new-born King; the Epiphany in which the Kings of the East, like tributary rulers, followed the appearance of a new Sun in the heavens in order to lay their offerings at the feet of the Son of God, the universal King; the Flight into Egypt in which the heir to the throne was received by the cities of his kingdom as a new Lord and Master; and both the Presentation in the Temple and the Entry into Jerusalem which had a special imperial importance in the Byzantine palace ceremonies.[18] In the Nativity, for example, on an eleventh century ivory from Darmstadt (Fig. 70) there is a *skene* form of baldachin over the gateway of Bethlehem, just as there is over the entrance to Jerusalem in the scene of the Doubting of Thomas (Fig. 72) on an ivory at Weimar.[19] It is to be noted that the walls in both instances are crowned with the domical towers of a heavenly castrum, as they were on the earlier representations of imperial cities (Figs. 60, 64), because the cities had been honored as royal residences by the presence of the King of Heaven and Earth. Furthermore, the residence of King Herod in the reception of the Magi on the ninth century Lorsch book cover and on a later ivory in the Louvre (Fig. 71) is symbolically presented as a palatium by means of the baldachin under a towered façade that has the imperial orb at the apex of the gables.[20]

The baldachin under which Simeon receives the Christ Child in the Presentation in the Temple is generally thought to refer only to the ciborium over the church altar, as it does in the Western representations of the Purification in the Temple. The very fact that this Eastern feast was not officially accepted by the Roman Church

[18] Grabar, *L'Empereur dans l'art byzantin*, pp. 212-230; E. Kitzinger, *Art Bulletin*, XXXI, 1949, pp. 279-283; at the Byzantine Court, where everything centered around the Basileus as "the living image of God" and the "earthly Christ," it was customary in nearly all the ceremonies to associate him dramatically with the Son of God and in the celebrations of the Entry into Jerusalem, the Washing of the Feet, and the enactment of the Last Supper in the Triclinium of the Nineteen Beds he took the part of Christ (O. Treitinger, *Die oströmische Kaiser-und Reichsidee*, pp. 125-129); at other times

his identification with Christ was more subtly implied, as at the time of a royal birth when everyone, in memory of the Magi, brought gifts and the high officials came to kneel at the cradle (Treitinger, *op.cit.*, p. 109 n. 314; Ebersolt, *Constantinople*, p. 11).

[19] A. Goldschmidt, *Die Elfenbeinskulpturen*, II, no. 103, pl. XXXII/b; also an ivory of Osnabrück, no. 102, pl. XXXI/b.

[20] Goldschmidt, *op.cit.*, I, no. 13, pl. VII (Lorsch book cover); no. 95, pl. XLII (Louvre).

and was celebrated as an Adventus, "The Coming of the Son of God" and his reception at the Door (i.e. the Gateway) of the Temple, suggest that the baldachin was originally intended to denote that the *Templum* was the *Sacrum palatium*. The interpretation of the baldachin as a mark of divine authority and as a traditional place of royal receptions, where a new ruler would be received, would make the scene conform not only to the way in which the Feast of the Hypapante (*Occursus Domini*) was enacted in the East, but also to the Byzantine conception of the Palace being over the Church and the Emperor being the "high priest" responsible for the recognition and obedience of the New Law.

It has already been pointed out by Grabar that there were imperial implications in the exceptional way that the earliest representation of the Presentation in the Temple on the fifth century Triumphal Arch of Santa Maria Maggiore at Rome depicts the Temple of Jerusalem by means of the columnar and gabled *Templum urbis*.[21] For very much the same reasons that several centuries later Charlemagne on his coins chose to symbolize his Palatium by means of the *Templum urbis*, here in a Christian mosaic the Temple of Venus and Rome, which was the place where the Romans celebrated the Birth of the Eternal City and the Coming of their divine emperors, was used to show that the young Jesus was accepted by the Ancient Law, which at Rome was still identified with the Imperator as the *Lex animata* and as the embodiment of both *imperium* and *sacerdotium*.

This imperial theory of sacred royal authority, which the Roman Church soon denied so vigorously, persisted in Byzantium where the Presentation in the Temple was celebrated like an Adventus with a triumphal processional entrance, lighted candles as in a royal ceremony, and a reception at the Door of the Temple.[22] It is, therefore, not unlikely that the ciborium, which by the eighth or ninth century begins to figure so prominently in the Byzantine representations, refers to the Sacred Palace as the Temple and reflects, as does the introduction of a domical baldachin into the palace versions of the Entry into Jerusalem, the way in which the feast was enacted in the palace ceremonies at the Byzantine Court. This assumption also helps to explain the symbolism of the few Western examples of the Presentation, rather than the Purification, which accentuate the palace implications of the scene by placing a towered façade over the ciborium.[23]

The most important example of this Western emphasis upon the towered façade is the scene of the Presentation in the Temple which Roger II had placed about

[21] Grabar, *L'Empereur dans l'art byzantin*, pp. 216-221; J. Gagé, "Le 'Templum Urbis' et les origines de l'idée de Renovatio," *Annuaire de l'Inst. de philologie et d'histoire orientales et slaves*, IV, 1936, pp. 151-186.

[22] D. C. Shorr, "The Iconographic Development of the Presentation in the Temple," *Art Bulletin*, XXVIII, 1946, p. 18; E. Kitzinger, *Art Bulletin*, XXXI, 1949, pp. 281-283.

[23] An ivory of the Metz School at Frankfurt, dating c. A.D. 850 has schematic towers over the fastigium of the temple (Goldschmidt, *Die Elfenbeinskulpturen.*, I, no. 75, pl. XXXI); ivory of Metz School in Victoria and Albert Mu., dating c. A.D. 900, has towered gateway (Goldschmidt, I, no. 118, pl. LI); eleventh century altar front of Salerno (Shorr, *op.cit.*, fig. 9); eleventh century Tropary of the Church of Autun (Shorr, fig. 11); eleventh century Golden Evangelistary of Henry III (Shorr, fig. 17); eleventh century Codex Aureus of Gniezno (Shorr, fig. 19); and twelfth century ivory of the Trier Cathedral (Goldschmidt, III, no. 35, pl. VIII).

A.D. 1140 among the other Adventus themes in front of his royal loge in the palace-chapel at Palermo.[24] The very presence of the scene in the Palatine Chapel, like the style of the mosaics, is evidence of Roger's interest in Byzantine precedents as a graphic affirmation of his own theocratic ideal of kingship. It is certainly to be deduced from the "Norman Anonymous of A.D. 1100" that Roger II, like his Carolingian and Norman predecessors, had inherited the conviction that *Rex sanctus est* and that he, as the *christus Domini*, was over the church.[25] Inasmuch, therefore, as the towered façade was a palace motif on the royal abbey churches of the north and on the later coins of the German emperors, it seems to follow that the Norman mosaic, where the palace towers dominate the ciborium, was a northern way of making more evident the Byzantine implication that the Sacred Palace was the Temple. Thus the Presentation in the Temple, along with the other Adventus subjects, comes more completely into harmony with Kitzinger's interpretation of the mosaics as a pictorial "Paean to the King."

The Entry into Jerusalem, the most important of all Adventus themes, is another scene in the Palatine Chapel which shows a somewhat similar modification of Byzantine palace iconography. What is exceptional in the Norman mosaic is the way that the entrance to Jerusalem is surmounted by a little tower with a conical roof, which recalls the reception vestibule sometimes depicted over the palace gateway (Figs. 83, 87) on the coins of the German emperors.[26] This unique representation of the city-gate is related to a few Byzantine examples of the Entry into Jerusalem which have a reception ciborium at the entrance to the city. From as early as the fourth century the event was customarily presented as a Royal Epiphany in which the populace, carrying palms of victory, welcome its Triumphant Lord on his lowly ass, instead of the imperial white charger. In the West, after the Frankish kings had come to celebrate their own entries like a Roman Adventus, having taken as their immediate precedent the ceremonial welcome at Rome of the Byzantine Exarch,[27] they and their people saw in the Entry into Jerusalem on Palm Sunday the prototype of their own receptions.[28] Hence any Adventus, but more especially the enactment of the Feast of Palms, came to have political connotations throughout the period when the popes and emperors were endeavoring to dramatize their contending claims to being the counterpart of Christ and the Vicar of God.

When the Pope and the Emperor took part together in an Advent or entry, it was not uncommon, although always dependent upon the convictions and relative dependence upon one another of the two great actors, for the Emperor to walk as the military servant of the Pope who rode.[29] There is, however, no artistic evidence before the thir-

---

[24] E. Kitzinger, "Mosaics of the Capella Palatina," *Art Bulletin*, XXXI, 1946, pp. 269-292; O. Demus, *The Mosaics of Norman Sicily*, 1949, fig. 11B.

[25] G. H. Williams, *Harvard Theological Studies*, XVIII, 1951.

[26] O. Demus, *The Mosaics of Norman Sicily*, pl. XX/B.

[27] Kantorowicz, *op.cit.*, p. 21 n. 23.

[28] *Ibid.*, pp. 210-211.

[29] In the West Pepin in 754 was the first to act as the Strator-servant by walking holding the reins of the Pope's horse; Emperor Louis II did the same for Pope Urban II; and Lothar of Supplinburg in 1131 acted as the Marshal-servant of Pope Innocent; but in 1155 Frederick Barbarossa forced Pope

teenth century to illustrate the extent to which issues of prestige, involving the conflict-ing papal and imperial policies of *imitatio imperialis* and *imitatio Christi*, were of im-portance in the enactment of an Entry. The papal conception of an Adventus as an Entry into Jerusalem, in which the Pontiff enacts the role of Christ, is pictured about A.D. 1248 in the St. Silvester chapel of the church of SS. Quattro Coronati at Rome.[30] Like the Lord, Pope Silvester is depicted on an ass being led by Constantine on foot; and as a further confirmation of the Pope's relation to both God and the imperial tradition he is covered by a divine umbrella, which the Church claimed to have in-herited from the first Christian emperor. Thus the scene is a graphic presentation of the papal contention, which went back to the eighth century and the forged "Dona-tion of Constantine," that the Emperor was only the Cursor of Christ and the Marshal of the Pope.[31]

At the Byzantine Court, on the contrary, there was never any question as to who was entitled to impersonate the Son of God, for in the ritual for Palm Sunday the "Book of Ceremonies" makes it clear that within the confines of the palace the Basileus was the exalted and adored figure in the elaborate procession with which the event was cele-brated.[32] He it was who was received as the Triumphant Lord by the whole cortege when he entered the "Hemicycle of the phiale of the Trichoncos" (Fig. 121) and was again acclaimed at the "exedra of the Trichoncos" after the procession had completed its round of the palace. Throughout this ceremony it is to be imagined that the Basileus in his divine role was received at the gateways, vestibules, and entrances to the various courts and churches of the palace either in a baldachinlike phiale or under a domical ciborium set up for the occasion. Hence, the few Byzantine representations of the Entry into Jerusalem which reflect this palace ritual in having a domical place of reception are evidence of there having been a palace tradition quite distinct from the customary iconography.

The earliest extant exception to the standard iconography in having a large dome, or symbolic reception baldachin, over the entrance to Jerusalem is the late eleventh century mosaic from the church at Daphni (Fig. 127), which was an imperial founda-tion and decorated, according to Demus, in a "Court Style."[33] Further evidence that this domical portal on the Daphni mosaic was based upon the prescribed provisions for the enactment of the Entry into Jerusalem in the palace ritual, and that it was copied from a similar scene in one of the palace churches at Constantinople, is indi-cated by the representation on the Pala d'Oro of San Marco.[34] The presumption that the iconography on the enamel (Fig. 169), which has an actual ciborium with twisted

Hadrian to act as his servant (Treitinger, *Die os-trömische Kaiser-und Reichsidee*, pp. 225-227).

[30] E. W. Anthony, *Romanesque Frescoes*, 1951, pp. 81-82, fig. 101.

[31] Kantorowicz, *op.cit.*, pp. 229-231; R. Holtz-mann, "Der Kaiser als Marschall des Papstes," *Schriften der Strassburger Wissenschaftlichen Ge-sellschaft in Heidelberg*, No. 8, 1928.

[32] A. Vogt, *Le livre des cérémonies, Texte*, I, ch.

41; Treitinger, *op.cit.*, pp. 125-126.

[33] E. Diez and O. Demus, *Byzantine Mosaics in Greece*, 1931, p. 62, fig. 92, p. 109 (Daphni an imperial foundation), pp. 96-101 (its "Court style" derived from the secular art of the Constantinopol-itan Court).

[34] A. Pasini, *Il Tesoro di San Marco*, Venice, 1885, pl. xv.

columns and a *skene* type of domical canopy under the gabled portal of the city, was based upon the Byzantine palace conventions is strengthened, if not confirmed, by the belief that the twelfth century enamels of the Venetian altarpiece were originally in the palace-church of St. Savior Pantocrator before they were brought to Venice sometime after A.D. 1254.[35] Since St. Savior was the very special imperial sanctuary of the Comneni family, and is the earliest known church (Fig. 140) to have a monumentalized version of an imperial baldachin, or parakyptikon, over its portal, it is significant to find that the mosaic representation of the Entry into Jerusalem in the Church of the Nativity at Bethlehem, which was executed in A.D. 1169 at the order of the Emperor Manuel Comnenus, has a bulbous dome over the gateway and a cupola on one of the towers.[36]

It is, therefore, not unlikely that the Entry into Jerusalem on the Pala d'Oro and in the Church of the Nativity were copied from a painting, or mosaic, in the Pantocrator, which was built in part by the Empress Irene, who is thought to figure in the panels of the Venetian altarpiece, and had a charter making it independent of the Patriarch.[37] Also during the period of the Latin occupation it was turned over to the Venetians, but under the Palaeologi it again became, as it had been under the Comneni, a mausoleum for the members of the royal family.[38] Even if the chronology makes it impossible to connect the Daphni mosaic directly with the Pantocrator church, the sequence of all the examples is evidence that a domical place of reception at the entrance to a royal and symbolic City of God was a feature taken over from the palace tradition. Hence, in returning to the palace-church of Roger II at Palermo, it is now more apparent why its Entry into Jerusalem, which has a royal tower, like an Islamic *majlis*, over the portal, is another example of the Norman ruler's interest in modifying the Byzantine Court iconography and associating the scenes with his own palace.

It is also of importance in studying the domical place of reception to note that the presence of a ceremonial or symbolic ciborium over the gateway in the palace versions of the Entry into Jerusalem is related to the symbolic palace frame for the Council of Antioch (Fig. 75) and the Byzantine palatium on the Troyes casket (Fig. 98), where the palace entrance is surmounted by a dome flanked by towers with cupolas. Furthermore, it recalls the architectural setting back of the figure of St. Gregory of Nyssa (Fig. 125) in the Menologium of Basil II. Although the miniature looks as if the copyist in depicting the *Domus Dei* misunderstood that the symbolic palace of God was intended to be represented by a gateway, and hence reversed the perspective of the two flanking towers, he was, nevertheless, fully aware of the importance of the baldachins as a means of showing that the royal and heavenly abode of the saint was like a Sacred Palace.

[35] O. M. Dalton, *Byzantine Art and Archaeology*, 1910, p. 512, fig. 297; C. Diehl, *Manuel d'art byzantin*, 1910, p. 656; N. Kondakoff, *Histoire et monuments des émaux byzantins*, 1892, p. 117; E. Molinier, *Le Trésor de la basilique de Saint Marc.*, 1885, p. 65; *Gazette des Beaux Arts*, I, 1889; G. Veludo, *The Pala d'Oro of the Basilica of St. Mark*, Venice (trans. W. Scott), 1887.

[36] R. W. Schultz, *The Church of the Nativity at Bethlehem*, pl. 11; for other bibliography see Ch. II n. 50.

[37] Van Millingen, *Byzantine Churches in Constantinople*, pp. 219-233.

[38] R. Janin, *La Géographie ecclésiastique de l'empire byzantin, III, Les églises et les monastères*, Paris, 1953, pp. 529-538.

During the Carolingian period in the West the clearest evidence that the Christian patrons of art were, like the Byzantine illuminators, interested in the expressive implications of the imperial ciborium and domical towers is recorded in the Bible of St. Paul at Rome and the Utrecht Psalter. Both were royal manuscripts of the ninth century whose illuminations were presumably executed under the supervision of the "Palace Clergy." The importance which is given to the various symbolic uses of the royal ciborium in the Bible of St. Paul has a particular historical significance when it is recalled that this manuscript was probably made for Charles the Bald in the Royal Abbey of St. Denis at the time when the emperor was the honorary abbot and the abbey was a royal residence.[39] Throughout the Bible the various representations of an imperial baldachin over the Throne of Solomon, over Antiochus at the siege of Jerusalem and over Holofernes record a thorough knowledge of the whole antique tradition of the king's tent, while the use of the baldachin over the Evangelists shows that the age still thought of the ciborium as a divine emblem over those who spoke with the authority of God.[40]

The most instructive pages in this Bible are those illustrating the Pentecost and the Life of St. Paul.[41] In the Pentecost (Fig. 126) a special distinction is given to Peter and Paul among the Apostles about to go forth to the conversion and spiritual conquest of the *orbis Romanorum*, for they are seated like the imperial rulers of the world under a large baldachin, which is set within the bulwarks of the Church and under a towered façade. Most of the towers of this symbolic castrum have the customary flat roof, except for the two flanking ones which are domical. The careful location of the central baldachin under a towered façade may have been purely accidental; and then again, in an age when visible forms were so important, it may have been intended to show that the ultimate authority in the Carolingian Empire came from the Palatium, just as it is possible that the towered façade of the *palatium regale* had a symbolic meaning over the ciborium in the scene of the Presentation in the Temple at Palermo.

Of equal interest are the various uses of the ciborium in the scenes from the Conversion of St. Paul (Fig. 128), which are divided into three vertical registers. In the upper zone Paul receives his orders to persecute the Christians from the High Priest, who sits like a ruler under a baldachin guarded by soldiers and flanked by domical towers to make it evident that the authorization came from the imperial Palatium. In the middle zone the blinded Paul is led into the city of Damascus where he is healed and converted by Ananias, whose source of power is made manifest by the heavenly ciborium under which he receives the new ambassador of God. Finally, in the bottom scene Paul speaks as the representative of the supreme King of Kings from a ciborium at the gateway, reminding us that in the West it was customary during the Middle Ages for a bishop to preach at times from the city-gate, and indicating that his *pulpitum*, as in a church, was a heavenly canopy from which one spoke in the name of the Lord.

[39] A. M. Friend, "Carolingian Art in the Abbey of St. Denis," *Art Studies*, I, 1923, pp. 67-75.

[40] Throne of Solomon (fol. 185), Holofernes (fol. 231), Antiochus IV (fol. 240), and St. John (fol. 284).

[41] Pentecost (fol. 293v) and Conversion of Paul (fol. 308v).

The illustrations of the Utrecht Psalter furnish the most striking confirmation that the Middle Ages were cognizant of the antique palace tradition, thought of a *palatium* in the architectural terms which were characteristic of late Roman and Byzantine palaces, and still visualized a domical vestibule as a celestial *skene* in which a *Dominus et Deus* was received and worshiped. "The House of the Lord" (Fig. 132), illustrating Psalm 133, is a literal interpretation of the words: "Behold, bless ye the Lord, all ye servants of the Lord, which might stand in the house of the Lord." The place "in the house of the Lord" where his subjects bow down and lift up their hands in adoration is pictured in imperial terms as a domical chamber with the sun and stars of heaven above it and the purifying waters of the River of Paradise, comparable to a *Lavacrum*, in front of it. This divine salutatorium, which is set into the porticos of a colonnaded court hung with royal curtains, is like the rotunda at the entrance to Diocletian's Palace (Fig. 133), the round vestibule of the *praetorium-palatium* at Treves (Fig. 131), the Chalce of the Imperial Palace at Constantinople (Fig. 130/B), and the palace on the Byzantine casket at Troyes (Fig. 98). There are also two other palaces in the Psalter, the sanctuary of the Lord in Psalm 28 and the palace in Psalm 111, which are very similar to the *palatium* on the Byzantine ivory and the mosaic at Bethlehem (Fig. 75) in having a domical vestibule with halls opening off from it, as if they extended down either side of an interior court.

This palace type with a domical vestibule, or *salutatorium*, which is given such marked importance in the Utrecht Psalter, was not merely a pictorial convention that the illuminators had obtained from Constantinople. Instead, it was probably based upon existing Carolingian palace architecture which was copied from the Late Antique and early Byzantine tradition. The palace at Farfa, where the Carolingian emperors resided with their Court before attending ceremonial functions in Rome, had, as the documents tell us, a *pro aulium*, or *Porta Prima*, leading to a great *salutatorium*, off from which there were a *consistorium* for audiences and a tri-apsidal triclinium, called a *trichorum* (Ch. V, n. 39). Furthermore, the manner in which the domes on the palaces in the Utrecht Psalter are drawn, when considered in relation to the palaces represented on the Bayeux tapestry and the *skene* domes pictured in mediaeval art, should be accepted as evidence as to how the Middle Ages constructed and thought of domical coverings. Also it should dispel any lingering doubts that the domical covering over a place of reception, whether a portable ciborium, or a permanent vault over a hall of state, was still considered to be a heavenly tent. On the "House of the Lord" (Fig. 132), and on the other palaces in the Psalter, the artist carefully drew the celestial canopy with the cusped edges and melonlike corrugations of a *skene* in the same way that it was depicted in the Hellenistic and Roman periods (Figs. 48, 105). Further evidence that the churchmen supervising the execution of the Psalter in the royal scriptorium of Reims were interested in the symbolism of the dome and were fully conversant with its imperial and divine connotations can be seen in the way they contrast the baldachin and *fastigium* in Psalm 1, and throughout the manuscript use the customary flat-roofed

161

towers on ordinary battlements, but depict domical towers over royal and divine gateways at the entrance to cities honored by the presence of God.

Domes, it has been seen, crown the towers, in the same way that they were used to commemorate a royal visitation on the Thracian coins, in the scenes of the Coming of the Lord (Fig. 54) in which the "King of Glory" with his military escort is being welcomed at the city-gate. Sion is pictured either as a castrum (Ps. 72) with domical towers at the four corners, or with *skene* cupolas on the towers of its principal gateway (Ps. 47, 64, 76). Domical towers flank the tabernacle within a castrum (Ps. 17) in the same way that they flank the baldachin within the battlements from the Bible of St. Paul (Fig. 126). "The City of God" (Ps. 45), which is made glad by angels blowing trumpets, has a royal portal with cupolas, and the "House of the Lord" (Ps. 121), which is pictured being built as the New Jerusalem, has the celestial cupolas on its gateway, while from outside the city, as in an Adventus, gather "the Tribes of God," all carrying palms, to give thanks to the Lord in a triumphal manner.[42]

It has already been seen how literally the rulers of the Holy Roman Empire followed Roman precedent by combining on their coins the heavenly ciborium, and its related orb, with the towers of the castrum-palatium gateway in order to picture their divine authority in terms of a *Sacrum palatium*. The persistent symbolic and ceremonial significance of the baldachin shape over a palace portal is proved by the bulla (Fig. 83) of Henry IV and the coin (Fig. 87) of Frederick I, which give so much importance to a *skene* cupola over the portal of the *aula regia*. The presence of a domical oratory over the gateway on these two coins also recalls the cupola over the royal chamber of the monastic *Porta curia* (Fig. 7) at Canterbury, and suggests a conceptual relation in the East to the palace versions of the Entry into Jerusalem which have either a dome or a ciborium over the gateway (Figs. 127, 169). Furthermore, the exact resemblance of the royal portal on the coins of the Germanic emperors to the domical parakyptikon, which was constructed as an imperial oratory over the entrance to some of the Byzantine palace-churches (Fig. 140, 156), is incontrovertible evidence that a domical place of reception was a ceremonial provision and a symbolic feature of the palace tradition in both the East and the West.

Because of the Adventus ceremonies during the Middle Ages, in which a ruler was still welcomed by the populace as a divine being, the history of the domical vestibule at a city and palace gateway suggests that this architectural feature, like the towered façade on the royal abbeys of the Carolingian emperors, had come to involve controversial issues as to whether it was only the heavenly Christ, or also the emperor, who was to be so honored. In view of this ever present issue it is possible to advance an explanation of why Innocent III (A.D. 1199-1216), at the height of his political and religious struggle with the German rulers of the Holy Roman Empire, changed the mosaic in the apse of Old St. Peter's. According to the Renaissance drawing of this now

---

[42] E. T. DeWald, *The Illustrations of the Utrecht Psalter*; it is also to be noted that "the Blessed Man," like an Evangelist, sits under a domical skene, while "the Prince" is under a royal *fastigium* (fol. 1v, pl. 1).

destroyed apse, he had introduced at the bottom (Fig. 129) the city of Jerusalem with a large domical vestibule and Bethlehem presented in royal terms with domes on its towered portal.[43] It is to be recalled that there are no other examples of a domical vestibule at the entrance to Jerusalem, except on the Carolingian ivories (Fig. 73), where the city is so distinguished because of the presence of Christ, and in the Byzantine palace version of the Entry into Jerusalem at Daphni (Fig. 127), Bethlehem, and on the Pala d'Oro (Fig. 169).

Before the architectural symbolism of the Cities of God can be dismissed as the fanciful elaboration of a Renaissance draftsman, or left uninterpreted because the architecture does not conform to what we are accustomed to associate with the gateways of mediaeval cities, palaces, and monasteries, some consideration should be given to the Pope's reasons for introducing this iconography into the already decorated apse of St. Peter's, which was the principal sanctuary to be visited by the German emperors when they made their processional Advent into Rome. Is it not possible that Innocent III had so much emphasis given to the royal portal of Bethlehem and the domical vestibule of Jerusalem, as places of honor from which emerges the symbolic Master of the World, in order to dispel any popular belief that these domical features implied the presence of the emperor as the earthly "Royal Christ"? Innocent III, as we know, was aggressively uncompromising in his opposition to the claims of the German rulers that they were comparable to the Son of God and the Master of Rome and the World. Hence the presumption that in his desire to disprove the ideas that the motifs were to be associated with secular rulers and that they stood for imperial authority, he had this mosaic executed in order to demonstrate how the architectural forms, in this spiritual version of a Roman *Profectio*, like the ceremonies which went with them, referred, not to earthly kings, but only to the Lamb of God, the Heavenly King.

Since the only architectural examples, other than the Roman and Byzantine palace vestibules, appear to be limited to some of the Mt. Athos monasteries and in the East to Islamic palaces, which will be discussed later, it may seem as if too much ideological importance were being attached to the domical vestibule at the entrance to the Celestial City on the Roman mosaic. Even though the monastic examples were undoubtedly added onto the existing buildings at a relatively late date, it is nevertheless necessary to find some precedent and explanation for the domical vestibule at the entrance to the convent of St. Panteleimon (Rousselon), which is pictured in the eighteenth century drawing of Baskii, and the ciboriumlike place of reception in front of the portal of the famous, imperial Lavra monastery.[44]

Before this evidence at Mt. Athos can be related to the thirteenth century Roman mosaic several factors in the development of architecture have to be taken into consideration. In the first place we cannot overlook the fact that we know so little about imperial palaces, that all the important mediaeval palaces in the West have been totally

[43] J. Wilpert, *Die Römischen Mosaiken und Malereien*, I, 1916, p. 358, fig. 14; Müntz, *Rev. arch.*, II, 1882, p. 143.

[44] L. de Beylié, L'habitation byzantine, 1902, p. 70; F. Perilla, *Le Mount Athos*, 1927, p. 58.

destroyed, and that the early monastic gateways have been either destroyed or rebuilt. Also it must not be forgotten that a domical vestibule was conceptually and traditionally a portable ciborium, or temporary structure, customarily set up at a gateway for the reception of honored guests. Hence there is no reason to expect architectural evidence of nonstructural baldachins and domical vestibules at the entrance to cities, palaces, and monasteries, except in those instances, as at Mt. Athos, where the traditional form of the place of reception was eventually translated into a permanent pavilion.

There may be no documentary proof that portable ciboria were set up when the Carolingian and Byzantine emperors visited their royal abbeys and imperial foundations, like the Lavra. At the same time it is reasonably certain that in the West it was customary for a whole chapter of monks to receive their rulers as the *christus Domini* and to conduct them, in what was a kind of Adventus ceremony, to their royal chamber either over the gateway, as was probably the case at Canterbury (Fig. 7), or in the upper story of a kind of triumphal arch, as at Lorsch.[45] Because of the important role which the royal abbeys played in the itinerant life of the Carolingian kings it may be surmised that the injunctions in the Rule of St. Benedict, which read, "Let all guests that come be received like Christ himself" and "Let fitting honor be shown to all," were instructions originally based upon the ceremonial honors accorded to the ruler as the Royal Christ.[46]

The influence of the Adventus tradition in the monasteries of the East is also implied by the words of St. Ephrem who wrote, "In the person of the stranger who presents himself, we receive not a man, but God himself."[47] That the early monastic rites of welcome were based upon the customary salutations and adoration of a divine emperor is more clearly indicated by the information that at one time the early monks were accustomed to go forth in a body to meet their guests with the instructions, "at the arrival or departure of all guests, by bowing the head or even prostrating with the whole body on the ground, let Christ be adored in them."[48] It is doubtful whether at any time "all guests" were actually received with the "fitting honors" accorded the emperor as the "image of Christ"; but it must be assumed that at any imperial monastery, like the Lavra at Mt. Athos, all visitors of any importance were welcomed, like the "Christos-Basileus," in the traditional ciborium of honor. This custom, therefore, would have resulted eventually in the building of a domical vestibule or pavilion, even though the monks of Mt. Athos, with their loss of imperial patronage and in their present isolation, no longer make any ceremonial use of these places for receptions. Nevertheless,

---

[45] See p. 91.

[46] Dom F. Delattre, *The Rule of St. Benedict*, 1921, p. 330; the two questions of whether monasteries received the emperor, like Christ, under a heavenly canopy and whether the royal Advent influenced the later monastic injunctions can only be settled by a competent investigation of the various *Ordines ad regem suscipiendum*, but they seem plausible in view of Kantorowicz's statement (*op.cit.*, pp. 208-209) that the king's liturgical reception was formulated in monastic circles and that the oldest known setting of these Orders comes from the Abbey of Farfa, which was the royal abbey where the Carolingian rulers resided prior to their ceremonial entrance into Rome.

[47] Delattre, *op.cit.*, p. 332.

[48] *Ibid.*, pp. 333-334.

it is the importance of the Adventus receptions at the monasteries, palaces, and cities during the Middle Ages which, when taken in combination with the ritualistic recognition of the Byzantine Basileus and German emperors as the personification of the Son of God, allows us to see a countersymbolism in the architectural iconography used by Innocent III on the mosaic of Old St. Peter's.

VII · THE IMPERIAL PARAKYPTIKON AND DOMICAL VESTIBULE IN BYZANTINE ARCHITECTURE

I T IS the survival in both the Byzantine East and Germanic West of similar and related architectural provisions for the imperial ritual which presupposes a common origin in the palace conventions of the Late Roman Empire. The validity of this assumption becomes more convincing when the ceremonial provisions for the Carolingian emperors in the towered *Westwerke* of their royal abbey churches, which they annually visited for designated festivals, are compared with the development and use of the imperial parakyptikon or koiton over the entrance to those Byzantine palace-churches at Constantinople which were honored on a special feast day by the Coming of the Basileus.

The domical vestibule, it has been deduced from the history of the Epiphany and Adventus, and from the plans and ceremonies of the Byzantine palaces, was originally a structural version of a reception *skene* which, like the towered façade of the castrum-palatium gateway on the Carolingian churches, had a conceptual as well as a ritualistic purpose. Having been from Hellenistic times a celestial form, the shape of the vaulted vestibule was visible proof of the heavenly nature of the divine honors conferred upon the ruler by the ceremonies. The account of the cupola which Justinian built after the fire of A.D. 532 in the narthex of the Senate House (Fig. 130/G) is evidence that the use and meaning of the domical shape in the ritual of the Byzantine Court was based upon Roman precedent. The six columns of the narthex of the Senate House were all white, "the largest of all columns in the whole world," and the porch back of them had, as we are told, "a roof curved into a vault *(tholus).*" What, then, was the precedent for this domical vault, if it was not to take the place of the portable ciborium which had previously been used in the ceremonies? Procopius certainly believed that this vestibule, and the ceremonies which took place in it, followed Roman tradition, because he wrote, "There the Senate of the Romans assembles at the beginning of the new year," which in both pagan and Christian times was associated with the coming of a god, "and celebrates an annual festival, observing always the ancient tradition of the State."[1]

At about the same time that Justinian, "observing always the ancient tradition of the State," added the "tholus" to the Senate House for the celebration of an "annual festival" in which he was undoubtedly the chief participant, he also built the palace church of SS. Sergius and Bacchus near the Hormisdas palace.[2] Here he had a shallow cupola constructed over the central bay of the narthex, or what was the vestibule in front of the "Imperial Door." According to the palace ritual, as later recorded in the "Book of Ceremonies," when the emperor visited this church on Easter Monday in order to celebrate the beginning of the Christian's New Year, he was received by the

---

[1] Procopius, VIII, *Buildings* (Loeb), 1940, Bk. I, x, 5 (p. 83); Ebersolt, *Le grand palais,* p. 14.

[2] J. Ebersolt and A. Thiers, *Les Églises de Constantinople,* 1913, pp. 27-36, pl. v.

Hegumen under the domical vestibule at the entrance to the Royal House of God. Then, in a ceremony that paralleled a liturgical Entrance the Hegumen, censing in front of him, led the emperor up the stairs to his seat in the tribune over the "Royal Door."[3]

After the entry the emperor lit candles, prayed, and received the Communion in the veiled oratory of the tribune, which is referred to in the texts as a parakyptikon ($\pi\alpha\rho\alpha\kappa\nu\pi\tau\iota\kappa\acute{o}\nu$). During the service and until after the Communion, he sat in this special place of honor from which he could look down into the naos. Then he was led to the *mitatorion*, which was either a private chamber, or a portable pavilion, at the east end of the south gallery where he changed his vestments before being led to the *triklinos* to partake of a ceremonial meal with the Hegumen and certain honored guests. When he had finished eating, preceded by dignitaries of the chamber, magistrates, and others of his personal service, the Hegumen, who again censed in front of him, led him back by way of the *catechumenia*, or galleries, to the narthex where he was received by his full entourage of nobles and officers.

In order to show the importance and architectural development of the imperial chapel in the tribune of the palace-churches, it is better to continue with the other references to a parakyptikon, or $\kappa o \iota \tau \acute{\omega} \nu$ as it was also called, before considering the significance of the domical vestibule in the narthex of SS. Sergius and Bacchus. With the exception of Hagia Sophia, where the parakyptikon used by the Basileus during the celebration of the Feast of the Raising of the Cross was probably in the south aisle, or possibly in the south gallery, and the Nea, which will be discussed later, the imperial chapel seems to have been always located in the middle of the tribune over the narthex.[4] Among the early sanctuaries of Constantinople, which are described as having had a parakyptikon in the tribune and a triklinos adjacent to the gallery, is the church of the Holy Reliquary, which was a round martyrium, probably dating from the time of Leo I (A.D. 457-474), connected with the palace-church of St. Mary Blachernae.[5]

Without the structural evidence from the later Byzantine churches it is difficult to reconstruct from the texts what a parakyptikon was like in either the destroyed churches or in SS. Sergius and Bacchus where it was not built of masonry. Taking only the usage of the word in the accounts of the palace ceremonies, where it is applied to balustrades in front of a throne, to a throne in a phiale and to the draperies held around the imperial seat in the *cathisma* of the Hippodrome, it seems to have been essentially a barrier of richly decorated fabrics which either marked the location of the throne by being thrown over the surrounding balustrade, or held around the

[3] A. Vogt, *Le Livre des cérémonies, texte*, I, pp. 79-80 and *Commentaire*, I, p. 119; Reiske, *Corpus script. hist. byzantinae*, II, *Constantinus Porphyrogenitus*, II, pp. 195 (88, 5), 209 (103, 18), 301 (266, 24); Ebersolt, *Le grand palais*, p. 101 n. 1; Ebersolt and Thiers, *Les Églises*, p. 32.

[4] Ebersolt, *Sainte-Sophie de Constantinople*,

1910, pp. 25 n. 7 (parakyptikon), 16 n. 1 (coronation), 27 (reception of ambassadors).

[5] Ebersolt, *Sanctuaries de Byzance*, 1921, pp. 48-49; J. B. Papadopoulos, *Les Palais et les églises des Blachernes*, 1928, p. 104; J. P. Richter, *Quellen der Byzantinischen Kunstgeschichte*, 1897, no. 355 (p. 169).

throne in order to veil the emperor while he was taking his seat.[6] It has, therefore, been variously interpreted as: a balustrade in front of a throne, a veiled and partly concealed place of distinction from which the Basileus could look out, hence a window or place of public appearances, and an oratory.

Because of the ambiguities in the usage of παρακυπτικόν, which usually seems to signify hangings, it may seem unjustified to refer to the imperial seat of honor in the tribune of the palace-churches as a parakyptikon after it was constructed as a domical oratory. There are several reasons why the term is used throughout this study. In the first place it is necessary to assume that when it was applied to the imperial chapel as the location of the royal seat it implied not only hangings, but also a baldachinlike structure with a domical canopy. Even though it was not a formal baldachin, its later translation into masonry and its sculptural treatment in Arta (Fig. 156) show that it must have been at first a light and portable pavilion, like a ciborium, with concealing portieres at the sides. Also the fact that this place of honor is frequently referred to in the texts as a koiton (κοιτών), signifying a "royal chamber" or "pavilion," is another indication that a parakyptikon, even when it was only a piece of ritualistic furniture, had all the distinguishing and symbolic features of a throne covering.[7] Furthermore, by referring to the imperial chapel as a parakyptikon, which of course continued to have portieres hanging at the sides after it was bulit into the tribune with a domical vault, the term emphasizes the general contention of this study that it was customary ever since Hellenistic times to translate portable canopies of reception, i.e. a *skene* pavilion with its symbolic shape, into a domical vestibule, a tetrapylon, and other ceremonial provisions of masonry construction.

There is the possibility that koiton was used instead of parakyptikon when the imperial oratory in the tribune of a palace-church was incorporated into the structure, instead of being a portable ciborium with veils. There is also the question of what distinctions should be made between a parakyptikon, or koiton, and a *mitatorion*, because in the scene from the History of John Skylitzes (Fig. 168), where Leo the Wise stands in the gallery of Hagia Sophia reading a defamatory libel on the worship of icons, the ciborium over the Emperor is designated in the text as a *mitatorion*.[8] Like the parakyptikon, the exact meaning of *mitatorion*, which is frequently mentioned in the rituals, is ambiguous. Not only does it refer to the place where the emperor changed his vestments and sat in the gallery, but in Hagia Sophia it is applied to the place in the south side-aisle, next to the sanctuary, where he listened to the reading of the Gospels, and also to various other locations in the church where the emperor took part in the ceremonies.[9] It has been argued that in Hagia Sophia it

---

[6] For various uses see Ebersolt, *Le grand palais*, p. 101 n. 1; for meanings see Ebersolt, Reiske (*op.cit.*, II, pp. 195, 209, 301) and Vogt (*op.cit.*, *Commentaire*, II, p. 118).

[7] Ebersolt, *Le grand palais*, p. 14 n. 2, pp. 54-55, and p. 70 n. i (koiton same as mitatorion); Ebersolt, *Sainte-Sophie*, p. 19 (koiton same as mitatorion).

[8] Folio 115v; de Beylié, *L'Habitation byzantine*, p. 102.

[9] Ebersolt, *Sainte-Sophie*, pp. 17-21, 25 (gallery); *Le grand palais*, p. 70 n. 1 (in Magnaura); Lethaby and Swainson, *St. Sophia*, p. 78; E. Mambourg, "Topographie de Ste-Sophie," *Atti d. V Congresso d. Studi bizantini e neoellenici*, v, 1940, pp. 240ff.; Richter, *op.cit.*, nos. 52 (p. 29), 90 (p. 84), 100-104

must refer to actual rooms which were originally connected with the church.[10] On the basis of the Skylitzes miniature and the different uses of the word, it is possible that *mitatorion*, signifying a "place of honor," was a more general term than either parakyptikon or koiton and was, therefore, applied to both special chambers and to a ciborium-like canopy set up in the side-aisles, galleries, and tribune of the church.[11] Although Hagia Sophia may have been the exception among palace-churches in not having a parakyptikon in the tribune, there must have been a portable veiled canopy, like a parakyptikon, which could be set up so that on such occasions as when a new emperor spent the night before his coronation in the tribune he could be appropriately secluded.[12]

Even without the evidence of the later Byzantine churches, in which the imperial chapel was constructed with a domical vault, the necessary assumption that it was always covered with a cupola, regardless of whether it was a veiled parakyptikon or a more permanent chamber over the Royal Portal, suggests some relation in form, symbolism, location and, perhaps, in ritualistic use to the ciboria-cupolas over the palatium portal on the fourth century coins. Certainly throughout Byzantine history the parakyptikon, and the ceremonies for which it was provided, were intended to dramatize the special sanctity of the Basileus and, like the *capella regia* at the entrance to the Carolingian churches, to show that the emperor's position in the church was second only to that of Christ. It is not only the domical parakyptikon which implies a derivation from a pre-Christian past. The ceremonial forms with which the Basileus was treated as a manifestation of God, was received at the entrance to his palace-churches and was conducted to his elevated seat over the "Imperial Door" all seem to have been Christian adaptations of features that went back in origin to the *parousia* of Hellenistic kings at a city and palace gateway.

On Sunday of Antipascha, for example, the emperor went to the church of St. Mokios, which was a fourth century sanctuary built on the foundations of a temple of Zeus and then later rebuilt by Justinian.[13] In a ceremony that recalls a Roman Adventus and a Hellenistic Apantesis the emperor arrived on horseback and was received by representatives of the political factions of the city while he sat in the phiales, which were the domical kiosks over fonts.[14] During the service in St. Mokios he sat in his oratory, which is described as the *koiton* in the tribune "over the royal doors"; and afterward he was conducted to the *triklinos* for the ceremonial repast. For the Feast of the Ascension he visited St. Mary of the Source where he went to the tribune over the narthex in order to receive Communion in the "koiton of the

---

(pp. 92-93), 107-109 (p. 95), 119 (p. 97), 304 (p. 156); E. Swift, *Hagia Sophia*, 1940, pp. 85, 102; Vogt, *Texte*, I, pp. 143, 147, 148 and *Commentaire*, I, pp. 61-62.

[10] D. Bjeljaev, *Byzantina*, II, pp. 128ff.

[11] du Cange, *Gloss. Lat.*, "Metatus"; Reiske, *op.cit.*, II, pp. 109-110.

[12] Ebersolt, *Sainte-Sophie*, p. 16 n. 1.

[13] Ebersolt, *Sanctuaires*, pp. 74-75; *Le grand palais*, p. 186; Richter, nos. 181-187 (pp. 120-122).

[14] The way in which the Byzantine emperors were received by the political factions in the domical phiale before entering a church is somewhat reminiscent of the probable ceremonial use of the *Lavacrum* at the entrance to the *Porta triumphalis* at Rome (see p. 27).

Emperor"; and later, while he was partaking of the special repast with the Patriarch, the political factions outside in the atrium chanted their praises of him.[15]

Another of the palace-churches visited by the emperor on several feast days was the old basilica dedicated to the Mother of God and connected with the Blachernae palace.[16] Although the original church dated back to the reign of Marcian (A.D. 450-457), it was largely rebuilt in the eleventh century after the disastrous fire of A.D. 1070. For the celebration of the Feast of the Dormition all the Senators, specially clad, sat at the border of the sea, outside the Porta, awaiting the arrival of the emperor by boat; and when he landed they prostrated themselves in adoration before him.[17] Following this ancient ritual of welcome he was conducted with great formality to the *koiton* in the tribune of the church. It was also in this church of St. Mary on February 2, the Roman month of purification, that the whole court took part with the Basileus in the celebration of the Feast of the Hypapante, or the Presentation in the Temple, which was presumably enacted as if the *apantesis* pertained to both Christ and the emperor.[18]

It is impossible to ascertain from the texts when a church was first honored with a prescribed imperial visitation and to know in the case of the now destroyed sanctuaries what provisions were made for the liturgical reception of the Basileus. It is reasonably certain, however, that in all the palace-churches there was either a portable canopy with hangings or an actual domical chapel to serve as the imperial chapel, even when the texts fail to mention either a parakyptikon or koiton. This is indicated for the church of the Holy Apostles by the reference to the emperor having taken a seat in the narthex before having been led to the tribune for the Communion and after the services having been conducted by way of the galleries to the *triklinos*.[19] At the same time, as in the church of Hagia Sophia, the location of the imperial place of honor must have varied with the different types of ceremonies. In San Marco, for example, which the Venetians copied from the Holy Apostles, after its rebuilding by Justinian, the Doge and the Patriarch had special thrones on opposite sides of the eastern sanctuary, but at the western end the staircases at either side of the Royal Door, which is set into an apsidal *Porta regia*, went up to a tribune now thought to have been covered by a dome.[20]

While Justinian's church of the Holy Apostles may have had a domical tribune similar to the one in San Marco there is no evidence prior to the Book of Ceremonies to show whether or not the early churches had a parakyptikon. Certainly the honors

[15] Ebersolt, *Sanctuaires*, pp. 61-62; *Le grand palais*, p. 187.

[16] R. Janin, *La Géographie ecclésiastique de l'empire byzantin*, III, 1953, "Les Églises et les monastères," pp. 169-174.

[17] Papadopoulos, *Les Palais et les églises des Blachernes*, p. 130; Richter, no. 356 (pp. 168-170, parakyptikon).

[18] Ebersolt, *Sanctuaires*, p. 48 and *Le grand palais*, p. 191; Vogt, *op.cit., Texte*, I, Ch. 36 p. 140.

[19] Ebersolt, *Le grand palais*, pp. 183-186 and *Sanctuaires*, p. 34 n. 4 and *Constantinople*, 1951,

p. 34 n. 3-4, p. 36 n. 2; Richter, *op.cit.*, no. 157 (p. 112). The tribune communicated with the "Bonus Palace" which was built by Romanus Lecapenus.

[20] The curious *pozzo*, or shaft, through the western tribune of San Marco, which is best illustrated by the eighteenth century section of Visentini (*Documenti per la storia dell' Augusta Ducale Basilica di San Marco in Venezia*, ed. Ongania, Tav. XL/122), presumably had a wooden floor and was, according to Demus, originally covered with a dome.

accorded to the Byzantine emperors in the church receptions were much older than the tenth century. If they were taken over quite literally from the palace ceremonies, when the emperor-liturgy was adjusted to the Christian services, then it is possible to argue that the ritual of reception, including a ciborium of reception, went back to the time of Constantine and was based upon the palace versions of the Adventus and Epiphany. The many features of the palace-church ceremonies, which must have been derived from the Roman and Hellenistic tradition, strengthens the presumption that the Byzantine parakyptikon was in some way related to earlier palace receptions in a domical vestibule and the importance of ciboria on the gateway coins of the fourth century. That the ceremonies were based upon precedent is perhaps illustrated by the repast in a triklinos.

By the Byzantine period there was no practical necessity for eating after a ceremony when the emperors had only a short journey from their palaces to an adjacent or nearby church. Earlier, however, when the Hellenistic and Roman rituals were formulated there would have been a real necessity for serving food and drink in a ceremony of welcome after a ruler had traveled from one city to another. Furthermore, a religious meal had always been an established feature in the celebration of Advents, triumphs, and anniversaries: in Egypt the *heb-sed* and triumphal festivals of the Pharaoh culminated in a ritualistic meal; in Assyria it was an essential rite in the seasonal celebration of the coming of a god; and at Rome a Triumph probably began with a breakfast outside the Porta Triumphalis and certainly ended with a state banquet. Some reflection of this pattern is preserved in the Christian sequence of the Entry into Jerusalem being followed by the Last Supper at Sion, which was traditionally the palace stronghold of the Hebrew kings.

One cannot attempt to trace the history of the parakyptikon and its influence upon palace-churches without asking when it was changed from a piece of liturgical furniture into a structural and domical chapel for the emperor. Could the change have taken place in the Nea, that palace-church built by Basil I and dedicated in A.D. 881, which no longer exists?[21] It seems as though there should have been an exceptional place of honor in this famous sanctuary, which acquired its distinction of being the "New Church" partly because it may have been the first church to adopt the palace design of a central dome over an audience hall with smaller golden cupolas at the four corners, and more especially because it was unique in having ceremonial portals on all except the east side. These were intended to reproduce the gateway and adventus symbolism of the temple of the Lord described in Ezekiel.[22] Unfortunately the Nea cannot be used to fill the gap in the evidence, since there is no justification for believing that it had either a tribune or a special oratory where the emperor received the Communion.

[21] Ebersolt, *Le grand palais*, pp. 130-135; Vogt, *op.cit.*, *Commentaire*, I, pp. 135-136; R. Janin, *Les Églises et les monastères*, pp. 374-378.

[22] My information, that the symbolic design and decorations of the Nea were based upon the temple of Ezekiel (chs. 40-44) and described by Photius, I owe to A. M. Friend.

All the imperial ceremonies in the Nea appear to have followed the ritual prescribed for the celebration of the Dedication of the church on May 1, in which the emperor and empress, after entering the church and visiting various chapels, were conducted to their seats in the south narthex where, protected by curtains which imply a portable parakyptikon, they listened to the reading of the Holy Scriptures.[23] In fact the account is very specific in stating that at the end of the service the emperor alone went up a hidden staircase to the terracelike roof of the narthex by which he returned to the palace. At the beginning of the ceremonies, however, which were conducted like an Adventus, the emperor was met by all the members of the Senate in front of the western narthex before he entered the church through the Royal Door. Partly because one is reminded of the Senate House, which had a domical vestibule for the reception of the Basileus, but also because in the course of the service the emperor and patriarch returned to the western narthex where they lit candles before the image of Basil, which was presumably over the Royal Door, we may assume that there was a cupola over the central bay of the narthex which served both as a place of reception and a kind of chapel in honor of the Founder.

The development of Byzantine church architecture after the ninth century shows that there was progressively marked emphasis upon all domical forms in order to make the church a more symbolic replica of God's universal dwelling. In the period between the ninth and twelfth centuries cupolas were added at the corners of the heavenly castrum-palatium, the central dome was elevated on a higher drum, its celestial shape was given more prominence on the exterior, and the imperial place of honor was not only incorporated into the vaulted construction, but was also raised up above the roof of the tribune. It was not, however, until after the twelfth century that the square bays of the narthex and exo-narthex were given a new distinction by having their cupolas elevated above the roof. This sequence raises a series of related questions: one, as to when the parakyptikon was translated into a structural oratory and its domical vault was elevated above the tribune roof; two, whether the use of a domical vault over the central bay of the narthex had any ceremonial significance; and three, whether the eventual adoption of elevated cupolas over a narthex and exo-narthex was influenced by the development of the structural parakyptikon?

The chronological problem of attempting to answer these questions is complicated by the total destruction of so many of the important palace-churches, by the successive rebuilding of the extant churches, and in many instances by the changes which were made when the churches were turned into Turkish mosques. Since there was no need for either a tribune or a parakyptikon in any but those churches regularly visited by the Basileus, the problem is limited to Constantinople until after the Latin conquest, except for those monastic churches at Mt. Athos which, as imperial foundations, enjoyed royal visitations. According to Millet, the texts indicate that there was an oratory in the tribune over the original narthex of the Lavra, which was a very

[23] Vogt, op.cit., Texte, I, p. 122; Richter, op.cit., nos. 948-961 (pp. 352-359).

172

special imperial structure first built at the end of the ninth century, and also in the eleventh century churches of Iviron and Vatopedi, which copied it.[24] Unfortunately, however, later changes, including the addition of an exo-narthex to these churches, have removed all traces of a structural parakyptikon at Mt. Athos.

The earliest example, therefore, is in St. Savior Pantepoptes (Fig. 139) at Constantinople, which was built by Anna Delassena, the wife of Alexis I (A.D. 1081-1118).[25] The fact that the vaulted cupola of the royal chapel is concealed under the roof of the tribune may imply that it is an early type of structural parakyptikon which was copied from an earlier palace-church. A much more developed and symbolically important treatment of the imperial chapel is preserved in the South Church of St. Savior Pantocrator, where the cupola of the parakyptikon is raised up on the exterior over the entrance (Fig. 140). The Pantocrator, located in the palace area, was a special monastic church and burial place of the Comneni family during the twelfth century and later a private mausoleum and imperial sanctuary of the Palaeologi. While there have been differences of opinion regarding the order in which the three contiguous parts were built, it is generally agreed that the South Church was the original section which was erected by Irene, the wife of the Emperor John II Comneni, sometime before her death in A.D. 1126.[26]

The section of the South Church (Fig. 141) is sometimes drawn as if there had never been a tribune and hence no parakyptikon to explain the cupola over the central bay of the narthex. This is surprising because, in addition to the raised cupola, both the construction and the later use of the church by the Turks prove that it originally had an imperial chapel. The section shows a ledge on the outer wall, exactly at the level where a wooden floor would have rested, and on the opposite wall, at the proper height, a customary royal window looking down into the naos. That there was a wooden floor at the tribune level, at least during the period when the Pantocrator was used as a Turkish mosque, is known from the fact that it was customary for the Sultan to sit in the gallery under the royal cupola of his Byzantine predecessors.[27] All that is doubtful is whether this new type of raised parakyptikon was part of the original construction, erected at the beginning of the twelfth century under the Comneni, or a later addition as van Millingen has suggested.

A twelfth century date for the imperial chapel of the Pantocrator is suggested by the curious emphasis upon the cupola over the gateway in the two scenes of the Entry into Jerusalem at Bethlehem and on the Pala d'Oro (Fig. 169), both executed under the Comneni, and by the equally exceptional chapel over the entrance to the City

[24] G. Millet, "Recherches au Mont-Athos," *Bull. Corr. Hell.*, XXIX, 1905, pp. 91-93, fig. 3; the elevated cupolas over the narthex vestibule at Iviron, Vatopedi, and Chilandari were a later addition (p. 74).

[25] A. van Millingen, *Byzantine Churches in Constantinople*, 1912, Ch. XIV, fig. 73; Ebersolt and Thiers, *Les Églises*, pp. 172-182, pls. XXXIX, XL.

[26] Ebersolt and Thiers, *Les Églises*, p. 185, pl. XLII; van Millingen, *op.cit.*, pp. 219-240, figs. 77 (plan), 80 (section); Janin, *Les Églises et les monastères*, pp. 529-537.

[27] van Millingen, *op.cit.*, p. 237; Ebersolt and Thiers in section (pl. XLIII) show the wooden floor of tribune in place.

of God in the Entry into Jerusalem at Palermo. On the contrary, there are several reasons, including the fact that all the other examples of a raised parakyptikon date from after the Latin conquest, for associating the new type with the Western masters of Constantinople. It has already been noted that there is a striking parallel between the imperial cupola raised over the seat of the Basileus on the façade of St. Savior Pantocrator (Fig. 141) and the *skene* cupola over the gateway of the *aula regis* on the bulla of Henry IV (Fig. 83) and the coin of Frederick I (Fig. 87), and the provisions for the Western emperors in the Westwerk, usually dedicated to St. Savior, of their royal abbey churches (Figs. 78, 80, 123). Furthermore, the symbolic intent of making the imperial seat of honor an architectural manifestation of the emperor's exalted position and authority over the Church seems much more typical of the West, where the controversy with the papacy forced the rulers to use every visible means of making their position manifest. In Constantinople, however, there was never any question, as there was in the West, regarding the supremacy of the Basileus as a throne-sharer with God and, therefore, no necessity to demonstrate the ruler's pre-eminence on the façade of the church, until after the Crusaders had usurped the power.

Following the sack of Constantinople and the conquest of the Byzantine Empire, the new Latin rulers, who shared with Henry VI the Hohenstaufen conception of the Emperor as over the Church, had every reason to strengthen their position by architectural symbolism. It has already been seen how the Latin kings of Jerusalem, and especially Jean de Brienne, made use of the Constantinian motifs on their seals (Fig. 97) and gave an exaggerated importance to the baldachin and globe over the gateway as imperial symbols of a ruler's mastery of the City and the World. One might, therefore, be tempted to attribute the addition of a raised parakyptikon over the façade of the Pantocrator to Jean de Brienne, who after the loss of his Palestinian kingdom was the regent for the young Baldwin II between A.D. 1228-1237, if it were true, as has been stated, that the Latin emperors lived in the monastery of St. Savior Pantocrator instead of in the Blachernae and Boucoleon Palaces.[28] At the same time that the date of the imperial chapel on the façade of the Pantocrator is still open to question, there being the possibility that the Latin rulers were the first to elevate the royal domical parakyptikon in order to assert their position of authority, it must be realized that the eleventh century illuminations of the Skylitzes manuscript (Figs. 162, 164, 165) are proof that raised cupolas over an imperial chamber were traditionally the architectural insignia of *auctoritas imperialis*.

Regardless of the date, the fact that the Pantocrator had a wooden floor for the tribune, which could be removed, may be of significance in the subsequent development of the Byzantine narthex. It was not uncommon for palace-churches, like the Pantocrator which was exempt from the building laws of Constantinople, to have wooden instead of vaulted tribunes and galleries. At Venice San Marco, which was

[28] Janin, *op.cit.*, p. 531.

rebuilt in the eleventh century in imitation of the famous palace-church of the Holy Apostles, had wooden galleries that were removed at a later date.[29] After the Pantocrator had been turned over to the Venetians, or when any palace-church was no longer visited by the emperor and hence had no need of a tribune, the removal of the wooden floor would have left the cupola of the parakyptikon as a lofty vault over the central bay of the narthex. Thus the two traditions of a domical place of reception, one in the tribune and the other in front of the "Royal Door," would have been combined into a new type of narthex, thereby accounting for the innovation of elevated cupolas, such as one seen on the exo-narthex which was built onto the church of St. Theodore (Fig. 146) in the fourteenth century. Certainly no examples appear before the thirteenth century, because the domical narthexes on the churches at Mt. Athos and the Kaisariani in Attica were later additions.[30] This possible explanation makes it desirable to interrupt the history of the parakyptikon and return to the question of when the Byzantine churches adopted from the imperial architecture the domical vestibule in front of the entrance to the Royal House of God.

Apart from the little cupola in front of the Royal Door of the sixth century church of SS. Sergius and Bacchus, and a possible domical vestibule in front of the entrance to the Nea, no other examples can be dated with any accuracy before the eleventh century.[31] There is a cupola over the inner narthex of St. Theodore (Fig. 145) which is usually dated in either the tenth or eleventh century.[32] Another example is found in the Myrelaion (Fig. 143) which is still thought to have been constructed by Roman Lecapenus (A.D. 919-944) and used as an imperial sanctuary and burial place, in spite of the fact that recent excavations have raised the question of whether its brickwork

[29] C. Boito (*The Basilica of S. Mark*, 1888, pp. 353-356) makes it clear that the eleventh century church had galleries, supported by timbers, which were later removed.

[30] Although it has been customary to assign the Kaisariani near Athens to the tenth century, the section of the church and the fact that the narthex was not decorated until 1682 are evidence that the narthex with its elevated cupolas was a later addition (O. Wulff, *Altchristliche und Byzantinische Kunst*, II, 1914, p. 459, Abb. 88; Strzygowski, *Ephemeris*, 1902, p. 54, figs. 2 (plan), 6 (section); J. A. Hamilton, *Scottish Ecclesiological Soc., Trans.*, 1916). The exo-narthex with its elevated cupolas on the Katholikon of Nea Moni at Chios, which was built by Constantine Monomachus sometime before A.D. 1054, is also probably a later addition (Wulff, *op.cit.*, II, p. 467, Abbs. 396-397; G. A. Sotiriou, *Deltion*, II, 1916, p. 30, fig. 8; Strzygowski, *Byz. Zeit.*, V, 1896, pp. 140ff.

[31] The church at Christianou (E. Stikas, *L'Église byzantine de Christianou*, Paris, 1951), dating from the middle of the eleventh century, has a shallow cupola not only in front of the Royal Door of the narthex, but also in front of the two side doors. In the church of Nea Moni of the eleventh century and in the Panaghia Krina and the Holy Apostles

of Pyrghi, all on the Island of Chios, there is a cupola in the narthex (A. Orlandos, *Monuments byzantins de Chios*, II, Athens, 1930). The domes over the narthex of St. Sophia at Saloniki are later additions (C. Diehl, Le Tourneau and H. Saladin, *Les Monuments chrétiens de Salonique*, 1918, p. 160). The domical vestibule shown by Strzygowski on the early church of the Dormition at Nicaea (*Kleinasian*, pp. 106-107) and reproduced in other books was actually a domed-up groin vault which, according to T. Schmidt (*Die Koimesiskirche von Nikaia*, 1927, p. 18) was the result of a rebuilding in the eleventh century. While there is a possibility that the domical vault in front of the central door in the narthex of St. Andrew in Krisei, which is supported like a ciborium on four columns, may date from the sixth century, it was probably built in the thirteenth century (van Millingen, *op.cit.*, pp. 106-118, fig. 40; Ebersolt and Thiers, *Les Églises*, p. 75, pl. XIX; A. Schneider, *Byzanz*, 1936, p. 52). Also the domical vestibule in the South Church of St. Mary Panachrantos was the result of later rebuilding (van Millingen, pp. 122-134, figs. 44-45).

[32] Ebersolt and Thiers, *Les Églises*, pp. 163ff., pl. XXXIV; van Millingen, pp. 243-250, figs. 84, 85; Schneider, *Byzanz*, p. 77, Abb. 9.

was earlier than the eleventh century.[33] Its section (Fig. 142), its fenestration in two stories on the façade, and the partial elevation of its concealed cupola under a gable, all suggest that the Myrelaion may have once had a low tribune with a wooden floor, which means that its royal window looking down into the naos is now concealed by Turkish alterations.

The comparatively late and infrequent appearance of a domical vestibule in the narthex may at first seem curious, especially since the Basileus was always received with great formality in the narthex of a church. We are told, for example, that in the ceremonies at the Holy Apostles and St. Mary Blachernae, he took his seat in the narthex before being conducted up the stairs to his place of honor in the tribune.[34] The probable reason, however, why it was so long before the domical covering was incorporated into the vaulting of the narthex, except in the private imperial sanctuaries like SS. Sergius and Bacchus, was that in the public churches, which were visited only once or twice a year by the emperor, the "Royal Door" was not reserved solely for the use of the Basileus. Instead he either took his seat, as we are told, in a domical phiale over the mystical waters of life or was probably received under a portable ciborium, which was set up for the occasion. Graphic evidence of the use of a ciborium as a place of reception, and of the way an imperial reception was enacted like a Royal Epiphany, is pictured in a miniature (Fig. 144) from the Skylitzes manuscript.[35] It shows the Emperor Theophilus, nimbed and escorted by his mounted entourage with banners flying, visiting the Holy Reliquary which was part of the palace-church of St. Mary Blachernae. In front of the domical reliquary chapel are a font, ciborium, and figures, presumably delegates of the political factions, receiving the Emperor with gestures of adoration.

It was not uncommon for a phiale, and there were sometimes two located either at the ends of the narthex or in the atrium, to be associated with a particular faction and used as a domical throne covering at the time of an imperial reception.[36] In fact, there is one reference to a parakyptikon, probably as an enclosing hanging, in connection with the imperial throne in a phiale.[37] While there seems to be no specific evidence that the cupola of the Byzantine phiale was thought of as a celestial tent, which would have made it a natural substitute for a baldachin, it may be significant to recall that the *Lavacrum* in front of the *Porta Triumphalis* at Rome is thought

[33] Ebersolt and Thiers, pp. 139-146, pls. xxxii-xxxiii; van Millingen, pp. 196-200, figs. 66 (plan), 67 (section), 68 (interior). The reasons for rejecting the early date and assigning the church to the eleventh century, which were advanced by G. Millet (*L'école grecque*, pp. 56, 110) and D. T. Rice (*Byzantion*, viii, 1933, pp. 152-158) have not been generally accepted (Brounov, *Akkitektoura Konstantinopolia*, XI-XIIth, ii, 1949, pp. 169-171; Janin, *Les Églises et les monastères*, p. 366).

[34] St. Mary Blachernae (Vogt, *Texte*, i, p. 139); church of the Mother of God (Vogt, *op.cit.*, i, p. 24); Holy Apostles (Richter, no. 157, pp. 112-114).

[35] Skylitzes Ms., Madrid, Bibl. Nat. 5.3.N.2, fol. 43r.

[36] Throne in phiale of Greens (Ebersolt, *Le grand palais*, p. 101 n. 1); receptions in phiales (*op.cit.*, pp. 100-103); reception of emperor at St. Mokios (*op.cit.*, p. 186); two phiales in atrium of Nea (*op.cit.*, p. 132); ceremonies at Holy Well of St. Sophia (Richter, no. 187) and at Theotokos (Richter, no. 437). Vogt, *Échos d'Orient*, xxxix, 1940, pp. 78-83. Theophilus seated in phiale while rendering justice (A. Rambaud, *Études sur l'histoire byzantine*, p. 194).

[37] Ebersolt, *Le grand palais*, p. 101 n. 1; Cer., i, pp. 286-288.

to have had a dome with concave gores like a *skene* and that the pagan font in the forecourt of the Great Temple of Jupiter Heliopolitanus at Ba'albek had its stone roof carefully carved to represent a *skene*.[38]

What becomes most apparent as one endeavors to trace the history of the domical vestibule and structural parakyptikon is that both these imperial features seem to have been much more important during the troubled period after the Latin conquest. As is so often true in history, it is the conquerors, usurpers, and those whose position has become less secure who attach the greatest value to established forms, which they feel will make their exalted position and authority more manifest. Some such explanation is necessary to account for the prominence which is given to the ritualistic architectural features in the churches of Mistra during the late and disastrous period when it was for a time the capital of the Despotate of Morea and then for a little while the residence of the Byzantine Court. At the time when the Empire had been broken up into small and independent states the churches both at Mistra and at Arta, which was the capital of a small principality, show that the rulers, whether Latins or Greeks, insisted upon being received and honored as the earlier emperors had been at Constantinople.

At Mistra the section (Fig. 147) and plan (Fig. 148) at the tribune level of the Metropole, which was built in A.D. 1310, make it clear that there was a domical chapel over the narthex, which was undoubtedly the traditional parakyptikon where the Despots of Morea sat during the services.[39] The modest way in which the royal chamber of the Metropole is concealed under the roof of the gallery makes one suspect that the more monumental parakyptikon in the Brontochion (Fig. 149), which is thought to have been built in A.D. 1311, may have been rebuilt at a later date because of the way in which it is raised up above the roof of the tribune.[40]

Changes presumably took place in both the ceremonial use and provisions of the various churches at Mistra, which seem to be more numerous than was at any time necessary. For example, it is curious that St. Sophia (Figs. 150-151), which was built about A.D. 1350 as the actual palace-church when the son of John Cantacuzene was the ruling despot, has no tribune, but instead has a lofty domical vestibule carried up above the roof of the narthex.[41] One might think, as in the case of the Pantocrator at Constantinople, that the tribune floor was removed at a later date, were it not for the way in which the royal window looking down into the naos comes so high in relation to the floor of a possible gallery as to indicate that the whole narthex was rebuilt at a later time when the royal favor had been transferred to one of the other churches.

This change at St. Sophia may well have taken place in the fifteenth century, because the imposing parakyptikon on the Pantassa (Figs. 152-154), which was built

---

[38] T. Wiegand, *Baalbek*, I, 1921, pp. 95-96, abbs. 67-71: a circular aedicula of six columns over a sacred well in the forecourt; its roof hemispherical on interior but on the exterior carved as a concave cone decorated with the folds of a *skene*.

[39] G. Millet, *Monuments byzantins de Mistra*, 1910, pls. 17/4 (plan), 17/1 (section).

[40] Millet, pl. 23/2; Wulff, *Altchristliche und Byzantinische Kunst*, II, p. 492, Abb. 421.

[41] Millet, pls. 31/1 (section), 31/4 (plan).

between A.D. 1428 and 1445 when John VII Palaeologus resided with his brilliant Court at Mistra, indicates that it had been made the official ceremonial church of the Emperor.[42] The façade of the Pantassa (Fig. 154), coming at the end of Byzantine architecture, is monumental proof that the symbolism of imperial palace architecture had persisted through the centuries: over the audience hall of Christ is the cosmic and celestial dome of the *Pater orbis*, at the corners are the smaller cupolas of the royal and heavenly castrum-palatium, and above the entrance to the *Porta coeli* is the elevated and structural version of the imperial baldachin as an emblem of the seat of authority.

The building which most clearly links the whole development of Byzantine church architecture with the palace symbolism of the Late Empire is the Panagia Paragoritissa at Arta, which was built in the thirteenth century by the Despot of the independent principality of Epirus.[43] Having been a palace-church, it has a domical vestibule in front of the Royal Door (Fig. 155) and on the exterior (Fig. 156) it has in the center of the façade an elevated parakyptikon, which is carefully differentiated as a ciborium-like structure from the great dome and the four domical towers at the corners of the palatial stronghold of God. The distinctive treatment of the royal chapel is by itself proof that the parakyptikon, as a place of honor and reception had always been thought of as a baldachin. Hence it is no flight of fancy to see in the Panagia a Christian version in brick and stone of an imperial palace, related by derivation and symbolic intent to the Olympian palatium of the *Pater orbis* on the mosaic of Carthage (Fig. 65), the Jovian castrum on the coins of Diocletian (Fig. 33) and the Apollonian abode of VIRTUS MILITUM (Fig. 41) and PROVIDENTIA (Fig. 44) on the coins of Constantine.

[42] Millet, pl. 35.   [43] Wulff, *op.cit.*, p. 469, fig. 398.

VIII · THE CONCLUSIONS AND THEIR ISLAMIC

IMPLICATIONS

MUCH of the proof, it has been seen, regarding the purpose and meaning of imperial architectural symbolism is cumulative rather than specific, since it has to be reconstructed from a historical pattern of persistent forms and ideas. Because of the inherent difficulties of presenting this kind of evidence there is an advantage in reviewing the conclusions so as to differentiate more clearly between those which are acceptable and those in need of further investigation. The reason for introducing into this summary parallels from Islamic architecture, which present the same combination of motifs as now appear to have been characteristic of late Imperial and Byzantine palaces, is to round out the evidence and, perhaps, get a new focus on the importance of the dome on imperial palaces. Regardless of whether the Islamic parallels are to be explained by dissemination, or accounted for in some other way, the similarities cannot be disregarded.

In the past most discussions of the origins and development of Islamic architecture have been based upon the assumption that the dome was peculiar to the Orient and that the imperial palace tradition in the Near East was essentially Classical, in the limited sense of being columnar with gabled roofs, until it came under the exotic influence of the East. Because there is little in the existing ruins of the late Roman and Byzantine palaces of Constantinople, Asia Minor, and other parts of the East Roman Empire to contradict this preconception, it is generally thought that there was no very direct relation between the Imperial tradition, going back to Hellenistic times, and the much later Islamic buildings in the use of domical halls with cupolas at the corners, towered gateways with arcades and the symbolic use of baldachins over royal portals.

The basic issue underlying many of the conclusions in this study is the question of whether we should not reformulate some of our preconceptions regarding the historical development, domical appearance, ceremonial purpose and heavenly symbolism of the *Sacrum palatium* at Constantinople. Much depends on whether it is granted that from the time when Constantine built his new capital the domical mausoleum had celestial and cosmic implications as the heavenly abode of a divine Kosmokrator, that domical vestibules and audience halls were already symbolic and ceremonial features of the architecture, and that the towered façade of the imperial castrum, the royal arcade, *skene* and bulbous cupolas, and sculptured baldachins were already recognized insignia of the imperial authority over heaven and earth.

If the major portion of this inclusive premise has already been proved tenable, then there is a justification for believing that imperial palace features and ceremonies had a lasting influence in the East and that the Islamic examples of this dissemination have some value in working back to a reconstruction of the now totally destroyed palaces of Constantinople. None of the presumptions of this study, even when they

179

read like Strzygowsky in reverse, is meant to imply a reversion to the old *Orient oder Rom* controversy and the Rivoira contention that everything started at Rome. After the fourth century in the East it was Constantinople that men thought of as Rum. Furthermore, the whole Hellenistic background of Roman palace forms and ceremonies is in itself evidence that from the time of Alexander the Great there were successive periods of both eastward and westward dissemination and that the development of architecture was never the result of any one-way transmission of ideas.

There are many obvious dangers in outlining, and hence in oversimplifying, the historical development of motifs in a summary, where it is impossible to evaluate properly the originality and contributions of Persian, Islamic, and Indian architecture. What must be an overemphasis upon the continuity of imperial forms and ceremonies has the value, however, of raising the question of whether successive Sassanian, Arab, and Turkish rulers were not motivated by a desire to make their palaces, mosques, and mausolea comparable to the structures of Rum, even when they were combining, in an eclectic way, only a few of the imperial motifs with other forms of royal architecture derived from Persia and India. Once the prevailing ideas about imperial palace architecture are modified it becomes apparent that throughout the development of Islamic architecture there was a persistent veneration and admiration for the outward manifestations of Roman prestige and precedent, that at no time was the spread of architectural ideas and the movement of itinerant craftsmen seriously limited by racial boundaries and political antagonisms, and that, as Creswell has pointed out, "architects in the East as well as in the West appear to have been a migratory race."

There are several reasons for including in the summary the survival of what are believed to have been imperial motifs in the late Islamic architecture of India, where the Moghul rulers with their eclectic interests are known to have imported Turkish architects from Constantinople and Asia Minor. Late as the evidence is, it brings the discussion back to Rum and the neglected question of how directly the Sublime Porte was influenced by the ceremonies and architectural forms of its Byzantine predecessors. There is also the possibility that the late Islamic and Turkish palaces, in spite of all their stylistic characteristics, may reflect enough of the past to help in reformulating our ideas about the appearance of the Imperial Palaces at Constantinople. Furthermore, even if the evidence for the dissemination of palace forms proves unconvincing, it does extend Sauvaget's arguments regarding the importance of the palace in the development of Islamic architecture.[1]

1. The palace-temple concept

It is axiomatic that from the remote time when men began to visualize their deities as like themselves in need of shelter, and then began to see in their rulers either priest-kings or god-kings, the palace and temple developed as interrelated forms of

---

[1] J. Sauvaget, *La Mosquée omeyyade de Médine*, 1947.

architecture. In every theocratic society, where the royal dwelling was revered as a sacred edifice, temples were customarily built like palaces, or palaces like temples. Throughout Antiquity and the Middle Ages there appear to have been recurrent parallels between kingly and divine dwellings, royal and religious ceremonies and the formal rituals pertaining to the adoration of godlike kings and kinglike gods. Hence the importance of the palace-temple concepts in the formation of architectural symbolism. As long as the human imagination was limited to thinking of the unknown in terms of the known, to conceive of the invisible only by means of the visible, it remained instinctive for the common man to see in the most memorable aspects of the Sacred Palace, the Royal Stronghold, and the King's Gate heavenly images, visions of paradise and cosmic forms. Even when this figurative imagery seems artificial in the Late Antique panegyrics and stereotyped in the iconography of the Middle Ages, it should not be forgotten that it was still vividly real to the uneducated masses and that to the authors of the Bible and to thinkers, like St. Augustine in his "City of God," it was a graphic means of conveying mystic ideas.

2. The city-gate

(a) Because the gateway of the king's stronghold in the Ancient East was the center of public life, the portal where god-images made their seasonal entrance, the place where the populace took part in the appearances and triumphal receptions of their divine rulers, and the archway where a king sat in judgment, its bounding towers and brilliantly decorated arched opening acquired royal, divine, celestial, and anagogical values. Partly because of this association of ideas the towered façade was transferred to palaces and temples, where it was seen and remembered as a mark of royal power, of a heavenly abode and of a seat of authority.

(b) The ancient gateway imagery not only persisted in the Greek world, but during the Hellenistic period it acquired additional imaginative values when the people throughout the Near East began to reenact an old religious festival when they went forth at the time of a Royal Epiphany to welcome their kings as the Lord of Heaven and Earth at the "Golden Gate" of their cities. Later, because of the prestige of Hellenistic forms, ruler concepts, and ceremonies, the monumental city-gate throughout the Roman Empire became a dramatic and memorable stage-set of imperial glory, where the people took part in the Adventus, Triumphs, and ceremonial receptions with which the imperial *Divus*, his statues and his official representatives were received. Imaginatively influenced by the theophanic honors and apotheosis implicit in the Triumph and Adventus, the people saw a celestial shape in the arched portal, an entrance to heaven in the triumphal arch and a symbol of an Olympian abode in the towered façade with its crowning arcade.

(c) *The crowning arcade*, which according to the numismatic evidence did not become a feature on city-gates until the close of the first century A.D. and on the coins was at first a mark of distinction for provincial capitals, soon took on celestial and

181

royal implications. These overtones of meaning, which were inherited by the Christians and which made the arcade so important in mediaeval art and architecture, were largely the result of the arcaded gallery being associated with the Palatium, as a heavenly abode, and seen on the gateways as a symbol of *Imperium Romanorum*. In addition to being thought of as the royal upper gallery, from which the Elect looked down, there is the possibility that the arcade over the gateways was actually used in the public ceremonies as a place of honor and appearances.

Before the possible ceremonial use of the arcade over Roman gateways is judged unlikely, because of the lack of any documentary evidence, more consideration should be given to the following traditional factors: the long history of windows, loggias, and balconies of appearance in the ritual of ancient temples, palaces, and gateways; the equally long association of a city-gate with a royal residence; and the persistent custom in the mediaeval West, Byzantium, and the Islamic East of conducting a ruler to his place of honor over an actual, or symbolic, gateway. In Egypt there are pictures of the royal box in the portal of the palace at Tell El-Amarna, while at Medinet Habou there were special ceremonial provisions for Rameses III in the upper story of the towered gateway at the entrance to the defensive walls surrounding his mortuary temple and temporary palace. In Palestine the *solarium* of the Latin kings of Jerusalem was in the "Tower of David," because it was customary for the palace to be either in or adjacent to the King's Gate.

The tentative conclusion that the Roman gateway arcade had a ceremonial, as well as symbolic, purpose is based upon the following evidence: 1) the loggia of appearances over the Porta Marzia (Fig. 3); 2) the heads looking down from the crowning arcade over the gateways on the coin of Bizya (Fig. 28) and in the Byzantine representation of the palace of Nineveh (Fig. 73); 3) the apsidal place of appearances in the arcade over the entrance to the Palace of the Exarchate (Fig. 6) at Ravenna; 4) the ceremonial custom of conducting a royal visitor at the time of his Adventus to the King's oratory, or "Heaven Chamber," over the monastic archway at Lorsch and over the "Porta curie" (Fig. 7) at Canterbury; 5) the royal balcony of the Carolingian and Germanic emperors in the towered façade over the *Porta coeli* of their royal abbey churches; 6) the imperial "parakyptikon" in the tribune over the "Royal Door" of the Byzantine palace-churches; 7) the "royal chamber" (*Regium cubiculum*) over the portal of the Triumphal Gateway of Frederick II at Capua; and 8) the persistence of a domical royal chamber, or *majlis*, over the portal of many Islamic palaces. Something of the importance of upper galleries and loggias of appearances in Byzantine palaces can be seen in the Skylitzes manuscript (Fig. 165) where the empress speaks to the people, or the emperor defends the palace from the people.[2]

The crowning arcade, regardless of its origin and ceremonial purpose over gateways, had unquestionably acquired an ideological association with a divine residence when it was made a decorative feature over the Golden Gate at the entrance to Dio-

---

[2] From the same manuscript the scene of Michael defending the palace (de Beylié, *L'Habitation byzantine*, p. 114) shows the Emperor shooting from a loggia which is covered with a cupola.

cletian's castrum-palatium at Salona (Fig. 5). That it continued to be a dominant and distinguished feature of a *Sacrum palatium* can be seen on the façade of the Palace of the Exarchate (Fig. 6) at Ravenna, the "Palatium" of William (Fig. 9) and the Palace of Edward (Fig. 10) on the Bayeux tapestry, and in the way that arched galleries and wall-arcading were given so much prominence on the upper story of every extant palace from the Tekfur Seray at Constantinople down to the mediaeval and Renaissance palaces at Venice.

Since the crowning arcade was so traditionally identified in men's minds with the *Sacrum palatium* of a Roman *Divus* and with the mediaeval dwelling of a "Throne-sharer with God" it was natural for the Christians to transfer it to their tombs, as heavenly abodes, and to their churches, as a *Domus Dei*. Thus the royal and celestial connotations of the imperial arcade, taken in combination with the mediaeval man's desire to make the House of God as heavenly as any kingly dwelling, help to account for the way in which wall-arcades, arched corbel-tables, and arcaded galleries were given so much emphasis on Romanesque apses, crossing towers and façades, once these arch motifs had spread from North Italy where they had been taken over from the brick architecture of the Byzantine Exarchate with its imperial heritage.

(d) The crowning arcade is the first of the Roman motifs to raise the question of the dissemination of palace symbolism in the East. Since there is no evidence of wall-arcading on the Achaemenid palace architecture of Iran, the exceptional appearance during the Sassanian period of superimposed arcades on the façade of the great palace at Ctesiphon, where they were executed in moulded brick and had only a decorative significance, is curiously inexplicable unless some credence is given to the later Byzantine record that Justinian sent craftsmen to assist Khusra in the construction of his palace.[3] Also, if precedent means anything, one must suspect Byzantine influence on the Sassanian fire-temples of the Gira valley, which are usually dated in the sixth century, because without following any existent precedent in Iran they have decorative wall-arcades around the top of the enclosing walls which, like Roman and early Byzantine construction, mask much of their masonry domes.[4]

It is equally suggestive to find that after the Arab conquerors of the Near East had begun in the Umayyad period to impose the ideas of *mulk*, or kingship, upon Islam, their rulers not only made use of arcading for interior decoration, but frequently had a crowning wall-arcade between flanking towers over the principal portal of their chateaux and palaces. The painted arcades around the top of the hall at Qaṣr Amra (c. A.D. 750), which are supported on columns with Byzantine stilt-blocks and were used as frames for figures largely of Classical derivation, have been generally accepted as evidence that the new rulers were more interested in the decorative conventions of late Roman palace architecture in Syria than in the nonfigurative injunctions of Islam.[5] Therefore, it seems more reasonable to see a Roman gateway

[3] Recorded in the ninth century by Theophylactus Simocatta, v, cap. 6; Creswell, *Early Muslim Architecture*, II, 1940, p. 90; A. Christensen, *L'Iran sous les Sassanides*, p. 392.

[4] E. E. Herzfeld, *Archaeological History of Iran*, 1934, pp. 91-93, fig. 12.
[5] A. Musil, *Kusejr 'Amra*, 1907, pl. XX; Creswell, *op.cit.*, I, pp. 262-271.

and early Byzantine palace tradition, rather than the influence of Ctesiphon, in the treatment of the gateway of the smaller of the two Umayyad palaces (c. A.D. 728) at Qaṣr al-Hair, which has flanking towers crowned with royal cupolas, an elaborate decorative arcade across the top of the wall and towers, and a machicolated balcony of appearances over the portal, and in the way so much emphasis is given the wall-arcade over so many Umayyad and Abbasid palace gateways, such as Qaṣr Khārāna, Qaṣr al-Hair al-Gharbi, Raqqa and Ukhaiḍir.[6] At the beginning of Islamic palace architecture it is difficult to believe that the builder of the gateway from Qaṣr al-Hair al-Gharbi, which has been reconstructed as the Museum entrance at Damascus, would have given so much importance to the painted stucco and moulded arcading, and to the two little windows over his palace portal, if he had not been aware of their royal significance in the Late Antique tradition.

The reason for extending the discussion to include the decorative use of crowning arcades over the Moghul, or late Islamic, portals of India is because the Indian arcades occur so consistently in combination with all the other imperial gateway motifs, such as flanking towers with cupolas, sculptural baldachins and domical entrance vestibules. If it is granted that these motifs were insignia of heavenly power on the Byzantine palaces, and probably on the late Roman palatia, it is neither unlikely, nor inexplicable, that they were transmitted to the Orient at different times, especially after Constantinople had become the Turkish capital and Turkish architects are known to have worked at the Moghul Court. The fact that the Muslim rulers were most interested in making their architecture as much like that of Persia as the native craftsmen and local conventions made it possible does not, however, mean that they did not consciously incorporate other features into their new style.

They were often traveled men of learning and artistic interests, who sent envoys to the Western centers of culture, collected illustrated manuscripts and surrounded themselves with scholars. Because they were above all else ambitious conquerors, still motivated by all the ideals of universal rule and divine prestige, they were deeply impressed by what they had seen, or been told, of the past and, therefore, attached great importance to the architectural forms which they knew had been an artistic manifestation of Rome's mastery of the world. At the end of the thirteenth century 'Alā-ud-din, the tyrant of Delhi, described himself as a second Alexander the Great on his coins; and in A.D. 1344 Muhammad, The Tughlug master of Old Delhi, when he received the envoys sent from Egypt by the Abbasid Caliph al-Hakim II in response to his request for religious recognition, had triumphal arches erected in the city and went forth to meet the envoy in a ceremony which recalls a late Roman triumphal

---

[6] Qaṣr al-Hair (Creswell, *op.cit.*, I, pp. 330-349, fig. 409, pls. 54-55); Qaṣr Khārāna which Creswell (*op.cit.*, I, pp. 283-284 and II, p. 86, fig. 70) thinks may have been pre-Islam; Qaṣr al-Hair al-Gharbi (D. Schlumberger, *Syria*, XX, 1939, pp. 194-238, 324, fig. 13); "Baghdad Gate" at Raqqa (Creswell, *op.cit.*, II, p. 44, fig. 32, pl. 2/e); and Ukhaiḍir (Creswell, *op.cit.*, II, p. 57, figs. 37, 39) which not only has a wall-arcade along the top of the principal gate, but in the Court of Honor (fig. 44) gives great importance to arcading around the sides, on the second story and along the top of the wall.

Adventus.[7] Two centuries later Akbar, the great builder, was influenced by the ruler traditions of Rome and Byzantium when in his "Infallibility Decree" of A.D. 1579 he imposed upon Islam an Imperator-Pontifex, Emperor-Pope and Caliph-Imān concept of theocratic power. That this learned, but very ambitious, Moghul knew and appropriated the architectural symbols of royal and divine authority does not seem unlikely when it is remembered that he called himself "the Shadow of God on Earth" and went so far as to stamp his coins with the legend "Akbar Allah," or "Akbar is Allah."

Long before Akbar, however, the imperial Roman features appear on the Islamic palaces of India. The walls of the palace stronghold (Fig. 170) of Man Singh (A.D. 1486-1516) at Gwalior are enriched by a crowning arcade in combination with domical towers, whose cupolas were originally made golden by a covering of copper gilt.[8] Also at the entrance is a domical place of appearances elevated on a tribunal terrace. Either this specific combination of symbolic and ceremonial features was derived from the earlier palace architecture of the West or the historian must find some other satisfactory explanation for the appearance of these forms on so many Moghul structures, such as the castrumlike walls of Amber where arcading and domical towers gave a royal distinction to the capital of the Jaiphur State.[9]

Also it is necessary to ask whether or not it was purely fortuitous that in the palace of the Great Moghul at Delhi the Nekare Chan (Fig. 171), which was the ceremonial gateway at the entrance to the Diwan-i-am court, has a large arcaded loggia of appearances over the portal and at either corner of the façade sculptural baldachins closely resembling the ciboria over the castrum-palatium gateways on the Constantinian coins?[10] Even the terrace in front of this Indian palace reminds us that ceremonial platforms were in front of some of the portals of the Fatimite Palace at Cairo and had a Byzantine prototype at the entrance to the Chalce at Constantinople. Still more striking and suggestive is the combination of motifs a century later on the "Delhi Gate" (Fig. 173) and the "Lahore Gate" of the Delhi Castle where the bands of both false and open arcading are crowned with a row of orbislike cupolas between slender decorative towers and there are large sculptural baldachins on the towers flanking the portals.[11] These monumental gateways, in spite of the fact that everything is exaggerated, multiplied, and decorated in the usual Indian fashion, have all the features which it has been insisted were characteristic of the Imperial Palace portals at Constantinople. Is it, therefore, merely arguing in a circle to suggest that

[7] Sir Wokeley Haig, *The Cambridge History of India*, III, 1928, pp. 102, 164.

[8] F. Fergusson, *History of Indian and Eastern Architecture*, II, 1910, p. 175, pl. XXVIII; O. Reuther, *Indische Palaste und Wohnhauser*, 1925, pl. 12; P. Brown, *Indian Architecture (Islamid Period)*, 1942, p. 120, pl. XCV/1. The Western tradition of golden towers and of a "Golden Gate" must have been taken very seriously by the Islamic rulers in India because E. Terry in 1616 (S. Purchas, *Hak-luytus Posthumus, or Purchas his Pilgrims*, Glasgow, 1905, IX, p. 32) tells how the Great Mogol at Agra "hath a Palace, wherein two large towers, the least ten foot square, are covered with plate of Purest Gold."

[9] Brown, *op.cit.*, p. 122, pl. XCIV; Reuther, *op.cit.*, pl. 79.

[10] Brown, p. 106, pl. LXVII, LXXXI; Reuther, pl. 62.

[11] Reuther, pl. 61.

the "Delhi Gate" is close enough in its essential elements to the Byzantine tradition to have some value in restoring the appearance of imperial portals like the Chalce?

The link between the palaces at the two ends of the Islamic world was not only the lasting veneration which ambitious world masters had for the traditions of Rum, but also the influence which Constantinople had after the Turkish Sultans established themselves as successors of the Byzantine emperors. Before drawing any parallels between Turkish and Indian architecture, the best Moghul monument to show that there must have been a relation with the imperial tradition is the triumphal portal (Fig. 172), known as the "Gate of Magnificence," or the *Buland Darwaza*, which Akbar had erected to commemorate his victories at the entrance to his Royal Mosque at Fathpur Sikri.[12] Although executed in an eclectic Persian-Indian mode, it has a crowning arcade beneath a cresting of little bulbous cupolas and between slender and decorative towers, while over the façade are three large sculptural baldachins. Even its lofty vestibule, which at first glance looks exactly like a Persian *liwan*, is polygonally semicircular like a *Porta regia* and is covered on the interior with a domical vault. In view of this curious eclecticism are we justified in assuming that this memorial was a purely accidental combination of palace and triumphal motifs?

3. The towered façade as a palatium motif

(a) The castrum portal, surmounted by either sculptural baldachins or flanking towers crowned with royal cupolas, had become by the time of Diocletian a universally recognized symbol of the *Sacrum palatium*, and as such exemplified the government, the virtues and godlike distinction of its *Pater urbis et orbis*. The towered façade, both as a portal and palace motif, acquired over the centuries its various overtones of meaning from such traditions and habits of thought as: 1) the eastern custom of associating a towered gateway with royal and heavenly strongholds; 2) the use of towers on Hellenistic palaces and the resultant habit of thinking of "turris" as a synonym for a royal residence; 3) the persistent custom in Roman Syria of erecting towers for ritualistic purposes at the four corners, or over the façade, of pagan temples and of building towered propylaea for ceremonial and ideological purposes at the entrance to the sacred residences of the great sky-gods; 4) the natural tendency in the Roman provinces to visualize the castrum as the seat of government, which resulted in the use of *castrum* and *praetorium* to designate a *palatium*; 5) Diocletian's adoption of the castrum-type of palace; and 6) the various ideas of celestial meaning which were attached to the arched and towered gateway as the place where the people welcomed the Imperator as a divine being.

The towered façade, as a numismatic motif, appears in the first century on the city-gate coins of Thrace, where it seems to have been used either to designate a seat of provincial government or to commemorate an imperial visitation. Towards the close of the fourth century gabled structures with flanking towers (Fig. 157), which

[12] Fergusson, p. 279, fig. 425; Brown, p. 100, pl. LXXIV; V. A. Smith, *Akbar*, 1919, pp. 437ff.

presumably refer to the praetorium as the headquarters of imperial rule, were used to designate the provinces in the Alexandrian World Chronicle. Also from the fourth century the "Basilica" (Fig. 8) and the so-called "Palace of Helena" (Fig. 76) at Treves are the two extant monuments which indicate that towers at the four corners had an imperial significance.

Because of the ruined condition of all Roman palaces it is difficult to bridge the gap between the Treves monuments and the Hellenistic use of towers, which had resulted in a palace, or a "mighty building," being designated by the word for tower ($\beta\hat{\alpha}\rho\iota\varsigma$). Nevertheless the way in which the Roman writers continued to use "turris" as the equivalent of palatium, when taken in combination with the indications of towers in the plans of Trajan's praetoriumlike structure at Pergamum (Fig. 136) and of Hadrian's villa at Tivoli (Figs. 137, 138) is evidence that towers were a customary mark of an imperial stronghold from the beginning of the Empire. The most convincing proof that there was in the Roman Empire a long-established usage associating a towered gateway with the residence of a divine ruler is the persistence of the towered façade concept during the Middle Ages.

(b) Towers during the fifth and sixth centuries were given marked symbolic importance on the churches of North Syria and Asia Minor at the time when the Christians were adapting the forms, ceremonies, music and iconography of an Imperator to the presentation of Christ as the heavenly King of Kings. The churchmen were in part influenced by the gateway traditions of the Near East and the anagogical significance of towers in the Bible; but their real incentive came from a desire to make the church a replica of God's cosmic *Domus*, an image of the "Celestial Jerusalem," a "Porta coeli," and a more manifest "Royal House," as can be seen on the fourth century mosaics of St. George at Saloniki (Fig. 74) where the palatium motifs were used to depict the glories of God's *Sacrum palatium*. Thinking almost instinctively in terms of imperial architecture, they had their builders construct towers at either side of the "Royal Door" at about the same time that they were introducing "the Great Entrance" into the liturgy of the mass. Also, as can be seen in the mosaic at Khirbit Mukhayyat (Fig. 2), they transformed the church into a heavenly castrum by erecting towers at the four corners. At the same time, in order to erect a martyrium and kingly mansion for their saints, as in the Church of the Apostles, Prophets, and Martyrs at Gerasa, they took over the palace plan of a central tower, probably domical, with four smaller towers at the corners.

(c) That the gateway design with its domical towers, or sculptural baldachins, continued to be an established feature of the Byzantine *Sacrum palatium* cannot be proved by any extant buildings, because nothing remains standing of any of the great Imperial Palaces at Constantinople. The evidence, however, is recorded clearly and consistently in the art, where it can be seen in the mosaic of Saloniki (Fig. 74), the Palace of the King of Nineveh (Fig. 73), the Byzantine palace on the Troyes ivory (Fig. 98), the symbolic palatium frame for the Councils at Bethlehem (Fig. 75), the representation of the Boucoleon Palace (Fig. 159), and perhaps, in the illuminations of the Skylitzes manuscript referring to the Chalce (Fig. 161) and the Chrysotriclinos (Fig. 166).

The real reason that the Syrian use of the towered façade had so little influence upon subsequent church architecture in the Near East was not because the Arab conquest so abruptly terminated the building of churches. Rather was it because in Byzantium, even though the palace churches took over from the *Sacrum palatium* the form of a heavenly castrum with little cupola towers at the four corners, there was never any necessity and desire, as there was in the West, to insist by means of the symbolism of the towered façade that the Church was subordinate to the Palatium.

(d) Towards the close of the eighth century in the West the Carolingian rulers, with their policy of *imitatio imperialis*, made the towered façade the dominant feature over the entrance to their royal abbey churches. As long as the northern masters of the Carolingian, Ottonian, and Holy Roman Empires were successful in their struggle with the Papacy in adhering to their theocratic conception of the ruler as both king and priest, their august and towered Westwerk served the double purpose of being a ceremonial *Capella imperialis*, or *palatium regale* at it was called, and of making apparent their hieratic preeminence in the Church. The graphic concept, based upon antique prototypes, that the towered façade stood for the palace as a source of divine guidance can be seen in the illumination of "Charlemagne" seated beneath the Hand of God in his *Sacrum palatium* (Fig. 158). What is equally convincing is the consistency and persistency of the evidence, which is illustrated by the representation of palaces on the Bayeux tapestry (Figs. 9, 10, 53) and by the way the German emperors made use of the towers of the *aula regia* on their seals and coins (Figs. 82-93).

The Roman Church, however, was successful before the end of the Middle Ages in transferring the symbolism of the towered façade from the majesty of the emperor, as the *christus Domini* and "Throne-sharer with God," to the greater glorification of Christ as the heavenly *Majestas Domini*. Because so much of the development of towered churches in northern Europe was influenced by the now veiled, but none the less determined, conflict of imperial and papal ideologies, it is possible that we should look not so much to economic conditions and aesthetic interests, but to political factors and the victory of the papal policies, to explain why the towered façade was never finished on some of the Romanesque and Norman churches in Southern France and Sicily.

4. Cupolas, baldachins, and globes

It has been argued that these related forms were insignia, intended to make manifest the heavenly and universal authority of the *Sacrum palatium*, which actually existed on the towers, gateways, and ceremonial vestibules of late Roman and Byzantine palaces.

(a) *Cupolas*, it has been seen, first appear at the beginning of the third century on the towers of the city-gate coins of Thrace (Figs. 20-24), where they were presumably imperial emblems intended to commemorate a royal visitation or to make apparent the heavenly distinction which a city enjoyed by the presence in it of a divine ruler. By the beginning of the fourth century the baldachinlike cupolas with global finials, which occur over the castrum portal on the coins of Diocletian (Figs. 31-38) and those of his successors (Figs. 39-46), were a means of showing that the Palatium was the residence of the *Pater urbis et orbis* who personified all the virtues desirable in the head of the state. Both the combination of cupola and orb, and more especially the way in which the ciborium-cupolas were transformed into globes not only on the fourth century coins of Diocletian and Constantine, but also on the coins of the German emperors of the Holy Roman Empire (Figs. 85-93) and the seals of the Latin kings of Jerusalem (Figs. 94-97), are proof that the two motifs were thought of together as denoting a ruler's godlike domination as a world master.

(b) The fact that nothing remains of any palace superstructures is an unconvincing reason for believing that the cupolas and baldachins, which are recorded on the Roman coins, were only numismatic conventions. Unless they were actual features, either carved in stone or made of wood sheathed in burnished metal, on late Roman and Byzantine palaces, they would have been incomprehensible on the coins, and there would be no reasonable explanation for their persistent appearance over palace portals of Byzantine, Islamic, and Turkish architectures. It has, therefore, been suggested that the staircases in the shoulders of Trajan's hemicycle at Pergamum (Fig. 136) and in the corners of the domical vestibule at the entrance to Diocletian's palace (Fig. 133) went up to towers with either golden cupolas or sculptural baldachins.

(c) Only the assumption that these motifs continued to be used over Byzantine palaces explains the importance which was attached to them in architectural representations throughout the history of Byzantine art. We might be suspicious of this conclusion if we had only the baldachins on the towers of the Saloniki mosaic (Fig. 74) and over the heavenly palace in the Menologium of Basil II (Fig. 125). But without some actual precedent the schematic drawings in the Skylitzes manuscript and the cupolas over the Gate of David on the Latin seals of Jerusalem (Figs. 94-97) would have been meaningless. It has been seen among the illuminations of the Skylitzes manuscript that little cupolas or diagrammatic baldachins crown the loggia from which the empress speaks (Fig. 165), mark the archway under which the emperor is enthroned (Figs. 162, 164), cap a triumphal arch (Fig. 167) and appear at the corners of buildings, one of which is the Chrysotriclinos (Fig. 166) and the other may be the Chalce (Fig. 161).

(d) In the West during the Carolingian period the churchmen and rulers revived, or took over from the Byzantine East, the use of cupolas as a mark of royal and divine presence. The ivory carvers were instructed to deck the towers of Bethlehem and Jerusalem (Figs. 70, 72) with *skene* cupolas to show that the cities were honored by the presence in them of the Christian King of Kings; the illuminators depicted domical towers on the Biblical cities of God (Fig. 54); and throughout the Middle Ages little baldachinlike cupolas with global finials were a distinguishing feature of the *Palatium*

(Figs. 71, 128), were used over the *aula regia* on the imperial seals and coins (Figs. 82-85) and were depicted in the illuminations over royal abbeys, royal halls (Fig. 53) and royal gateways (Fig. 7). Therefore, in restoring the architecture of the early Middle Ages the manuscripts, ivories, and coins should be accepted as evidence that cupolas with *skene*like striations once crowned the towers of many of the churches and palaces, before it became customary to substitute the more easily constructed spire for the domical shape.

(e) The *bulbous dome*, which appears so frequently on late Roman coins, could not have originated in the Islamic East, but was presumably a symbolic shape on East Roman towers where it was intended to express more fully the cosmic significance of the combined *skene-sphaera*. From Hellenistic times the celestial ciborium and world globe, as can be seen on the frescos of Pompeii and Herculaneum (Fig. 48), were related emblems denoting the scope of a Helios-Kosmokrator's domination over heaven and earth. The way that the baldachin-cupolas on the coins of Diocletian and Constantine were given a sphaeralike bulge (Figs. 36, 40), or transformed into globes with supporting uprights and finials (Figs. 35, 42-46), is proof that the bulbous shape was intended to make clear the imperial idea of universal rule.

Since domes of this shape were at first constructed of wood and then sheathed with gilded metal, there is no reason to expect archaeological evidence of bulbous domes on late Roman towers. Instead we have the references to bulbous domes of wood on the pagan Marneion at Gaza and on the later Christian churches in Syria.[13] There are also the bulbous domes pictured on the city towers of the *Corpus Agrimensorum Romanorum* (Figs. 61-64), the domes depicted on Early Christian martyria, the emphatically bulbous cupolas on the "Palatium" frame for the Council of Antioch (Fig. 75) and the shape of the domes on the bulla of Frederick I (Fig. 87), who was politically interested in reviving Roman symbolism, but who would have objected to having his palace symbolism associated with the architecture of Islam.

(f) The *skene* dome and corrugated apsidal vault were developed in Roman architecture to express the old idea of heaven as a cosmic tent. It was from the Hellenistic East that the Romans learned to see in the ciborium (Fig. 48) a celestial canopy and to use the *skene* with its convex gores and cusped edges as a symbolic covering for an heroön (Fig. 105), tholus, royal triclinium, and palace vestibule. Much of the imperial interest in the *skene* concept of a heavenly vault presumably came from the importance of the tent in both the cosmogony and palace decorations of Alexandria. In fact, this interest may have been initiated by Nero who, in his effort to emulate the Hellenistic kings, adopted the tent pattern as a ceiling decoration in his Golden House, with the result that the painted *skene* became a standard motif, as Lehmann has shown, on subsequent Roman and Christian domes. Since little is known about the forms of the Alexandrian palaces, except what is reflected in the frescos of the fourth Pompeian style, it is impossible for us to know whether the Romans were imitating Hellenistic wooden domes when they translated the *skene* shape into permanent masonry con-

---

[13] Smith, *The Dome*, pp. 14-44.

struction by making their domes and half domes, as can be seen in Hadrian's villa, with concave gores on the interior, which for structural reasons they masked on the exterior.

It was this masonry type of *skene* dome that the Byzantine architects continued to use on imperial structures such as SS. Sergius and Bacchus and the Chrysotriclinos at Constantinople because they wanted to show the celestial import of the vault over the House of God and the *Sacrum palatium*. As early as the fifth century, however, the Early Christian representations of the Holy Sepulchre and other martyria, which were undoubtedly influenced by imperial architecture, picture another type of *skene* dome with the convex gores showing on the exterior. This free-standing and unbuttressed type of corrugated dome, which is commonly called a "melon dome," had to be constructed in wood sheathed with burnished metal. Although it is not known whether the wooden dome on the pagan Marneion at Gaza had melonlike corrugations, Choricius' account of the fifth or sixth century martyrium of St. Stephen at Gaza and the many Syrian and Alexandrian representations of gored domes imply that there must have been in the Near East on old tradition of building *skene* domes in wood, which because of their light construction could make their heavenly and tent symbolism visible on the exterior.[14] Hence it is possible that this type of *skene* covering, which the later Islamic architects succeeded in reproducing in brick, may have had its origin on the Alexandrian palaces and antedated the gored masonry domes which the Romans used.

The clearest proof that there was an old and persistent custom of thinking of domes and cupolas as cosmic and celestial tents comes from the Middle Ages. The mediaeval evidence of this tradition is best illustrated by the cusped edges and gores of the domes in the Utrecht Psalter, especially the one over the *salutatorium* of the House of God (Fig. 132). Therefore, the way cupolas are pictured throughout the Middle Ages with the radiating striations of a *skene* on churches (Fig. 79), palaces (Figs. 9, 10, 75), and coins (Figs. 83, 86, 87, 93) should be more fully accepted as a record of how domes were constructed as symbolic forms.

(g) Granting the previous conclusions that sculptural baldachins, like the one over the parakyptikon in the center of the façade of the palace-church at Arta (Fig. 156), had continued to be actual features of Byzantine palace architecture, one way of raising the question of whether these imperial insignia influenced Islamic architecture is to work backward from the fountain house and gateway which Achmed III (A.D. 1703-1730) had built in Constantinople.[15] The fountain house back of Hagia Sophia, which is almost directly in front of the "Imperial Gate" of the Turkish palace, reminds us somewhat by its location and domical form of the "Lavacrum" in front of the Porta Triumphalis at Rome and the Byzantine palace phiales which were used

---

[14] *Ibid.*, pp. 14-15 (Marneion), 38-39 (Choricius' account of church at Gaza), figs. 6, 15, 16, 41, 152, 153, 168, 188 (melon domes).

[15] E. Diez and H. Gluck, *Altkonstantinople*,

1920, fig. 64 (Fountain), fig. 68 (Gateway); C. Gurlitt, *Die Baukunst Konstantinopels*, 1912, II, pl. 35c.

by the Basileus in the palace ceremonies. Its design, with a central dome and little decorative cupolas at the corners, is that of the old Byzantine palace *pentyrigion*. Since there seems to be no record of its having been used by the Sultan, the gateway (Fig. 174), which Achmed built as the royal entrance to the court at the side of the mosque of Hagia Sophia, is more important to the present problem.

The gateway, if we disregard the far from successful effort of a Turkish architect to translate a Byzantine-Turkish convention into a Western style, is interesting because its canopylike roof is surmounted by three decorative cupolas, which recall the similar insignia over the palace-castrum portals on the Roman coins of the fourth century. Two centuries earlier than Achmed we find that there were three cupolas over the Sultan's private portal on the north side of the Mosque of Suleiman and that the two gateways through which the Turkish rulers entered the courts of Hagia Sophia were always domical.[16] This evidence, therefore, takes us back not only to the period when the Sublime Porte at Constantinople was taking over the Byzantine palace tradition, but also to the time when sculptural baldachins began to appear over the Moghul portals in India, such as the Nekare Chan (Fig. 171), the "Delhi Gate" (Fig. 173) and the Buland Darwaza (Fig. 172) of Akbar.

Fortunately there are historical facts to bridge the gap between the opposite ends of the Islamic world. Writers on India agree that Yûsuf 'Âbdil Khan, the founder of a new dynasty at Bijapur in the sixteenth century, even if it is unlikely that he was the son of Sultan Muhrad II of Turkey, was a Turk from Constantinople who, according to the Persian Firishta, "invited to his court many learned men and valiant officers from Persia, Turkistan and Rum, and also several eminent artists."[17] At about the same time Barbar (A.D. 1483-1530), the most successful founder of a Moghul Empire in India, relates in his Turki *Memoires* that he imported from Constantinople Yousouf and Isa, the talented pupils of Sinan.[18] Later in the seventeenth century the recorded presence at the Moghul Court of the Venetian Geronimo Veronea and the Frenchman Austin of Bordeaux does not mean, as some writers have suggested, that these Western artists could have designed the Taj Mahal, the "Crown of the Palace" which Shah Jehan, "The Just Emperor and Protector of the World," built as a heavenly and palatial tomb for his wife. It does mean, however, that there was a very direct and close link between India and Constantinople where these Western craftsmen presumably worked for the Turkish Sultan before they were sent out to India.[19]

[16] In his engraving of the Mosque of Suleiman G. C. Grelot (*Relation nouvelle d'un voyage de Constantinople*, Paris, 1681, p. 279) shows the three striated cupolas at "N" over the Sultan's private portal; also in engraving (p. 117, "D") he depicts the domical "Porte au le Grand Seigneur entre à Sainte Sophie" on the side towards the palace; and in his view of the northwest side of the "Templum Sanctae Sophiae" (p. 255, "K") he shows the domical baldachin in front of the portal through which the Sultan entered the west court of the sanctuary.

[17] Fergusson (*History of Indian and Eastern*

Architecture, II, p. 199) says a pure Turk born in Constantinople; V. A. Smith (*The Oxford History of India*, 1923, p. 291) probably the son of Sultan Murad II; and Haig, *The Cambridge History of India*, III, 1928, p. 416 n. 2.

[18] S. M. Jaffar, *The Mughal Empire*, 1936, p. 27; M. A. Chaghta, *Le Tadj Mahal d'Agra*, 1938, pp. 13, 122.

[19] Chaghta, *op.cit.*, pp. 69-82; V. A. Smith, *History of the Fine Arts in India*, pp. 416-419; E. B. Havell, "The Taj and its Designers," *The Nineteenth Century and After*, 1903.

Envoys, scholars, craftsmen, and hence ideas traveled back and forth across Asia, regardless of time and the lack of railroads, just as easily as Thomas Croyat, that peripatetic Englishman, in the seventeenth century succeeded in walking every step of the way from Constantinople to Delhi without any serious mishaps.[20] Therefore, when we learn that the Turkish architect Ahmad was a distinguished artist, scholar, and mathematician at the Moghul Court, and that he and his sons worked on the mausoleum of Horshang Shah at Mandu, the Palace Fort at Delhi, the Taj Mahal and the Royal Mosque at Delhi, it no longer seems unlikely that the sculptured baldachins and cupolas over the Moghul buildings were adopted, with inevitable mutations, from the Byzantine palace tradition.[21]

5. The *pentyrigion*, or five-towered palatium

It is assumed that a *pentyrigion*, or a five-towered structure with a central dome and smaller domical towers, or cupolas, at the four corners, such as can be seen on the late palace-church at Arta (Fig. 156) and the fountain kiosk of Achmed, was originally a type of palace. While it is impossible to prove that it had a Roman prototype, the ruins of Hadrian's domical audience hall at Tivoli (Fig. 138/B) show that there could have been towers at the four corners, and it has been suggested that the staircases in Diocletian's palace (Fig. 133) went up to little towers with either cupolas, or sculptured baldachins, at the corners of the dome over the entrance rotunda. The value of this hypothetical assumption is that it presupposes a palatium precedent for the "Palace of Helena" in the fourth century at Treves (Fig. 76) and makes possible a logical explanation for the subsequent survivals and dispersion of this palace concept.

(a) Working from the same premise for Byzantine palace architecture, it has been argued that both the Chalce (Fig. 161) and the Chrysotriclinos (Fig. 166), as pictured in the Skylitzes manuscript, had little domical towers at the corners and were the two ceremonial structures of the Imperial Palace most likely to have been the immediate prototype of the *pentyrigion* as a palace design in Constantinople. This contention is sustained by the way in which a generalized palace is represented by a domical hall with flanking towers, or cupolas, on the Bethlehem mosaic (Fig. 75) and the Byzantine casket (Fig. 98).

At the same time that it is necessary to conjecture that the Nea of Basil I was the first palace-church to emphasize the four cupolas at the corners of a central dome, thereby establishing a "New Church," there is also evidence to indicate that the basic palace design back of the Nea had already influenced the Byzantine palace-church. Hagia Sophia, as it was first built by Justinian, is restored by Antoniadi with little towerlike cupolas over the pendentives at the corners of the great dome, and

[20] W. Foster, *Early Travels in India (1583-1619)*, 1921, p. 248 "spent in my ten moneths travels betwixt Aleppo and the Moguls court but three pounds sterling, yet fared reasonable well everie daie."

[21] Chaghta, *op.cit.*, pp. 113-126.

recent studies of the sixth century church have shown that there were always stone cupolas over the stair-wells which flank the half dome on the entrance side of the church.[22] It is equally significant to find on the somewhat fanciful drawings of Hagia Sophia in the Skylitzes manuscript that considerable importance is given either to slender decorative towers at the corners (Fig. 165) or to cupolas flanking the central dome (Fig. 168).

(b) Later in the history of Constantinopolitan architecture, regardless of whether it is thought that the Turkish mosques were copied directly from Hagia Sophia, or instead were based upon the imperial palace precedents, it is important to find that all the early mosques have *skene* cupolas at the four corners of the central dome. The survivals of an imperial palace-castrum type of structure with cupolas at the corners can be seen on the Bayazit mosque (A.D. 1501-1505) of the architect Hayreddin and, what is of far greater significance, on the Sehzade (1548), Mihrimah (1555), and Suleiman (1557) mosques, all built by the great Turkish architect Sinan, whose pupils, it will be recalled, went to India to work for Barbar, the founder of the Moghul Empire.[23]

(c) If the *pentyrigion* with its central dome and corner cupolas exemplified the idea of a *Sacrum palatium*, that is the cosmic house and heavenly dwelling of the Late Antique and Early Byzantine Kosmokrators, then it is possible to explain the exceptional building on the bronze salver in the Berlin Museum and the Mausoleum of Sammanid Isma'il (A.D. 849-907) at Buchara, which is the earliest royal tomb to have its walls decorated with arcades and to have its square plan surmounted by a central dome and small corner cupolas. Now that Sauvaget, followed by Grabar, has shown that the Persian dish is post-Sassanian and of the same period as the Mausoleum, it is no longer necessary to think of the pavilion engraved upon it, which is pictured with a crowning arcade, a central dome and corner cupolas, as the Throne of Khusra, a fire-temple, or a Sassanian garden kiosk.[24] Instead, we may see in it a somewhat fanciful, but nonetheless learned, artistic creation, illustrating one of the pictorial ways that later Islamic rulers became acquainted with the architectural vocabulary of the imperial palace tradition.

The Mausoleum of Sammanid Isma'il is as exceptional in the Islamic architecture of the tenth century as is the building on the salver. There is nothing comparable to it in the mortuary architecture of Iran, and the Qubbat aṣ-Sulaibaīya at Samarra (A.D. 820) is the only earlier domical mausoleum of any Islamic ruler.[25] In concept,

[22] Antoniadi, *Hagia Sophia*, I, 1907, p. 18; W. Emerson and R. L. van Nice, "Hagia Sophia and the first minaret," *A.J.A.*, LIV, 1950, pp. 28-35; Salzenberg, *Altchristliche Baudenkmale von Constantinople*, Berlin, 1854, pl. XI.

[23] A. Vogt-Göknil, *Türkische Moscheen*, Zurich, 1953, figs. 54 (Bayazit), 52 (Sehzade), 51 (Mihrimah), 22 (Suleymaniye), 41 (Azap-kapisi built by a pupil of Sinan); M. A. Charles, "Hagia Sophia and the Imperial Mosques," *Art Bulletin*, XII, 1930,

pp. 321-344.

[24] A. Grabar, *Münchner Jahrb. d. Bildenenkunst*, 1951, p. 52 n. 25; Sauvaget, *Journal Asiatiques*, CCXXXII, 1940, pp. 19-33.

[25] Mausoleum of Isma'il (Creswell, *Early Muslim Architecture*, II, pp. 367-369, fig. 261, pl. 118; E. Cohen-Wiener, *Turan*, 1930, p. 12, pl. 1; Pope, *Survey of Persian Art*, pl. 264/a); Qubbat aṣ-Sulaibīya (Creswell, *op.cit.*, pp. 283-285).

both of these mausolea were similar to the cosmic and heavenly tombs of Diocletian and Constantine, the typical imperial sepulchres pictured in the *Corpus Agrimensorum Romanorum* (Figs. 162-164) and the domical *aeternae memoriae* stamped on the Constantinian coins.[26] In fact, the coins were undoubtedly one of the means by which the domical form of an eternal memorial became known to the later Eastern monarchs who had never seen the tomb of Constantine and such derivative monuments as the Holy Sepulchre. There was nothing new, however, in thinking of an everlasting abode in terms of palace architecture; and the only innovation in the design of Isma'il, who was a traveled and learned king, was that it went further than his predecessor at Samarra. By having the enclosing walls of his mausoleum crowned with arcading and by erecting little cupolas at the corners of the central dome Isma'il made his own resting place as heavenly and palatial as the *Sacrum palatium* of the early Kosmokrators at Rum. That there were Armenian and Persian palaces of the same period with multiple domes would have been only an additional reason for making his tomb like the most renowned royal residence.

This explanation may seem too theoretical, but it helps to account for the fact that it was not until about five hundred years later, during the Moghul period in India, that this type of tomb was again used with the same combination of motifs for such royal mausolea as those of Hushan Shah (c. 1440) at Mandu,[27] Humâyûn (1530-1536) near Delhi,[28] the Taj Mahal, the Gol Gumbaz (c. 1659) at Bijapur[29] and the mausoleum of Nawab Salfdar Jang (c. 1750) near Delhi.[30] It is difficult to believe that the interest of the Great Moghuls of India in this type of tomb came from Indian prototypes or from the isolated tenth century example at Buchara, especially at a time when they had so many contacts with Constantinople. It is possible, therefore, that in tracing the development of architectural forms we have overlooked the fact that the Asiatic monarchs and their advisors were well informed about the past and deeply interested in the traditional architectural language of kingship, which they believed would exalt them in their earthly palaces and give celestial glory to their palatial memorials.

(d) Returning to Turkish Constantinople, where the Chalce at the entrance to the Imperial Palace had once been the most memorable example of a domical *pentyrigion*, we should expect to find some evidence of the influence of this Byzantine ceremonial gateway on the Turkish palace architecture, especially since the "Porte" was so important in the early ceremonies and the metaphorical designations of the government.[31] An early seventeenth century drawing of the "Old Palace," which was the first official residence of Mehmed II, shows that the entrance gateway was a large

---

[26] Smith, *The Dome*, pp. 24-25, figs. 17-21; H. Koethe, "Das Konstantinsmausoleum und verwandte Denkmäler," *Jahrb. d. deutschen archaeologische Institut*, XLVIII, 1933, pp. 185-203; C. Cecchelli, "Mausolei imperiali e reale di basso impero e dell'alta medioevo," *Saggi sull'architettura etrusca e romana*, Rome, 1940, pp. 142ff.

[27] P. Brown, *Indian Architecture (The Ismaic Period)*, pl. XLIII.

[28] Brown, *op.cit.*, pl. LXII.

[29] Brown, *op.cit.*, p. 77, pl. LI.

[30] Brown, *op.cit.*, pl. XCI.

[31] Von Hammer, *Histoire de empire ottoman* (trans. by J. J. Hellert from the German), III, pp. 298-299; B. Miller, *Beyond the Sublime Porte*, New Haven, 1931, pp. 43-45.

square tower in two stories with a central dome and slender round towers at the four corners.[32] Before his death Mehmed turned the "Old Palace" into a harem and built his new palace, which the Turks call *Top Qapu Saray*, or the "Palace of the Canon Gate," next to Hagia Sophia, but on the opposite side from the ruins of the Byzantine palace.

That Mehmed thought of himself as the successor of the divine Imperators of Rum and saw in his palace gateway the old celestial symbolism is recorded in the inscription, dated 1478-1479, which he had carved on the "Imperial Gate" at the outer entrance to his New Palace.[33] It describes him as, "The Shadow and Spirit of God among men, Monarch of this terrestrial orb, Lord of two continents and of two seas, and of the East and the West" and then, in words which recall Martial's praise of Domitian's palace, it ends, "May God exalt his residence above the most brilliant stars in the firmament." But that he originally made his "Imperial Gate" a Turkish version of the Chalce is difficult to prove, because it was periodically rebuilt and changed after successive earthquakes and fires.

It is reasonably certain, however, that the "Imperial Gate" was a two-storied structure, that in the upper story was a chamber for the use of Mehmed, which was called a "kuishk," thereby implying a dome, and that over the building there were four minaretlike Turkish versions of round towers at the corners.[34] By the seventeenth century, when the upper story was no longer used by the sultan and the building had been repaired and changed several times, Grelot's engraving of it shows: a large central portal flanked by very deep niches, which were probably the smaller passageways of the original structure; a second story with only windows and no arcading; and an ugly, overhanging, and flat hip-roof, in place of a hypothetical dome, out of which rose in a very makeshift manner four slender towers with conical caps.[35]

Some vague realization that the towers had an imperial significance must have survived because Grelot wrote, "Quatre tourelles qui sont comme autant de petites cheminées rondes, elles ne servent que d'ornement et de marque que cette porte est l'entrée d'une Maison Royalle." The subsequent history of the "Imperial Gate" shows that any symbolism once associated with the towers was eventually forgotten, because in the course of time first two, and then the remainder, of the four "chimneys" were removed from the roof.[36]

[32] Miller, *op.cit.*, p. 26; Wilhelm Dilich, *Eigentliche Kurtze beschreibung . . . stadt Constantinople*, Cassell, 1606.

[33] Miller, *op.cit.*, p. 42.

[34] *The Guide to the Museum of the Topkapu Saray*, 1936, p. 2, says, "in the time of the Conqueror the gate was surmounted by a pavilion." Miller, pp. 141-147; N. M. Penzer, *The Harem*, 1936, p. 82; an account of this gateway "par un Solitaire Turc" (*État général de l'empire otoman*, trans. by M. de la Croix and presented to the French King in 1695, pp. 357-359) says it was called Bab Umaïoum because of the present use of its apartment for Mohammed II as a "Bureau des Finances," and refers to a tower, "not twenty steps from this apartment," as "la tour du Grand Seigneur, un mieux bâtei que les autres" in which was a "kiost cabinet" where the Sultan watched processions and the entrance of ambassadors.

[35] G. J. Grelot, *Relation nouvelle d'un voyage de Constantinople*, Paris, 1681, pp. 116-117; Miller, *op.cit.*, p. 142.

[36] Engraving with two towers by Mouradja d'Ohsson, 1781-1820 (Miller, p. 142), and drawing of 1852 by Fossati with no towers (Miller, p. 166).

6. The ciborium

The ciborium, or baldachin, was in origin a portable canopy supported on four uprights which was derived from the various tent traditions of the Ancient East. As an inner sanctuary, portable shrine and place of public appearances over the cult images of sky-gods it had very specific celestial implications, which gave it a symbolic value when it was used as a ceremonial covering over a divine ruler.

(a) It is still very doubtful whether this sky covering was used in Ancient Egypt, Mesopotamia, and Persia as a throne-tabernacle, or royal baldachin, when the king was seated in his palace on the dais of his audience hall. At a very early date, however, it was set up over rulers to serve both as a protection from the sun and as a mark of heavenly distinction when they made their public appearances. By far the earliest known and most direct antecedent of the royal baldachin, with a symbolism of cosmic and heavenly power, was the *heb-sed* tent under which the Egyptian Pharaohs and their statues were seated at the time of a Jubilee Festival, and in which the rulers appeared as the living Horus, or Ra, when they visited their cities.

(b) Throughout the East the sacred ciborium became a Tent of Appearances and an emblem of honor over a godlike ruler when he gave public audiences, transacted business, and prescribed justice, usually at the royal gate of his palace stronghold. During the Hellenistic period the celestial *skene* was taken over as the place of receptions, salutations and adoration in the Royal Epiphany ceremonies with which the coming of the godlike Greek kings were celebrated. According to the graphic evidence of the fourth Pompeian style (Fig. 113), which reflects the palace conventions of Alexandria, there was not only a domical vestibule at the entrance to a palace, but there was also a royal ciborium set up for festivals and receptions in the apsidal *Porta regia*, so that the king would be identified with a deity, usually a sun-god, and adored as the universal ruler of heaven and earth.

(c) After the conquest of the Near East the Roman generals of the Republic, and then the subsequent emperors, presumably became accustomed to being enthroned under a ciborium when they were received at the city and palace gateways of the Hellenistic cities with all the ceremonial provisions of an Epiphany. Prior to Diocletian, however, there is no evidence that the emperors ever appeared at Rome under a baldachin. This was not because the domical ciborium was not known at Rome, where from the beginning of the Empire it was used for shrines and the covering of a fire-altar. For a long time, perhaps as late as the beginning of the fourth century, the imperial policy of taking over the oriental conventions of ruler-worship never went further at Rome than to set up the emperor statues, usually in the vestibule of the Palatium, under a celestial canopy.

(d) One may suspect that the central baldachinlike cupola over the portal on the gold coins of Diocletian, which were issued at Rome and Pavia when the monarch first visited those cities, refers to the ciborium of reception, while the corner cupolas were meant to show that the building was an imperial castrum. Undoubtedly the ap-

197

pearance of the baldachins over the palatium-castrum on the coins of the fourth century is proof that by this time the *skene* was recognized throughout the Empire as an imperial emblem, symbolically associated with the universal globe. At the same time the coins show that the *skene* was still a palace gateway feature intended to mark the portal as the place where Adventus and Epiphany ceremonies were publicly celebrated. Since there are no references to a throne-tabernacle before the sixth century it is problematic as to when and where the ciborium was transferred from its customary use as a Tent of Appearances and public receptions and made a Baldachin of State over the ruler in his audience halls. It is tentatively suggested that this innovation took place under Diocletian in his palace at Nicomedia.

(e) Apart from the frescos of the second and fourth Pompeian styles (Fig. 113) there is very little graphic evidence that the royal *skene* was traditionally a place of appearances and receptions at city and palace entrances until we come to the Middle Ages when the use of canopies of reception in the royal and ecclesiastic ceremonies is reflected in the art.

7. The domical vestibule

The old Eastern custom of presenting a ruler under a canopy of honor, when he was sitting in judgment or being received with acclamations in his palace and city gateways, resulted in the symbolic shape of the ciborium being translated into a domical vestibule, as a place of salutations, at the entrance to the Hellenistic palaces of Alexandria. Because of the desire of the Roman emperors to emulate the Ptolemaic kings this domical place of reception was taken over into the Roman palace architecture. In fact, it must be assumed that the domical vestibule with its *skene*like vault at the entrance to the Great Palace of Hadrian at Tivoli (Fig. 138) is evidence not only of Alexandrian influence on the architecture, but of the introduction of palace ceremonies of ingress and egress which were the antecedents of the reception rituals which later took place in the domical *salutatorium* of Diocletian's palace and in the Chalce of the Imperial Palace at Constantinople.

(a) Further evidence that the royal ciborium was traditionally a Tent of Appearances and a Canopy of Honor at the King's Gate and in the *Porta regia* of the palace is the way in which either the ciborium, or the domical vestibule, continued throughout the Middle Ages to be associated with ceremonies based upon the Hellenistic Epiphany and Roman Adventus. This association of ciborium and gateway explains the baldachins over the symbolic portal on the imperial coins of the fourth century, the Carolingian emphasis upon a *skene* covering over the gateways of royal cities, such as Bethlehem and Jerusalem (Figs. 70, 72), the presence of either a reception ciborium, or domical vestibule, in the scene of Christ's Entry into Jerusalem (Figs. 127, 169), and the actual construction of a domical pavilion, in place of a portable ciborium, at the entrance to the Byzantine monasteries, where at one time it had been customary to receive all guests, but more especially the emperor, "like Christ himself."

(b) The Byzantine parakyptikon, which was at first a portable covering and later a structurally domical oratory for the Basileus in the tribune over the portal of his palace-churches, is another architectural manifestation and survival of the same ceremonial tradition. Furthermore, the similarity between the parakyptikon over the façade of such palace-churches as St. Savior Pantocrator (Fig. 140) and the Panagia Paragoritissa at Art (Fig. 156) and the baldachins, or cupolas, over the palace gateways on the coins of the German emperors (Figs. 83, 87) leads to the conclusion that in both the East and West the symbolic and ceremonial association of a domical sky-covering with a royal gateway had persisted since the time of Diocletian.

(c) Before attempting to outline the extent to which Islamic architecture took over the domical vestibule and the ceremonies that went with it, special attention should be given to the third century, Roman "Palace of Dux-Ripae" at Dura-Europos, which was one of the headquarters of imperial authority on the eastern border of the Empire.[37] The shape and location of its entrance vestibules, which if restored with domes as their square plans imply, are evidence that it was not necessarily from the great Roman and Byzantine palaces that the later Islamic rulers derived the imperial forms. The plan of this ruined castrum, which the inscriptions call a "Principia," has a square, protruding vestibule in front of the portal of the outer, western court and a second similar vestibule at the entrance to the inner court. Also on the south side of the main court it has a rectangular structure with a square vestibule, which Rostovtzeff identified as either a "Pro-tribunale" for public audiences, or a "Vexilla" where the imperial standards and the emperor-cult were enshrined.[38]

First, because it has been recognized that square chambers in Roman and Christian Syria were frequently roofed with light domical vaults of either wood or volcanic scoria, second, because of the importance of domical vestibules in both Roman and Byzantine palaces and, third, because of the persistent use of similar vestibules in Arab and Turkish palaces, it is necessary to restore the square vestibules at Dura-Europos with cupolas and to assume that the "Vexilla" was also domical like the *kalubé* of Umm-iz-Zetum, which was a shrine dedicated to the worship of Fortuna and the Emperor.[39]

(d) At the same time that it is suggested that Roman and Byzantine seats of government, like the castrum at Dura-Europos, had a very direct influence upon subsequent Islamic palaces, one has to be cautious about implying only a one-way dispersion of gateway forms and ceremonies in the successive periods of Islamic culture. The fact that much of the Roman-Byzantine tradition of palace architecture originated in the Near East means that during the centuries following Alexander the Great and the Hellenistic kings there were various recurrent tides in the eastward and westward movements of royal rituals and architectural symbolism. Nevertheless, the consistent

[37] M. Rostovtzeff, "The Palace of Dux-Ripae," *The Excavations at Dura-Europos*, New Haven, III, 1952, fig. 1 (plan), fig. 2 (restoration without domes).

[38] For a discussion of the Vexillum as a sacred *signum* with the *imago* of the emperor, which was set up as a shrine in the Temple at Jerusalem, opposite to the eastern gate, see K. Kraeling, *Harvard Theological Studies*, XXXV, 1942, pp. 263ff.; and M. Rostovtzeff, *J.R.S.*, XXXII, 1942, pp. 92ff.

[39] H. C. Butler, *Syria*, II, A, p. 361; Smith, *The Dome*, pp. 70-71, figs. 120-121.

and persistent nature of the Islamic evidence forces one to the conclusion that the enemies and conquerors of the East Roman Empire, which survived until the fifteenth century, were not unlike the barbarian invaders of the West Roman Empire in the way they preserved a lasting veneration for the concepts, ceremonies and architectural manifestations of emperor-worship and continued to adopt them with some modifications. It is also to be hoped that this evidence will show that it is no longer possible to disregard the domical ideology of Roman palaces because Strzygowsky and others have insisted that everything domical came from the Orient.

As early as the Umayyad period, when the new Arab rulers were beginning to adapt their palace architecture and court rituals to the non-Islamic concepts of kingship, it is not surprising that only a few of the extant palaces and chateaux have domical vestibules. As yet these potentates, whose residences we know, were not in a position to aspire to the ceremonial and architectural provisions of a heavenly and universal authority. Yet, for this very reason, the early Islamic examples have an added importance in linking up the consistent use of domical vestibules in the late Islamic palaces with the earlier traditions of Rome and Byzantium. At Qaṣr Khārāna, which Creswell believes to have been pre-Islamic and Sauvaget attributes to the Umayyad period, the principal hall is not only domical but is located directly over the gateway.[40] This architectural provision for audiences and receptions recalls: (1) the persistent evidence from both the East and the West of a *regium cubiculum* having been customary over a portal, (2) the Eastern tradition of associating the gateway with the seat of the king, and (3) the eastern custom of locating the king's room in the gateway, which went back to such Hellenistic palaces as at Arak el-Emir where there was over the portal a chamber with a loggia, or window of appearances, between flanking lions.

There is an Umayyad gateway with a domical vestibule at Khirbit al-Minayah;[41] and at Khirbit al-Mafjar excavations have uncovered the remains of a domical vestibule at the entrance to the baths with stucco decorations showing that it had a celestial symbolism.[42] Of even greater interest is the castrum-stronghold of Qaṣr ar-Ribāṭ at Sūsa, where the elevated cupola directly over the portal, which is approached by staircases on the interior, is suggestively similar to the central cupola over the castrum portal on the coins of Diocletian (Figs. 33, 34), and the gateway cupolas on the imperial German coins (Fig. 83) and to the imperial Byzantine loge surmounted by

[40] Sauvaget, *La Mosquée omeyyade*, pp. 127-128, fig. 17; Jaussen and Savignac, *Mission archéologique en Arabie*, Paris, 1922, III, pp. 51-77, 114-121, fig. 11, pls. xx (façade), xxiv (plan); Creswell, *Early Muslim Architecture*, I, pp. 283-284; in the castellum at el-Qaṣṭal, which most authorities believe was late Roman or pre-Islamic, but Stern considers to have been Umayyade, there was probably a ceremonial room over the entrance (Brünnow and Domaszewski, *Die Provincia Arabia*, 1905, II, pp. 95-102, pl. XLIV; Stern, *Ars Islamica*, XI, 1946, p. 47; Sauvaget, *op.cit.*, p. 129, fig. 18).

[41] A. M. Schneider and O. Püttrich-Reignard,

"Ein frühislamischer Bau am See-Genezareth," *Palätinahefte des Vereins vom Heiligen Lande*, Cologne, 1937; Stern, *Ars Islamica*, XI, 1946, p. 92, figs. 3-4; it is possible that Qasr eṭ-Ṭuba with its almost square projecting vestibule between square towers may have had a dome (Creswell, *Early Muslim Architecture*, I, p. 377, fig. 461).

[42] D. Baramki, *Quarterly of the Dept. Antiq. in Palestine*, VIII, 1939, p. 51; R. W. Hamilton, *Palestinian Exploration Fund Quart.*, 1949, pp. 40-51, pl. v, and *Quarterly of the Dept. of Antiq. in Palestine*, XIV, 1950, pp. 100ff.

cupolas on the Skylitzes manuscript (Fig. 165). Against the background of the long history of reception ciboria and domical vestibules, which this study has endeavored to trace back to Hellenistic palaces, it is impossible to agree with Stern that the few domical vestibules of the Umayyad palaces were taken over from the Sassanian palace architecture, because in the Palace at Kaṣr-i-Shīrīn the domical hall at the end of a typical Persian *liwan* is in no way an entrance vestibule.[43]

As is to be expected, the importance of the domical place of reception, either in or over a royal gateway, becomes more apparent after the Umayyad period when the Abbasid Caliphs drew upon Imperial, Sassanian, and Mesopotamian precedents in order to make their palaces and ceremonies show their universal and theocratic pre-eminence. In the new Royal City of al-Mansūr (A.D. 754-775) at Baghdad there were four ceremonial gateways in the circular walls which gave access to two main avenues that intersected one another, as in a Roman castrum, at the center of the city, where the palace and the royal mosque stood in monumental and commanding isolation.[44] That al-Mansūr's residence, with its entrance porticos facing the avenue from the northern gate, was known as the "Palace of the Golden Gate" recalls the Hellenistic-Roman tradition going back to the "Golden Gate" of Alexandria, through which Anthony made his triumphal entry, and also to the Pharaonic custom of referring to "his Majesty on his throne in the Golden Gateway."

Each of the four gateways, which were constructed like the much earlier Mesopotamian strongholds with a small reception court, had over the inner portal an upper chamber, known as a *majlis*, that was a royal audience hall covered by a free-standing golden dome. These elevated and shining domes are enough like the cupolas over the palace portals on the coins of Diocletian and Constantine to suggest that they were still thought of as symbols of celestial authority. The other type of domical entrance is found at Ukhaiḍir, which Creswell attributes to the Abbasid ruler 'Isa sometime after A.D. 775-776, where, in addition to the arcading already noted over the entrance tower, there is a fluted, or *skene* type, dome over the vestibule leading into the "Court of Honor."[45] Much later in the palace architecture at Baghdad we are told that there was a *manẓarah*, or domical belvedere, over the palace gate.[46]

If these domical provisions for royal ceremonies at a palace and city gateway were peculiar to any one period and region of Islamic architecture there would be far less reason for presenting them as survivals of a long-established imperial tradition. The evidence, however, is cumulative and has become much more convincing since Canard has shown the relations between the Fatimid and Byzantine palace ceremonies.[47] Concerning the Great Palace of the Fatimids at Cairo he says that six of

[43] H. Stern, "Architecture des châteaux omeyyades," *Ars Islamica*, XI, 1946, pp. 72-97.

[44] Creswell, *Early Muslim Architecture*, II, pp. 10-30, figs. 3-5; J. B. Bury, *A History of the Eastern Empire*, 1912, pp. 239-240; Le Strange, *Baghdad during the Abbasid Caliphate*, 1900, Ch. II.

[45] Creswell, *op.cit.*, II, pp. 57-62, figs. 40, 64.

[46] Le Strange, *op.cit.*, p. 273.

[47] M. Canard, "Le cérémonial Fatimite et le cérémonial Byzantin," *Byzantion*, XXX, 1951, pp. 355-420; for the architecture: Creswell, *The Muslim Architecture of Egypt*, 1952, pp. 33-34; E. Pautry, "Les palais et les maisons d'époque musulmane au Caire," *Mém. de l'Institut français d'arch. orientale*, LXII, 1932, pp. 31-38.

its pavilions were each called a "Palace Gate" and that of these the most important was the "Palace of Gold," which was located at the "Golden Gate" where the most formal ceremonies took place. It was in a domical *manẓarah* at the "Golden Gate" that the Caliph made his public appearances and was acclaimed on such occasions as the celebration of the birth of the Prophet and the anniversary of his own birthday. "The Gate of Festival," we are told, had a domical pavilion, as did in all probability the Onopodion in front of the Augusteus of the Byzantine palace and the "Gate of Felicity" in front of the throne room of the Turkish palace at Constantinople. Also at the entrance to the Great Iwan there was a special place of honor, called a *sidillā*, where the Caliph was enthroned and which was surmounted by three cupolas, reminding us of the cupolas over the imperial loge in the Skylitzes manuscript (Figs. 162, 165) and the three cupolas over the royal portals of Suleiman and Achmed (Fig. 174).

The extent to which domical vestibules were characteristic features of Fatimid architecture is illustrated by the towered gateways of the Bāb al-Futuh and the Bāb-Zuwayla at Cairo.[48] The royal provisions of the early Fatimid architecture were continued in the Palace of Mohummid 'Ali in the Citadel at Cairo, where there was a basin of water in front of the domical pavilion under which the Caliph was enthroned.[49] Certainly this type of royal stage-set, which is best preserved in the beautiful Court of the Lions in the Alhambra with its lovely font in front of the domical pavilion that stands over the royal doorway, is too similar to what we know of the ceremonial provisions in the Imperial Palace at Constantinople to be disregarded. Before turning, however, to the influence of the Byzantine tradition on the Turkish palace architecture in Constantinople and the dissemination of the domical vestibule in the architecture of India, it should be noted that the Muslim mosque, like the Byzantine church, took over the domical vestibule from the palace architecture.

While it is unnecessary to review the mosques with domical entrances, some consideration might be given to the eighteenth century drawing by the Russian Baskii of a mosque which not only has domes over each of the three entrance archways opening, into the court, but also shows over each dome a small lantern cupola with a global finial that closely resembles the ciboria on the Constantinian coins.[50] Also it is suggestive to compare the entrance to the Mosque at Qairawan, which Creswell says was added to the existing structure in A.D. 1249, with the square vestibule in front of the entrance to the "Palace of Dux-Ripae" at Dura-Europos, because the Islamic portal with its royal arcade and its gored *skene* dome may be a survival of what was once the portal of the Roman palace.[51]

(e) It is possible that not enough attention has been given to the over-all pattern of evidence which shows that the new Turkish masters of Constantinople were interested in appropriating the architectural symbolism of their predecessors as they were in surrounding themselves with all the formal authority, ritualistic sanctity, and ceremonial

[48] Creswell, *op.cit.*, pp. 177, 197, figs. 84, 97.
[49] Pautry, *op.cit.*, p. 64, pl. L.
[50] de Beylié, *L'Habitation byzantine*, p. 61.
[51] Creswell, *Early Muslim Architecture*, II, p.

216, pls. 45/f, 46/e; A. Fikry (*Le grande mosquée de Kairouan*, Paris, 1934, p. 122) attributes the gateway to the ninth century.

pomp of the Byzantine emperors. It is true, of course, that long before the conquest of New Rome the Turkish builders had been influenced by the Islamic architecture of Iran and the Near East and hence brought to Constantinople an interest in domical forms. At the same time it is realized that it was not until after the Ottoman rulers had established their capital at Adrianople that they gave up their informal Turkish customs. Certainly Mehmed II, with his knowledge of Greek and Latin, his group of Greek scholars, and his instinctive desire as a conqueror to invest himself with all the manifestations of divine authority, began to cultivate the Roman idea that he and his palace were sacred. Just how much these interests of the Conqueror signify that he and his immediate successors were directly influenced by architectural precedents is problematic and depends upon how we visualize the now destroyed imperial palaces.

It has been noted that the Sultan's private entrance to a royal mosque was domical, and it has been suggested that the early mosques, which emphasized the *skene* cupolas at the four corners of the central dome, were following an imperial palace design. By this period of Turkish architecture there was nothing exceptional in the fact that the royal mosques like so many Byzantine palace-churches, had a cupola over the bay of the narthex in front of the entrance, or even that the font in the forecourt was covered by a domical kiosk like a Byzantine phiale. It is a little more significant, however, that a lofty domical gateway stood over the entrance to the garden court in back of the Mosque of Suleiman, where in form and location the domical mausolea of the Sultan and his wife are not unlike the tomb of Constantine in back of the Church of the Holy Apostles. It is also interesting to see in Grelot's drawing of the Mosque of Achmed I that there was a series of domical vestibules along a processional axis: the first in the outer enclosure, the second at the entrance to the forecourt, and the third in front of the central portal of the mosque, which is elevated like the imperial loge over the narthex of St. Savior Pantocrator.[52]

When it comes to comparing the New Palace, which Mehmed had built on the northeast side of Hagia Sophia, with the *Sacrum palatium* of the Byzantine emperors it must be admitted that its arrangement of parts and its at present tawdry buildings are usually considered to have been derived from oriental Persian and Islamic sources. In spite of its having been periodically rebuilt after a succession of fires and earthquakes, at no time could the Top Qapu Saray have had anything like the magnitude, monumentality, and specific buildings of the great Byzantine palace. And yet there are relations between the two, especially in the ceremonial importance of the gateways and the axial divisions of the palaces.

The "Imperial Gate," which was the first gateway of the Turkish palace, has already been discussed. The second, which separated the outer court, or "Place of Processions" where the palace guard was quartered, from the middle court with the Diwan and other buildings, was the "Gate of Salutations" and "Gate of Peace." This "Central

[52] Grelot, *op.cit.*, p. 329; for other examples of elevated domical vestibules at the entrance of Turkish mosques and gateways with a domical upper chamber see C. Gurlitt, *Die Baukunst Konstantinopels*.

Gate," or *Ortakapi*, although rebuilt more than once, has always consisted of a central portal, which is once pictured as a triumphal arch, between polygonal towers with sharp conical roofs.[53] On the side facing the second court the *Ortakapi* has today a portico with a cupola over the central bay in front of the portal. An eighteenth century painting from the Ducal Palace at Venice depicts this gateway in a processional scene with each of its dividing pilasters surmounted by a small pine-cone finial, not unlike the finials in the Skylitzes manuscript (Fig. 165) and the bulbous cupolas over the Moghul gateways.[54]

At the end of the middle court, which was like a *paradisus* or deer-park and called the "Court of the Diwan," is the "Gate of Felicity," or what was sometimes known as the "Gate of the Throne," the "King's Gate" and the "Royal Gate." Since it gave access to the last and most sacred section of the palace, where the domical throne-hall was located, one wonders whether the symbolism of this arrangement may not account for the reference to "the gate of felicity leading to the sanctuary of celestial happiness."[55] The Gate of Felicity, set into a portico of royal porphyry and verdi-antique columns, has a domical pavilion in front of its portal and was the place where the most distinguished ambassadors were received before being led in solemn silence to the inner throne-room.[56] At the time of the accession of the Sultan a golden throne was placed in the pavilion of this gateway so that the dignitaries of the empire could pay their homage to the ruler; it was also in this domical place of appearance that the Sultan was enthroned during the Bayram ceremony, when the officials and dignitaries of the Court kissed his hand, vest, and the steps of his dais, depending on their rank; and it was here, as in the Chalce of the Imperial Palace, that at his death farewell prayers were said over his body.[57]

Inasmuch as similar domical pavilions existed much earlier in front of the Fatimid palace gateways and were part of the Islamic palace tradition, as can be seen in the Court of the Lions of the Alhambra, it is impossible to argue, except in terms of the whole history of palace architecture, that the Gate of Felicity with its domical pavilion was a modified version of some part of the Byzantine palace, such as the Onopodion in front of the Augusteus. Yet the more one learns about the Turkish ceremonies, the more one comes to believe that Mehmed and his successors were endeavoring to adhere

[53] B. Miller, *Beyond the Sublime Porte*, pp. 158, 170 (drawing of Melling in 1819); Penzer, *The Harēm*, pp. 97-98 (woodcut from H. Schedel's *Nuremberg Chronicle* of 1493 showing conical towers; C. Gurlitt, *op.cit.*, I, p. 93 and II, pl. 12e. A miniature in the Hünername (*Guide to the Topkapu Saray*, pl. IX) depicts the gateway surmounted by a round tower with a conical roof.

[54] T. Bertelè, *Il Palazzo degli ambasciatori di Venezia a Constantinople*, 1932, fig. 69.

[55] Von Hammer, *Histoire de l'empire ottoman*, III, p. 299.

[56] Miller, *op.cit.*, pp. 206f.; Penzer, *op.cit.*, pp. 106-107 (drawing by Melling); the "Solitary Turk," whose history was translated into French in 1695 (note 34), says (p. 370) that it was called the Gate of Felicity because at one time the Diwan was

held in it. According to the *Guide to the Topkapu Saray*, p. 27, in the pavement of door to the throne-room there was a circular slab of porphyry, reminding us of the similar stations of the Byzantine emperor at the entrance to the Chalce and in the pavement at the east end of the south aisle of Hagia Sophia where it presumably marked the place where the Emperor sat while listening to the reading of the Gospels.

[57] Von Hammer, *op.cit.*, p. 300; account of ceremony by R. Withers in 1620 (S. Purchas, *Hakluytus Posthumus*, IX, p. 387); a detailed account of the ceremony and the procession afterward to the mosque of St. Sophia by the "Solitary Turk" (note 34, pp. 184-192); painting of ceremony in the *Guide to the Museum of Topkapu Saray*, Istanbul, 1936, p. 25, pl. XV.

to the Byzantine palace tradition. It was the Conqueror who initiated the Bayram ceremony and imposed upon his court the ideas of pomp, silence, seclusion, and sacredness of his person.[58] When it comes to the architecture the evidence is suggestive, but inconclusive. For example, we are reminded of the ceremonial importance of the phiales in the Imperial Palace by the way in which the Sultans used the domical "Kuishks" of their Seray to give audiences, meet their entourage before visiting a mosque, and to watch ceremonies.[59]

The most important single piece of evidence, however, is an early engraving (Fig. 175), perhaps of the sixteenth century, which pictures the reception of the Venetian ambassador at the Sublime Porte.[60] It is obviously somewhat fanciful and its architecture does not agree with what we know about any one of the specific gateways in the Turkish palace. And yet it is a graphic summary of this study, because it curiously combines every one of the symbolic provisions for a royal reception at a palace gateway which have been traced back to Roman and Hellenistic times. The sultan is pictured sitting at the entrance to his palace on his divan, which although covered by a flat canopy is also surmounted by a somewhat misunderstood and towerlike baldachin with a *skene* dome. At the same time the traditional idea of a towered façade being a palatium symbol is pictured, more symbolically than architecturally, by flanking towers at either side of the double archway, which are purely decorative in scale, but nevertheless capped with *skene* cupolas.

While we may suspect that the engraving was not done by an eye witness, it is impossible to believe that it did not have a basis in fact. Fortunately we have some proof that it records actual ceremonial conventions in the "Travels of Bertrandon de la Brocquière," who between 1432 and 1433 officially visited the Turkish palace at Adrianople.[61] In his account of the court, which he says the Turks call "porte du seigneur" the Burgundian Ambassador writes, "Every time the prince receives a message or an embassy, which happens almost daily, *il fait porte*," because "*faire porte* is for him the same as when our Kings of France hold royal state and open court." He goes on to relate how "after the ambassador had entered they made him sit down near the gate" and that then the Prince "walked across an angle of the court to a platform, where a seat had been prepared for him." The seat "was a kind of couch with velvet, with four

[58] Miller, *op.cit.*, pp. 28-31; A. H. Lybyer (*The Government of the Ottoman Empire in the time of Suleiman the Magnificent*, Cambridge, 1913, p. 134) say Mohammed's "Law of Ceremonies" was based on imperial forms.

[59] Describing the principal entrance to the palace from the harbor, presumably the Canon Gate, the "Solitary Turk" (note 34) says (p. 349) that there was a domed kiosk in front of it where the Sultan received the homage of his naval forces and at times granted audiences. He also says (pp. 169, 188) that when the Sultan rode through the city in a formal procession the streets were cleaned and sanded, a custom that went back to Roman triumphal entries. According to John Sanderson in

1546 (S. Purchas, *op.cit.*, IX, p. 430), at the time of a triumphal entry the route of the Sultan was lined on both sides by people holding strips of cloth of gold, velvet and damask.

[60] Bertelè, *Il Palazzo degli ambasciatori di Venezia a Constantinople*, fig. 9; a somewhat different version was published in 1612 in *Illustrations . . . sur l'histoire de Chalcondile*, see C. W. Rouillard, *The Turk in French History, Thought and Literature (1520-1660)*, p. 87, 236 n. 1, fig. 11.

[61] *The Travels of Bertrandon de la Brocquière to Palestine and his Return from Jerusalem overland to France during the years 1432-1433* (trans. T. Johnes), 1808, pp. 253-258.

or five steps to mount it." During the ceremony the prince did not speak, but after the presentation food was served and "on his going away the musicians, who were placed in the court near the buffet, began to play." Also regarding the importance of gateways the Burgundian writes, "The chief cadi, with his assessors, administered justice at the outward gate of the palace."[62] After reading this fifteenth century French account of a rather ordinary gateway ceremony, which the engraving so clearly illustrates, it is less difficult to understand why over the centuries gateway rituals and symbolism were so important to the popular conceptions of a palace.

(f) The fact that by the Late Islamic period in India, when Turkish architects worked for the Great Moghuls, domical vestibules, such as those in the gateways of the Delhi Palace and the triumphal portal of Akbar (Fig. 173), occur in combination with all the imperial symbols of universal and heavenly ruler—that is, sculptural baldachins, crowning arcades, and purely decorative flanking towers—would seem to imply a direct relation to the tradition which went back to the palace portals, like the Chalce, at Constantinople. By this late date, however, it is impossible to differentiate clearly between the various domical traditions in India. The consistent use of domical vestibules at the entrance of the mosques presumably reflects the influence of the Islamic architecture of the Abbasid Caliphate.[63] The clearest indication of Muslim dissemination from the Near East is to compare the elevated cupola over the gateway of Sikandra Bei Agra with an Abbasid *majlis*, the domical tower over the portal of Qaṣr ar-Ribāt at Sūsa and the cupola-baldachins over the palatium gateway on the coins of Diocletian.[64]

What complicates this question of dissemination is not only the destruction of practically all the native palaces before the Moghul period, but the temple architecture which shows that India had its own domical tradition. The principal reason for further involving this summary with peripheral issues is that India, like the West, had its own gateway symbolism; and in its development of gateway rituals, like that which has been assumed to have been true in the Near East, gave at an early date, a celestial meaning to either a domical tent, or wooden canopy, of reception and then translated it into a monumental pavilion of stone at the entrance of temples which were derived from palace architecture. This means that the so-called "Celestial Pavilion," or *Swarga Vilâsam*, at the entrance of late Moghul palaces, like that of Tirumalai Nâyyah at Madurâ, was not necessarily based upon Muslim precedent.[65] Proof that there was an early custom of setting up a round tent or wooden canopy as a "Celestial Pavilion" and at a later date reproducing it as an elaborately decorated domical structure is preserved in the temple architecture of the Jains, which originated long before the earliest extant monuments of the eleventh century.

The most significant example for the purpose of this study is the temple built by Vimala in A.D. 1031 at Mount Abu.[66] Here there are two very large and richly carved

---

[62] *Op.cit.*, p. 263.

[63] For example, the thirteenth century mosque of Gutbu-d-Dîn at Old Delhi (Fergusson, II, p. 199, fig. 369) and the fourteenth century Kalan Masjid at Shahjahanabad (Brown, *op.cit.*, pl. xv).

[64] Reuther, *op.cit.*, pl. 37.

[65] Fergusson, I, p. 417, fig. 240.

[66] *Ibid.*, II, pp. 36ff., figs. 283 (plan), 284; Brown, *Indian Architecture*, 1942, p. 147.

mandapas or domical pavilions, one at the entrance to the shrine and the other outside the walls and directly in front of the entrance to the castrumlike enclosure. The ceremonial purpose of these magnificent heavenly pavilions is made evident by a long rectangular structure located in front of the outer pavilion. This hall was constructed for the sole purpose of protecting the statues of Vimala and his family, who are all mounted on elephants and lined up in a processional order, just as they would have been in actual life when they approached the place of reception at the entrance to the temple-palace of their god.

Beginning with the Temple of Somnath, which has only one pavilion, down to the fifteenth century Temple of Adrinatha at Ranpur, which has a series of pavilions on all four sides of the central shrine, the Jain temples preserve what must have been in the beginning a palace plan and its ceremonial provisions.[67] Always in the center of the enclosing walls there is a *sikara*, like a throne-room in which the god-image is enthroned, and in front of its entrance a large *mandapa*, which is sometimes referred to as a "canopy of gems," that is a sculptural version of what was at one time a wooden domical structure. There is, therefore, a distant parallel between these Indian *mandapas* and the development in the Near East of a ciborium of reception into a domical palace entrance.

In addition to the Jain pavilions India had other forms of gateway symbolism which attributed heavenly values to the towers and arched portals of temples, palaces, and royal cities. For example, in regard to the various meanings of the Hindu word "torana," which was used for a gateway, a kind of triumphal arch and the ornamental entrance of temples and palaces, Archarya says that Chaṇḍi-Síva "built a beautiful torana, which contains all the gods like a portico of heaven made by the Creator himself."[68] He also illustrates the Hindu word "pratoli" as a kind of towered "Gateway leading to heaven."[69]

Although little seems to have been written about the architectural symbolism of the early Indian palaces, the elaborate and detailed cosmic symbolism of the Imperial Palace at Peking is proof that the Orientals, like the peoples of the Roman Empire, were accustomed to see a microcosm and replica of heaven in the sacred dwellings of their rulers.[70] It may help, therefore, in realizing that there was nothing exceptional in the thinking of the antique and mediaeval West, which attached mystic and heavenly meanings to the *Sacrum palatium* of a divine Kosmokrator, if this study is terminated with the inscription that Shah Jehan had carved on his Palace at Delhi, for it reads, "If there is a Heaven on earth, this is it, this is it."[71]

[67] Temple of Somnath (Fergusson, II, p. 35, fig. 282); Chaumukh Temple of Adinatha at Ranpur (Brown, *Indian Architecture, Islamic Period*, p. 164, pl. cv).

[68] P. K. Acharya, *An Encyclopaedia of Hindu Architecture*, VII, 1946, pp. 664, 216-221; reference to a Jain "Canopy of gems" (p. 402, nos. 29, 30).

[69] *Op.cit.*, p. 321, illustration opp. p. 309.

[70] For the cosmological and architectural symbolism see: H. G. Creel, *Sinism, a Study of the Evolution of the Chinese World-view*, Chicago, 1929; O.

Franke, "Der kosmische Gedanke in Philosophie und Staat der Chinesen," *Vorträge der Bibl. Warburg*, 1925-1926; A. Forke, *The World-conception of the Chinese*, London, 1925; M. Granet, *La Pensée Chinoise*, Paris, 1934; C. Ito, *Architectural Decoration in China*, I, Tokyo, 1941 (English summary by J. Harada); W. E. Soothill, *The Hall of Light, a Study of early Chinese Kingship*, London, 1951.

[71] Fergusson, II, p. 11.

INDEX

INDEX

211

E. Baldwin Smith, *Architectural Symbolism of Imperial Rome and the Middle Ages*
(Princeton: Princeton University Press, 1956)

ERRATA CORRIGE

Final work on this posthumously published book was completed by the author during what proved to be his last illness. A list of errata, subsequently noted by two of his colleagues, has therefore been prepared in accordance with what undoubtedly would have been his wish.

p.4, n.1, col.1, line 3: for *impérial romain* read *impériales romaines*
     line 6: for *byzantine* read *byzantin*
     line 7: for culturel read cultuel
     line 8: for *del'Ac.* read *de l'Ac.*
p.7, n.3, col.2, line 1: for Europapäischen read Europäischen
     line 4: for *Historische* read *Historisches*
p.14, n.18, col.1, line 1: for Antiquities read Antiquités
p.15, n.19, col.1, line 4: for romains read romaines
     line 7: for "Turres" read "Turris"
   n.21, col.2, line 1: for Bishofs read Bischofs
p.19, n.34, line 1: for *Real-Encyclopädia* read *Real-Encyclopädie*
p.22, n.47, col.2, line 2: for triumph read triomphe
p.25, n.62, col.1, lines 2-3: for *Humanistika, Abhandlungen* read *Humanistiska Avhandlingar*
     line 15: for Iulia read Iulium
p.26, n.63, col.1, line 3: for *archaeologica* read *archeologica*
   n.63, col.2, lines 6-7: for *Vesonius Primus* read *Vesoni Primi*
p.27, n.67, col.1, line 1: for Triumpstrasse read Triumphstrasse
   n.69, col.2, line 3: for "Apotheosi" read "Apoteosi"
     line 4: for *Osloensis* read *Osloenses*
p.28, n.70, col.1, lines 14-15: for *altestamentliche* read *alttestamentliche*
p.29, line 10: for "phiale mysticum" read "phiale mystica"
   n.74, col.1, line 3: for Wasserspier read Wasserspeier
p.30, n.76, col.2, line 1: for *"Universitets Årsskrift"* read *"Uppsala Universitets Årsskrift"*
p.34, line 36: for *salam regalem* read *sala regalis*
p.36, n.93, col.2, line 9: for Trèves dans le read Trèves dans la
   n.94, col.2, lines 1-2: for Theodorichgraber read Theodorichgrabes
p.37, n.95, line 1: for *als Besichte an Architektur,* 1936 read *als Bereiche der Architektur,*
   1939
p.38, n.97, col.1, line 5: for Gierstad read Gjerstad
p.40, line 17: for Diodochi read Diadochi
   n.111, col.1, line 1: for *Antiquites* read *Antiquités*
p.44, n.128, col.2, line 1: for Diocletienischen read Diocletianischen
     line 3: for *Description* read *Déscription*
p.45, line 16: for Cyzica read Cyzicus
p.47, n.138, col.1, line 15: for *Domus iustini* read *Domus Iustini*
   n.139, col.2, line 6: for Crispus read Crispi
p.49, line 18: for *Sacritissime* read *Sacritissimus*
   n.152, col.2, line 2: for *Fitswilliam* read *Fitzwilliam*
p.50, line 30: for was called *Apollo tuum* read was called *Apollo*
p.52, line 25: for *orbs* read *orbis*
p.55, lines 14-15: for *Mater Deus* read *Mater Deum*
   n.16, col.2, line 5: for *praetoria* read *praetorio*
p.56, n.20, col.1, line 2: for impérieux read impériaux
p.61, n.40, col.1, line 2: for Sainte Georges read Saint Georges
p.62, line 3: for *scaena frons* read *scaenae frons*
p.64, n.45, col.1, line 3: for *Sizungsberichte* read *Sitzungsberichte*

p.66, n.50, col.1, line 1: for *Gebürtskirche* read *Geburtskirche*

n.56, col.2, line 2: for *Atti delle* read *Atti della*

line 4: for *storice* read *storiche*

line 5: for Mintorno read Minturno

line 6: for Brixentes read Bressanone

p.68, n.64, col.2, line 6: for *Vercingetorix* read *Vercingétorix*

p.70, n.74, col.2, line 5: for Paribene read Paribeni

p.73, n.80, col.1, line 1: for *païen* read *païens*

line 4: for Vinnalia read Vinalia

p.75, n.2, col.1, line 6: for *Stauronika* read *Stauronikita*

p.76, n.5, col.1, line 3: for "turres" read "turris"

line 10: for *Xth Jahrshunderts* read *X. Jahrhunderts*

p.77, line 28: for *Aula Palatinis* read *Aula Palatina*

n.9, col.1, line 5: for *Enstehung* read *Entstehung*

n.10, col.2, line 3: for Baukunst des 11 Jahrhunderts read Baukunst des 11. Jahrhunderts

p.78, line 8: for *capella regale* read *capella regalis*

n.13, col.2, line 7: for *Constantine* read *Constantin*

p.79, line 24: for *Porta curia* read *Porta curiae*

n.14, line 1: for *Ravenna* read *Ravenne*

p.80, n.15, col.1, line 2: for "Zur des römischen Kernes" read "Zur Deutung des römischen Kernes

p.81, n.21, col.2, line 2: for *Sonderdruck aus Westfälische Zeitschrift,* read *Westfälische Zeitschrift*

p.83, n. 26, col.1, line 2: for *Karolingischenkunst* read *Karolingischen Kunst*

n.29, col.2, line 1: for *Westfälischen Zeitschrift* read *Westfälische Zeitschrift*

p.84, n.30, col.1, line 6: for Karolingischen Bäu read Karolingischen Bau

n.34, col.2, line 1: for Fuchs, *Zeitschrift* read Fuchs, *Westfälische Zeitschrift*

p.85, n.34, col.1, line 3: for *auditorio regali* read *auditorium regale*

line 8: for *colloquo* read *colloquio*

n.35, col.1, line 1: for and *Zeitschrift* read and *Westfälische Zeitschrift*

n.37, col.2, line 2: for *romanische und frühgotischen* read *romanischer und frühgotischer*

p.86, n.39, col.2, lines 6-7: for Erdiözese read Erzdiözese

line 10: for Denn in diesen read Denn in diesem

line 12: for bestaltet read bestattet

p.87, n.42, col.1, line 5: for *Kunst des X Jahrb.* read *Kunst des X. Jahrh.*

col.1, line 11: for *beschichte* read *Geschichte*

col.2, line 1: for *Plastik der früheren Mittelalters* read *Plastik des früheren Mittelalters*

line 5: for *Kunst des X Jahrb.* read *Kunst des X. Jahrh.*

p.88, n.46, col.1, line 4: for *administration dans* read *administration byzantine dans*

n.47, col.2, line 5: for *Kunst des xth Jahrsh.* read *Kunst des X. Jahrh.*

line 10: for *salam regalem* read *sala regalis*

line 12: for *Glossarium Lat.,* vi read *Glossarium Lat.,* iv

n.49, col.2, line 2: for *12 Jahrsh.* read *12. Jahrh.*

p.90, n.54, col.1, lines 5-6: for Mittelalterlichen im Deutschland," *Westfälischen* read Mittelalterlichen Deutschland," *Westfälische*

p.91, n.57, col.2, line 4: for *capellam* read *capella*

p.92, line 3: for *Porta curia* read *Porta curiae*

n.59, col.1, lines 6-7: for *Römanischen Zeit,* read *Romanischen Zeit*

p.93, n.61, col.2, line 1: for *Westfälen* read *Westfäl.*

line 3: for Fuchs, *Zeitschrift* read Fuchs, *Westfäl. Zeitschrift*

p.94, n.63, col.2, lines 2-3: for R. Janin, *Les Églises et les monastères* read R. Janin, *La géographie ecclésiastique de l'empire byzantin,* iii, *Les églises et les monastères*

p.95, n.64, col.1, lines 2-3: for *Kaiser und Königer* read *Kaiser und Könige*

col.2, line 3: for *mediovale* read *medioevale*

n.65, col.2, line 1: for *L'Habitation byzantin* read *L'habitation byzantine* p.97, n.68, col.1, line 1: for *Deutschen Kaiser und Könige* read *Deutsche Kaiser und Könige*

p.98, n.72, col.1, line 3: for *sous le race* read *sous la race*

p.102, n.91, col.1, line 5: for *Kaisermystick* read *Kaisermystik*

p.106, n.110, col.1, line 1: for *Kaiser Friedrichs* read *Kaiser Friedrich*

p.107, line 19: for *urbis* read *urbs*

p.110, n.6, col.1, line 19: for οὐρανίσκον read οὐρανίσκος

p.111, n.7, col.1, line 5: for Banketthauser read Banketthäuser

n.8, col.1, line 3: for heroä read heroa

p.114, n.18, col.1, line 4: for *Agyptische Sprache* read *Aegyptische Sprache*

p.115, n.21, col.1, line 23: for *Preuss. Kunstlg.* read *Preuss. Kunstsammlungen*

col.2, line 22: for *Antike und der Mittelalters* read *Antike und des Mittelalters*

p.117, n.28, col.1, lines 6-7: for *Le légende phénicienne de Danel* read *La légende phénicienne de Daniel*

p.119, n.43, col.2, line 1: for *Inventaire des mosaïque* read *Inventaire des mosaïques*

p.121, n.46, col.2, line 2: for *in regis theatri* read *in regia theatri*

p.125, line 15: for NER(O) read NER(ONIS)

n.60, col.1, line 7: for Varro, *Apud non*, c.6 n.2 read Varro, *De lingua latina*, v, 146

line 12: for *Acc. romana de archeologia*, Ser. III, VIII, 1944 read *Acc. romana di archeologia*, Ser. III, Memorie vol. VII

col.2, lines 1-2: for Wulzinger, "Die Marcellum Dupondieu des Nero," *Num. Int. Monatschrift*, 1933 read Wulzinger, "Die Macellum-Dupondien des Nero," *Numismatik*, 1933, pp. 83-95, 116-138

n.61, col.2, line 2: for *I Campi flagrei* read *I Campi Flegrei*

p.126, n.66, col.2, line 1: for *Du caractère religieux de la rayauté* read *Du caractère religieux de la royauté*

p.128, n.73, col.1, line 10: for Maximian Hercules read Maximianus Herculeus

p.131, n.1, col.1, lines 1-2: for *l'empire byzantium* read *l'empire byzantin*

line 3: for vies privée read vies privées

n.2, col.2, line 8: for *Vorarbeiten zur iconographie und archäologie* read *Vorarbeiten zur Iconographie und Archäologie*

p.134, line 11: ανατολή read ἀνατολή

p.137, n.19, col.1, line 2: for *Byzance* read *Byzanz*

line 4: for Aachen Pfalz read Aachener Pfalz

p.140, P.2, line 3: for *Tribunali triclinii* read *Tribunal triclinii*

line 8: for *in coelo aurea* read in *coelo aureo*

n.34, col.1, line 1: for Osservazioni sur frontone read Osservazioni sul frontone

n.35, col.2, line 2: for *Schrit.,* read *Script.,*

p.141, n.37, col.2, line 5: for Jocopi, "Galatea [Forli]," *Mon. Scavi Antiq.* read Jacopi, "Galatea [Forli]," *Not. Scavi di Antichità*

n.38, col.2, line 4: for *Diokletiens* read *Diokletians*

line 6: for Spolato read Spalato

line 7: for *Sprogog Oldtidsforskning* read *Sprog og Oldtidsforskning*

p.142, n.39, col.1, line 13: for *pro aulium* read *proaulium*

n.40, col.2, line 10: for *basilica impetrale* read *basilica ipetrale*

p.143, n.45, col.1, lines 4-5: for portano alle luce read portano alla luce

col.2, line 3: for *dei Lancei* read *dei Lincei*

p.144, line 15: for *tribunale triclinii* read *tribunal triclinii*

line 39: for Pergamine read Pergamene

p.146, line 17: for *scena frons* read *scaenae frons*

n.49, col.2, lines 1-2: for *Das Trier Kaiserthermen* read *Die Trierer Kaiserthermen*

p.147, n.51, col.2, line 1: for J. Lindos read K.Lehmann-Hartleben and J. Lindros

p.148, n.52, col.1, line 6: for Biancini read Bianchini

n.54, col.2, line 10: for Biancini read Bianchini

p.149, n.55, col.1, line 9: for *Bauten im Latium* read *Bauten in Latium*

p.150, n.58, col.1, line 1: for Paulys-Wissowa read Pauly-Wissowa

n.61, col.2, line 1: for *Exarchate de Ravenna* read *Exarchate de Ravenne*

p.151, line 15: for *Capitoleum aureum* read *Capitolium aureum* p.153, n.6, col.1, line 2: for *Studien den Bibl.* read *Studien der Bibliothek*

n.7, col.1, line 1: for del'ipogee read dell'ipogeo

lines 5-6: for *Monumenti Christiano-eretici* read *Monumenti Cristiano-eretici*

n.8, col.2, line 1: for *Const. Porph. di Cer.* read Const. Porph., *De caer.*

p.162, line 23: for *Porta curia* read *Porta curiae*

p.163, n.44, col.2, line 1: for L'habitation byzantine read *L'habitation byzantine*

line 2: for *Le Mount Athos* read *Le Mont Athos*

p.171, n.21, col.1, lines 2-3: for R. Janin *Les Églises* read R. Janin, *La géographie ecclésiastique de l'empire byzantin*, III, *Les églises*

p.173, n.26, col.2, line 1: for *Les Églises* read *Les églises de Constantinople*

p.175, n.31, col.2, line 9: for *Kleinasian* read *Kleinasien*

p.176, n.33, col.1, line 8: for *Akkitektoura* read *Arkhitektoura*

line 10: for R. Janin, *Les Églises* read R. Janin, *La géographie ecclésiastique de l'empire byzantin*, III, *Les églises*

p.185, n.8, col.1, line 3: for *Indische Palaste* read *Indische Paläste*

p.191, n.15, col.1, line 1: for *Altkonstantinople* read *Altkonstantinopel*

p.194, n.22, col.1, lines 4-5: for *Constantinople* read *Constantinopel*

n.24, col.2, lines 1-2: for *Bildenenkunst* read *Bildenden Kunst*

lines 2-3: for *Asiatiques* read *Asiatique*

p.195, n.26, col.1, lines 3-4: for *archaeologishe Institut* read *archäologischen Instituts*

lines 5-6: for "Mausolei imperiali e reale di basso impero e dell'alta medioevo" read "Mausolei imperiali e reali del basso impero e dell'alto medioevo"

p.196, n.32, col.1, lines 1-2: for *Eigentliche Kurtze beschreibung . . . stadt Constantinople*, Cassell, 1606 read *Eigentliche kurtze Beschreibung . . . Stadt Constantinopel*, Cassel, 1606.

p.200, n.41, col.2, line 2: for *Palätinahefte* read *Palästinahefte*

p.204, n.54, col.1, line 2: for *Constantinople* read *Constantinopoli*

p.205, n.60, col.2, line 2: for *Constantinople* read *Constantinopoli*

INDEX

p.211, col.2, line 43: for *auditorio regali* read *audiorium regale*

col.3, line 48: for *impetrale* read *ipetrale*

p.213, col.3, line 15: for *iustini* read *Iustini*

p.215, col.1, line 8: for *Imperator coelistis* read *Imperator coelestis*

col.3, line 4 from bottom: for *in praetoria* read *in praetorio*

p.216, col.1, line 4: omit

line 42: for *ad Locutio* read *adlocutio*

p.217, col.1, line 9: for Domus Vesonius read Domus Vesonii

col.1, line 25: for *Porta curia* read *Porta curiae*

line 17 from bottom: for *pro aulium* read *proaulium*

col.3, line 26: for *sacritissime Imperator* read *sacritissimus Imperator*

line 4 from bottom: for *salam regalem* read *sala regalis*

p.218, col.1, line 36: for *scaena frons* read *scaenae frons*

col. 3, insert between lines 17 and 18 from bottom: Tiridates, coronation of, 124

p.219, col.1, line 17 from bottom: for *Tribunali triclinii* 140, read *Tribunal triclinii* 140, 144

FIGURE CAPTIONS

Figure 7, line 1: for Porta curia read Porta curiae

Figure 14: for Caesaria read Caesarea

Figure 27: for Elagabulus read Elagabalus

Figures 60, 63, 64: for *Wölfenbeitel* read *Wolfenbüttel*

Figure 69: for Kunsthistorische read Kunsthistorisches

Figure 70: for Hessischeslandes Museum read Hessisches Landesmuseum

Figure 72: for Kunsthistorische read Kunsthistorisches

Figure 116: for DIVA CLAUD read DIVA CLAUDIA

ILLUSTRATIONS

1. Roman temple, Djmer, Syria
2. Church of St. Lot, mosaic from Khirbit Mukhayyat, Syria
3. Porta Marzia, Perugia
4. Porta Triumphalis, *Forma urbis*, Rome
5. Porta aurea, palace of Diocletian, Salona (after Clérisseau)
6. Palace of the Exarchate, Ravenna
7. Norman manuscript showing King's Gate, Porta curia, and royal Guest House at Canterbury
8. "Basilica" of Constantine, Treves (after Krencker with cupolas added)
9. PALATIUM of William the Conqueror, Bayeux tapestry
10. Palace of Edward the Confessor, Bayeux tapestry

11. Roman gateway, Nîmes
12. Coin of Augustus, Emerita, Spain
13. Ceremonial gateway, Perge, Asia Minor
14. Coin of Titus, Caesaria (Germanica), Bithynia
15. Coin of Sauromatis I, Bosphorus
16. Coin of Hadrian, Bizya, Thrace
17. Coin of Caracalla, Trajanopolis, Thrace
18. Coin of Septimius Severus, Isauria, Asia Minor
19. Coin of Commodus, Anchialus, Thrace
20. Coin of Septimius Severus, Anchialus, Thrace
21. Coin of Septimius Severus, Anchialus, Thrace
22. Coin of Caracalla, Anchialus, Thrace
23. Coin of Caracalla, Anchialus, Thrace
24. Coin of Gordianus, Anchialus, Thrace
25. Coin of Geta, Callatia, Thrace
26. Coin of Gordianus, Marcianopolis, Thrace
27. Coin of Elagabulus, Nicopolis, Thrace
28. Coin of Philippus Senior, Bizya, Thrace
29. Coin of Gordianus, Nicopolis, Thrace
30. Coin of Trajan Decius (?), Philippopolis (?), Thrace

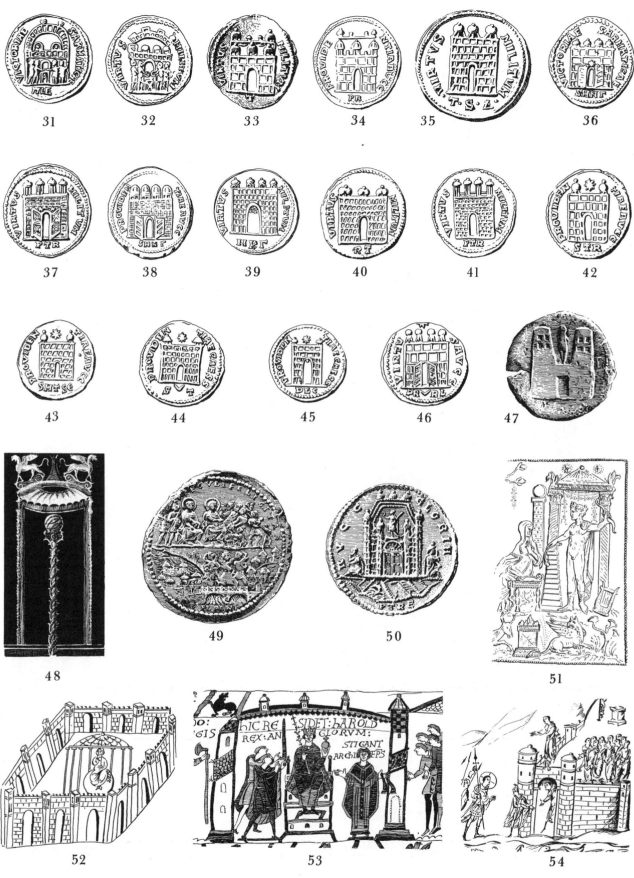

31. Coin of Diocletian
32. Coin of Maximianus
33. Coin of Diocletian, Ticinum
34. Coin of Diocletian, Rome
35. Coin of Diocletian
36. Coin of Diocletian, Nicomedia
37. Coin of Maximianus, Treves
38. Coin of Diocletian, Nicomedia

39. Coin of Galerius as Caesar, Cyzica
40. Coin of Constantine as Caesar, Treves
41. Coin of Constantine as Caesar, Treves
42. Coin of Constantine, Treves
43. Coin of Constantine, Thessalonica
44. Coin of Crispus as Caesar, Tarragona
45. Coin of Constanins as Caesar, Lyon
46. Coin of Constantine, Arles
47. Coin of Trajan, Alexandria

48. Fresco, Casa del Argo ed Io, Herculaneum
49. Lead medallion, Morgantiacum (Mainz)
50. Gold medallion of Constantine, Treves
51. Silver lanyx, Corbridge
52. "Sapientia seated in the temple," Psychomachia of Prudentius, University Library, Leyden
53. Harold enthroned in palace, Bayeux tapestry
54. "The Advent of the Lord," Utrecht Psalter

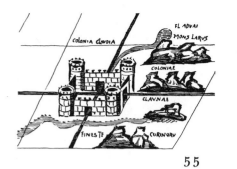
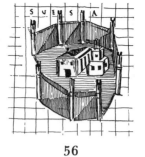

55

56

57

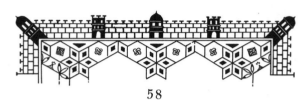

59

58

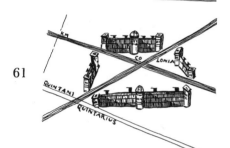

61

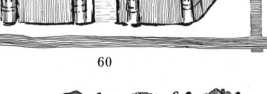

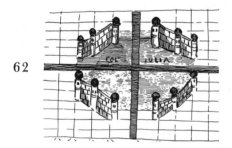

60

62

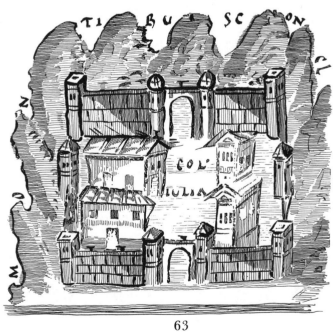

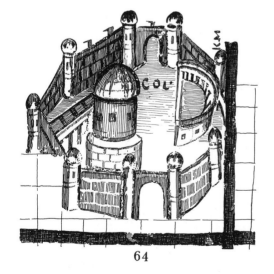

63

64

55. "Colonia Claudia," *Ms. Hyginus Gromaticus, Corpus Agrimensorum Romanorum*

56. "Suessa," *Ms. Agennius Urbicus, Cor. Agr. Rom.*

57. "Colonia Auxurnas," *Cor. Agr. Rom.*

58. Mosaic, Auriol, Bouches-du-Rhône

59. "Colonia," *Ms. Hyginus, Cor. Agr. Rom.*

60. "Col," *Ms. Wölfenbeitel, Cor. Agr. Rom.*

61. "Colonia," *Cor. Agr. Rom.*

62. "Colonia Iulia," *Cor. Agr. Rom.*

63. "Colonia Iulia," *Ms. Wölfenbeitel, Cor. Agr. Rom.*

64. "Col," *Ms. Wölfenbeitel, Cor. Agr. Rom.*

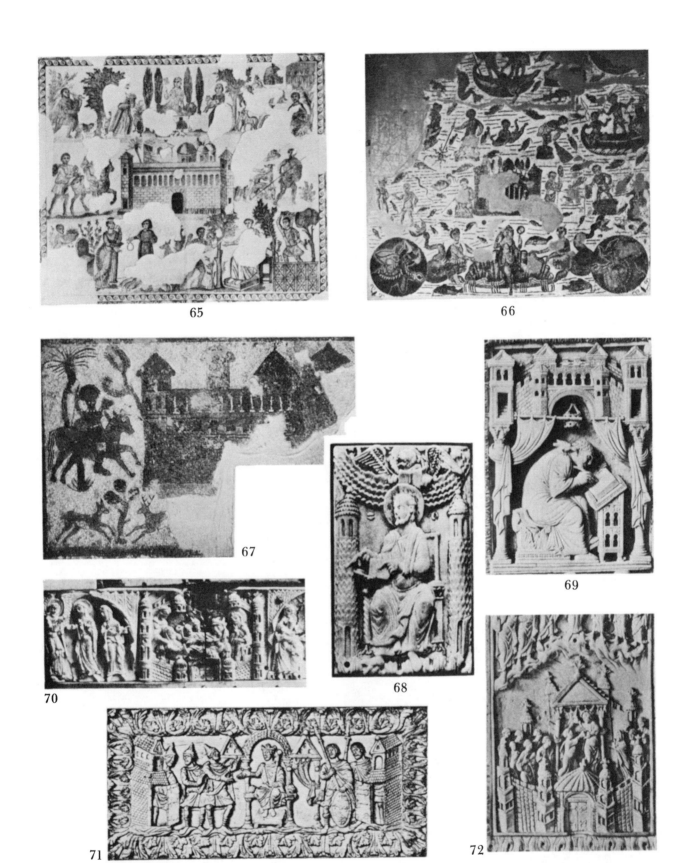

65. Roman mosaic from Carthage, Bardo Museum
66. Roman mosaic from Carthage, Bardo Museum
67. Roman mosaic from Carthage, Bardo Museum
68. Evangelist Mark, ivory, Victoria and Albert Museum, London
69. The Holy Gregorius, ivory, Kunsthistorische Museum, Vienna
70. Nativity, ivory, Hessischeslandes Museum, Darmstadt
71. Magi before Herod, ivory, Louvre, Paris
72. Doubting of Thomas, ivory, Kunsthistorische Museum, Weimar

73

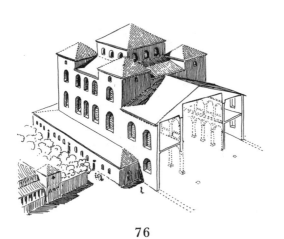

74

75

76

77

78

79

80

73. Jonah speaks to King at city-gate of Nineveh, *Ms. gr. 510*, Bibl. Nat., Paris

74. Mosaic, St. George, Saloniki

75. Mosaic, Church of the Nativity, Bethlehem

76. Treves, restoration of fourth century east end of Cathedral (after Krencker)

77. Treves, fourth century plan of Cathedral

78. Corvey, Abbey church, section of Westwerk (after Fuchs)

79. Royal abbey church of St. Peter, Bayeux tapestry

80. Corvey, Abbey church, façade

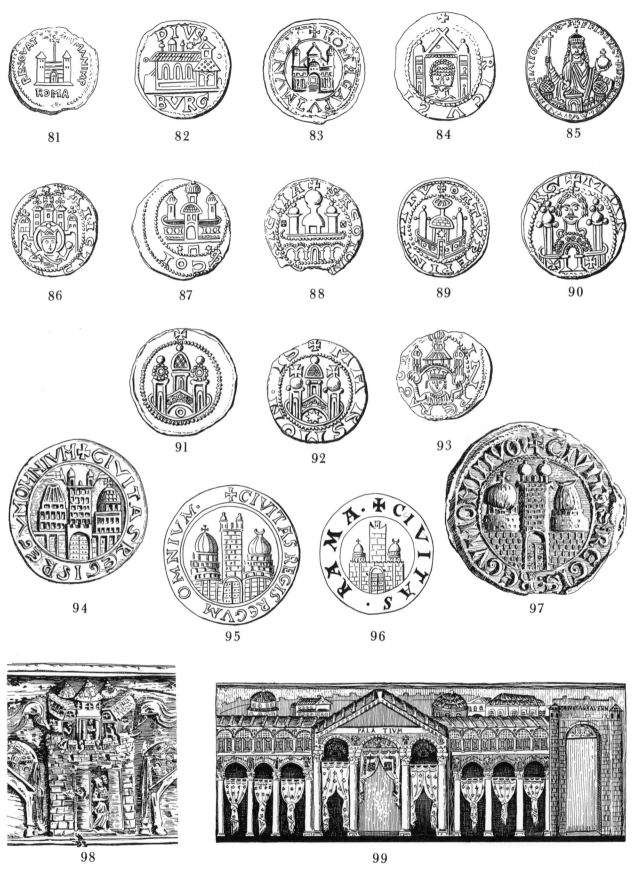

81. Seal of Charlemagne
82. Coin, Henry III
83. Metal bulla, Henry IV
84. Coin, Henry IV

85. Gold bulla, Frederick I
86. Coin, Frederick I
87. Coin, Frederick I
88. Coin, Henry VI

89. Coin, Henry VI
90. Coin, Otto IV
91. Coin, Otto IV
92. Coin, Otto IV

93. Coin, Frederick II
94. Seal, Amaury I, Jerusalem
95. Seal, Baldwin V, Jerusalem
96. Seal, Baldwin I, Ramah
97. Seal, Jean de Brienne, Jerusalem

98. Byzantine palace, ivory casket, Cathedral, Troyes
99. Theodoric's palace, mosaic, Sant'Apollinare Nuovo, Ravenna

100. Throne of Theodosius, *Ms. gr. 510*, Bibl. Nat., Paris
101. Byzantine Empress, ivory diptych, Mus. Nat., Florence
102. Doors of Balawat, British Museum, London
103. Audience tent of Emperor Kienling (after eighteenth century engraving)
104. Assyrian relief, Brit. Mus., London
105. Heroön of Meleager and Dioscurides, Etruscan mirror

106. Tent-shrines, coin of Trajan, Lycia
107. Tent-shrine, coin of Gordianus, Antioch in Pisidia
108. Tent-shrine, coin of Alexandria
109. Tyche shrine, coin of J. Domna, Damascus
110. Altar of Zeus, coin of Septimius Severus, Pergamum
111. Shrine of Mars Ultor, coin of Augustus, Rome
112. The Macellum, coin of Nero, Rome

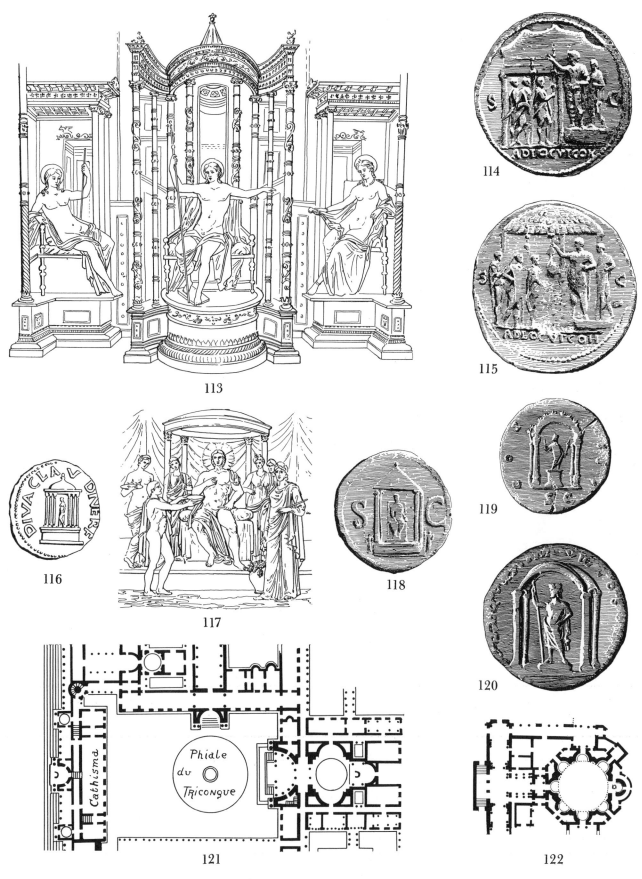

113. "Porta regia," fresco, Casa di Apollo, Pompeii
114. Coin of Nero, Rome
115. Coin of Nero, Lugdunum
116. Coin of Nero, DIVA CLAUD
117. Helios enthroned with Seasons and Phaeton, *Domus aurea* of Nero (after eighteenth century drawing)
118. Statue of Emperor enthroned, coin of Domitian, Rome

119. Statue of Emperor under baldachin, coin of Antoninus Pius
120. Statue of Emperor as Ianus under baldachin, coin of Commodus
121. Constantinople, plan of the Trichoncos and Court of the Phiale in Imperial Palace (after Vogt)
122. Constantinople, plan of Chrysotriclinos in Imperial Palace (after Ebersolt)

124

123

125

126

127

128

129

123. Sint Servaas, Maastricht, restoration of interior in A.D. 1180
124. Advent of the Soul, fresco, Hypogeum of Aurelius Felicissimus, Rome
125. St. Gregory of Nyssa, Menologium of Basil II
126. Ascension and Pentecost, Bible of St. Paul, fol. 293v, Rome
127. Entry into Jerusalem, fresco, Daphni
128. Conversion of St. Paul, Bible of St. Paul, fol. 308v, Rome
129. Drawing of lost mosaic, apse of Old St. Peter's, Rome

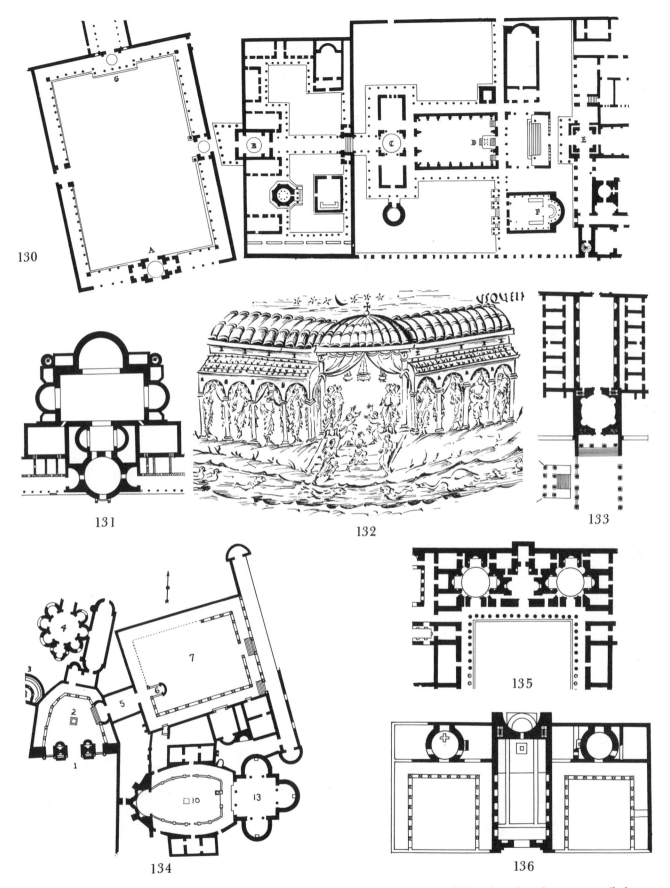

130. Constantinople, plan of Imperial Palace (after Ebersolt)
131. Treves, plan of "praetorium-palatium" (after Krencker)
132. "House of the Lord," Utrecht Psalter

133. Salona, palace of Diocletian, plan of entrance vestibule
134. Piazza Armerina, Sicily, plan of villa of Maximianus
135. Rome, plan of ceremonial court in palace
136. Pergamum, plan of "praetorium-palatium" of Trajan (?)

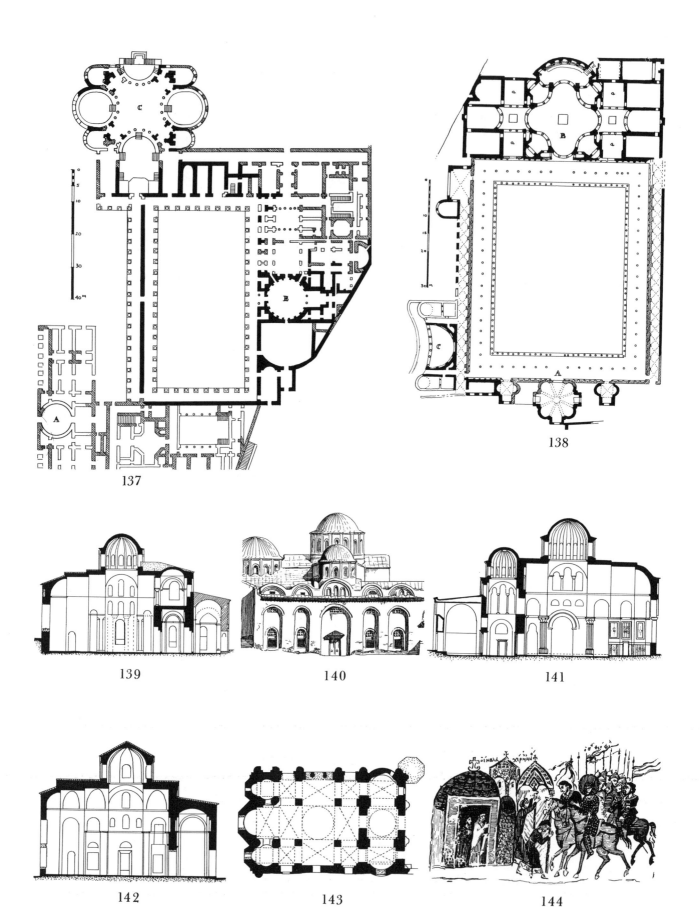

137. Tivoli, Small Palace of Hadrian
138. Tivoli, Large Palace of Hadrian
139. Istanbul, St. Savior Pantepoptes, section
140. Istanbul, St. Savior Pantocrator, façade
141. Istanbul, St. Savior Pantocrator, section

142. Istanbul, "Myrelaion," section
143. Istanbul, "Myrelaion," plan
144. Istanbul, Emperor Theophilus visiting St. Mary Blachernae, *History of John Skylitzes*, Madrid, Bibl. Nat. 5.3.N.2,
fol. 43r

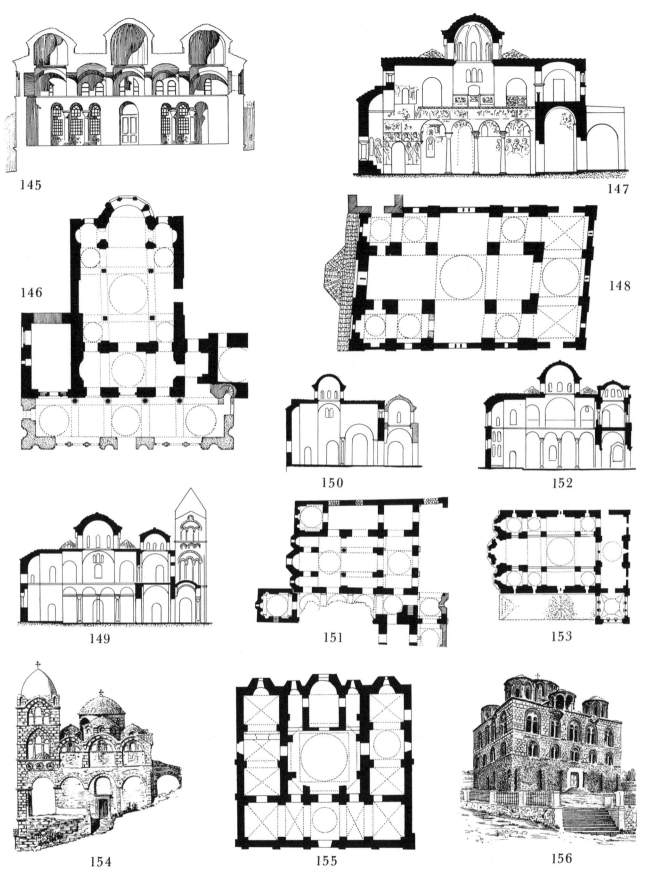

145

146

147

148

150

152

149

151

153

154

155

156

145. Istanbul, St. Theodore, section through exo-narthex
146. Istanbul, St. Theodore, plan
147. Mistra, Metropole, section
148. Mistra, Metropole, plan at tribune level
149. Mistra, Brontochion, section
150. Mistra, St. Sophia, section

151. Mistra, St. Sophia, plan
152. Mistra, Pantassa, section
153. Mistra, Pantassa, plan at tribune level
154. Mistra, Pantassa, façade
155. Arta, Panagia Paragoritissa, plan
156. Arta, Panagia Paragoritissa, façade

157. Praetoria (?), World Chronicle of Alexandria

158. "Charlemagne" in his palace, seventeenth century engraving copied from a Carolingian illumination

159. Boucoleon palace, Skylitzes Ms., Bibl. Nat. 5.3. N.2, fol. 157r, Madrid

160. Death of Romanus Lecapenus, Skylitzes Ms., fol. 133v

161. Romanus receiving the veil with the image of Christ, Skylitzes Ms., fol. 131r

162. Basil enthroned in palace, Skylitzes Ms., fol. 105v

163. Palace-church at Preslau, plan

164. Samonas before the Emperor Leo, Skylitzes Ms., fol. 113r

165. Empress Theodora leaves St. Sophia and goes to the palace to speak to the people, Skylitzes Ms., fol. 220v

166. Queen of Georgia led before Romanus III in Chrysotriclinos, Skylitzes Ms., fol. 206r

167. Triumph of Basil, Skylitzes Ms., fol. 183r

168. Leo the Wise in *mitatorion* of St. Sophia reading in front of Pantocrator icon, Skylitzes Ms., fol. 115v

169. Entry into Jerusalem, Pala d'Oro, San Marco, Venice

170

171

172

173

174

175

170. The palace of Man Singh with royal cupolas, wall-arcading and a domical place of appearances on a platform, Gwalior, India

171. The Nekare Chan, or the gateway of the court of the Diwan-i-am, in the Palace of the Great Moghul, Delhi Castle, India

172. "The Gate of Magnificence," or *Buland Darwaza*, of Akbar, Fathpur Sikri, India

173. "Delhi Gate" of the Moghul Castle, Delhi, India

174. Istanbul, eighteenth century gateway of the Sultan at the entrance to the court of St. Sophia

175. Reception of an ambassador by the Turkish Sultan, sixteenth or seventeenth century engraving